With *Reason, Faith, and Tradition: Explorations in Catholic Theology, Revised Edition*, Martin Albl has written a timely book that corrects the increasingly prevalent assumption that faith and reason remain antithetical to each other. Lucidly written, this learned but accessible book provides a thoroughgoing analysis of the best arguments on all sides in an effort to demonstrate the reasonableness of faith; a rational person may indeed believe in God. More than that, however, Albl writes perceptively about our inherent desire for the transcendent, that foundational awareness that one has been called beyond the finite realm to participate in an infinite good.

—Ian Christopher Levy
Providence College

Martin Albl's *Reason, Faith, and Tradition, Revised Edition*, offers a brilliantly written text that serves well for in-class use. Professors and students will benefit from the additional chapters and the helpful links to videos and websites that offer supplementary content. The extended discussion and guided reading questions draw out key ideas and can be used for class discussions. The chapters do an impressive job of highlighting the historical development of key theological concepts without simplifying the complex history of thought in the Catholic tradition.

—Randall Woodard, PhD
Saint Leo University

I've been teaching Introduction to Catholic Theology for the past eighteen years, and I only wish that Martin Albl's *Reason, Faith, and Tradition: Explorations in Catholic Theology, Revised Edition* had been there from the beginning! Albl's book has a central argument—that faith and reason, which have been tragically separated in modernity, are compatible by nature—which it makes while introducing all manner of doctrines, theologians, controversies, etc. This second edition contains significant improvements over the first. I can't imagine using anything else in my introductory courses.

—Rodney Howsare
DeSales University

Author Acknowledgments

No book is written in complete isolation. For this one, I am indebted to the help of many people. Interaction with students and colleagues at Marquette University, Mount Marty College, and Presentation College has helped me to sharpen my own thinking and understanding of these theological issues.

Thanks are due to the publishing team at Anselm Academic, especially to Leslie Ortiz for first accepting this book for publication and to editors Jerry Ruff and Beth Erickson for their critical insight, sensitivity to reader perceptions, and improvement of the writing style. Thanks also to Maura Hagarty for her role in the process.

I appreciate Rodney Howsare's helpful suggestions for improving the first edition.

I'm grateful to my wife, Judy, and son, Dan, for their steady love, support, and patience in the writing process.

My final debt of gratitude is to my father, Ludwig Albl. His love of learning and culture, his ethic of hard work, and his openness to ecumenical understanding have shaped not only my thoughts but also and more essentially, who I am. I dedicate this book to his memory.

Publisher Acknowledgments

Our thanks to the following individuals who advised the publishing team or reviewed the first edition of this work while in progress:

Professor Mara Kelly-Zukowski
Felician College, Lodi, New Jersey

Susie Paulik Babka
University of San Diego, California

Reason, Faith, and Tradition

EXPLORATIONS IN CATHOLIC THEOLOGY, *REVISED EDITION*

Martin C. Albl

Created by the publishing team of Anselm Academic.

Cover images: Statues of Saint Peter and Saint Gregory. © Bradley Harmon. All other images royalty free from *iStockphoto.com*.

Printed in the United States of America

7065

ISBN 978-1-59982-632-5

Contents

Abbreviations

BCE before the Common Era, referring to dates before the birth of Jesus

ca. circa, meaning "approximately"

CCC *Catechism of the Catholic Church*, 2nd ed.

CDF Congregation for the Doctrine of the Faith, a Vatican office

CE Common Era, referring to dates after the birth of Jesus

par. parallels. When given with a Gospel passage, *par.* indicates the passage has parallels in other Gospels.

PBC Pontifical Biblical Commission

SCG *Summa contra Gentiles* by Thomas Aquinas

ST *Summa Theologica* by Thomas Aquinas

Documents of the Second Vatican Council

All references are to the translations available on the Vatican website, *www.vatican.va/archive/hist_councils/ii_vatican_council/index.htm.*

DV *Dei Verbum* (*Dogmatic Constitution on Divine Revelation*)

LG *Lumen Gentium* (*Dogmatic Constitution on the Church*)

NA *Nostra Aetate* (*Declaration on the Relation of the Church to Non-Christian Religions*)

UR *Unitatis Redintegratio* (*Decree on Ecumenicism*)

Papal Encyclicals and Apostolic Exhortations

EG *Evangelii Gaudium* (*On the Proclamation of the Gospel in Today's World*) by Francis

SS *Spe Salvi* (*On Christian Hope*) by Benedict XVI

UUS *Ut Unum Sint* (*On Commitment to Ecumenism*) by John Paul II

VD *Verbum Domini* (*On the Word of God in the Life and Mission of the Church*) by Benedict XVI

Introduction

One of the tragedies of our modern world is the widespread belief that faith and reason are opposites. In more than fifteen years of teaching theology at the college level, I have taught numerous students who assume that a person must choose between a rational, scientific view of the world and a worldview based on faith. The message of this book is that this is a false dichotomy. In the Christian understanding of reality, a scientific worldview and a faith perspective, properly understood, are in perfect harmony. The ultimate goal of Christian theology is to demonstrate the harmony of faith and reason, and this book, I hope, makes a small contribution toward achieving that goal.

This book is not intended as a comprehensive introduction to all aspects of Christian or Catholic theology. Rather, I hope to introduce students to the Christian and Catholic theological tradition by exploring some key questions involving the relationship between faith and reason. This approach allows us to go straight to the heart of Christian theology: the deep conviction that faith and reason are harmonious.

To help illustrate the organic nature of the centuries-old Christian theological tradition, I include a fair amount of cross-referencing within the text. Students need not look up each cross-reference to understand any particular topic, however. Rather, the references serve as a reminder that Christian theology is best understood as a whole and as an aid to studying a specific topic in further depth if the student so desires.

Key theological terms are defined within the text; some of them also are defined in a brief glossary. Terms included in the glossary are highlighted in bold at first use in the text.

The text includes numerous links to print and video resources for further study that are available on the Internet. Descriptions of these resources and the URLs where they can be found are presented in footnotes in the print version of the text and in either footnotes or endnotes in the digital versions of the text. Readers of digital versions with Internet access can use the hyperlinks in the text to access the resources.

An introductory book such as this one can only skim the surface of many deep and complex issues. However, if it can help motivate students to continue their efforts to recognize the deep harmony between faith and reason, this book will have achieved its purpose.

Faith and Reason I

Reason and Christian Faith   1.1

The title of this book includes two terms that may seem incompatible: *reason* and *faith*. Many people assume that religious beliefs or faith can only be opinions and conjectures about the unknown and unknowable. The very fact that there are so many different religions, often with widely differing beliefs and practices, seems to prove that religious beliefs are simply opinions and are not open to reasonable discussion and investigation.

The central aim of this book is to show that reason and Christian belief are neither contradictory nor mutually exclusive. In fact, the two are inseparable. Reason, aided by Christian faith, reveals truths about the universe and humans that reason alone could never have reached. Conversely, Christian faith needs reason to communicate its beliefs clearly, to arrange those beliefs systematically, to guard it from straying into fanaticism or error, and to provide answers to reasonable objections to those beliefs.

Specifically, this study considers Christian **theology**—the reasonable study of the Christian faith. Theological studies have sometimes been mocked as useless theoretical debates about such topics as "how many angels can dance on the head of a pin." The argument of this book is that theology is intensely practical, because religious beliefs, or lack of beliefs, profoundly shape the way people understand the world and how they live in the world. Theology helps clarify basic religious beliefs and explores how they influence all aspects of life.

The third main word in the book's title, *tradition*, essentially means "a way of life" or "customs" passed down through the generations. This word is used in different ways: A family has certain holiday traditions; different nations and peoples have traditional music, dances, or food.

In this book, *Tradition* refers to the specific way of thinking that is the Roman **Catholic** theological tradition—a way of combining reason with religious faith that has been passed down from generation to generation for two thousand years. This raises some questions: In a world full of many different religious and theological traditions, isn't it rather narrow-minded, or even prejudiced, to focus on just the Catholic tradition? Wouldn't it be better to be more inclusive, and study a diverse range of theological ideas?

The reasons for focusing specifically on the Catholic tradition will be discussed in detail in section 1.11. For now, consider three brief points:

1. Any theological thinking must be thinking within a specific theological tradition: it is simply impossible to think theologically in general.

2. The Catholic theological tradition has a rich, two-thousand-year-old intellectual and spiritual heritage that has profoundly influenced Western culture and, through Western culture, the rest of the world. Anyone wishing to gain a clear understanding of that culture must also consider this heritage.

3. While this study focuses on Roman Catholic thought, it does not exclude important contributions from non-Catholic thinkers (for example, C. S. Lewis and Hans-Georg Gadamer).

This study is not technical, explaining in detail what theology is, or how theology works. Rather, the text addresses certain basic theological issues and questions (for example: Can one prove that God exists? Do science and religion contradict one another?) and considers how the Catholic tradition combines faith and reason in its response to these questions. The text also considers some basic Christian beliefs (for example: that God is a Trinity, that the Bible is God's word, that people spend eternity in either heaven or hell after death) and explores how faith and reason relate in these specific beliefs.

Before discussing Christian theology specifically, however, the text explores how reason relates to human religious belief in general. Trying to gain a better understanding of that sometimes-strange human activity called religion is a good place to start.

Why Study Religious Beliefs?   1.2

People wishing to understand the world and its inhabitants must consider the influence of religious beliefs. Billions of people throughout the world identify themselves as members of religious traditions,[1] following major religious traditions such as Judaism, Christianity, Islam, Hinduism, and Buddhism as well as countless smaller or lesser-known traditions. Every society in human history has had some kind of religious belief. One has only to follow the news to know that religion and religious beliefs play a central role in a variety of national and international issues: the conflicts in the Middle East, political debates on the role

---

1. The interactive chart "Major Religions of the World Ranked by Number of Adherents" is accessible at *http://chartsbin.com/view/3nr*.

of Hinduism in Indian society, the discussion on teaching evolution in public schools, and public policy debates on same-sex marriage and abortion.

At the personal level, the majority of people, even those who do not regularly attend religious services or follow an organized religion, sooner or later confront "religious" questions. For example, when a close friend or family member passes away, one may wonder, "What happened to my loved one? Is she in a better place? Will I see her again?" As young people consider which career to pursue or which college major to choose, the question may arise, even if vaguely, "What is the purpose of my life?" or, more specifically, "Does God have a plan for me?" Perhaps as a couple considers marriage, each may wonder, "Is this the person whom I was meant to marry?"

These questions are religious to the extent that they all imply the existence of a supernatural reality—a reality completely different from one's everyday experience in this world. Such questions ask whether everyday life has a meaning given to it by a supernatural power. Notice that even atheists face religious questions, even if only by the choice not to believe in a reality beyond this world.

From these general and personal considerations, it is clear that religion is a central dimension of human life and, thus, an important subject of study.

The Heart of Religion: Encountering the Transcendent ⠀⠀⠀⠀⠀⠀⠀⠀⠀⠀⠀⠀⠀⠀⠀⠀1.3

Defining the term *religion* more closely is the next step. Buddhism, Hinduism, Judaism, Christianity, and Islam are commonly referred to as religions. People such as the Lakota and the Hopi, and various indigenous groups throughout the world have religious traditions. History tells of ancient Greek, Roman, and Babylonian religions. However, it is difficult to identify what exactly makes all of these religions. What do they have in common?

Clearly it is not just a belief in God. While Jews, Christians, and Muslims are monotheists (believers in one God), the ancient Greeks were polytheists (believers in many gods). Other traditions speak not of gods but of spirits or other supernatural beings. While Buddhism accepts the existence of gods and spirits, the Buddha's teaching focused not on these supernatural powers but on the ability of humans to achieve a state of perfect peace known as Nirvana. So once again the question arises: Is there a common link that unites these various beliefs?

In his classic study *The Idea of the Holy*, German philosopher, theologian, and historian Rudolf Otto (1869–1937) claims to have found the common link.[2] Otto identifies the primary source of all religious feeling in the common human encounter with what he calls "the numinous." The Christian writer C. S. Lewis summarizes Otto's concept well:

---

2. Rudolf Otto, *The Idea of the Holy* (London: Oxford University Press, 1923).

Suppose that you were told that there was a tiger in the next room: you would know that you were in danger and would probably feel fear. But if you were told "There is a ghost in the next room," and believed it, you would feel, indeed, what is often called fear, but of a different kind. It would not be based on the knowledge of danger, for no one is primarily afraid of what a ghost may do to him, but of the mere fact that it is a ghost. . . . Now suppose that you were told simply, "There is a mighty spirit in the room," and believed it. Your feeling would then be even less like the mere feeling of danger; but the disturbance would be profound. You would feel wonder and a certain shrinking—a sense of inadequacy to cope with such a visitant and of prostration before it . . . This feeling may be described as awe, and the object which excites it as the Numinous.[3]

Otto uses the Latin phrase *mysterium tremendum et fascinans* to sum up his understanding of the numinous. *Mysterium* refers to the "wholly other": something people experience as completely different from ordinary human knowledge and experience. *Tremendum* refers to the overwhelming power of the numinous presence: people become acutely aware of their human limitations and can only react by falling to their knees in worship. Otto illustrates this term with two biblical examples: When Moses encounters God in the burning bush, "Moses hid his face, for he was afraid to look at God" (Exod 3:6). After Jesus had performed a miracle, Simon Peter fell before Jesus and said, "Depart from me, Lord, for I am a sinful man" (Luke 5:8).

However, the numinous is also *fascinans*—it attracts a person in spite of the person's fear and dread. This double reaction can be illustrated in that most people, even while experiencing some fear, are

© Alfredo Dagli Orti / Art Resource, NY

In this terracotta relief, eighteenth-century Italian artist Angelo Bigari captures the ambiguity of religious experience: Moses is attracted to, yet overwhelmed by, the mysterious power of God's presence.

---

3. C. S. Lewis, *The Problem of Pain* (New York: Macmillan, 1978), 17.

attracted to and even fascinated by ghost stories or other paranormal accounts. At more developed levels, Otto finds the *fascinans* in the Christian's desire for the beatific vision of God (seeing God "face-to-face") and in the Buddhist's desire for Nirvana—that state of pure peace and bliss that is beyond all human language and even conception.

Scholar of world religions, Mircea Eliade[4] (1907–1986), agrees that all religions share a common belief in a realm of otherworldly, numinous reality, a realm he calls the "sacred," in contrast to the realm of the profane (everyday, visible reality).[5] Religions, Eliade adds, use this distinction to divide the world into sacred space (such as temples, altars, or sacred places in nature where the numinous may be encountered) and profane space (all other places of ordinary human activity); they divide time into sacred time (such as special times of year marked by festivals and religious rituals) and profane time (all other times of ordinary human activity).

A general term that covers both Otto's concept of the numinous and Eliade's concept of the sacred is the word ***transcendent***, referring to a reality that transcends, or goes beyond, natural, everyday human experience. The belief in the transcendent is at the heart of all religions.

Transcendence and the Meaning of Life   1.4

The personal religious questions mentioned in section 1.2—"What is the purpose of life?" or "Is this the person whom I was meant to marry?"—are questions about *meaning*, and they are clearly transcendent questions. They presume that life has a meaning beyond itself.

Consider how some common, everyday expressions also presuppose that life has a transcendent meaning. When one experiences an unpleasant or even tragic event, a friend may try to offer comfort by saying, "Everything happens for a reason." In the face of a disappointment, one might say, "I guess it wasn't meant to be." Notice that such statements seem to imply that a transcendent power has a plan.

Philosophically inclined people might ask themselves if human life has meaning and purpose rather than being the result of a random collection of cells, tissues, and organs that, through blind chance, evolved the ability to think. (This question will be discussed in chapter 4.)

Raising questions about meaning is an essential human characteristic, and a central function of any religious tradition is precisely to provide believers with a sense of meaning. The person who encounters the numinous is not left with

---

4. An overview of the life and thought of Mircea Eliade by Brian Rennie in the 1998 Routledge *Encyclopedia of Philosophy* is accessible at *www.westminster.edu/staff/brennie/eliade/mebio.htm*.

5. Mircea Eliade, *The Sacred and the Profane: The Nature of Religion* (New York: Harcourt, Brace, 1959).

only fear and terror but is given an orientation and a mission that help to make sense of daily life. To return to Otto's examples, after Moses' encounter with God, Moses is sent to free his people from Egypt; after Peter's encounter with Jesus, Peter is sent out as an apostle. Eliade describes how discovering a sacred space—a manifestation of the sacred—gives structure and meaning to life. He equates this discovery with the creation of the world because it helps make sense of a world that can seem chaotic and even terrifying.[6]

All societies have asked questions about the meaning of human life; countless millions have asked and continue to ask questions about the meaning of their individual lives. The question is a transcendent one because it is oriented toward ultimate meaning, a meaning that transcends that which any individual person or group can give to human life.

People, then, have a sense that a transcendent reality gives meaning to visible reality. However, this sense raises questions: Why? What gives people the idea that the invisible gives meaning to the visible?

Moral Law: Sign of the Transcendent   1.5

The first part of C. S. Lewis's[7] book *Mere Christianity* is titled, "Right and Wrong as a Clue to the Meaning of the Universe."[8] Lewis points out that all humans of every culture have the same basic sense of right and wrong. Some details vary, but all cultures share the sense that such actions as lying, stealing, and committing adultery are truly wrong—not just wrong in the opinion of some people. Notice that when people do lie or steal, they often try to rationalize or justify their behavior—proving that they accept the common standards of right and wrong but are simply arguing that their particular behavior qualifies as an exception. Lewis calls this common set of ethical standards the Moral Law.

What is the ultimate source of this Moral Law? Lewis shows that individual societies could not simply have invented it—or else how could one explain why the basic ethical standards of the ancient Egyptians, ancient Chinese, medieval Europeans, and modern Americans (all cultures that developed with no direct contact with one another) are essentially the same?

Nor can the Moral Law simply be based on instinct, because natural instincts are often contradictory. When another person is in danger, for example, one has a natural instinct to offer help, but one also has an equally natural instinct of self-preservation that prompts one to avoid danger. The Moral Law helps people decide which instinct to follow.

---

6. Eliade, *Sacred and Profane*, 20–22.

7. A video overview of the life and work of C. S. Lewis is accessible at *https://www.youtube.com/watch?v=YHCztUy3kGU* (time 0:24:21).

8. C. S. Lewis, *Mere Christianity* (London: HarperCollins, 2001; orig. pub. 1952), 1–32.

The Moral Law, Lewis concludes, can only come from a transcendent source—a supernatural power. Humans did not invent it but feel obligated to obey it. The Moral Law, then, is a sign that a transcendent power, the author of the Moral Law,[9] really does exist.

Personal Experience: Sign of the Transcendent
1.6

Perhaps you have stood outside in the evening, watching a sunset. The air is still and cool; the light on the distant horizon is streaked with a palette of soft colors. A feeling of infinite peace comes over you; however, the feeling only lasts a moment—a child asks you a question, you hear the sound of an airplane overhead, you recall a bill you forgot to pay—and the spell is broken. You have had an experience of the transcendent—a sense of peace and beauty that does not seem to belong to everyday reality but seems to point beyond it.

A feeling of unlimited love and a sense of responsibility for new life overwhelm many parents holding their newborn babies for the first time. The biological facts of how babies are conceived and born cannot describe or even begin to explain the experience. Parents speak of being overcome with the wonder of a new life that they did not create but that was given to them as a gift. Babies are commonly described as "little miracles." This description expresses the feeling that some experiences are simply beyond the ordinary—they touch on something transcendent.

At times the experience of the transcendent can take the form of dissatisfaction with this world, restlessness, a longing for something more, something better. People are often frustrated with their lack of ability to communicate, to find meaning in school or work, to find peace in their family life. This dissatisfaction comes not only at times of frustration or unhappiness but also at times of contentment, when life is good. Following experiences of the best of what life can offer—love, beauty, peace, deep joy—people often find themselves longing for more. Those moments of happiness don't last, but they do awaken a desire for something on a completely different scale: perfect, lasting love and perfect, eternal peace.

The great Christian theologian Augustine (354–430 CE) describes that experience of longing and desire with these words, "Our hearts are restless until they rest in thee, O Lord" (*Confessions* 1.1.1). Even the atheist philosopher Friedrich Nietzsche (1844–1900) knew this longing. In his most famous work, *Thus Spoke Zarathustra*, the line "All joy wants eternity—wants deep, deep eternity" is repeated several times.

---

9. An excerpt from *Mere Christianity* (book 1, chapter 2) in which C. S. Lewis argues that Moral Law is a sign that absolute truth exists is accessible at *www.pbs.org/wgbh/questionofgod/ownwords /mere1.html*.

If people have a longing for something that this world seemingly cannot provide, a longing for a perfect world, from where did that longing come?

Transcendence and Death   1.6.1

An elderly man wakes up suddenly in the middle of the night, thinking about an old friend with whom he has lost contact. He cannot get back to sleep, so he reads some magazines, gets a drink, and finally goes back to bed—all the while still thinking of his friend and wondering how he is doing. In the morning, he calls his friend's sister. "I'm so glad you called," she tells him, "John just passed away last night."

Over the course of two years during World War II, a woman lost three sons who were serving as soldiers. On each occasion, she had a vivid dream and knew even before she received the news that one of her sons had fallen.

I have heard these stories from reliable sources; many have heard similar accounts. While these and similar stories can be dismissed as coincidence or exaggeration, one wonders if that is the most reasonable explanation? When faced with events that have no natural explanation, perhaps the most sensible response is to admit that reason is limited and leave open the possibility of an explanation that transcends ordinary experience.

Reason and Truth: Signs of the Transcendent   1.7

The Catholic theologian Karl Rahner argues that the experience of transcendence is found not only in special encounters with the numinous but also in the very structure of the human person.[10] In every experience, people are aware not only of their own human limitations but, at the same time, of the possibility of transcending those limitations. Human experiences—the ordinary as well as the extraordinary—point beyond themselves to a "transcendent horizon." Consider a hypothetical example:

Jeff claims to be a complete skeptic: He denies that any absolute, objective truth exists. "Truth," he claims, is really based on people's perceptions. Every

---

10. See Karl Rahner, *Foundations of Christian Faith: An Introduction to the Idea of Christianity* (New York: Seabury Press, 1978), 14–35.

society, he insists, has had its own subjective opinions about truth, and strong or ruthless societies usually impose their version of truth on weaker societies.

But notice the logical problem in Jeff's analysis: if it is true that there is no such thing as truth, then there is at least one statement (Jeff's) that is in fact true. However, if Jeff's statement is true, then Jeff's claim that there is no truth makes no sense. By the very act of denying truth, Jeff in fact shows that absolute truth must exist.

Most people realize that their own thoughts and opinions will always be limited (whether because of their prejudices, lack of knowledge, or limited experiences). At the same time, most are also aware that it is necessary for this absolute truth to exist, or humans would never be able to think at all. How else would people know that their grasp of truth is limited, unless they had a sense of an absolute truth? With this intimation, this glimpse into absolute truth, people transcend themselves—they know there is an absolute horizon of truth that is infinitely beyond their (or any other human's) knowledge and control. They become aware of the transcendent.

Is Belief in the Transcendent Just Wishful Thinking? Responding to Some Challenges 1.8

Thus far, it's been noted that all societies known to historians have expressed belief in the existence of a transcendent realm. While it's true that they have described this realm in different ways (e.g., as Nirvana or heaven or as Mount Olympus), in every case, these societies have agreed that a realm beyond everyday, visible reality does exist, and that this transcendent realm gives meaning to human life.

It's also been noted that people encounter the transcendent through their deep desire to find meaning in life (e.g., "Does everything happen for a reason?") or through experiencing things that defy ordinary explanations. The sense of the transcendent is also manifest in the experience of a moral law not invented by humans, in the restless desire for deep, lasting peace and perfect joy, and in one's implicit sense that absolute truth must exist.

Various sociologists and psychologists have put forth theories attempting to explain the universal human awareness of and desire for the transcendent. Karl Marx (1818–1883) believed that the ruling classes fabricated religious beliefs to keep the oppressed working classes in a passive state. Religion, Marx asserted, is "the opium of the people," the false promise of an invisible world of peace and justice that distracts workers from demanding their rights in this world.[11]

---

11. Karl Marx, "Introduction" to *Critique of Hegel's Philosophy of Right*, trans. A. Jolin and J. O'Malley, Cambridge Studies in the History and Theory of Politics (Cambridge: Cambridge University Press, 1977; orig. pub. 1844).

Sigmund Freud (1856–1939) argued that religious beliefs arose as civilizations projected their need for a protective father figure onto a supernatural realm. In order to feel better in a dangerous, unpredictable world, humans invented the myth of a kindly father in the sky who watches over them.[12]

Such explanations are far too simplistic. Neither Marx nor Freud addressed a basic question: why do humans insistently seek meaning beyond the boundaries of this world? One can agree with Marx that many humans suffer under oppressive working conditions, but why would they seek escape from these conditions in a transcendent realm? There are plenty of earthly escapes, after all. One can agree with Freud that humans have a deep desire for security, but why seek that security in an invisible world? Doesn't it make more sense to look for security in a world one can see? Why and how did people come up with this belief in this other world in the first place?

Commenting on this persistent belief in a transcendent world, Lewis reflects that

> Creatures are not born with desires unless satisfaction for those desires exists. A baby feels hunger: well, there is such a thing as food. A duckling wants to swim: well, there is such a thing as water. Men feel sexual desire: well, there is such a thing as sex. If I find in myself a desire which no experience in this world can satisfy, the most probable explanation is that I was made for another world.[13]

Such arguments suggest that it is reasonable to take the world of the transcendent seriously as an object of study.

Religious Studies and Theology   1.9

If indeed it is important to study religious beliefs, then how should one undertake such a study? Two general approaches are religious studies and theology.

The first approach, religious studies, has had many labels: *history of religions, philosophy of religions, comparative religions*, or simply *religious studies*, the term that will be used in this text. The religious studies scholar focuses on human religious experience as a specific field of academic study. A common procedure is to gather data on religions from various times and places and then study and interpret this data, focusing especially on beliefs and practices shared by all religious traditions. Eliade's *The Sacred and the Profane* is a classic work in this discipline. From his studies of a variety of religions, Eliade identifies common beliefs, such as the division of the world into the sacred and profane, and common practices,

---

12. See, for example, Freud's book, *The Future of an Illusion* (New York: Norton, 1989; orig. pub. 1927).

13. Lewis, *Mere Christianity*, 136–37.

such as rituals marking sacred times, which give deep insight into the nature of religion as a human activity.

The goal of religious studies is to describe religious beliefs and actions as objectively as possible.[14] This makes the approach of religious studies departments, found in many state universities, similar to approaches taken in departments of sociology or **anthropology**. Scholars and students working in the area of religious studies avoid the question of whether a transcendent world exists. They aim to keep personal views about the transcendent apart from their analysis of religions and religious beliefs.

In contrast, the second approach—theology—begins by accepting the reality of the transcendent and attempting to better understand that reality. In other words, the theologian begins with a faith commitment to a specific religious tradition (e.g., Jewish, Muslim, Christian, Lakota), and uses reason to better understand that tradition's beliefs. Saint Anselm[15] (ca. 1033–1109 CE) offered a definition of theology that has been widely embraced: "faith seeking understanding."

Breaking down the word *theology* into its two Greek root words gives further insight into the task of this discipline. In Greek, *theos* means "God" or "a god"; the related adjective *theios* refers to divine things. The root word **logos** means a "study" or "disciplined use of reason." *Logos* is a familiar term for many as it is a common part of many English words, such as bio*logy*: the study of life.

It would be easy to conclude from this comparison that religious studies deals with *facts* (e.g., some societies believe in God; others believe in many gods) while theology deals with unprovable *opinions* (e.g., there is one God; Jesus is divine). It would be more accurate, however, to conclude that theology is concerned with *meaning*, in particular, with ultimate meaning. Does human life have a transcendent meaning or not? Did a transcendent power create the universe and give it meaning? These are not simply interesting but, ultimately, pointless speculations about things one can never truly know. Rather, they are serious questions about the ultimate nature of reality and human life. If God really does exist, if there really is a heaven or hell, they make a difference in how one lives. Such questions lie at the heart of the theologian's work.

Although theology deals with beliefs about the transcendent, theologians insist that one can deal with this "other world" by using reason. While the

---

14. Two classics in the field illustrate this procedure: William James, *The Varieties of Religious Experience*, Great Books in Philosophy (Amherst, NY: Prometheus Books, 2002; orig. pub. 1902), analyzes various religious experiences from a psychological point of view without raising the question of their objective reality; G. Van der Leeuw, *Religion in Essence and Manifestation*, trans. J. E. Turner (Princeton: Princeton University Press, 1986; orig. pub. 1933), uses a "phenomenological" approach—a method that attempts to give an exact description of the data without imposing value judgments on it.

15. An overview of the life and work of Saint Anselm is accessible at *plato.stanford.edu/entries /anselm/*.

starting point of theology is in faith—the faith that a transcendent world does exist—once this starting point is granted, the theologian aims to apply reason in a way that is just as rigorous and disciplined as in other academic fields of study.

The essential difference between theology and other academic disciplines lies less in its methodology than in its subject matter. Theology insists on the reasonable examination of *all* reality—both this-worldly and transcendent. Theologians believe access to the transcendent, however, cannot come directly through reason. It comes only through faith, a faith that is reasonable.

The Role of Traditions in Theological Thinking   1.10

In his book *Truth and Method*, the philosopher Hans-Georg Gadamer argues that while the scientific method (observation, hypothesis formation, testing) is appropriate for understanding and attaining truth in the natural sciences, truth and understanding are attained in a fundamentally different way in other fields of study such as art, history, or philosophy.[16] Gadamer insists that one can arrive at real truth and understanding, not just opinions, in these latter fields; one simply can't get there by using methods designed for the natural sciences. The method appropriate for seeking truth within humanities and fine arts involves accepting a certain tradition and thinking within it.

Take the discipline of history, for example. A historical event, such as the Cuban revolution of 1959 when the Communists under Fidel Castro took power, cannot be replicated in the laboratory or scientifically tested. People know about this event only through material evidence or the oral or written testimony of eyewitnesses. How they *interpret* that event, however, is shaped by particular traditions. If interpreted from within a Western tradition that values individual freedom and free markets, one may see it as a great disaster and loss of freedom for Cubans. If interpreted from within a socialist or Communist tradition that prioritizes the good of the community and centralized economic planning, one may to see it as an improvement for Cuba.

The same type of understanding applies to philosophical texts. The Western philosophical tradition, for example, shapes the way Westerners think about the world. Thinkers such as Plato, Aristotle, Thomas Aquinas, and Descartes have shaped how Westerners think about good and evil, cause and effect, and even science and religion. In contrast, a person influenced by Eastern tradition would think about these topics differently. Thus when studying a philosophical text, one cannot pretend to be a scientifically objective and neutral observer. One must be aware that one's perception and understanding of the text has been

---

16. Hans-Georg Gadamer, *Truth and Method*, 2nd rev. ed. (New York: Continuum, 1994).

fundamentally shaped by a particular tradition. People always read with certain prejudices, literally "prejudgments."

Most people are taught that prejudice is a bad thing. However, Gadamer's point is that certain prejudices, or prejudgments, are necessary; otherwise, one couldn't begin to think at all.

At the same time, this does not mean that a person's thoughts and beliefs are simply imprisoned within a particular tradition. Rather, as people become more self-aware of how traditions have shaped their basic assumptions, they are able to think critically about them. Encounters with other traditions, other ways of thinking, may lead people to rethink certain assumptions or see them in a new light. Here Gadamer[17] speaks of a "fusion of horizons"—an insight from one tradition (horizon) can "fuse" or merge with an insight from another tradition (horizon), producing a deeper understanding than could be gained through thinking in either tradition alone.

Theology's Method: Thinking within a Theological Tradition   1.11

Using a hypothetical example shows how Gadamer's insights might apply to understanding within the Christian theological tradition. Jane, a college freshman, although from a Christian background, doesn't attend church regularly, and doesn't consider herself particularly religious. One Friday night, she learns that her best friend Maureen has been killed in a car crash. A thousand thoughts and emotions begin to race through Jane's mind: shock, disbelief, confusion, anger, guilt. Some of her thoughts take a theological turn: "Where was God when the accident happened?" "How could God take Maureen's life when she was still so young?" "Why does God allow such terrible things to happen?" She is angry with God but, at the same time, feels guilty about her anger. She feels that she should pray, but doesn't know what to say.

Jane's questions and emotions are complex and even confused. Notice, though, that simply by asking certain questions, Jane shows that she is already thinking within a certain theological tradition and assumes that certain beliefs about God are true. She assumes, first, that there is one God, rather than many gods or other spiritual powers. When she wonders why God did not prevent the accident, she seems to assume that God is all-powerful, that God can control all events in the world. Jane also seems to assume that God is generally kind and caring toward humans. This is the source of her confusion and anger: If God is good and all-powerful, how could he allow an innocent person's life to be taken in such a senseless way?

---

17. An overview of the life and work of Gadamer is accessible at *plato.stanford.edu/entries /gadamer*. See especially section 3.1 on the positivity of prejudice and 3.2 on the fusion of horizons.

Jane's thinking, then, is shaped by several fundamental theological assumptions. Why does she have these unquestioned assumptions? Despite not attending church regularly or participating in formal religious education as a child, Jane had learned certain beliefs from her family. Then, as she grew older, she was influenced by ideas she picked up in school, from her own reading, and from everyday interactions with friends and other peers.

Where did her family, peers, and teachers pick up their religious ideas? The short answer is from the Christian tradition, or, more precisely, the Judeo-Christian tradition.[18] Through thousands of years of history, **Jewish** and Christian theological ideas have spread in myriad ways through many nations in the world and have shaped the thinking, directly or indirectly, of billions of people, including Jane's family, peers, teachers, community, culture—and, thus, Jane herself.

If Jane had been raised in a different tradition, for example, Buddhist, she would have asked different questions. She would have experienced the same basic human emotions of shock and sadness, but the way in which she reflected on her friend's death would have been shaped by such traditional Buddhist concepts as reincarnation (the idea of rebirth into another life), good and bad karma, and Nirvana. She would not have asked how the one creator, God, could allow her friend to die, because Buddhists do not believe in an all-powerful creator God.

The example supports the idea that thinking in fields such as theology *must* be guided by a particular tradition—Jane cannot simultaneously accept the Christian belief that Maureen is in heaven and the Buddhist belief that Maureen will be reborn in another life-form according to her level of karma.

At the same time, following Gadamer's thought, Jane still has the freedom to think critically about her own tradition. For example, Jane might question the traditional view that God is all-powerful and all good in the light of her friend's seemingly senseless death. If she seeks answers within the Christian tradition (for example, through reading the Bible or speaking with a pastor), she will ask her questions in a more theological way—using reason to try to better understand traditional beliefs. Gadamer's point is that even in questioning a traditional view, Jane should be aware that the very questions and the way in which these questions are asked have already been deeply influenced by that tradition. A person simply cannot approach the basic questions of the meaning of life except by means of a particular tradition.

---

18. The Christian theological tradition is founded on Jewish conceptions of God and God's relationship with humans. However, as it developed, the Christian theological tradition quickly took on a distinctive shape (e.g., in conceiving of God as a Trinity); and this fact justifies reference to the "Christian theological tradition" throughout the book.

Studying the Catholic Tradition in a Pluralistic World   1.12

The study of religious traditions—especially the study of the major religious traditions such as Judaism, Islam, or Hinduism that have influenced and shaped the thoughts and actions of countless millions of people—helps people understand both human societies and their own search for meaning.

Why then study the Christian theological tradition in particular? The reasons are many. The tradition is two thousand years old, not counting its deep roots in the Jewish tradition, and it has produced, and continues to produce, a rich theological reflection on the transcendent. Christian theological ideas have deeply influenced every aspect of Western culture, and many non-Western cultures. Because the Christian tradition is closely related, historically and theologically, to the Jewish and Muslim traditions, the study of Christian theology can shed light on these other traditions as well.

Yet the Christian tradition is made up of a vast variety of more specific traditions. There are various **Orthodox** traditions, the Roman Catholic tradition, traditions arising from the Protestant **Reformation**, and many more. Why focus on the Catholic tradition in particular? Like the Orthodox traditions, the Catholic tradition traces its beginnings to the earliest years of Christianity. The Catholic **Church** has been enormously influential in shaping religious, political, and cultural history, especially in the West, and remains a powerful spiritual and cultural force to this day. In addition, the Catholic theological tradition continues to shape Christian thinking and culture.

Although this book focuses on the Catholic theological tradition, it will draw on insights from other theological traditions. Already the text has considered the thought of Otto, Eliade, Lewis, and Gadamer, all non-Catholics. Openness to recognizing truth in other traditions is a fundamental characteristic of Catholic theology.

More specifically, this book frequently uses the term *traditional* or *orthodox Christianity* to refer to beliefs and practices shared by Catholic, Orthodox, and many Protestant and **evangelical** churches. Many of these shared beliefs are expressed in the Apostles' and Nicene Creeds—important early Christian summaries of beliefs.

Because it is impossible to cover the entire Catholic theological tradition, this book focuses on a central theme of the tradition: the relationship between reason and faith. Serious study of the relationship between faith and reason within the Catholic tradition leads not to pointless speculations about angels dancing on pins but to a deeper, truer, more beautiful, and more satisfying understanding of the world and of human life than can be obtained through reason alone.

Questions about the Text

1. Why have all known human cultures developed religious beliefs?
2. What does the word *transcendent* mean and how is it related to religious beliefs?
3. What does it mean to ask whether human life or the universe as a whole has a transcendent meaning?
4. What are some reasons for thinking that a transcendent realm exists?
5. What is the root meaning of the word *theology*? How does the academic discipline of religious studies differ from theology?
6. Explain Gadamer's claim that truth in artistic, historical, philosophical, or religious experience can only be attained by following a certain tradition.

Discussion Questions

1. Have you had a personal experience of the transcendent? Explain.
2. Do you think that all people wonder about religious questions—questions about the transcendent—at some point in their lives? Why or why not?
3. Do you agree that it is reasonable to believe in a transcendent reality? Why or why not?
4. What are some characteristics that all religions seem to share? Why do all religions share these characteristics?
5. Has the Christian tradition shaped the way in which you think about the existence of God, life after death, or the meaning of life? Explain.

Faith and Reason II

What Is Reason? What Is Faith? 2.1

The relationship between faith and reason is the theme of this entire book; further defining these terms is the purpose of this chapter. Though it may seem, at first glance, that the meanings of *reason* and *faith* are obvious, this is not at all the case.

The first chapter (secs. 1.10–1.11) addressed the influence of traditions on the way people look at reality—the basic questions they ask and the assumptions they make about the world. This chapter explores how one's very understanding of the terms *reason* and *faith* is profoundly influenced by particular traditions. Two types of tradition are particularly influential: (1) traditions that are open to the transcendent, and (2) traditions that are closed to the transcendent. The chapter aims to demonstrate that traditions closed to the transcendent produce a narrow view of both reason and faith that distorts the meanings of both. A fuller, more accurate understanding of reason and faith can only be regained by viewing the world from traditions open to the transcendent.

A key concept in this chapter is *worldview*, a term meaning the way one looks at the world and one's assumptions about reality. Notice how closely **worldview** and tradition are related. One's tradition influences one's worldview, and so one can speak, for example, of a Christian or Buddhist worldview.

Traditions Closed to the Transcendent: Rationalism, Materialism, and Determinism 2.2

First, a caution: The following description of traditions closed to the transcendent is simplified. Intellectual traditions are complex, so the labels used—*rationalism,* *materialism,* and *determinism*—are general. Few individual thinkers, for example, are purely rationalistic, materialistic, or deterministic. Nevertheless, the terms accurately describe highly influential trends in modern thinking, and one needs to be aware of how these trends affect modern thinking about faith and reason.

Rationalism   2.2.1

The French philosopher René Descartes[1] (1596–1650) is usually considered a primary catalyst in the development of the rationalist tradition. Dissatisfied with the conflicting philosophical opinions of his time, Descartes wished to get back to basics: he wanted to establish true knowledge on a solid basis. His first step was a negative one: to "reject as absolutely false everything in which I could imagine the least doubt, in order to see whether, after this process, something in my beliefs remained that was entirely indubitable [incapable of being doubted]."[2]

Descartes's method is sometimes called methodological doubt—the process of sweeping away all uncertain ideas so that only solid knowledge remains. After doubting everything, including the trustworthiness of his own sense observations (one sometimes sees optical illusions or mirages, for example), Descartes found he was sure of only one thing: that he doubted! If he could raise these doubts, he must exist as the subject raising these doubts. This train of thought led to Descartes's famous conclusion, "I think, therefore I am."[3] Descartes' focus on how a person (the subject) can know objects external to himself is sometimes called modern philosophy's "turn to the subject." In other words, philosophy since Descartes no longer takes for granted the common-sense notion that we perceive external reality as it actually is; modern philosophy tends to focus on how the human mind shapes reality.

Because he could not be sure that his senses gave him true knowledge of reality, Descartes turned to mathematical knowledge for his model of sure and accurate knowledge. Everyone agrees, after all, that 2 + 2 = 4. "In seeking the correct path to truth we should be concerned with nothing about which we cannot have a certainty equal to that of the demonstration of arithmetic and geometry."[4] This paradigm of true knowledge is also evident in the title of a work by Descartes's contemporary, the Dutch Jewish philosopher Baruch Spinoza[5] (1632–1677), *Ethics: Demonstrated in Geometric Order.*

---

1. An overview of Descartes' thought and life is accessible at *http://plato.stanford.edu/entries/descartes*. See especially section 1.2 on the claim that mathematical knowledge should be the model for all knowledge.

2. René Descartes, *A Discourse on the Method of Correctly Conducting One's Reason*, trans. I. Maclean, Oxford World's Classics (Oxford: Oxford University Press, 2006), 28. The Project Gutenberg version of this text is accessible at *www.gutenberg.org/files/59/59-h/59-h.htm*.

3. Ibid.

4. René Descartes, *Rules for the Direction of the Mind*, in René Descartes, *Philosophical Essays: Discourse on Method; Meditations; Rules for the Direction of the Mind*, trans. L. J. Lafleur (Indianapolis: Bobbs-Merrill, 1964), 152.

5. An overview of Spinoza's life and work is accessible at *http://plato.stanford.edu/entries/spinoza/*.

Following in the tradition of Descartes, rationalists tend to define *true knowledge* as scientific knowledge of the physical world, because this knowledge is based on the mathematically exact laws of physics and chemistry. Any other claims to knowledge that do not measure up to this standard cannot be called true knowledge, only opinion. The rationalist[6] thus denies that true knowledge about the transcendent world is possible: How can one truly know something that one can't even see or measure?

Descartes's thought was a precursor to the highly influential intellectual movement known as the **Enlightenment**. Partly in reaction to the bloody religious conflicts of the Thirty Years' War (1618–1648), Enlightenment[7] rationalists such as David Hume (1711–1776) attacked belief in the supernatural as irrational; and thinkers such as Voltaire (1694–1778) criticized religious belief as blind obedience to church authority. Rationalists in the Enlightenment tradition viewed reason and faith as opposites. They associated the term *reason* with strictly logical, empirical, mathematically based thinking, and *faith* with a blind adherence to traditional doctrine.

Materialism and Determinism 2.2.2

The materialist worldview is one logical extension of the rationalist worldview. The rationalist claims that the material, physical world is the only basis of true knowledge; the materialist goes a step further by insisting that the material world is the only reality. The influence of materialist thinking is evident in many fields of study. In psychology, a strict behaviorist rejects concepts such as *mind* and *thought* as ultimately meaningless. (Where exactly is the "mind" located? Can one measure a "thought"?) Instead, behaviorists focus strictly on the facts of observable behaviors that can be understood as responses to external stimuli. Karl Marx claimed that his economic philosophy was based on "scientific materialism"[8]—a view of the world that rejects such vague notions as *spirit* and *soul* in favor of observable, physical realities that provide real explanation of human behavior.

In neuroscience, research into genetics and brain function is increasingly revealing the physical foundations for mental processes in the brain and in genetic makeup. For example, scientists can identify which parts of the brain control certain functions and which specific genes are associated with specific character traits. From this, the materialist concludes that there is no difference between mind and thoughts and their physical foundation. Thoughts are simply

---

6. A video presenting examples of contemporary rationalist thinking is accessible at *www.youtube.com/watch?v=EuxgdkqvuRE* (time: 0:09:59).

7. An overview of the Enlightenment is accessible at *http://plato.stanford.edu/entries/enlightenment*.

8. For more information about scientific materialism, see David H. Bailey, "What Is Scientific Materialism, and How Does It Enter Into the Science-Religion Discussion?" (2014) accessible at *www.sciencemeetsreligion.org/theology/scientific-materialism.php*.

electronic signals sent by the brain along the human nervous system. For Sir John Maddox, former editor of the premier scientific journal *Nature*, an explanation of what is meant by *mind* "must ultimately be an explanation in terms of the way neurons function."[9]

Implications of Worldviews Closed to Transcendence   2.2.3

Ethical relativism is one natural consequence of rationalist, materialist, and determinist views. For the rationalist, ethical standards of right and wrong cannot be objectively true statements, because they are not based on physical facts. They must simply be matters of opinion. For the strict materialist and determinist, ethical right and wrong can have no meaning, as actions are not chosen but determined by forces beyond human control. One cannot hold people accountable if their actions aren't the result of freely made choices.

As noted earlier, although few people are pure rationalists, materialists, or determinists, the influence of these worldviews is apparent everywhere. Consider these examples of common statements, followed by the rationalist or determinist logic behind each.

- "Teens are going to have sex because of their 'raging hormones.'" *Translation*: Teens don't have free will; their hormones determine their behavior.

- "I'm not a morning person." *Translation*: Certain genetic factors determine whether people function well in the morning.

- "It's all about the money." *Translation*: In business transactions, people may speak of ethical qualities such as honesty and integrity, but their actions are determined by the desire for money.

- "I think abortion is wrong, but I can't judge anyone who thinks it is right." *Translation*: True, objective, ethical standards do not exist: standards of right and wrong are only matters of opinion.

While few people see themselves as strict materialists or determinists, many think and act in ways that presume materialistic and deterministic principles, whether they recognize them as such.

---

9. John Maddox, *What Remains to be Discovered: Mapping the Secrets of the Universe, the Origins of Life, and the Future of the Human Race* (New York: Simon and Schuster, 1999), 281.

Similarly, emotions can be broken down to their "true" material basis: they are simply the result of certain chemical reactions that take place in the stomach or other bodily organs.

Francis Crick, one of the discoverers of DNA, nicely sums up the materialist conclusion: "'You,' your joys and your sorrows, your memories and your ambitions, your sense of personal identity and free will, are in fact no more than the behavior of a vast assembly of nerve cells and their associated molecules."[10]

The strict materialist view is closely related to a determinist view. If the material world is all that exists, then it is obvious that everything that happens in the universe is a result of the strict laws of cause and effect that govern the physical world. If this is true, human free will must be an illusion. Crick writes: "What you're aware of is a decision, but you're not aware of what makes you do the decision. It seems free to you, but it's the result of things you are not aware of."[11] An individual's choices are determined by genetic makeup and the influence of environment, according to the determinist.[12] If one takes away genetics and environmental stimuli, there is no mind or will left over to make a choice.

Rationalist and Materialist Definitions of Faith   2.3

How is religious faith understood within traditions that are closed to the transcendent? For the materialist or rationalist, the concept of a transcendent God who created the universe is meaningless. Because all things in the universe can be explained by material causes, there is no need for God.[13] Religious knowledge, for the rationalist, is not true knowledge, as it is not based on observable, testable evidence. Thus invisible realities such as spirits, the soul, heaven, and hell can only be accepted by a blind faith that is the opposite of reason. British biologist Richard Dawkins speaks of the "overweening confidence with which the religious assert minute details for which they neither have, nor could have, evidence."[14]

For the materialist, there can be no ultimate meaning to the universe. Ultimate reality is matter, and matter can have no higher purpose or goals.

---

10. Francis Crick, *The Astonishing Hypothesis: The Scientific Search for the Soul* (New York: Scribner, 1994), 3.

11. Private conversation noted in John Horgan, *The Undiscovered Mind: How the Human Brain Defies Replication, Medication, and Explanation* (New York: Free Press, 1999), 247.

12. An overview of causal determinism is accessible at *plato.stanford.edu/entries/determinism-causal*.

13. When Napoleon asked the Enlightenment mathematician Pierre-Simon Laplace why he did not mention God in his five-volume study of heavenly bodies, Laplace famously replied, "I have no need of that hypothesis."

14. Richard Dawkins, *The God Delusion* (Boston: Houghton Mifflin, 2006), 34.

In a rationalist worldview, religious thinking is based on a prescientific view of reality. Religion arose as a way of explaining natural phenomena. For example, with no scientific understanding of electrical charges, the ancients imagined that Zeus hurling thunderbolts across the sky was the source of lightning. As science advances, the need for "religious" explanations will shrink and eventually vanish.

For thinkers such as Dawkins, faith is an irrational way of thinking that can only be imposed on people by authoritarian churches. Dawkins writes, "Faith is an evil precisely because it requires no justification and brooks no argument."[15]

For worldviews closed to the transcendent, scientific knowledge can only advance when it is free of religious interference. Proponents of these worldviews often cite the example of the Roman Catholic Church forcing Galileo to deny his scientific conclusion that Earth revolved around the sun, because such a conclusion contradicted the literal meaning of some biblical passages. Dawkins also cites the more contemporary example of strictly literal interpretation of the Bible leading people to reject any scientific evidence for evolution.[16]

To sum up, within traditions closed to the transcendent, faith and reason have specific meanings. *Reason* is defined as "logical thinking based on sure, physical, and scientifically provable evidence." *Faith* is defined, at best, as "unprovable opinions about highly speculative subjects." At worst, faith (especially if associated with organized religions) is narrow-minded, judgmental, resistant to scientific truth, and insistent on blind obedience to its authority.

Is the Rationalist View of Reason Reasonable? 2.4

The Judeo-Christian worldview's understanding of both reason and faith differs from the rationalist's and materialist's, whose definition of reason can be critiqued as excessively narrow, distorting, and in the end, unreasonable. As the Jewish theologian Abraham Joshua Heschel wrote, "Extreme rationalism may be defined as the failure of reason to understand itself."[17] The following sections explore an understanding of reason that is broader than the rationalist's view that reason is strictly logical and scientifically based.

Reason Is Broader than Strict Logic and Scientific Proof 2.4.1

Human knowledge is based on far more than scientifically observable facts; one comes to know things in a variety of ways. Recall Gadamer's point (sec. 1.10)

---

15. Ibid., 308.

16. Ibid., 282–86.

17. Quoted in Rodney Stark, *For the Glory of God: How Monotheism Led to Reformations, Science, Witch-hunts, and the End of Slavery* (Princeton, NJ: Princeton University Press, 2003), 201.

that humans acquire aesthetic, historical, or philosophical knowledge in ways that cannot be based on strictly scientific methods, and yet such knowledge is accepted as reliable truth. Reason involves more than scientific reasoning. Consider the following examples:

Reasoning Based on Trust in Authority   2.4.1.1

The word *authority* can have a negative ring to it when associated with blind trust. Many people prefer to develop knowledge through experience and thinking rather than by blindly trusting someone else. However, the fact is that the vast majority of knowledge is based not on personal experience but on reasonable acceptance of someone else's authority. C. S. Lewis writes:

> Do not be scared by the word *authority*. Believing things on authority only means believing them because you have been told them by someone you think trustworthy. Ninety-nine percent of the things you believe are believed on authority. I believe there is such a place as New York. I have not seen it myself. I could not prove by abstract reasoning that there must be such a place. I believe it because reliable people have told me so. The ordinary man believes in the Solar System, atoms, evolution, and the circulation of the blood on authority—because the scientists say so. Every historical statement in the world is believed on authority. None of us has seen the Norman Conquest or the defeat of the Armada. None of us could prove them by pure logic as you prove a thing in mathematics. We believe them simply because people who did see them have left writings that tell us about them: in fact, on authority.[18]

Lewis's point is that it is reasonable to accept knowledge from trustworthy authorities.

Reasoning Based on Probability   2.4.1.2

The many decisions people must make are rarely based on scientific evidence; usually they are based on probabilities.

Consider some examples: Reflecting on her interests and abilities as well as on the current job market, Jill decides to major in nursing. Her choice is reasonable, yet she cannot prove scientifically that her choice is correct. Given what Jeff knows about Martha's good character, their common interests, and their five years of dating, he feels certain that his marriage to Martha will be a happy one. His conclusion is reasonable but again not strictly scientific.

The English theologian John Henry Newman shows that, in many practical cases, knowledge based on probability is certain, even without strictly logical

---

18. C. S. Lewis, *Mere Christianity* (London: HarperCollins, 2001; orig. pub. 1952), 62.

proof.[19] For example, an Englishman is certain that Great Britain is an island. Yet how can he be sure, as he has never personally sailed around it? He was taught at school, Britain appears as an island on maps, and he has never heard anyone deny that Britain is an island. Although none of these points is logical proof, when all these probable arguments converge, he concludes that his knowledge is certain.[20]

Reasoning Based on Experience   2.4.1.3

People often make reasonable decisions and judgments based on what Newman calls the "illative sense," a type of reasoning that is based on personal, implicit knowledge.[21] Again, this type of decision making and judging is not strictly logical or provable, but it is still reasonable and reliable.

Thus a farmer may be able to make highly accurate predictions about the weather based on his long years of observations, but he might not be able to articulate his reasons logically. A chef, based on many years of experience, may have a highly developed sense of just which seasonings to put in a soup and in what amounts, but she might have a hard time writing out an exact recipe.[22] The personal knowledge of the chef and farmer cannot be demonstrated scientifically; nevertheless, their conclusions are reasonable and accurate.

Historical Reasoning   2.4.1.4

Knowledge of historical events is by definition nonscientific. As C. S. Lewis points out, historical knowledge comes primarily through individual trust of authorities.

Historians cannot prove scientifically that George Washington was the first president of the United States. However, there is no serious doubt about this statement: all credible eyewitness accounts and reports from that time agree that Washington was the first president. It is a certain fact.

Historical knowledge is not limited to simple matters such as identifying the first US president. It also involves interpretation, as discussed in the example of the Cuban revolution (sec. 1.10). One's interpretation, even the questions one asks about a historical event, are shaped by certain traditions, whether they are capitalist, socialist, or other traditions of understanding. However, as Gadamer insists, historical interpretation is not a matter of opinion. Good historians are aware of how their own traditions shape their thinking and attempt to fuse two

---

19. John Henry Newman, *An Essay in Aid of a Grammar of Assent*, ed. I. T. Ker (Oxford: Clarendon Press, 1985), 187–213. A version of this text is accessible at *www.newmanreader.org/works/grammar/*.

20. See Ibid., 191–92.

21. Ibid., 222–47.

22. Kathleen Fischer and Thomas Hart, *Christian Foundations: An Introduction to Faith in Our Time*, rev. ed. (New York: Paulist Press, 1995), 19.

horizons: 1) their own thinking and 2) the different horizons from the past encountered in historical research.

Why Strict Determinism and Materialism Are Unreasonable　　2.4.2

Strict materialists and determinists pride themselves on their strict use of reason, yet the question about whether such thinking is reasonable remains.

A strict materialist asserts, "My thoughts are simply a firing of neurons, nothing more." However, how can that thought, "My thoughts are simply a firing of neurons," be merely a firing of neurons? Logically, people thinking this are, so to speak, standing apart from their neurons and thinking about them. In other words, in their thinking, people transcend the physical structures with which they think. This point is similar to the earlier point (sec. 1.7) that by the very act of thinking, people presuppose that a "transcendent horizon of truth" exists.

Similarly, a strict determinist says, "My every thought is determined by my genetics or my environment, my thoughts and choices are not truly free." If this were true, how would the person ever have become aware that his thought was determined? If all thoughts were truly determined by outsides forces, one would never know it. That humans can think about their own thoughts and actions shows that they have the freedom to stand apart from themselves and consider the causes that influence, but do not fully determine, their beliefs and behaviors. In the very act of freely thinking about outside forces that supposedly determine behavior, a person shows that she transcends those forces.

The materialist and determinist have difficulty in explaining self-awareness or self-consciousness. Although consciousness has a material basis in the physical functioning of the brain, it cannot reasonably be reduced to this physical phenomenon and nothing more.

The newly developing science of neuroplasticity also challenges materialist thinking. Conventional neurology had assumed that adult brains in particular are "hardwired, fixed in form and function."[23] However, recent research and practice is showing that carefully planned mental exercises can change the structure of the brain in significant ways.[24] This research has caught the attention of religious leaders such as the Dalai Lama, who finds in it confirmation of his belief that not only does the brain affect the mind, but also "how people think really can change their brains."[25] Our thinking transcends our brains and neurons.

Stephen Barr shows that faith has a role in the materialist's thinking. The materialist belief that all reality is simply physical reality is an article of faith that

---

23. Sharon Begley, *Train Your Mind, Change Your Brain* (New York: Ballantine Books, 2007), 6.

24. A video animation demonstrating how the brain changes is accessible at *www.youtube.com/watch?v=ELpfYCZa87g*.

25. Quoted in Begley, *Train Your Mind*, viii.

cannot be proven. The materialist assumes that no reality exists beyond material reality—that which can be observed scientifically. However, if a transcendent, nonmaterial reality does exist, then by definition, it could not be observed scientifically, because scientific observation is able to examine only material reality. It is illogical to assert that because something cannot be scientifically observed, it, therefore, does not exist.[26]

The Insanity of Rationalism and the Sanity of Faith   2.4.3

G. K. Chesterton shows that the commonly accepted idea that the religious worldview is irrational and the rationalist worldview is reasonable has it exactly backward. In fact, argues Chesterton, rationalism is more closely related to insanity than to healthy reasoning.

In his book *Orthodoxy*, Chesterton discusses a paranoid man who is convinced that everyone is secretly plotting to kill him. It is impossible, using strict logic alone, to convince the man that he is wrong. If someone points out that other people deny that they want to kill him, he responds, "Of course, they deny it, because they are trying to conceal their plot." His version of reality logically explains the facts.

The real problem with his paranoid view of reality is not that it is irrational but that it is *too narrowly* rational—it takes a single idea and uses it in a strictly logical way to explain all events. The only way to restore the paranoid man—and indeed the strict rationalist and materialist—to sanity is to help him see how cramped and narrow his worldview is.

Chesterton contrasts the narrow rationalism of the logician with the imagination of the poet. The poet knows that life is complex and mysterious and, therefore, cannot be defined completely with strict reason; the rationalist logician insists that everything must have a logical explanation. Who is mentally healthier?

The poet only desires exaltation and expansion, a world to stretch himself in. The poet only asks to get his head into the heavens. It is the logician who seeks to get the heavens into his head. And it is his head that splits.[27]

26. Stephen Barr, *Modern Physics and Ancient Faith* (Notre Dame, IN: University of Notre Dame Press, 2003), 15–18.

27. G. K. Chesterton, *Orthodoxy* (Peabody, MA: Hendrickson, 2006; orig. pub. 1908), 13, accessible at *www.ccel.org/ccel/chesterton/orthodoxy*.

Faith plays a role in the strict determinist's thinking too. The geneticist and evolutionary biologist J. B. S. Haldane observes,

> If my mental processes are determined wholly by the motion of atoms in my brain, I have no reason to believe that my beliefs are true . . . and hence I have no reason for supposing my brain to be composed of atoms.[28]

Reason and Faith in the Christian Worldview   2.5

Rationalism and materialism understand faith as, at best, a harmless opinion about matters that are not real. At its worst, religious faith is actively evil: it is intolerant of other beliefs, obstructs rational and scientific thinking, and demands slavish and blind obedience. How differently do faith and reason look when considered from a Christian worldview?

Reason Is Ultimately Based on Faith   2.5.1

Faith and reason, for Christians, are not mutually exclusive: they, in fact, can work well together. Chesterton shows that reason itself is based on faith: "It is idle to talk always about the alternative of reason and faith. Reason is itself a matter of faith. It is an act of faith to assert that our thoughts have any relation to reality at all."[29]

Consider Chesterton's point: How can people be sure that what they think they know about the world is actually true? When looking at a tree, how do people know they are really seeing a tree? Isn't it possible that their senses or minds are deceiving them? After all, people do see mirages or suffer delusions, don't they? Yet even if individuals can trust their senses and minds, how do they know that their perception of the tree actually gives them true information about the tree? After all, they're only seeing the surface of the tree: isn't its true nature (for example, its molecular structure, the relationships of its subatomic particles) still hidden?

These questions could drive one crazy because they suggest the mind isn't connected with reality. (After all, the insane person is one whose mind is disconnected from reality.) Most people simply *take it on faith* that their minds are connected with reality. One's thinking, including scientific thinking, is really based on two articles of faith: (1) trust in the human ability to accurately perceive and reason about reality, and (2) trust that the true nature of reality is accessible to people. In other words, people trust that reality has an ordered structure that can be understood by reason.

---

28. Quoted in C. S. Lewis, *Miracles* (New York: Macmillan, 1960), 15.

29. Ibid., 28.

Rationalists and materialists also accept these two articles of faith, because one simply cannot think without them. However, rationalists and materialists don't admit that faith is actually the starting point of reason.

God: The Transcendent Source of Reason and Meaning   2.5.2

Why trust reason, and why trust that the world is reasonable? For Christians, this trust is rooted in the belief that God, the creator of all, is the source of reason itself.

According to Christian Scripture: "In the beginning was the Word, and the Word was with God, and the Word was God. . . . All things came to be through him" (John 1:1–3). A key term in this passage is *Word*. In Greek, the original language of the Gospel of John, the term translated as *Word* is *Logos*, a central concept in ancient Greek philosophy. The meaning of the *Logos* is "reason, or study" (recall from sec. 1.9 that *theology* is derived from *theos* and *logos*). So what is the Gospel saying? Essentially, it says that God's reason is integral to God's nature (the Word was God), and that God created all things through his reason. John 1:14 goes on to say that "the Word became flesh"—indicating the belief that the Word took human form in Jesus Christ. This belief, known as the Incarnation, is a central belief of Christians.

If God created the universe through his Word, the universe itself is reasonable and open to human understanding. God's Logos is the reason why matter has a clearly structured molecular order and why the universe functions according laws of nature. In the Christian view, these laws of nature reflect God's Logos.

According to the biblical creation account, humans were created in God's image (Gen 1:26–27). In other words, humans reflect or mirror the Creator in significant ways. One of these ways is reflecting God's Logos by thinking and reasoning. Humans can trust their reasoning ability because God, the transcendent source of all reasoning and meaning, created it.

A Classic Definition: Thomas Aquinas on Faith   2.5.3

Christian faith, then, involves a fundamental trust in the goodness and rationality of God and of God's creation. To gain a deeper understanding of the Christian understanding of faith, consider a more technical definition of faith from a well-known representative of the Catholic theological tradition, the medieval theologian Thomas Aquinas (1225–1274).[30]

In his *Summa Theologica*, regarded by many as the most influential work in Catholic theology, Aquinas writes, "Now the act of believing is an act of the

---

30. A brief video overview of the life of Aquinas is accessible at *www.youtube.com /watch?v=nxZfgawlf-0* (time 0:01:36).

intellect assenting to the divine truth at the command of the will moved by the grace of God" (*ST* 2–2.2.9).[31] The *Catechism of the Catholic Church* (no. 155) used Aquinas's definition in its discussion on faith. The following sections consider each part of Aquinas's important definition in turn.

Faith Involves Intellect and Will   2.5.3.1

Faith, Aquinas teaches, involves the will and intellect. In other words, religious faith is not just a matter of intellect, the mind alone. Rather, the act of faith begins with the will, including emotions and desires. When people take the time to think about a topic, whether football, volleyball, or God, it is because the will motivates them—the will, their desire, is attracted to that topic, and so the will "commands" our intellect to consider that topic.

The will is attracted to something because one perceives it to be good. In Aquinas's terms, the good is the object of the will (*ST* 2–2.4.1). People's perception of the good differs, whether that good is fishing, gardening, or basketball. As noted in chapter 1 (secs. 1.6–1.8), however, all people desire not just *a* good, but rather *the* good; not just temporary good things, but the perfect, permanent happiness, truth, and peace that cannot be achieved in this imperfect world. People desire God, although many don't usually consciously recognize that desire.

"Moved by the Grace of God": Faith and God's Grace   2.5.3.2

According to Aquinas, the will does not seek God on its own power. Rather, it is "moved by the grace of God." What exactly does this mean? According to the *Catechism of the Catholic Church* (no. 1996), "Grace is favor, the free and undeserved help that God gives us to respond to his call to become children of God, adoptive sons, partakers of the divine nature and of eternal life." In other words, **grace** is God's free gift that allows humans to fulfill their purpose: to enter into that perfect peace and happiness that they will experience in heaven. One cannot have faith in God, then, without the help of God's grace: "Believing is possible only by grace and the interior helps of the Holy Spirit" (*CCC*, no. 154).

Faith, Nature, and Grace   2.5.3.3

Aquinas' definition of faith raises a topic much debated by theologians: the relationship between nature and grace. *Nature* refers to the natural, this-worldly realm, while *grace* refers to the supernatural, transcendent realm. The relationship between the two requires careful thought. If, on the one hand, one sees the two realms as too closely related, then it seems that one doesn't really

---

31. Thomas Aquinas, *Summa Theologica*, trans. Fathers of the English Dominican Province, Christian Classics (Notre Dame: Ave Maria Press, 1981; orig. pub. 1911). All quotes from Aquinas's *Summa Theologica* in this book are from this translation.

need the transcendent, eternal God. One could achieve perfect happiness in this world. If, on the other hand, one sees the two realms as essentially separate, then it is difficult to explain how the transcendent God can have any effect on this world.

Theologians such as Henri de Lubac offer a solution: Human nature "is by nature ordered to an end that it is not equipped by nature to attain."[32] In other words, humans naturally desire, and in fact, their natural purpose is to attain the perfect peace and happiness that can only be found in God (compare Lewis's comment in sec. 1.8). However, they cannot reach that purpose by their own natural abilities. Humans have to accept God's help; they must allow the free gift of God's grace to work within them to reach that goal.

Faith, Grace, and Free Will 2.5.3.4

Rossetti, Dante Gabriel Charles (1828–82) / Fitzwilliam Museum, University of Cambridge, UK / Bridgeman Images

How exactly is a person's will "moved by God's grace"? Does this mean that God simply takes over the will, so individuals are no longer free? This question of the will's relationship to God's grace was the focus of a great debate between Reformers, such as Martin Luther and John Calvin, and the Catholic Church (see sec. 7.17.2). At this point, however, it is enough to note that the Catholic theological tradition has always insisted that humans truly have the free will to cooperate, or to refuse to cooperate, with God's grace.

The Catholic imagination sees the classic example of this cooperation with God's grace in Mary's (the mother of Jesus) acceptance of God's plan for her life. When the angel Gabriel told Mary that she would have a child, Mary was confused; she didn't understand how this would be possible, as she had no relations with a man. In the end, however, she agreed to cooperate with God's mysterious plan for her, proclaiming, "I am the handmaid of the Lord. May it be done to me according to your word" (Luke 1:38).

In this depiction, Mary's open-handed gesture reflects her openness to God's will. The dove symbolizes the Holy Spirit's role in Mary's conception of Jesus (see Luke 1:35).

---

32. For a discussion on this point, see Rodney A. Howsare, *Balthasar: A Guide for the Perplexed* (London: T & T Clark, 2009), 15.

The Divine Truth: Object of Faith   2.5.3.5

We now return to the last part of Aquinas's definition of faith. The intellect, motivated by will, which was moved by God's grace, assents "to the divine truth."

What exactly is this "divine truth"? In another passage of *Summa Theologica*, Aquinas clarifies: "The formal object of faith is the First Truth as manifested in Holy Writ and the teaching of the Church, which proceeds from the First Truth" (*ST* 2–2.5.3). The primary object of faith, in other words, is God, considered as the source of all truth. The person trusts God, and because God is trustworthy, he can believe in what God communicates in Holy Writ (Scripture) and the teaching of the Church.

For Aquinas, God communicates the specific content of faith through Scripture and Church teachings. These teachings are expressed as articles of faith (for example: "God is a Trinity," or "the Second Person of the Trinity became human"); these articles, in turn, are expressed in the church's **creeds**— brief summaries of basic beliefs (*ST* 2–2.1.6–10).

In the modern era, many challenge the idea that religious faith can be summed up in articles or statements of belief. Many argue that religion should be a matter of the heart and that precise creedal definitions make religion too abstract and intellectual and thus dampen true religious spirit. The Catholic tradition argues, however, that theological propositions are necessary because people cannot love what they don't know. Before one can have a loving faith in God, one needs some knowledge of God, and theological ideas expressed through creedal statements contribute to this knowledge.[33]

C. S. Lewis makes a similar point in his response to an air force officer who rejected theological ideas as "petty and pedantic and unreal" in comparison to his real experience of the tremendous mystery of God when he was out flying alone in the desert at night. Lewis agreed that such an experience was more real than a theological statement, just as the Atlantic is more real than a map of the Atlantic.[34]

Yet the map analogy supplies Lewis with a further point: theology functions as a good map. First, maps, like theological propositions in creeds, are based not on the experience of a single person but on the combined experience of numerous people. Second, just as when one wishes to leave the beach and travel on the ocean, a map is necessary; so too if one wishes to make any progress in growing closer to God, then one cannot rely on personal feeling alone; one needs a more objective guide. The officer's experience of God in the desert may have been very real, but

> It leads nowhere. There is nothing to do about it. In fact, that is just why a vague religion—all about feeling God in nature, and so on—is so

33. Newman, *Grammar of Assent*, 82–83.
34. Lewis, *Mere Christianity*, 153–54.

attractive. It is all thrills and no work: like watching the waves from the beach. But you will not get to Newfoundland by studying the Atlantic that way, and you will not get eternal life by simply feeling the presence of God in flowers and music.[35]

Lewis's last point is that theology is practical. Lewis writes (and his point is even more true in today's Internet-centered culture), that people have access to a great variety of (often contradictory) theological ideas. Even if people never study theology directly, they cannot avoid forming some theological ideas. Recall our example of Jane (sec. 1.11): even though she did not attend church or read the Bible on a regular basis, she had beliefs about God. However, without disciplined theological study, by picking up a few ideas here and a few ideas there, one's theological beliefs are virtually certain to be muddled and confused.[36]

Returning to Aquinas's definition, notice that belief in the articles of faith is based not only on a trust in God as the "first truth" but also on a fundamental trust in the authority of Scripture and of Church teachings as accurate reflections of God's communication. This should come as no surprise, however, because knowledge in any field is based largely on trust in authorities (sec. 2.4.1.1). One can think theologically, moreover, only if one thinks within a certain theological tradition, and this implies accepting the authorities of that tradition (secs. 1.10–1.11).

One authoritative Catholic teaching, the Second Vatican Council's document *Dogmatic Constitution on Divine Revelation (Dei Verbum)* emphasizes this aspect of faith as an obedient acceptance of God's revelation:

> "The obedience of faith" (Romans 16:26, cf. Romans 1:5; 2 Corinthians 10:5–6) "is to be given to God as he reveals, and obedience by which man commits his whole self freely to God, offering the full submission of his intellect and will to God who reveals" and freely assenting to the truth revealed by Him. (*DV*, no. 5, citing Vatican I's *Dogmatic Constitution on the Catholic Faith*, ch. 3)

Theological statements of faith found in the creeds (such as "I believe in one God,") or in the Bible (such as "Christ died for our sins"), form the objective aspect of Christian faith. They are necessary expressions of faith that all believers can use as a reference point to clarify the beliefs they share. They sum up the centuries-old religious experience and insights of the Christian tradition.

---

35. Ibid., 154–55.
36. Ibid., 155.

Intellectual Conversion as a Step
toward Faith

Aquinas's definition of faith involves God's grace, the will, and the intellect. So although God's grace and human will are indispensable, the act of faith itself is "an act of the intellect" (*ST* 2–2.2.9). This should drive home how closely faith and reason are bound together in Catholic thinking: faith itself is an act of reason. So it is fitting to conclude this study of the Catholic understanding of faith with some specific reflections on the role of reason.

One's faith is closely connected with one's fundamental way of understanding reality—one's worldview (sec. 2.1). Christians have a worldview rooted in faith that the world makes sense because a good God created it through his Word. The materialist worldview is also ultimately based on the faith that the only reality that exists is material reality. The change from one worldview to another, from accepting one faith to accepting another faith, is known as conversion, derived from the Latin *converto*, "to turn around."

In the Christian worldview, the fundamental "turnaround" is when a person turns from a worldview closed to the transcendent to one open to the transcendent. To believe, writes Joseph Ratzinger (later Pope Benedict XVI),[37]

> . . . means that man does not regard seeing, hearing and touching as the totality of what concerns him, that he does not view the area of his world as marked off by what he can see and touch but seeks a second mode of access to reality, a mode he calls in fact belief, and in such a way that he finds in it the decisive enlargement of his whole view of the world.[38]

But far from being an irrational turn from the world of the senses to a worldview of blind faith, the Catholic understanding of conversion includes a rational dimension, what Jesuit theologian Bernard Lonergan calls "intellectual conversion."[39]

Intellect alone cannot lead one directly to faith, because faith also involves God's grace and human will. However, an intellectual conversion might help prepare the way for a faith conversion. For example, if a person has a rationalist or materialist worldview, that person may be intellectually converted from that worldview by reason alone (e.g., by some of the arguments considered in sec. 2.4).

Two well-known conversions to the Christian faith involved this preliminary intellectual conversion. In his *Confessions*, Augustine describes how, as a

---

37. For a biography of Pope Benedict XVI, see *www.vatican.va/holy_father/benedict_xvi /biography/documents/hf_ben-xvi_bio_20050419_short-biography_en.html*.

38. Ratzinger, *Introduction to Christianity*, 50.

39. Bernard Lonergan, *Method in Theology* (Toronto: University of Toronto Press, 1990; orig. pub., 1971), 238.

youthful follower of the materialist-oriented Manichean religion, he had been unable to conceive of nonphysical existence. His reading of non-Christian, Platonist philosophy, however, encouraged him "to look for truth as something incorporeal" (*Confessions* 7.20).[40] This intellectual conversion prepared him to later accept Christian beliefs about the nonmaterial world.

C. S. Lewis too describes his intellectual conversion from an atheistic materialist view to a non-Christian, idealist philosophy as an important step in his eventual conversion to Christianity.[41]

For Lonergan, the intellectual worldview of today's Christian should be a "critical realism." The rationalist (Lonergan uses the term *empiricist*) restricts reality to what he can see and touch. The idealist takes the opposite view: our mind shapes our view of reality, so what we know is really a mental construction, not reality. Critical realism takes a middle path, insisting that we do have true knowledge of the world outside of ourselves but recognizing that this knowledge is always shaped in certain ways by our worldview. One must have a critical awareness of that influence.[42]

Catholic Faith: Between Fideism and Rationalism   2.6

In Catholic understanding, faith cannot be separated from reason. Not all Christian traditions have taken this approach, however. Some traditions are suspicious of reason: they believe that human reason can lead to questioning that may cause a person to lose faith. Faith, they insist, is a matter of personal experience and feeling, not intellect. Although they accept that reason is good in other areas of life, reason should not influence the life of faith.

This tendency of some Christians to sharply separate the realm of faith from the realm of reason is known as *fideism*.[43]

Ironically, even though fideistic persons are typically very pious and devout, they share with rationalists the same definition of faith: faith is a realm of personal feelings that is completely separate from the realm of reason.

The Catholic Church, however, has insisted that fideism is an error. Religious faith can never contradict natural human reason because God created human reason. In the words of the Vatican I Council (1870):

---

40. Saint Augustine, *Confessions*, trans. R. S. Pine-Coffin (New York: Penguin 1961), accessible at *www.ccel.org/ccel/augustine/confessions.x.html*.

41. C. S. Lewis, *Surprised by Joy: The Shape of My Early Life* (New York: Harcourt, Brace, 1955), 208–11.

42. Lonergan, *Method in Theology*, 238–39.

43. Avery Dulles refers to these traditions as "paracritical"; he notes the influence of Kant's philosophy on them and lists Lutheran pietism and nineteenth-century liberal Protestantism as examples (*The Craft of Theology: From Symbol to System* [New York: Crossroad, 1995], 4). An overview of fideism is accessible at *http://plato.stanford.edu/entries/fideism/*. See especially section 4, "A Rational Fideism?"

Though faith is above reason, there can never be any real discrepancy between faith and reason. Since the same God who reveals mysteries and infuses faith has bestowed the light of reason on the human mind, God cannot deny himself, nor can truth ever contradict truth.[44]

The Catholic tradition rejects both rationalism and fideism in its insistence that faith and reason cannot be separated.

Questions about the Text

1. What are some of the common characteristics of the *rationalist, materialist,* and *determinist* worldviews?
2. How are *faith* and *reason* defined within rationalist and materialist worldviews?
3. In what ways is a strictly rationalist view actually unreasonable?
4. What are some nonscientific ways by which one can gain sure knowledge?
5. How does the Word (Logos), mentioned in the Gospel of John, relate to the human ability to understand the world?
6. What roles do God's grace, the human will, and the human intellect play in Aquinas's definition of faith?
7. In the Catholic worldview, why does faith involve not only faith in God, but also faith in the creeds of the Church?
8. In what way can an "intellectual conversion" be a step toward faith?
9. Why does the Catholic tradition reject both fideism and rationalism?

Discussion Questions

1. Do you see examples of the influence of rationalism, determinism, or materialism in your daily life?
2. In your field of study, how much information do you accept on faith from trusted authorities without proving it for yourself?
3. To what extent are your daily decisions based on strict logic? What other factors influence your choices?
4. In your experience, do religious people tend to be fideistic, or are they open to rational discussions of faith?
5. Why do some people have a strong faith in God and others do not? Consider how your answer relates to Aquinas's definition of faith.

---

44. *Dei Filius*, no. 4 quoted in *CCC*, no. 159, accessible at *www.vatican.va/archive/ccc_css/archive/catechism/p1s1c3a1.htm*.

Doing Theology

Faith and Reason in Theology

This chapter considers how representative Catholic theologians have viewed the relationship among faith, reason, and tradition in their theological thinking. As the role of tradition is essential to theological thinking (secs. 1.10–1.11), the chapter begins with one of the most influential theologians of the Catholic tradition, Thomas Aquinas. Contemporary examples are then considered: the approaches of the American theologian Avery Dulles (1918–2008) and the Swiss theologian Hans Urs von Balthasar (1905–1988). In addition, the thought of the French Protestant philosopher Paul Ricoeur is examined, as he, like Hans Georg Gadamer (sec. 1.10), helps illuminate the issues involved in interpreting traditional texts like the Bible in modern times—issues that all theologians must face.

Reason, Faith, and Tradition in Thomas Aquinas   3.1

Knowing God through Reason and Faith   3.1.1

Given that *theology* literally means "study of God," a fundamental question for the theologian is, how do people know about God? Essentially, there are two ways: (1) knowledge gained using one's reason, and (2) knowledge that God reveals to people.

Aquinas, reflecting the Catholic view that reason and faith are compatible, believes people can know that God exists using reason alone. This conviction is reflected in the *Catechism of the Catholic Church*: God "can be known with certainty from the created world by the natural light of human reason" (*CCC*, no. 36, quoting the Vatican Council I document *Dei Filius*, no. 2). Aquinas discusses five "ways" in which one's reason can lead to knowledge of God's existence. (secs. 3.2.1–3).

Yet says Aquinas, the knowledge gained from reason alone is not adequate. Humans also need communication from God, in other words, God's **revelation**. Why is this necessary? First, reason itself can only show *that* God, defined as the eternal, transcendent source of all other things, exists; but it tells little about God's nature (e.g., Does God answer prayers? Does God care about people and love them? Does God forgive sins, and, if so, how?) God's direct revelation, accepted by faith, is needed for a more complete picture of God. Second, using reason to prove that God exists, while possible, is a challenging intellectual task, and therefore, such knowledge "would only be known by a few, and that after a long time, and with the admixture of many errors" (*ST* 1.1.1). To make things easier, then, according to Aquinas, God reveals divine truth, which Scripture and church teaching express.

Theology Is a Science   3.1.2

In modern culture, many people assume theology consists of discussions about religious opinions and is, therefore, unscientific. Aquinas, however, insists that theology is a science (*ST* 1.1.2; in Latin: *scientia*).

Although Aquinas did not, of course, have a modern understanding of experimental science, he did understand the term as a rigorous, systematic investigation into truth.

Any science, Aquinas says, begins by accepting certain first principles as its starting point, and then using logical deductions to build further knowledge from these first principles. First principles are truths that are so obvious they do not need further proof. In logic, for example, a first principle is that every change must have a cause. In geometry, the first principles are called axioms; theorems are then derived from these axioms. In political science, a first principle in theories of democracy is that "all men are created equal." The US Declaration of Independence, for example, asserts that this principle is "self-evident," requiring no further proof.

The first principles of theology are the basic articles of faith as expressed in Scripture and church teaching, especially in the creeds (*ST* 1.1.2) These articles (e.g., There is one God who created all things; Jesus rose from the dead.) are accepted on faith, just as a scientist in any field of study accepts that field's first principles without further proof. From the foundation of these first principles, the theologian deduces further theological knowledge in a rational, systematic way.

As Aquinas noted, every science takes for granted certain first principles. Many sciences take for granted the principles established by other sciences: the study of music depends on principles established by mathematics. No scientist personally verifies every scientific principle; rather, the scientist accepts on authority a large body of previously established scientific knowledge (sec. 4.3). So theology is comparable to other sciences in beginning with unproven first principles.

Reason Answers Reasonable Objections 3.1.3

Aquinas realizes that non-Christians would not accept the Christian articles of faith as their first principles. So is it possible to have further dialogue between Christians and non-Christians, if their starting point is not the same?

Yes, says Aquinas. Although theological reason cannot *prove* the truth of an article of faith to a nonbeliever, it can answer a nonbeliever's objections that a particular article of faith is illogical or unreasonable. For example, a non-Christian might argue that the Christian belief that God is a Trinity (three persons—Father, Son, and Holy Spirit—in one God) is a logical contradiction. How can three things be one? Although Christian theologians cannot logically prove that God is a Trinity, they should be able to show, by reason alone, that belief in the Trinity is not illogical (for example, by showing that the three persons of God are unified by sharing one divine nature) (*ST* 1.1.8).

Aquinas's confidence that Christian beliefs can be defended with reason is unshakeable: "Since faith rests upon infallible truth, and since the contrary of a truth can never be demonstrated, it is clear that the arguments brought against faith cannot be demonstrations, but are difficulties that can be answered" (*ST* 1.1.8).[1] Thus every reasonable question about Christianity has a reasonable answer.

Reason Prepares for Faith 3.1.4

Reason can also prepare a person to have faith. In fact, a person can begin with natural knowledge that can be attained by reason alone and then move on to theology. Human intelligence "is more easily led by what is known through natural reason (from which proceed the other sciences) to that which is above reason, such as are the teachings of this science [theology]" (*ST* 1.1.5 ad. 2). Aquinas holds that "faith presupposes natural knowledge, even as grace presupposes nature, and perfection presupposes something that can be perfected" (*ST* 1.2.2 ad. 1). Just as natural experiences in this world can point one away from this world toward transcendent meaning and happiness (secs. 1.4–1.8), so too, a natural knowledge of this world may lead one to seek the higher knowledge of God. Reason led people such as Augustine and C. S. Lewis to question their materialist worldviews, and prepared them intellectually to accept faith (sec. 2.5.4).

Reason Is Open to Learning from Non-Christian Sources 3.1.5

Aquinas's trust in reason is demonstrated by his willingness to recognize and accept truth apart from the Christian articles of faith. In fact, Aquinas's primary

---

1. On these points, see Peter Kreeft, *A Summa of the* Summa: *The Essential Philosophical Passages of Saint Thomas'* Summa Theologica (San Francisco: Ignatius Press, 1990), 45 no. 32.

guide in his philosophical thinking, for example, in his description of causes and effects, was the non-Christian philosopher Aristotle. In the *Summa*, Aquinas simply refers to Aristotle as "the Philosopher." Aquinas also interacts with the thought of the Muslim philosophers who commented on Aristotle: Avicenna (e.g., *ST* 1.71.1 ad. 1) and Averroes (e.g., *ST* 1.117.1) and the Jewish philosopher Maimonides (e.g., *ST* 1.68.1; Aquinas calls him "Rabbi Moses").

© Neftali / Shutterstock.com

Other sciences can help clarify theological teachings; Aquinas calls them the "handmaidens" of theology (*ST* 1.1.5). Theology properly makes use of these sciences, each of which is competent in its own realm of expertise: "Hence sacred doctrine makes use also of the authority of philosophers in those questions in which they were able to know the truth by natural reason" (*ST* 1.1.8). Applying Aquinas's point to a modern con-

In his *Guide for the Perplexed*, Jewish philosopher and rabbi Moses Maimonides (1138–1204) strives to show the harmony of the Jewish faith with reason, especially as expressed in Aristotle's philosophy.

text, it is acceptable for a theologian to use insights from anthropologists, historians, and astrophysicists in his thinking about God, although such sources do not have the same theological authority as Scripture.

Faith Builds on Tradition   3.1.6

As Aquinas discusses theological questions in the *Summa*, he deliberately thinks within the Christian tradition (sec. 1.11). As he considers possible answers, he cites the teachings of an array of Christian theologians, including John Chrysostom (ca. 347–407 CE), Augustine (354–430 CE), John of Damascus (ca. 675–ca. 749 CE), and Anselm (ca. 1033–1109 CE), as well as the teachings of Church councils and popes. Aquinas realizes that he is not the first to ponder theological questions, so he studies and builds on the past.

Theological Method in the *Summa*   3.2

Aquinas's *Summa Theologica* is a summary of theology designed for beginning students of theology.[2] The work is carefully structured: it consists of four main parts, with each part divided into treatises (such as, "On the Creation"), and each treatise in turn divided into questions. Finally, each question is divided into articles.

---

2. The Prologue to the *Summa* states: "the Master of Catholic truth ought not only to teach the proficient but also to instruct beginners."

The article is the heart of the *Summa*'s method. It consists of five steps:

1. **Focusing the question.** A specific question is narrowed so it can be answered either yes or no. Aquinas does this to focus and sharpen the issue and avoid vague conclusions.

2. **Listing objections.** Aquinas was convinced that the only way to grasp the truth is by seriously considering all sides of an issue. He lists several objections to his conclusion, stating them in a fair and balanced way.

3. **Statement of Aquinas's answer, backed by authority.** After considering various points of view, Aquinas gives a reasonable answer. He always cites other authorities to support his thinking, both on theological questions (citing Scripture, theologians such as Augustine and Anselm, and official Church teachings) and on philosophical questions (citing authorities such as Aristotle). Aquinas is careful to point out, however, that the conclusions of Christian theologians are only probable. He considers only the authority of Scriptures to be unquestionable (*ST* 1.1.8 ad. 2). This step illustrates how Aquinas thinks within the tradition. He does not aim to express his personal opinion; he intends to think along with tradition in order to discover the truth on any given issue.

4. **Detailed explanation of Aquinas's position.** This is the main part of the article in which Aquinas rationally justifies his answer, providing any necessary explanations and clarifications.

5. **Specific answer to the objections.** The objections to Aquinas's position (stated in step 2) are answered in detail.

The theological method of the *Summa* is thus diametrically opposed to a model of blind faith. It is true that the Christian articles of faith are the unquestioned starting point of Aquinas's thinking, but from that starting point, he proceeds with the most rigorous regard for exact and precise thinking.

Proving God's Existence   3.2.1

The best known of Aquinas's articles in the *Summa* is his response to the question of God's existence. Aquinas responds following the five steps outlined in the previous list.

1. **Focusing the question.** The first two articles of this question had focused the discussion by dealing with preliminary questions: (1) Is the existence of God self-evident? and (2) Can the existence of God be demonstrated? Once Aquinas has shown that God's existence is neither (1) so obvious that any reasonable person must accept it nor (2) so far beyond reasoning ability that it must be accepted on faith alone, he is then ready to ask the specific question: Does God exists?

2. **Listing objections.** Aquinas considers the other side of the argument: possible reasons why God does not exist.

   - Objection 1 (summary): If two things are opposites and one is infinite, then its opposite would be canceled out and cease to exist. Because God is infinitely good, then logically the opposite of good—evil—should not exist. However, evil does in fact exist. Therefore, God does not exist. (This objection is basically a variation of that commonly asked question: If God is all powerful and all good, why do terrible things happen?)
   - Objection 2 (summary): Everything that occurs in the world can be explained without referring to God. Events in nature can be explained by natural causes; events caused by humans can be explained by human causes. Therefore, there is no need to suppose God's existence.

3. **Statement of Aquinas's position, backed by authority.** Aquinas refers to God's own witness to his existence in Exodus 3:14, in which God tells Moses from the burning bush, "I am who am."

4. **Detailed explanation of Aquinas's position.** Aquinas sketches out five ways by which the existence of God can be proved; details follow.

5. **Specific answer to the objections.**

   - Reply to Objection 1: God would not allow evil to exist, unless God's goodness and power could bring good out of evil.
   - Reply to Objection 2: It is true that one can find either a natural or a human cause for any event. However, neither nature nor the human will can explain its own existence. For example, how was the universe created, because logically it cannot have caused itself? Both nature and human free will point beyond themselves to a cause that transcends this universe (i.e., God).

Aquinas's Five Ways 3.2.2

All of Aquinas's five ways[3] of proving God's existence begin with empirical observations of the physical world—observing reality that can be seen, heard, smelled, tasted, and touched. By thinking rationally about physical reality, Aquinas concludes that its very existence points beyond itself to a transcendent cause. In this sense, Aquinas's ways are a philosophical expression of the human experiences of transcendence described in sections 1.4–8. Aquinas explains, in philosophical terms, the common human experience that all reality in this world, because it is limited, points beyond itself to the transcendent.

---

3. A video that introduces Aquinas's five ways in the context of an overview of his life and work is accessible at *www.youtube.com/watch?v=EPnfDgNy1dU* (time 0:06:29).

Each of the five ways starts by observing the nature of physical reality and then draws reasonable conclusions from those observations that point toward the existence of God.[4] The following summaries use modern examples to illustrate Aquinas's points.

1. **Argument from motion.** It is an observable fact that things move and that nothing moves itself. For example, a ball can't move itself; it can only be moved by a force outside of itself (e.g., a child kicks it, or the force of gravity moves it). Consider the very first thing that ever existed in the universe, whether it was a molecule, atom, or subatomic particle. How did it first move, as there is no force outside of itself to move it? Yet motion must have started somewhere, as it's an observable fact that things move. If nothing started the first things in motion, there would be no motion now. Therefore, a logical conclusion is that a First Mover, which first caused things in this universe to move, exists outside, or transcends, this universe.

2. **First Cause argument.** It is an observable fact that all things in the universe have a cause. Nothing causes itself to exist; things do not suddenly appear out of thin air. How, then, did the universe itself first begin, as nothing else exists outside of it, and yet it did not cause itself? A logical conclusion is that a transcendent, eternal First Cause must exist that created the universe.

3. **Argument from contingency and necessity.** It is an observable fact that all things in the world are contingent, not logically necessary. In other words, it's not logically necessary that any particular thing exists. Any existent thing—a person, cabbage, or star—might very well have not existed if other factors had been different. Its existence is contingent, not necessary. If there is no necessary existence then, at some point, all contingent things would cease to exist. Because things do in fact exist, a reasonable conclusion is that one Necessary Being has existed from the beginning.

4. **Argument from degrees of quality.** It is an observable fact that degrees of quality in physical things can be compared. For example, some things are better, stronger, or more beautiful than others. The fact that this comparability is so implies that a fixed standard of measure exists by which all other things are measured. Otherwise how could one know that one thing is truly better or stronger than another? Because it measures all existent things, the standard itself must be transcendent.

5. **Argument from design.** It is an observable fact that physical things are structured with an order and design. For example, a plant cell is a complex

---

4. See also the clear explanation of Thomas Aquinas's ways in Kreeft, *Summa of the* Summa, 60–70.

system composed of many parts, including nucleus, protoplasm, and membrane that function together as a system. The cell did not design itself, nor did any human design it, so it is reasonable to conclude that a transcendent "intelligence" designed it.

The First Cause Argument: Some Clarifications   3.2.3

It is easy to misunderstand Aquinas's five ways, because they are so abstract. The following points should help clarify one of Aquinas's best-known ways: the First Cause argument.

There are only two options: (1) Either a transcendent First Cause created the universe, or (2) the universe exists without an outside cause. Option 1 seems more reasonable, because the idea that the universe exists without a cause or that it caused itself to exist contradicts basic scientific principles.

A person might be tempted to object, "What caused the First Cause?" In other words, Who or what made God? Did he just pop out of thin air? By definition, the First Cause cannot have any other cause—otherwise it would not be the first! Thinking of the First Cause means trying to conceive the absolute, ultimate starting point of all existence. Whatever that starting point was, logically, it must have existed by itself: Nothing else caused it, because nothing else was there. To put it in another way: If something or someone else made God, that something or someone is the true God. The word *God,* in this argument, means the ultimate source of all existence.

If one accepts that a First Cause caused the universe, this First Cause must be a *transcendent* cause—something that is qualitatively and absolutely different from anything else in the universe. It is different because (1) it is the one thing that does not have a cause outside itself and (2) it caused all other things to exist. Notice that these two points correspond with traditional Christian language: the First Cause, God, is (1) eternal and (2) all-powerful. In other words, the First Cause cannot simply be the first cause in a chain of causes, like the first billiard ball striking a series of other balls and causing them to move. It must be a cause *outside* of, *transcending* the universe.

Aquinas's First Cause argument is not meant to prove all aspects of the Christian view of God. It does not prove that God is kind, loving, listens to prayer, or judges sin. It just demonstrates that some kind of transcendent, eternal power must have brought the universe into existence. In the context of Aquinas's argument, it means simply calling that eternal transcendent power by the name of *God.*

Can Medieval Ideas Apply in
the Modern World?   3.2.4

Many people today assume that an argument developed by a medieval theologian can carry no weight in the modern, scientific world. In his book *The God Delusion*, for example, Richard Dawkins dismisses Aquinas's "ways" as unconvincing. Dawkins asserts that the first three ways, for instance, "rely upon the idea of a regress and invoke God to terminate it. They make the entirely unwarranted assumption that God himself is immune to the regress."[5] In other words, Dawkins argues, Aquinas traces the chain of causes (*A* was caused by *B*; *B* was caused by *C*; *C* was caused by *D*) all the way back to the very first cause. Then Aquinas simply assumes without proof that the first cause cannot itself have a cause.

Dawkins fails to understand Aquinas's point—Aquinas is *not* claiming that God is simply the first in the series of causes (like a first billiard ball causing all the other billiard balls to move) and subject to the law of causation. Aquinas's point is that, logically, the ultimate first cause of all existence cannot be caused, because nothing else exists to cause it. In fact, it must be transcendent—it must stand completely outside the chain of causation.

Dawkins again misses the point when he argues that there is no reason to ascribe, to this First Cause, any of the attributes normally attributed to God—such as goodness or the ability to listen to prayers. Aquinas's argument *does not claim* to prove these other attributes: it is limited to showing that God is the first cause.

If Dawkins finds Aquinas to be unconvincing, how would he himself explain how the universe came into being? He writes, "it is more parsimonious to conjure up, say, a 'big bang singularity,' or some other physical concept as yet unknown."[6] But this is simply to say that science cannot currently explain how the universe began—how it went from not existing to existing.

Dawkins seems to miss the point that science, by definition, cannot explain how the universe first came into being. Science, by its nature, deals with questions of cause and effect within the physical universe—it shows how one physical reality causes another; for example two hydrogen atoms combine with an oxygen atom to form water. It cannot answer the question of how the physical universe itself came into existence. The movement from nonexistence to existence obviously cannot have a physical cause. The question of how reality first came into existence, then, is outside the realm of science.

Aquinas's First Cause argument, then, holds up well in the face of modern criticism, which illustrates an essential claim of this book—that tradition, the voice of the past, still has much to teach the modern world. Some of Aquinas's

---

5. Richard Dawkins, *The God Delusion* (Boston: Houghton Mifflin, 2006), 77.

6. Ibid., 78.

thinking, however, is indeed outdated. Aquinas lived in a prescientific world, and so he thought of fire, for example, as a basic element that causes all heat. Yet theologians continue to regard his fundamental insights on how reason is consistent with faith in God as valid.

To practice theology responsibly in the world today, then, the theologian must be willing to learn from the past but, at the same time, be willing to engage critical modern developments. The task is double: listening to the past and engaging the present.

Contemporary Examples of Theological Method   3.3

Responding to Modern Challenges: Three Options   3.3.1

How is thinking about God in a modern setting different from thinking about God in Aquinas's time? The modern world, according to the American Catholic theologian Avery Dulles,[7] is characterized by the rise of a critical worldview, and different contemporary[8] approaches to theology can be characterized by how they react to this critical worldview.[9]

By "critical worldview" Dulles refers to Enlightenment thinkers such as Hume and Voltaire who directly attacked the authority of traditional Christian beliefs (sec. 2.2.1). The rejection of religious authority continued with critics such as Karl Marx and Sigmund Freud. These thinkers share the critical assumption that "nothing is sacred" and all authority can be questioned, including the authority of the Bible and of the Church (sec. 1.8). People should not take things on faith, these thinkers asserted, but rather think critically for themselves. This worldview is also critical in the sense of critically thinking about how true knowledge is attained, following the tradition of Descartes's "methodological doubt" (sec. 2.2.1).

How can the modern theologian respond to these radical challenges? One option is that of fideism: believers refuse to answer critical questions and instead retreat into their own world of faith (sec. 2.6). Fideists tend to respond to critical questions with, "I can't explain it, but I know in my heart that it's true." Some historical traditions, such as nineteenth-century Lutheran pietism, chose this option.

---

7. A video of Avery Dulles commenting on his career as a theologian is accessible at *www.youtube .com/watch?v=6W4-khADBg8* (time 0:04:04).

8. In many theological and philosophical discussions, the term *postmodern* is used to describe a variety of contemporary intellectual trends. The term is sometimes used in rather vague ways, however, and is often associated with ethical relativism. Therefore, here the term *contemporary* or simply *modern* is preferred.

9. Avery Dulles, *The Craft of Theology: From Symbol to System* (New York: Crossroad, 1995), 3–15.

Dulles contrasts the fideist approach with what he calls countercritical theology. In the latter approach, the theologian tries to answer the critic with rational arguments alone. A countercritical theologian is convinced, for example, that he can prove that the Gospel stories about Jesus' life are completely accurate, or that Jesus' miracles, confirmed by many witnesses, prove that Jesus was divine. Dulles notes that Catholic neo-scholastic theology of the late-nineteenth and early-twentieth centuries tended toward such rationalistic views.

For Dulles, the fideistic option does not trust reason enough, while the "countercritical" approach trusts reason *too* much—or, rather, trusts a rationalistic understanding of reason too much (secs. 2.2.1 and 2.4 on rationalism and critiques of rationalism).

Dulles identifies the Catholic approach as a postcritical theology. It does not ignore the critical challenges, as fideism does; but at the same time, it does not pretend that it can prove the truth of the Christian faith in the same way as one does a geometric proof. It accepts the broader definitions of faith and reason as presented in chapter 2. The following sections outline some characteristics that, in Dulles's view,[10] a postcritical theology should have.

Aspects of a Postcritical Theology 3.3.2

Postcritical Theories of Knowledge 3.3.2.1

Fideists "know" things in their hearts; rationalists "know" things through logical proof. In rejecting both approaches, a postcritical theology must show how theological knowledge and understanding are possible and rationally defensible. It must be able to answer rationalist criticisms by showing how theological understanding fits into a more general theory of how humans know and understand anything.

Some aspects of postcritical theories of knowledge and understanding were discussed earlier in the book. Postcritical theories recognize that reasonable knowledge is wider than pure logic: it is often based on authority, tradition, probability, and personal experiences (sec. 2.4). Fields of study such as art, history, and philosophy have their own legitimate ways of knowing and understanding: they need not try to copy the methods of the physical sciences (secs. 1.10–1.11). Reason includes an element of faith (sec. 2.5.1). Asking theological questions is legitimate because such questions are part of the universal human experience (sec. 1.6). With this type of reflection, the postcritical theologian can justify theological study as a legitimate field of inquiry, understanding, and knowledge.

A postcritical theory of knowledge would also include developing a hermeneutical theory—a set of guidelines for validly interpreting texts, especially traditional texts such as the Bible.

---

10. See Thomas G. Guarino, "Why Avery Dulles Matters," *First Things*, May 2009, accessible at *www.firstthings.com/article/2009/04/why-avery-dulles-matters-1243317340*.

A Hermeneutic of Trust   3.3.2.2

Dulles accepts that purely objective, or "neutral," thinking about God and religious questions is impossible. Rather, all thinking must begin from fundamental "prejudgments" about the nature of God, life and death, and reality that are taken from a particular religious or philosophical tradition (secs. 1.10–1.11). For Dulles, then, Christian theologians should begin by clearly acknowledging their commitment to the Christian faith tradition. "Recognizing that every affirmation rests upon some kind of faith, postcritical theology frankly relies on convictions born of the Christian faith."[11]

The Christian theologian begins with a "**hermeneutic** of trust" in the reliability and validity of the Christian tradition.[12] This does not mean that the theologian will never question or even criticize certain aspects of the tradition but simply that one's fundamental orientation is to trust the tradition. This hermeneutic of trust contrasts with a hermeneutic of suspicion with which, for example, a Marxist would approach a traditional text like the Bible. The Marxist, with his atheistic prejudgments, interprets the text not as an account of God's revelation but as the attempt of the ruling classes to maintain their power using theological language. From the beginning, the Marxist assumes that the claims of the text cannot be trusted because the authors have a hidden agenda. The Christian theologian's hermeneutic of trust includes trusting Church authorities (sec. 2.4.1.1). "[Catholic] Theology itself demands a basic confidence in the Church and its official leadership as the transmitters of the heritage of faith."[13]

Understanding through Living the Tradition   3.3.2.3

The Christian theologian comes to a deeper understanding of the articles of faith not simply through intellectual study or purely rational understanding but also by participating in Christian worship and the life of the Church. Theology "is done in the Church because the Church is the primary bearer of faith. . . . If theology is not to regress, it must retain its close bonds with prayer and worship."[14]

The point ties in with the earlier discussion about the many ways people gain knowledge beyond strict logic (sec. 2.4). As Newman wrote, "Man is *not* a reasoning animal; he is a seeing, feeling, contemplating, acting animal."[15] It is only through the commitment of the whole person—engaging not just reason but also emotions and imagination—that more profound depths of

---

11. Ibid., 13.

12. Ibid., 7.

13. Ibid., 14.

14. Ibid., 8–9

15. Newman, *An Essay in Aid of a Grammar of Assent* (London: Longmans, Green, and Col., 1910), 94 is accessible at *www.newmanreader.org/works/grammar/chapter4-2.html#section3*.

understanding can be reached. Dulles believed that it is only through an active participation in the Christian community, the Church, that the theologian can develop the tacit knowledge and skill (Newman's "illative sense") that is necessary for making valid theological judgments.

Consider a quick example. A Catholic theologian may understand, at the intellectual level, the belief in the Real Presence: that Christ is truly present, not just symbolically present, in the Eucharist. However, the theologian's writing on that topic will be much fuller, more understandable, more convincing, if that theologian has personally experienced the truth of that theological teaching through the personal experience of seeing, receiving, tasting, and reflecting on the Eucharist.

Scriptural Hermeneutics   3.4

Aquinas expressed the traditional Catholic understanding that Scripture is the foundational authority for a Christian: "For our faith rests upon the revelation made to the apostles and prophets who wrote the canonical books" (*ST* 1.1.8 ad. 2). Christian faith, then, involves trust in Scripture.

This raises a problem for the postcritical theologian: since the time of the Enlightenment, Scripture has been subjected to critical scrutiny. Do we really know who wrote the books of the Bible? Were mistakes made as books were copied and passed down over the years? Weren't these books all written by men in patriarchal societies and thus reflect patriarchal bias? How can books that were written thousands of years ago in a very different time and culture still be relevant today?

A central task for the postcritical Christian theologian, then, is to work out a valid scriptural hermeneutics—guidelines for interpretation that approach Scripture with a fundamental trust but, at the same time, do not ignore critical questions.

Becoming Aware of Prejudgments   3.4.1

A fundamental concept in modern hermeneutical theory is that humans come to understanding through a "hermeneutical circle." This theory begins with the insight that all readers bring certain "prejudgments" or preconceived ideas to their reading of a text (sec. 1.10).

Consider a reader who reads the first chapters of the Bible (Gen 1–3). Here is the story of God's creation of the universe and of the first humans, Adam and Eve, and of Adam and Eve's disobedience to God.

A person raised in a Christian environment brings certain prejudgments about God, creation, sin, good, and evil to the reading, even if reading Genesis for the first time. The reader, for example, might associate the snake mentioned in the story with the devil, although the text does not actually say this. A Muslim reader brings other prejudgments to the reading, influenced by how Adam and Eve are portrayed in the Qur'an. A reader influenced by feminist thought assumes that the story is written from a patriarchal perspective, because it was written in an ancient, male-centered society. One influenced by a rationalist worldview assumes the story is a childish myth and has nothing to teach the reader. A person influenced by a tradition in which the Bible is read literally assumes that the text must be understood in that way.

The first step, then, for a valid interpretation of Genesis, is for readers to become aware of their own prejudgments. This does not mean that they will reject these prejudgments, only that they become aware of them and realize how strongly these prejudgments influence their understanding of the text.

Interacting with Scripture 3.4.2

In the second movement of the hermeneutical circle, readers actively engage their own worldview, including its prejudgments, with the worldview of the text. Genesis presents a definite worldview: It assumes that the universe is created by God; that all of creation is good; and that humans originally had a close and trusting relationship with God, but that trusting relationship was broken when humans disobeyed God.

Understanding, as Gadamer describes it, occurs when two worldviews, one's own and the worldview of the text, are allowed to meet. Understanding occurs in the dialogue between the two. The dialogue, of course, presupposes that the reader is willing to listen to the claims of the text and approaches the text, at least to some extent, with a hermeneutic of trust.

For example, the feminist reader presuming the biblical text is completely patriarchal might reconsider that presumption in light of the text's assertion that God created both male and female in God's image (1:27). A person presupposing that the Bible must be understood literally might rethink the validity of that presumption when encountering the text's statement that "God rested on the seventh day" (Gen 2:2)—a statement whose literal meaning is difficult to square with the traditional belief that God is all-powerful.

If readers encounter the traditional text more than once, the process of understanding will be ongoing. Readers first encounter Scripture with certain prejudgments, but if they are open to learning from the text, they may come away from their reading with their prejudgments changed and see and experience events in their daily life in a different way. These new experiences and perspectives on daily life will, in turn, influence their reading when they return to the biblical text. The hermeneutical circle is an ongoing process.

Paul Ricoeur   3.4.3

The philosopher Paul Ricoeur[16] raises a critical question regarding the hermeneutical circle and the interpretation of Scripture: How can modern readers
truly engage the biblical worldview when it is so foreign to their way of thinking
and perceiving?

Let's say that Roger has been reading accounts in the daily news of suicide
bombings, school shootings, and corrupt politicians. He begins to wonder why
there seems to be so much evil in the world. In an attempt to find answers,
Roger turns to reading the Bible, because he knows it is a major source for the
teachings of the Christian tradition. A friend advises him to read the story of
Adam and Eve in Genesis, as it provides the Christian explanation of how evil
came into the world.

Roger does so but is disappointed. Rather than shedding light on the problem of suffering, it adds to his confusion. How is he supposed to believe a story
in which a snake talks and a woman is formed out of a man's rib? It seems to
have nothing to do with his concerns.

In Ricoeur's view, this example illustrates that modern readers can no longer
directly encounter a biblical text such as that found in Genesis 1–3 simply because
the worldviews of the biblical text and modern people are literally worlds apart.
The biblical worldview is prescientific and symbolic; a fundamentally scientific and literal understanding of reality shapes modern readers. For Ricoeur, a
meaningful encounter between reader and traditional text is still possible, but it
can only come *indirectly*. The reader must first go through a conscious process
of interpretation.

The first stage involves the use of critical reason, as modern readers do not
accept certain elements of the story that are based on prescientific understandings of reality. For Ricoeur, this includes the story's reference to snakes crawling
on their bellies due to God's curse (Gen 3:14). This should be recognized as a
prescientific explanation for why snakes crawl and is considered irrelevant for
modern readers.

Next, modern readers develop a critical awareness of the type of language
the story employs. It is not a historical, literal account; rather, it is the language
of mythic and symbolic foundational stories through which all ancient societies
expressed their encounters with the divine.

Once readers have passed through this critical phase, they can once again
take a trusting, open approach to understanding and learning from the text.
Ricoeur calls this the "second naiveté." The "first naiveté" is the approach of
a child—simply accepting the story as it is, without question. In the second
naiveté, after having asked the critical questions, the reader is again ready to

---

16. An overview of Ricoeur's life and philosophy is accessible at *http://plato.stanford.edu/entries
/ricoeur/*.

listen in a trusting way to the insights of the text. No longer focused on questions such as whether snakes really talk, the reader is better prepared to understand some of the deeper claims of the text.

At this stage, then, the reader might accept that Adam and Eve are not meant to be understood as literal, historical figures; rather, their lives symbolize the experiences of all humans. The exile from the Garden of Eden is not a literal, historical event. It is one of the biblical symbols used to express the human experience of sin.

The reader is now open to better hearing some of the fundamental claims of the text: that God created the entire universe (it is not the result of blind chance), that God created all things good, that humans are created in God's image and have been entrusted by God to care for his creation (Gen 1:26–28), that humans are free and can misuse this freedom to turn away from their Creator (Gen 3).

Ricoeur sums up the process of the hermeneutical circle in the following way, "We must understand in order to believe, but we must believe in order to understand."[17] By "understand in order to believe," Ricoeur means that for modern Christian believers the traditional text can only be accepted or trusted after passing through the critical questions raised by modern thought. However, Christians are drawn to the text in the first place (they "believe in order to understand") because of the traditional belief in its meaningfulness and power.

The process is similar for non-Christians. They, too, will need to "understand in order to believe." They, too, will need to ask critical questions before considering the truths within the text. Because they are not part of the Christian tradition, the biblical text cannot have the same meaning for non-Christians. However, if they are open to bringing their worldview into an encounter with the biblical worldview, then they may experience a deepened understanding of the human encounter with the divine.

Faith, Reason, and Tradition in Hans Urs von Balthasar 3.5

Theologian and Swiss native Hans Urs von Balthasar (1905–1988)[18] made a significant contribution to Catholic thought during the twentieth century. His life and writings[19] illustrate an influential approach to the relationship of reason, faith, and tradition in contemporary Catholic theology.

---

17. Paul Ricoeur, *The Symbolism of Evil*, trans. Emerson Buchanan (New York: Harper & Row, 1967), 351.

18. Karen Kilby introduces the life and work of von Balthasar in a video accessible at *www.youtube.com/watch?v=uT1Bg0YI6QE*. (time 0:08:27).

19. An archive of books, articles, and videos on von Balthasar is accessible at *http://hansursvonbalthasar.blogspot.com*.

A Holistic Approach to Theology 3.5.1

When Balthasar began his formal studies in theology as part of his preparation for ordination to the priesthood, Catholic theology was dominated by neo-scholastics, an approach Dulles labeled as countercritical (sec. 3.3.1). Neo-scholastic study focused on tracts that summarized each major belief of the Christian creed, supporting each belief with "proofs" from Scripture or church tradition. The approach tended toward rationalism: It assumed that theological knowledge could be summed up in neat propositions that could be proven in a way analogous to scientific and mathematical proofs. The approach also tended to sharply separate theological knowledge from other, **secular** branches of knowledge and, similarly, to separate the natural world from the supernatural.

Balthasar's theological approach reacts against the neo-scholasticism in important ways. Balthasar refused to separate theology from other fields of study. Theology deals with transcendent questions (the existence of God; the deeper, transcendent meaning of human life), but so do other branches of study. Great poets such as Dante, great playwrights such as Shakespeare, and great philosophers such as Plato have always been concerned with theological questions (e.g., What is the meaning of life? What is the ultimate nature of reality?), and thus theologians should consider insights drawn from other fields in their own work.

Balthasar's education reflected this holistic approach. As a young man, he was an accomplished musician and seriously considered a career in music. Before he began his formal theological studies, Balthasar had already earned his doctorate in "German studies," an interdisciplinary course of studies including philosophy, language, literature, and art.[20]

For Balthasar, theology was not merely an academic, intellectual process, what Balthasar calls a "sitting theology." Theologians are to be actively engaged in the worship and life of the church and seek to grow closer to God through their studies, an approach Balthasar calls a kneeling theology. The theologian is to maintain a humble attitude of seeking knowledge by being open to hearing God's revelation: "Knowledge must never be separated from the attitude of prayer with which it began."[21]

Again, Balthasar's life illustrates his belief: In addition to writing on philosophical topics, Balthasar wrote on contemplative prayer and translated Ignatius of Loyola's *Spiritual Exercises*[22] into German. He also led more than 100 spiritual retreats based on the *Exercises*. With the Swiss physician, writer, and mystic, Adrienne von Speyr, Balthasar founded the Community of St. John,

---

20. Peter Henrici, "A Sketch of Von Balthasar's Life," in *Hans Urs von Balthasar: His Life and Work*, ed. D. L. Schindler (San Francisco: Communio Books/Ignatius Press, 1991), 8–11.

21. Hans Urs von Balthasar, "Theology and Sanctity," in *Explorations in Theology, Volume I: The Word Made Flesh* (San Francisco: Ignatius Press, 1989), 207.

22. Articles and videos on Loyola's Spiritual Exercises are accessible at *www.ignatianspirituality.com/ignatian-prayer/the-spiritual-exercises*.

a secular institute, whose members dedicated themselves to a closer following of Christ (emphasizing the traditional monastic values of poverty, chastity, and obedience) while still pursuing secular careers.[23]

Dialogue with the Tradition   3.5.2

Like Thomas Aquinas, Balthasar continually drew on the insights of past thinkers. He was convinced that Christians and interested non-Christians needed to hear the insights of patristic theologians such as Origen (ca. 185–ca. 254), Gregory of Nyssa (ca. 330–ca. 395), Maximus the Confessor (ca. 580–662), and Augustine (354–430); medieval thinkers such as Anselm (ca. 1033–1109), the English mystic Julian of Norwich (ca. 1342–ca. 1416), and Catherine of Sienna (ca. 1347–1380); as well as more modern writers such as Thérèse of Lisieux (1873–1897). Balthasar not only included the insights of these authors in his work but also translated, edited, and published editions and anthologies of their writings.

In this, Balthasar, along with theologians such as Henri de Lubac and Jean Daniélou, was associated with a Catholic theological movement of the mid-twentieth century known as the *nouvelle théologie* ("new theology" in French). Like Balthasar, de Lubac[24] and Daniélou criticized neo-scholastic theology and encouraged theologians to "return to the sources" (*ressourcement* in French), especially to writings from the patristic era.

Why are Balthasar and others so concerned with rediscovering the past? In their view, theologians are able to uncover prejudices and gain insights about contemporary times by engaging with the past and discovering how Christian beliefs have developed. Also, theologians today view the work of patristic-era theologians as important sources, even authoritative, because of the role these theologians played in shaping Catholic thought.

Yet this encounter with the past cannot consist of simply repeating what past theologians have said. Rather, it means entering into a dialogue with them—allowing modern questions, concerns, and insights to interact with earlier thought.

This dialogue is a critical one. Every theologian works within a certain cultural worldview, and sometimes a particular worldview can obscure the authentically Christian message. Balthasar notes that even well-known theologians such as Gregory of Nyssa and Maximus the Confessor at times allowed their Platonist presuppositions to obscure the doctrine of the Trinity in their works.[25]

23. Maximilian Greiner, "The Community of St. John," in *Hans Urs von Balthasar: His Life and Work*, ed. D. L. Schindler (San Francisco: Communio Books/ Ignatius Press, 1991), 87–101.

24. See Michael Deem, "Part II: The Ressourcement Movement: Henri de Lubac," for an introduction to de Lubac's role in the ressourcement movement, accessible at *http://percaritatem.com/2006/10/25/part-ii-the-ressourcement-movement-henri-de-lubac/*.

25. Hans Urs von Balthasar, "The Fathers, the Scholastics, and Ourselves," 1939; repr., Communio 24, no. 2 (Summer 1997), accessible at *www.communio-icr.com/articles/view/the-fathers-the-scholastics-and-ourselves*.

In his theological work, Balthasar engaged extensively not only with Protestant theologians, most notably Karl Barth, but also with non-Christian thinkers, including Jewish philosopher Martin Buber; Buddhist thinkers, and even the anti-Christian philosopher Friedrich Nietzsche. Here, Balthasar worked with his conviction that because every person is oriented toward God, there is no such thing as a purely "natural" religion or philosophy. God can work, in mysterious ways, through these non-Christian traditions as well. "Every religion stands in a more or less direct, more or less oblique, light of Christ's revelation, even if it does not expressly know of Christ and his coming."[26] Balthasar points out that Christians have often engaged in fruitful ways with non-Christian thought: Thomas Aquinas built on Aristotle's philosophy; the Gospel of John adapts the Greek philosophical concept of the *logos*.

In keeping with his holistic approach to theological thinking, Balthasar also wrote on, translated, and published the works of poets, playwrights, and novelists such as Dante, Dostoyevsky, Gerard Manley Hopkins, Goethe, Georges Bernanos, and Paul Claudel.

The Starting Point of Balthasar's Theology: Human Experience and the Transcendent   3.5.3

What is the starting point for Balthasar's theology? He writes, "We start with a reflection on the situation of man. He exists as a limited being in a limited world, but his reason is open to the unlimited, to all of being."[27] The task of theology is to show how the "limited being" of things in this world, especially the human being, is related to transcendent, unlimited being: God.

As a person grows, he or she learns all too well that the being of this world is limited: plants grow and wither, pets get sick and die, a favorite grandparent passes away. Yet at the same time, that person intuitively knows that because all of these limited beings did not create themselves, they can only exist if there is an unlimited being that is their ground and source. This person experiences the same intuition in an emotional way—longing for this unlimited being in the desire for the eternal peace and happiness of the eternal world (sec. 1.4–1.8). Humans transcend their limitations: the very act of thinking implies that an absolute truth exists (sec. 1.7); our awareness of the forces that limit and shape us shows that we transcend those limitations (sec. 2.4.2). This is Balthasar's starting point—the limited human being who is aware of, and oriented to, infinite being.[28]

---

26. Ibid.

27. Balthasar, "A Résumé of My Thought, " in *Hans Urs von Balthasar: His Life and Work*, ed., David L. Schindler (San Francisco: Ignatius Press, 1991), 1.

28. Balthasar calls this starting point, "meta-anthropology," see Rodney A. Howsare, *Balthasar: A Guide for the Perplexed* (London: T & T Clark, 2009), 50–53.

For Balthasar, that distinction between finite being and infinite being "is the source of all the philosophical and religious thought of humanity"; all religions and philosophies are attempts at explaining the relationship between this finite world and the transcendent world of the infinite.[29] Plato, for example, conceived of infinite being as the transcendent realm of the ideas; physical objects in the world are merely the shadows of those pure Ideas. For Buddhism, finite reality is actually an illusion; the only true reality is infinite being. How does the Christian understand this relationship?

Balthasar's Focus: God's Self-Revelation through Beauty, Goodness, and Truth   3.5.4

To understand the relationship of infinite and finite being, Balthasar sought to understand being itself. Medieval philosophy, building on ancient Greek thought, identified four transcendental properties of being: the one, the good, the true, and the beautiful. These properties are transcendental not in the sense that they exist only in a transcendent world, but that they transcend all individual categories and apply to all of being in this world.

Balthasar finds that an infant begins to develop an intuition of these transcendentals in its very first experience of reality—via the relationship with the mother. The infant experiences unity with her in the mother's unconditional love and senses that reality, or being, is one. The infant experiences this love as good; thus his or her first intuition is that the world, being, is good. The infant experiences a mother's love as true, sensing that all being is true. Finally, her love evokes a response of joy, and the infant feels that life is beautiful.[30]

As children grow up, they realize that the beautiful, the good, and the true are limited in this world. The world's reality is also ugly, evil, and deceitful. In Balthasar's view, the fullness of the good, the beautiful, and the truth exist only in God.

For the Christian, the truth, beauty, and goodness of this world, though limited, are nevertheless real, not illusory. Building on Aquinas's work, Balthasar describes the relationship between the finite and the infinite as an analogy of being. The goodness, beauty, and truth of this world are similar or analogous to God's infinite goodness, beauty, and truth because God is the source of those qualities in this world.[31]

The theologian can show, then, how limited beauty, goodness, and truth point beyond themselves toward God.

---

29. Ibid.

30. Balthasar, "A Resume of My Thought," 3.

31. Howsare, *Guide for the Perplexed*, 6–8, 40–43.

Following Beauty, Goodness, and Truth to God

3.5.5

The centerpiece of Balthasar's theological writing is his trilogy based on the transcendentals: *The Glory of the Lord: A Theological Aesthetics*, focusing on beauty;[32] *Theo-Drama: Theological Dramatic Theory*, focusing on the good;[33] and *Theo-Logic*, focusing on the true.[34] The infinite God reveals himself through the limited beauty, goodness, and truth of this world.

Limited Being Reveals God's Glory

3.5.5.1

Aesthetics is the study of how humans perceive reality, especially how they perceive beauty. In Balthasar's view, the modern world has great difficulty perceiving beauty and great difficulty perceiving the ultimate source of beauty: God.

A rationalist might try to analyze the beauty of a painting by identifying the colors and types of brushes the artist used. An aesthetic approach, in contrast, argues that beauty cannot be assessed in this manner. People recognize beauty when they allow the whole, which is greater than the sum of its parts, to have its effect on them.[35]

In general, materialist and rationalist thought perceives reality as a collection of parts functioning in a mechanical way: People, for example, can be defined in terms of the molecules, nerve cells, and genes that compose them. An aesthetic perspective reminds one that the true essence of each person can only be perceived as a whole, not as a combination of parts.

Modern thought is pragmatic and controlling when it studies how nature functions in order to manipulate it for the benefit of humans. An aesthetic approach is receptive: It receives, with a sense of wonder, the beauty that nature reveals.

Modern thought tends to focus on how the human mind perceives and shapes reality. The influential Enlightenment philosopher Immanuel Kant,[36] for example, taught that one can never know the true nature of an object one perceives, "the thing in itself." Instead one can only know how one's mind perceives it by organizing reality into certain mental categories.

---

32. Balthasar, *The Glory of the Lord: A Theological Aesthetics*, 7 vols. (San Francisco: Ignatius Press, 1982–89).

33. Balthasar, *Theo-Drama: Theological Dramatic Theory*, 5 vols. (San Francisco: Ignatius Press, 1988–98).

34. Balthasar, *Theo-Logic*, 3 vols. (San Francisco: Ignatius Press, 2000–2005).

35. On this point, see Howsare, *Guide for the Perplexed*, 80.

36. An overview on Immanuel Kant's life and philosophy is accessible at *http://plato.stanford.edu/entries/kant/*. See especially sec. 4, "The Transcendental Deduction," which discusses Kant's theory of perception through certain mental categories.

The aesthetic view a fundamentally different persupposition: One is able to know the essence of things because they reveal their true nature. A person is able to perceive a tree as a tree and not merely a collection of branches, leaves, and bark because, in a sense, the being of the tree reveals itself to that person. It shows itself as more than a collection of its separate parts.[37] Balthasar does not envision the subject (e.g., the person seeing) dominating the object (e.g., the tree that is seen). Instead, in his view, knowledge develops through an encounter between the knower and the known.

If a person can learn to perceive beauty in the world despite its limitations, that person will be more open to sensing the Infinite Beauty that reveals itself through limited being. For Balthasar, God's revelation surpasses beauty, and reveals itself as the glory of the Lord. Glory, in the Old Testament (*kabod* in Hebrew), is a visible manifestation on Earth of the invisible God. This glory is often associated with the Jerusalem Temple: "the glory of the Lord had filled the house of the Lord" (1 Kings 8:11). In the New Testament, however, the glory of the Lord takes a paradoxical turn: For now the ultimate manifestation of God's glory is Jesus Christ, God's divine Son taking on human form to suffer and die for the sake of sinful humanity.

Balthasar on Dante: Earthly Love Leading to Heaven 3.5.5.2

In his famous poem, *The Divine Comedy*, Dante journeys through hell, purgatory, and heaven. The pagan Roman poet Virgil, symbolizing human reason, is his guide through hell and purgatory; Beatrice, a resident of Dante's native Florence, leads him from the end of purgatory to the heights of heaven. Beatrice is modeled on an actual woman who inspired Dante to write a series of love poems.

For Balthasar, Dante's poetry expresses deep theological insight. Balthasar writes, "Dante's daring act of taking before the throne of God the earthly love between man and woman and of purifying *Eros* [earthly love] so as to make of it something akin to *Agape* [divine love] is a theological event of the first order."[38] Dante expresses, poetically, how **salvation** does not involve abandoning earthly goods, but with the help of God's grace, it involves purifying them.

Continued

37. Howsare, 70.

38. Balthasar, *My Work: In Retrospect* (San Francisco: Communio Books/Ignatius Press, 1993), 83.

Balthasar on Dante Continued

Private Collection / The Stapleton Collection / Bridgeman Images

Beatrice's guidance of Dante through heaven symbolizes the transformation of earthly love into heavenly love. Scripture often compares these two loves: the husband-wife relationship reflects God's love for Israel; the Church is described as the "Bride of Christ."

As they near the highest levels of heaven, Dante describes how Beatrice, her beautiful face reflecting God's glory, points him onward toward God:

> While the Eternal Joy, which shone directly
> on her, contented me with Its aspect,
> reflected in her beautiful face
> Overwhelming me with the light of a smile,
>   she said to me, "Turn and listen,
>   for not only in my eyes is Paradise."[39]

Limited Being Reveals God's Goodness and Freedom   3.5.5.3

Balthasar next studies the transcendental characteristic of goodness. In its experience of a mother's unconditional love, the child already has an intuition of the goodness of being and the goodness of infinite being.[40]

---

39. Paradise 18.16–21. Dante Aligheiri, *The Divine Comedy*, trans. H. R. Huse (New York: Holt, Rinehart and Winston, 1954).

40. Balthasar, "A Résumé of My Thought," 3.

Humans are free to choose the good or to reject it. This question of freedom is what gives human life its truly dramatic character: Will humans freely choose to follow God, or will they use their freedom to reject God?

How do finite freedom and infinite freedom relate to each another? Some worldviews stress the free will of God, or the gods, so much that they deny the reality of human free will. The Catholic tradition, in contrast, insists on the reality of human free will (sec. 2.5.3.4).[41]

In reflecting on the relationship of divine and human freedom, one must answer a fundamental question: What is freedom? In modern thought, the ideal model of freedom is a completely independent person who does whatever he or she wishes—free from any authority. The continuing influence of the Enlightenment, which tended to reject all religious authority in the name of individual freedom, is seen here.

Is freedom from all authority a true or false freedom? A theoretical example of two teenagers will illustrate the point. Imagine that Maria has been given total freedom from authority: She doesn't have to work, go to school, or follow anyone's rules. So she eats whatever she wants—soda, chips, and cookies—and spends all day on Facebook and watching soap opera reruns. Carmen, on the other hand, has little freedom. She must follow her parents', teachers', and coaches' rules about eating balanced and nutritious meals, attending classes, studying at certain times, and exercising regularly.

At the end of two years of following these lifestyles, who has more freedom? Because she is physically healthy, Carmen has the freedom to play basketball or hike in the mountains. Because she is intellectually prepared, she has the freedom to continue her studies, apply to a variety of colleges, and consider several career options. Maria, although she is still free from authority, is no longer free to play basketball or hike, as she has damaged her health. Without an education, she is also not free to apply to college and her career choices are very restricted. It's clear that Carmen has true freedom, but she gained it, paradoxically, by following the rules of others.

Balthasar sees this same paradox played out in the drama of Jesus Christ's free choices. For Balthasar, the answer to the problem of the relationship between finite and infinite freedom can be found only in Jesus, whom Christian faith has revealed as both human and divine. Only in Jesus do human and divine freedom meet.

A central Christian belief is that God the Father sent his divine Son into the world to become human and to suffer and die for the sake of other humans. Jesus freely surrendered his own will out of obedience to the Father. He gave up his own will, and yet, paradoxically, he retained his freedom, because he *freely* chose to obey the Father. Jesus' life illustrates the paradoxical teaching he gave to

41. For a discussion on limited and absolute freedom in Balthasar's thought, see Howsare, *Guide for the Perplexed*, 96–120.

his own disciples, "whoever wishes to save his life will lose it, but whoever loses his life for my sake will find it" (Matt 16:25). One who wishes to control her life and live in absolute freedom, as in the case of Maria, in the end loses her life and her true freedom; one who chooses to give up control and accept the authority of another, as in the case of Carmen, finds her life and her true freedom in the end.

Christ, then, is the model for all humans: Paradoxically, humans must freely give up their desire to control their own lives and submit themselves to following God's will. Humans can make this surrender to God, not out of a blind faith, but based on the intuition that ultimate being is good and can be trusted. In an analogous way, Carmen chose to obey her parents, teachers, and coaches because she believed that they had her best interests at heart.

Limited Being Reveals God's Truth and Love   3.5.5.4

How does the limited being of this world point to God as absolute truth?

At the level of limited being, humans can only truly know things in this world if they have some kind of rational structure that the mind can grasp. Modern science describes this rational structure as the "laws of nature." One could have no scientific knowledge if things behaved in completely arbitrary, unpredictable ways. Science is only possible because nature reveals predictable laws that humans can grasp with their minds. Ancient Christians accounted for this rational structure through their belief that God had created the world through his Word (*logos*) (John 1:1–3) (sec. 2.5.2).

However, if the being of this world is rationally structured, then in some real sense, it "speaks" to people. It gives people more than its surface appearance: It gives its "word" as well. But this word, this rational structure, would not be there unless God, the infinite source of all reason and truth, had placed it there in the creation. When one knows something, even if it's only a rock, one implicitly knows something about its creator.

Balthasar argues that the limited being of this world not only points beyond itself to a creator, but also it hints at two essential Christian beliefs: that God became human (the **Incarnation**) and that God is a Trinity.

Balthasar observes that, in this world, being exists only in limited things: in stones, stars and planets, humans. So in this sense, limited being is "full"—it accounts for all worldly being. At the same time, it is evident that worldly being is still limited, because it did not create itself and depends completely on infinite being (God) for its own existence. In this sense, worldly being is at the same time full, and empty.

Balthasar finds here an analogy for both the Incarnation and the Trinity. In the Incarnation, God the Son, sharing the fullness of divinity with the Father and the Spirit in the Trinity "emptied himself" to become human (Phil 2:7, while at the same time, paradoxically, remaining God. (Balthasar's Trinitarian thought is discussed more fully in chapter 6.)

What is the importance of these reflections? In Balthasar's view, these points reveal the essential nature of God as love. The Son's willingness to empty himself for the sake of humans reveals, in the strongest possible terms, that the Christian God is a God of love—complete, unreserved, sacrificial love. This self-giving love in turn is reflected in the very structure of his creation.[42]

Questions about the Text

1. Briefly explain the roles of reason, faith, and tradition in Aquinas's approach to answering theological questions.
2. Summarize Aquinas's method of posing and answering questions in the *Summa*.
3. Which of Aquinas's "five ways" of proving God's existence is the most convincing? Explain your choice.
4. Summarize the First Cause argument. Why must the First Cause be a transcendent one?
5. In what three ways do modern theologies respond to the critical questions about religious faith, according to Dulles?
6. Explain the difference between a hermeneutic of trust and a hermeneutic of suspicion in interpreting a text.
7. Name two ways in which Balthasar's approach to theology is holistic.
8. Summarize Balthasar's approach to the Christian tradition.
9. Define these terms from Balthasar's theology: *limited being, infinite being, analogy of being.*
10. Explain how an "aesthetic approach" differs from a rationalist approach in perceiving reality. Why does Balthasar think that taking an aesthetic perspective to reality is a good preparation for faith in God?
11. What is the difference between true freedom and false freedom? How does this question relate to Jesus' obedience to God's will?
12. What does it mean to say that reality has a rational structure? How do science and Christian faith interpret this rational structure in different ways?

Discussion Questions

1. Is Aquinas's method of asking and answering theological questions still valid today? Why or why not?
2. What are the advantages, and what are the dangers, of taking a fideistic approach to one's faith?

---

42. For a discussion of these points, see Howsare, *Guide for the Perplexed,* 121–44.

3. Do you agree with von Balthasar that there is a close connection between theology, art, and literature? Why or why not?

4. In your own experience, do you find that following rules can lead to a greater freedom? Explain.

Science and Christian Faith

Does Modern Science Contradict Christian Faith?   4.1

Chapter 2 considered some critiques of faith from a rationalist and materialist worldview (sec. 2.3). To review,

1. Religious thought contradicts and impedes scientific thought. When one observes lightning, scientific thought seeks rational causes. Religious thought invents myths about gods throwing lightning bolts.

2. Religious authorities impede the free progress of science. The Catholic Church, for example, persecuted Galileo for claiming that Earth moved around the sun.

3. Scientific thought relies on provable evidence; religious thought relies on unprovable, blind faith.

Richard Dawkins contrasts religious belief with scientific method in the following way:

> Fundamentalists know they are right because they have read the truth in a holy book and they know, in advance, that nothing will budge them from their belief. . . . The book is true, and if the evidence seems to contradict it, it is the evidence that must be thrown out, not the book. By contrast, what I, as a scientist, believe (for example, evolution) I believe not because of reading it in a holy book but because I have studied the evidence. . . . Books about evolution are believed not because they are holy. They are believed because they present overwhelming quantities of mutually buttressed evidence. In principle, any reader can

go and check that evidence. When a science book is wrong, somebody eventually discovers the mistake and it is corrected in subsequent books. That conspicuously doesn't happen with holy books.[1]

This chapter argues that Dawkins's characterization of both Christian faith and science is overly simplistic and misleading. Science is not purely objective, nor is Christian faith purely subjective. The two have far more in common than Dawkins and other rationalist thinkers imagine.

Intuition and Personal Insight in Science   4.2

The chemist and philosopher Michael Polanyi has shown that even in the physical sciences, scientists do not gain knowledge by strictly following the explicit rules of the scientific method. Polanyi shows how scientists often work with what he calls "tacit knowledge"—an intuitive, personal way of understanding. Consider two questions:

1. How do scientists begin their scientific research? When narrowing down a problem to be investigated or forming an initial hypothesis, scientists draw heavily on previous personal experiences and intuition. They do not proceed by following strict rules.

2. How do scientists observe data? Consider an astronomer recording observations of a planet's velocity. Due to a variety of factors, such observations will always vary to some degree from predicted values. The astronomer must then determine whether the pattern of variations is due to chance or is a clue to investigate other possible causes. No precise statistical rule of variations can help the astronomer, who must rely on personal scientific intuition to decide whether to follow up this clue.[2]

Newman also notes how scientists are not restricted to pure logic in their work, referring to Sir Isaac Newton's illative sense in perceiving mathematical and physical truth without strict proof.[3]

Authority and Tradition in Science   4.3

In contrast to Dawkins's idealized model of completely free scientific inquiry, both Polanyi and Thomas Kuhn have shown that science typically operates with a heavy emphasis on authority and tradition. Polanyi writes that science must be

---

1. Richard Dawkins, *The God Delusion* (Boston: Houghton Mifflin, 2006), 282.

2. Michael Polanyi, "The Unaccountable Element in Science," in *Knowing and Being: Essays*, ed. Marjorie Grene (Chicago: University of Chicago Press, 1969), 105–20.

3. John Henry Newman, *An Essay in Aid of a Grammar of Assent*, ed. I. T. Ker (Oxford: Clarendon Press, 1985), 215, accessible at *www.newmanreader.org/works/grammar/chapter8-3.html*.

"disciplined by an orthodoxy which can permit only a limited degree of dissent, and . . . such dissent is fraught with grave risks to the dissenter."[4] Scientific orthodoxy is based on the scientific beliefs of a particular time and culture. This orthodoxy determines, for example, whether certain research projects will be funded or papers accepted for publication based in large part on whether the proposals follow current scientific paradigms—the theoretical frameworks in which various sciences operate. Polanyi argues that such orthodoxy is necessary to weed out nonsensical theories, but it operates at the cost of occasionally ignoring or resisting legitimate scientific insights that go against the reigning paradigm.[5]

Kuhn describes scientific development as "a succession of tradition-bound periods punctuated by non-cumulative breaks."[6] A scientific community can only gain knowledge if it shares a certain paradigm of how the universe operates. Challenges to the reigning traditional paradigm are resisted: "Normal science, for example, often suppresses fundamental novelties because they are necessarily subversive of its basic commitments."[7] However, eventually, when the reigning paradigm encounters problems it cannot solve, a new theory will succeed in challenging the orthodoxy, and the scientific community will then undergo what is known as a paradigm shift, a change in the theoretical framework in which that science operates.

The Myth of Medieval Ignorance: Science in the Middle Ages   4.4

Consider another variation of the rationalist claim that faith hinders the free inquiry of science. A common belief today is that the Middle Ages, because it was so dominated by the authority of the Catholic Church, was a time of ignorance and superstition hostile to scientific thought. This assumption is evident in phrases commonly used today: labeling the Middle Ages, especially their early centuries, as the Dark Ages, and using the term *medieval* to describe unenlightened and unscientific thinking.

The reality, however, is quite different from the myth.

The medieval period had a sophisticated sense of science. Thinkers, such as Aquinas, understood science (*scientia*) as sure knowledge based on logical deductions from first principles. First principles were understood as the basic starting points of any science for which no further proof is needed; axioms,

---

4. Polanyi, *Knowing and Being*, 94.

5. Ibid., 79.

6. Thomas Kuhn, *The Structure of Scientific Revolutions*, 2nd enlarged ed., Foundations of the Unity of Science 1–2 (Chicago: University of Chicago Press, 1975), 208.

7. Ibid., 5.

for example, are the first principles of geometry (sec. 3.1.2). Aquinas writes, "There are two kinds of science. There are some which proceed from a principle known by the natural light of the intelligence, such as arithmetic and geometry and the like. There are some which proceed from principles known by the light of a higher science: thus the science of perspective proceeds from the principles established by geometry, and music from principles established by arithmetic" (*ST* 1.1.2).

While it is true that medieval science did not employ the modern scientific method with its emphasis on experimental verification, it is also true that medieval thinkers were taking steps in that direction. Roger Bacon[8] (ca. 1214–1292), educated at Oxford, a professor at the University of Paris, and later a Franciscan friar, published a treatise, "On Experimental Science," (*De scientia experimentali*) in 1267. In this and other writings on scientific method, Bacon holds that logical argument alone is not enough to verify knowledge; one needs a method combining mathematics with detailed observations of nature. The role of experiment, for Bacon, is "to confirm, refute, or challenge theoretical claims." Bacon was one of the first authors to speak of the "laws of nature." Bacon's scientific studies were largely in the field of optics; he calculated accurately that the maximum height of the arch of a rainbow is 42 degrees above the horizon.[9]

Bacon's older contemporary, Robert Grosseteste (ca. 1168–1253), taught at Oxford and later become bishop of Lincoln. He wrote a number of scientific treatises, including "On the Generation of Sounds," "On Comets," "On Lines, Angles, and Figures," "On the Rainbow," "On Color," "On the Heat of the Sun." Again, while Grosseteste was far from operating within the scientific method as it is understood today, he "did introduce to the Latin West the notion of controlled experiment and related it to demonstrative science."[10]

Like Aquinas, both Grosseteste and Bacon drew freely on the pagan philosopher Aristotle and Aristotle's Muslim interpreters, Averroes and Avicenna, in their writings.

Because of men like Grosseteste and Bacon, the environmental scientist and philosopher of science, Hugh Gauch Jr. does not hesitate to call the thirteenth century the "golden age of scientific method. No other century has seen such a great advance in scientific method."[11]

---

8. An overview of the life and work of Roger Bacon is available in the Stanford Encyclopedia of Philosophy, accessible at *http://plato.stanford.edu/entries/roger-bacon/*.

9. Jeremiah Hackett, "Roger Bacon," *The Stanford Encyclopedia of Philosophy* (Winter 2012 ed.), ed. Edward N. Zalta, *http://plato.stanford.edu/archives/win2012/entries/roger-bacon/*. Sec. 5.4.3.

10. Neil Lewis, "Robert Grosseteste," *The Stanford Encyclopedia of Philosophy* (Summer 2013 ed.), ed. Edward N. Zalta, *http://plato.stanford.edu/archives/sum2013/entries/grosseteste/*.

11. Gauch, *Scientific Method in Brief* (Cambridge: Cambridge University Press, 2012), 41. See also Gauch's brief discussion of the contribution of the medieval scientists to scientific method.

Harmony of Faith and Science: Historical Examples

4.5

The following examples demonstrate that science and Christian faith have existed harmoniously.

- Nicole Oresme (ca. 1320–1382) was a doctor of theology and a bishop. He wrote on the nature of motion (including acceleration and velocity), refraction of light, and presented mathematically based arguments against astrological beliefs. Professor Stefan Kirschner concludes, "His work provided some basis for the development of modern mathematics and science."[12]
- Nicolaus Copernicus (1473–1543) who first published the heliocentric theory that the sun, not Earth, is at the center of the universe, had a doctorate in Church law and worked as a church administrator. He dedicated the work advancing the heliocentric theory to Pope Paul III; the work was published by a Lutheran press.[13]
- Johannes Kepler[14] (1571–1630) was a Lutheran well known for developing Copernicus's heliocentric model and discovering laws of planetary motion, including their elliptical orbits of the sun. A student of theology in his youth, Kepler believed that God created the universe using the pattern of the five regular polyhedra.[15]
- Sir Isaac Newton[16] (1642–1727) formulated fundamental laws of motion and universal gravitation. Although he held some unorthodox religious views, he firmly believed that his work pointed toward God's existence, "This most beautiful system of the sun, planets, and comets, could only proceed from the counsel and dominion of an intelligent Being."[17]

Continued

12. Stefan Kirschner, "Nicole Oresme," *The Stanford Encyclopedia of Philosophy* (Fall 2013 ed.), ed. Edward N. Zalta, *http://plato.stanford.edu/archives/fall2013/entries/nicole-oresme/*.

13. Sheila Rabin, "Nicolaus Copernicus," *The Stanford Encyclopedia of Philosophy* (Fall 2010 ed.), ed. Edward N. Zalta, *http://plato.stanford.edu/archives/fall2010/entries/copernicus/*.

14. An overview of Kepler's life and work is accessible at *http://plato.stanford.edu/entries/kepler.*

15. Daniel A. Di Liscia, "Johannes Kepler," *The Stanford Encyclopedia of Philosophy* (Summer 2011 Ed.), ed. Edward N. Zalta, *http://plato.stanford.edu/archives/sum2011/entries/kepler/*.

16. George Smith, "Isaac Newton," *The Stanford Encyclopedia of Philosophy* (Fall 2008 ed.) ed. Edward N. Zalta, *http://plato.stanford.edu/entries/newton/*.

17. Isaac Newton, *The Mathematical Principles of Natural Philosophy*, trans. Andrew Motte, vol. 3 (New York: Daniel Adee, 1848), 504.

> ### Harmony of Faith and Science *Continued*
>
> - The papacy established an astronomical observatory in 1774; the Vatican Observatory,[18] founded in 1891, remains active. The Jesuit Angelo Secchi (1818–1878) was the first to classify stars according to their observed spectra; he is only one of a distinguished tradition of Jesuit astronomers.[19]
> - The Austrian Augustinian monk Gregor Mendel[20] (1822–1884), whose experiments on pea plants uncovered basic laws of heredity, is generally considered the founder of modern genetics.
> - The Belgian priest and physicist Georges Lemaître (1894–1966) was one of the originators of the big bang theory.[21]

Christian Worldview as the Foundation for Modern Science   4.6

The previous examples show that Christian faith and scientific investigation are not inherently contradictory. In fact, a reasonable argument can be made that Christian faith is the foundation of modern science.

In sociologist Rodney Stark's words, "Christianity depicted God as a rational, responsive, dependable and omnipotent being and the universe as his personal creation, thus having a rational, lawful, stable structure, awaiting human comprehension."[22] Stark argues that far from suppressing scientific inquiry, *"Christian theology was essential for the rise of science."*[23]

Professor Hugh Gauch, commenting on the development of scientific method in the Middle Ages, reaches a similar conclusion: "The world was comprehensible to humans because the same good God made both the physical world

---

18. "Part 1: A Vatican Scientist." A video interview about science and faith with Jesuit Brother Guy J. Consolmagno, a research astronomer at the Vatican Observatory, is accessible at *www.youtube.com/watch?v=u8wLH4z7tn4* (time: 0:05:00).

19. "Pietro Angelo Secchi," *Encyclopedia Brittanica* is accessible at *www.britannica.com/EBchecked/topic/531286/Pietro-Angelo-Secchi.*

20. A video of the life, work, and legacy of Gregor Mendel is accessible at *www.youtube.com/watch?v=O4drel1JYmk* (time: 0:30:23).

21. Stephen M. Barr, *Modern Physics and Ancient Faith*, 10. A video discussing Georges Lemaître and the big bang theory, "Father of the Big Bang," is accessible at *www.youtube.com/watch?v=x-hLQ_b3bKdI* (time: 0:05:49).

22. Rodney Stark, *For the Glory of God: How Monotheism Led to Reformation, Science, Witch-hunts, and the End of Slavery* (Princeton, NJ: Princeton University Press, 2003), 147.

23. Ibid., 123. Italics original.

and those humans, with their senses and minds suitable for comprehending the world around them. Confidence that nature was open to human investigation tremendously encouraged the growth of science in the great universities of Western Europe."[24] Notice the point that not only is the physical world rational, but also the human mind itself is oriented toward understanding the world: The Christian can trust that his rational mind is truly in touch with rational reality (sec. 2.5.2).

Albert Einstein, though not a traditional religious believer, echoes this conviction.

> What a deep conviction of the rationality of the universe and what a yearning to understand, were it but a feeble reflection of the mind revealed in this world, Kepler and Newton must have had to enable them to spend years of solitary labor in disentangling the principles of celestial mechanics![25]

It can be argued further that modern science developed not merely because of trust in a "higher power" but very specifically because of the trust in the Judeo-Christian God. The philosopher Alfred North Whitehead argues that religious traditions that believed in inscrutable impersonal powers or in gods that acted arbitrarily could not inspire "the same confidence as in the intelligible rationality of a personal being."[26] It is for essentially these same reasons that science did not develop in otherwise highly sophisticated ancient civilizations such as China or Greece, according to Stark. Even the Islamic tradition, with its belief in a personal Creator, did not provide the foundations for modern science, because Islamic thought tends to conceive of events in the universe as shaped directly by God's will rather than through natural laws established by God.[27]

The Galileo Affair   4.7

Solid evidence thus supports the idea that the Christian worldview contributed to the development of modern science, and that the medieval Church in particular was not opposed to the use of reason and experimental science. Yet if this is true, how can one explain the undeniable fact that the Catholic Church, in 1633, forced Galileo to recant his scientifically-based belief that Earth revolved around the sun?

First, as Stephen Barr notes, one should recall that the Catholic Church's condemnation of Galileo is an anomaly: it is the only case in which the Catholic Church has condemned a scientific theory.[28] The Catholic Church has often condemned what it considers *theological* errors, but not scientific ones.

---

24. Hugh G. Gauch Jr., *Scientific Method in Practice* (Cambridge: Cambridge University Press, 2003), 54.

25. Albert Einstein, *Ideas and Opinions* (New York: Bonanza Books, 1954), 39.

26. Quoted in Stark, *Glory of God*, 148.

27. Ibid., 150–56.

28. Barr, *Modern Physics*, 8.

Second, one needs to understand the Galileo affair in its historical context.[29] Copernicus's heliocentric theory, *On the Revolutions*, was published in 1543. The Church did not condemn it, but many in the Church were uneasy about it because it contradicted the literal meaning of scriptural passages that state that Earth is immovable (e.g., Ps 93:1: "The world will surely stand in place."

Galileo, a renowned teacher and experimental scientist, had published a work in 1613 explicitly supporting the Copernican theory, bolstered by his recent observations with the telescope. Aware of objections to the theory's perceived contradiction of Scripture, Galileo published letters defending the compatibility of Copernicus and the Bible. Scripture is concerned with issues regarding human salvation, Galileo insisted, not with issues involving how nature works. In other words, "the intention of the Holy Spirit is to teach us how one goes to heaven and not how heaven goes."[30]

Galileo was far from being a radical freethinker. He was genuinely concerned to show that scientific research did not contradict a correct understanding of Scripture. He closely connected his scientific research with an appreciation of God's creation: "the book of nature is a book written by the hand of God in the language of mathematics."[31]

In 1616, the Church's top doctrinal body, the Congregation of the Holy Office, condemned Copernicus' heliocentric theory as contrary to Scripture and banned Copernicus' writings until they were "corrected." Scholars debate about why this condemnation was delayed; it may have been a reaction to Galileo's outspoken support of the theory. The condemnation did not mention Galileo by name, but Pope Paul V instructed that the astronomer be ordered privately to abandon the Copernican theory.

In 1623, Pope Urban VIII, who had been a friend and admirer of Galileo, allowed Galileo to again discuss the theory on the condition that he portray it only as a hypothesis. In 1632, however, Galileo published a book strongly implying that the theory should be taken as fact. The pope felt betrayed, and ordered Galileo to Rome for a trial.

At Rome, a Holy Office tribunal convicted him of violating the 1616 decree, forced him to recant his views publicly, and placed him under house arrest for the remainder of his life. He died in 1642.

---

29. The following summary is based on *The Church and Galileo*. ed. Ernan McMullin (Notre Dame, Ind.: University of Notre Dame Press, 2005); George V. Coyne, "Science Meets Biblical Exegesis in the Galileo Affair," *Zygon* 48 (2013): 221–29; Peter Machamer, "Galileo Galilei," *The Stanford Encyclopedia of Philosophy* (Summer 2013 ed.), ed. Edward N. Zalta, *http://plato.stanford.edu /archives/sum2013/entries/galileo/*.

30. Galileo, "Letter to the Grand Duchess," quoted in Coyne, "Biblical Exegesis," 225.

31. Galileo, *Confessions* 12.23–24, cited in Stark, *Glory of God*, 165.

Debate on the precise legal issues involved and the motivation for the pope's actions continues today. A key point to consider is that members of the tribunal believed, along with most people in Galileo's time, that the Copernican theory was factually false or at least unproven. It seemed to contradict the common-sense notion that the sun did move, and Galileo had not been able to produce convincing evidence in favor of the theory. Galileo sought to prove Earth's motion by the movement of tides—a theory that is scientifically incorrect. Had Galileo been able to produce convincing proof, the case may have been very different. Cardinal Robert Bellarmine, a leading Catholic official who had delivered the 1616 warning to Galileo, responded to one of Galileo's supporters:

> I say that if there were a true demonstration that the sun is at the center of the world and the earth in the third heaven, and that the sun does not circle the earth but the earth circles the sun, then one would have to proceed with great care in explaining the Scriptures that appear contrary; and say rather that we do not understand them than that what is demonstrated is false. But I will not believe that there is such a demonstration until it is shown me.[32]

Bellarmine upheld the traditional Catholic belief that the truths of reason can never contradict the truths of faith.[33] If the heliocentric theory had been clearly demonstrated, Bellarmine argues, this would have caused the Catholic Church to rethink its interpretation of scriptural passages that seemed to demonstrate that the sun revolved around Earth, perhaps concluding that such passages were meant metaphorically.

Long before Bellarmine's time, Augustine (354–430 CE) had articulated this same principle: "If it happens that the authority of Sacred Scripture is set in opposition to clear and certain reasoning, this must mean that the person who interprets Scripture does not understand it correctly."[34] This Catholic principle, then, is the exact opposite of the rigid and unreasonable fundamentalism described by Dawkins and cited at the beginning of this chapter.

In addition to the factual questions, Church officials were doubtless also concerned with broader issues. In the context of the ongoing tension with Protestant groups over proper interpretation of Scripture, the Church was understandably sensitive about Galileo's public challenge to its 1616 decree. Galileo's challenge had deeper implications as well: Galileo deliberately wished to discredit the entire Aristotelian view of the physical universe with its Earth-centered cosmology, doctrine of four basic elements, and sharp distinction between earthly and

---

32. Quoted in S. J. Coyne, "Biblical Exegesis," 225.

33. See Thomas Aquinas, *Summa contra Gentiles* 1:7: "It is impossible that truth of faith should be opposed to those principles that the human reason knows naturally."

34. Augustine, *Letter* 143.7.

heavenly (i.e., stars and planets) matter, and replace it with a more unified theory of matter. Because Aristotelianism had been, since the time of Albert the Great and Aquinas, closely tied with Catholic theology, an attack on that philosophy could be interpreted as an attack on the Catholic Church.

Lessons of the Galileo Affair   4.8

Pope John Paul II, having a particular interest in the relationship of faith and science, appointed a commission in 1979 to study the Galileo affair and suggest lessons that could be drawn from it. In its 1992 report, the Pontifical Academy of Sciences Commission identified problems associated with scriptural interpretation: "Theologians . . . failed to grasp the profound non-literal meaning of the Scriptures when they described the physical structure of the universe. This led them unduly to transpose a question of factual observation into the realm of faith."[35]

In his reflections on the report, John Paul II reiterates this point. The Catholic Church officials who condemned Galileo failed to distinguish between two realms of knowledge: knowledge based on divine revelation and knowledge that can be discovered by human reason. Scripture is not a reliable source for judging the nature of the physical universe. Such judgments should be left to the experimental sciences and philosophy, both of which are competent within their own respective realms. John Paul II was careful to add that, although the two realms of revelation and reason should be distinguished, they should not be separated. On the contrary, the two fields should be in close communication, as advances in one field of knowledge should affect knowledge in all other fields.

Thus the scientific evidence for the truth of the Copernican system should have caused theologians to question whether their literal interpretation of scriptural passages apparently opposed to the Copernican system were accurate. John Paul insisted that the principle still applies today. "It is a duty for theologians to keep themselves regularly informed of scientific advances in order to examine . . . whether or not there are reasons for taking them into account in their reflection or for introducing changes in their teaching."[36]

---

35. Cardinal Poupard, "Galileo: Report on Papal Commission Findings," *Origins 22* (November 12, 1992): 374–75. Quoted in Coyne, "Biblical Exegesis," 226.

36. John Paul II, "Faith Can Never Conflict with Reason," *L'Osservatore Romano* 44 (November 4, 1992), accessible at *www.its.caltech.edu/~nmcenter/sci-cp/sci-9211.html*.

The Big Bang and the Christian Doctrine of Creation 4.9

The most commonly accepted scientific theory of the origins of the universe is the big bang theory. According to this theory, about 14 billion years ago the visible universe began expanding from a single, extremely hot and dense point.[37]

Are the big bang theory and the Christian belief that God created the universe contradictory? Again, the answer depends on one's worldview. From a rationalist worldview, they are contradictory because there is no scientific evidence of God's intervention in the big bang. For a person who interprets the creation accounts in Genesis literally, they are also contradictory because Genesis says nothing about God creating a single hot, dense mass of energy that then expanded.

The Catholic tradition does not necessarily insist on a literal interpretation of biblical passages, because in seeking to understand a biblical author's intentions, "the reader must take into account the conditions of their time and culture, the literary genres in use at that time, and the modes of feeling, speaking, and narrating then current" (*CCC*, no.110). There are good reasons for not understanding the Genesis creation accounts as scientifically accurate descriptions of how the universe began. (See sec. 8.14.2 for more detail about biblical interpretation).

If one understands Genesis in a nonliteral way, it is possible to recognize noteworthy similarities between the biblical accounts of creation and the big bang theory.

The Christian View of Creation and the Big Bang 4.9.1

Assessing the scientific validity of the big bang theory falls outside the field of theology; however, many theologians who enter into dialogue with science recognize some similarities between the big bang theory and traditional Christian belief.

First, both the big bang theory and the Christian doctrine of creation agree that the universe had a specific beginning point. Previous to the big bang theory, a common scientific assumption was that the universe simply had no beginning—one version of this idea was the "steady state" model of the universe, which held that matter was continually being created as the universe expanded. In fact, many scientists were originally quite resistant to the big bang theory when it was first proposed, as it sounded suspiciously religious.[38]

---

37. "Big Bang Cosmology," *http://map.gsfc.nasa.gov/universe/bb_theory.html*.

38. See Barr, *Modern Physics*, 43, and Robert Jastrow, *God and the Astronomers* (New York: W. W. Norton, 1978), 112–13.

Second, the big bang theory and the Christian doctrine of creation agree that time itself has a beginning. The common sense experience of time is that it flows at an unchanging, constant rate, by minutes, hours, days, and years. The work of Einstein and others, however, has has demonstrated that time is not a fixed constant. Rather, "time, like space, is a measure of the intervals between things and events in the physical universe."[39] It makes no sense to speak about time before the universe began, because time as a function of the physical universe did not yet exist.

The insight that time has a beginning is not new—it was advanced centuries ago by Augustine. In the ancient world, the eternity of the universe was a common assumption (a view held by Aristotle, for example), and Augustine relates how some critics mocked the Christian belief that creation occurred at a specific time when they asked, "What was God doing before the creation?" If God had created the universe immediately, these critics argued, the universe would also be eternal, but if God had waited some time before creating, why was he waiting?[40]

Augustine replies that the critics' question is based on a misunderstanding of time. Time is a constant flow of past, present, and future, while God is eternal and outside of—transcends—time. God is the creator of time, and in Augustine's view, time did not exist before creation. Addressing God, Augustine writes, "But if there was no time before heaven and earth were created, how can anyone ask what you were doing 'then'? If there was no time, there was no 'then.'"[41]

The big bang theory is not a proof for God's existence. However, it does offer striking support for the *reasonableness* of the Christian view that the universe began at a specific point in time, the result of an act of creation by a transcendent cause. Science cannot offer a truly alternative explanation of how energy or matter first came into existence before they began to expand in the big bang (sec. 3.2.4). According to the scientific law of the conservation of energy, energy can be neither created nor destroyed. If that is true, how did energy appear in the first place?

Arguments from Design 4.10

Aquinas's "fifth way" of proving the existence of God is sometimes called the **"argument from design"** (sec. 3.2.2). This way coincides with a common biblical belief that the Creator can be known from observing the creation. In the New Testament, the apostle Paul writes that even Gentiles who know nothing about the God of Scripture still know God: "Ever since the creation of the world, his invisible attributes of eternal power and divinity have been able to be understood

39. Barr, *Modern Physics*, 47.

40. Augustine, *Confessions* 11.10, *www.ccel.org/ccel/augustine/confessions.xiv.html*.

41. Ibid., 11.13, *www.ccel.org/ccel/augustine/confessions.xiv.html*.

and perceived in what he has made" (Rom 1:20). In making this point, Paul is drawing on previous Jewish tradition, as found, for example, in the Book of Wisdom, "For from the greatness and beauty of created things their original author, by analogy, is seen" (Wis 13:5). The psalmist also maintains, "The heavens declare the glory of God; the firmament proclaims the works of his hands" (Ps 19:2). The premise of these various arguments from design is the same: if one sees evidence of a plan or design in nature, this implies the existence of an intelligent planner or designer who is ultimately responsible for that design.

Perhaps the best-known modern form of the argument from design comes from William Paley's book *Natural Theology*, published in 1802. Paley uses the example of a person finding a watch in a field. If the person carefully examines the watch, he will find many intricately designed gears and springs that function together to make the watch work. Although the person has never seen the designer of the watch, he knows that an intelligent designer must have made it because it is impossible that such intricate pieces could come together spontaneously to form a functioning watch.

Paley then turns to examples of design from nature. A person observing the human eye, for example, finds many intricately designed parts (the retina, rods, cones, optic nerve) that function together for a purpose: to allow a person to see. By **analogy** with the watch, then, it seems reasonable to conclude that an intelligent designer must have designed the eye. Now obviously the designer of the human eye could not have been a human, and so, one is led logically to the conclusion that the designer must be an intelligent power that transcends the natural world. This intelligent designer is called "God."

Section 4.10.2 will consider challenges to Paley's argument from the theory of evolution. First, however, the text explores another variant of the argument from design.

Cosmic Argument from Design 4.10.1

Barr rightly notes that there are actually two arguments from design: a biological design argument, seeing evidence for design in animate nature, and a cosmic design argument, seeing evidence for design in inanimate nature.[42]

The cosmic design argument often focuses on the *"regularity, pattern, symmetry, and order"* in nature, for example, in the regular movement of the heavenly bodies or in the symmetrical growth of crystals.[43] In the biblical understanding of nature, this regular order is a reflection of the divine Logos through which the universe was created (John 1:1; see sec. 2.5.2).

---

42. Barr, *Modern Physics*, 69.

43. Ibid. Italics original.

This spiral galaxy, photographed by the Hubble Space Telescope, is located in the constellation Ursa Major and is known as M101. Measuring 170,000 light years across, it is estimated to contain at least one trillion stars. The beautifully symmetrical, orderly design of such natural structures has long been regarded by both Christian and non-Christian traditions as evidence for a divine mind that orders the universe.

However, just as biological order might be explained by the theory of evolution through natural selection (sec. 4.10.2), so too, cosmic order may be explained as the result of natural physical laws: Planets orbit the sun in regular patterns because they are obeying the laws of gravity. The need for the "God hypothesis" is removed. The cosmic order is simply the result of the working out of impersonal physical laws.

At this point, however, Barr asks a basic metaphysical question: *Why* do these laws exist in the first place?

Consider the scientific facts: Throughout the twentieth century, physicists were able to discover ever-deeper levels of reality. Moving beyond the surface order displayed in the movement of the planets or the growth of crystals, scientists penetrated to the molecular and atomic levels. Here, too, they discovered a precise mathematical order in which, for example, each of the elements is distinguished from the others by a precise number of protons.

Earlier, James Clerk Maxwell (1831–1879), a Scottish physicist and elder in the Presbyterian Church, discovered that the apparently separate forces of electricity and magnetism were joined in a unified field, and he was able to express the fundamental laws of light, magnetism, and electricity in a few mathematical formulas. Though quantum and relativity theories have revolutionized twentieth-century science, these advances proved to be only new methods of further understanding the profound unity and order in the universe. Again physicists are able to describe these relationships in exact mathematical terms; Einstein's $E = MC^2$ is only the most famous of these equations. Today, scientific research is still stimulated by the search for a "grand unified theory" that would unite all partial theories into one. With their deep faith in the rationality of the universe, researchers are confident that such a theory will eventually be articulated.

Consider also the very first moments of the universe. According to standard scientific theories, the universe began as a chaotic mixture of subatomic particles. Why did these subatomic particles spontaneously begin to combine in an orderly fashion, forming atoms and molecules and eventually the entire ordered, predictable universe observable today? Does this spontaneous combining imply that in the very nature of matter itself there must exist a plan, a *logos*, an inherent tendency toward order and meaning?

The Rational Human Mind and the Rational Universe   4.10.1.1

The Reformed theologian and philosopher of science Thomas F. Torrance comments, "There is a fundamental harmony between the 'laws of the mind' and the 'laws of nature': that is, an inherent harmony between how we think and how nature behaves independently of our minds."[44] The mind has an inherent drive toward making sense of things, finding or creating order, understanding, and categorizing the realities in this universe. Why is it that the same rationality and order, expressible in precise mathematical laws, exists outside of the mind? If nature was not rational in itself, then one could never have understood its rational laws. "We could not know anything unless the universe itself had been created by a rational mind."[45] Because the same rational order of one's mind is reflected in nature, is it really so far-fetched to assume that a rational mind outside of oneself created nature's rational order?

---

44. Thomas F. Torrance, *The Christian Frame of Mind: Reason, Order, and Openness in Theology and Natural Science* (Colorado Springs, CO: Helmer and Howard, 1989), 26.

45. Christoph Schönborn, "The Designs of Science," *First Things* (January 2006), accessible at *www.firstthings.com/article.php3?id_article=71*.

In the materialist or determinist worldview, this profound order in the universe is accepted as a given. However, from a worldview open to the transcendent, the Christian allows him- or herself to step back and ask the metaphysical question: *Why* is reality like this? Why *should* it possess such a profoundly rational order that it can be described with exact mathematical formulas? It is surely not unnatural or unreasonable for the scientist to agree with the biblical worldview: This order is evidence of the divine Logos permeating all reality.

In the words of the Anglican priest and theoretical physicist John Polkinghorne,[46] "I would like to understand why the world is so rationally transparent. An explanation would be that the physical world is shot through with signs of mind because behind it is in fact the mind of the Creator."[47]

Biological Argument from Design 4.10.2

The Darwinian Challenge 4.10.2.1

Paley discussed the human eye as an example of intricate design that points toward the existence of a transcendent designer. Modern science offers another explanation: the **Darwinian theory of evolution**. Briefly stated, the Darwinian theory holds that all forms of life on Earth have evolved over billions of years from a single common ancestor. The mechanism that allows for this evolution is natural selection, the natural process by which advantageous genetic qualities are passed on and less advantageous traits gradually disappear.

All species have a certain DNA code, and as the DNA of any growing organism replicates itself, chance mutations in the code occur. Most of the time, these mutations are harmful to a species, but occasionally they are beneficial and allow the species a better chance at surviving. Members of the species with the beneficial mutation thrive and reproduce themselves, eventually replacing the non-mutated members of the species. In this way, species evolve different traits (e.g., a fish species evolves more efficient fins to help it swim faster). Over long periods, one species can eventually evolve into another species. Evolution of traits within a species is known as microevolution; the theory that one species can evolve into another is known as macroevolution.

The great majority of scientists today accept the Darwinian theory of evolution. Since Darwin's time, the field of genetics has provided particularly striking corroborating evidence for the theory of evolution from a common ancestor. Comparison between the DNA sequences of humans with those of various animals, for example, show convincingly that humans and nonhumans share a common ancestor; at the DNA level, humans and chimpanzees are 96 percent

---

46. A video interview with Polkinghorne is accessible at *www.testoffaith.com/resources/resource.aspx?id=640* (time: 0:01:32).

47. Polkinghorne, *Serious Talk: Science and Religion in Dialogue* (Valley Forge, PA: Trinity Press International, 1995), 4–5.

identical.[48] The combination of the new genetic insights with traditional Darwinist theory is known as neo-Darwinism.

For neo-Darwinian scientists such as Richard Dawkins,[49] the implications of Darwin's theory of evolution are clear: Paley's (and any similar) argument from design for the existence of God has been demolished. Paley's analogy of God as the Divine Watchmaker, according to Dawkins, has been replaced by the universe itself, evolving through random mutation and natural selection, as the "Blind Watchmaker." Because the complexity of all life can be explained through natural evolution, there is no need to believe in a higher power guiding the process—no need for the "God hypothesis." For Dawkins, "Darwin made it possible to be an intellectually fulfilled atheist."[50]

Reponses to Darwin: Creationism   4.10.2.2

Some Christians, known as "creationists," have responded to the Darwinian challenge by insisting on the literal truth of the creation stories in Genesis.[51] There is some variety among the creationist schools of thought, including "old Earth" proponents, who accept that Earth is billions of years old, and "young Earth" proponents, who believe it is only a few thousand years old. The young Earth school of thought has been the most influential and will be considered here.

Basic tenets of young Earth creationism are (1) Earth is no more than ten thousand years old, and (2) microevolution can occur within a species, but there is no true scientific evidence for macroevolution. Young Earth creationists attempt to refute Darwinian evolution on scientific grounds, arguing, for example, that there is no fossil evidence for transitional forms that indicate one species evolving into another or that carbon-14 dating methods—used to show that prehistoric animal remains are millions of years old—are flawed.

The scientific claims of the creationists have not been convincing—fossils of transitional forms showing evolution from one species to another, for example, have in fact been found.[52] In addition, the creationists' implicit assumption that the creation account in Genesis is a scientifically reliable account is highly misleading. In contrast, the Catholic tradition does not assume that the Genesis creation stories were intended as scientific accounts (sec. 8.15.1).

---

48. See Francis S. Collins, *The Language of God: A Scientist Presents Evidence for Belief* (New York: Free Press, 2006), 137.

49. A video of Richard Dawkins presenting his arguments is accessible at *www.youtube.com /watch?v=tDdn0UPDjmk* (time: 0:08:38).

50. Richard Dawkins, *The Blind Watchmaker: Why the Evidence of Evolution Reveals a Universe without Design* (New York: Norton & Co., 1986), 10.

51. For an overview of creationist beliefs, see Ted Peters and Martinez Hewlett, *Can You Believe in God and Evolution? A Guide for the Perplexed* (Nashville: Abingdon, 2006), 35–43.

52. Ibid., 43.

Reponses to Darwin: Intelligent Design   4.10.2.3

Another challenge to the Darwinian model comes from a school of thought known as intelligent design (ID).[53] It is associated with the Discovery Institute and its subsidiary the Center for Science and Culture. ID thinkers accept that evolution does occur, but find that it is an inadequate explanation for more complex cases. According to the concept of "irreducible complexity," for example, a system such as the human eye is too complicated to have evolved through natural selection. Its existence can only be explained by the intervention of a transcendent intelligence. The ID concept of specified complexity is similar: Molecular sequences such as DNA point toward a transcendent intelligent designer

As does scientific creationism, ID presents itself as a scientific alternative to the Darwinian theory. However, ID is not a science in the modern sense of the term, because its claims of supernatural intervention cannot be tested or verified and because it does not predict new findings or suggest areas for further experimentation.[54] More generally, ID is open to criticism for its conception of the intelligent designer as a "God of the gaps." Whenever science cannot find natural causes for certain phenomena, thus leaving a "gap" in scientific knowledge, religious believers have a natural tendency to see this as evidence of divine intervention in nature. The problem with the "God of the gaps" approach is that science is constantly discovering natural explanations for events previously thought to have been caused by God or other supernatural causes. The result is that God plays an increasingly smaller role as new discoveries are made. So, theoretically, if science one day provides satisfactory explanations for all natural phenomena, there will no longer be a need for an intelligent designer at all.[55]

Responses to Darwin: NOMA   4.10.2.4

The biologist Stephen Jay Gould coined the acronym NOMA (nonoverlapping magisteria) for the relationship between religion and science.

> To summarize, with a tad of repetition, the net, or magisterium, of science covers the empirical realm: what is the universe made of (fact) and why does it work this way (theory). The magisterium of religion extends over questions of ultimate meaning and moral value. These two magisteria do not overlap, nor do they encompass all inquiry (consider, for example, the magisterium of art and the meaning of

53. Ibid., 47–52.

54. Ibid., 50; Collins, *Language of God*, 187.

55. See Collins, *Language of God*, 93, 194–95. Dawkins (*God Delusion*, 119–34) also rightly critiques the "God of the gaps" theory.

beauty). To cite the old clichés, science gets the ages of rocks, and religion the rock of ages; science studies how the heavens go, religion how to go to heaven.[56]

From a Catholic perspective, there is some truth in Gould's assertion. Pope John Paul II wrote, "Both religion and science must preserve their own autonomy and their distinctiveness."[57] Yet the bald statement that the two magisteria do not overlap is profoundly at odds with the Catholic tradition. All truth, both theological and scientific, is from God, and to separate them into mutually exclusive compartments is to distort the meaning of both. As John Paul II emphasized, there is an urgent need for dialogue between theology and science, as they are both ways of understanding the world. "A divided community fosters a fragmented vision of the world; a community of interchange encourages its members to expand their partial perspectives and form a new unified vision."[58]

Toward a Christian Response to Darwin 4.10.3

Acceptance of Evolutionary Theory as a Scientific Explanation 4.10.3.1

The Catholic tradition is open to accepting Darwinian evolution as a scientifically established theory for physical evolution. Already Pope Pius XII, in his 1950 encyclical *Humani Generis* (no. 36), taught that evolution could be investigated as a scientific hypothesis for the physical development of the human body, as long as it was not used to explain the development of the spiritual soul, which Catholic doctrine insists is "immediately created by God."

In 1985 Pope John Paul II stated,

A belief in creation, rightly understood, and a rightly understood doctrine of evolution, do not stand in each other's way. Evolution presupposes creation; creation, seen in the light of evolution, appears as an event extended over time—a *creatio continua*, as a continuing creation—in that God becomes visible, to the eye of faith, as the "creator of heaven and earth."[59]

56. Stephen Jay Gould, *Rock of Ages: Science and Religion in the Fullness of Life* (New York: Ballantine, 1999), 6.

57. John Paul II, "Letter to Reverend George V. Coyne, S.J., Director of the Vatican Observatory" (June 1, 1988), accessible at *www.vatican.va/holy_father/john_paul_ii/letters/1988/documents/hf_jp-ii_let_19880601_padre-coyne_en.html*.

58. John Paul II, "Letter to George V. Coyne."

59. John Paul II, remarks at a 1985 Rome symposium "Christian Faith and the Theory of Evolution." Quoted in Christoph Schönborn, *Chance or Purpose: Creation, Evolution, and a Rational Faith* (San Francisco: Ignatius Press, 2007), 30.

Recent Catholic teaching, then, clearly recognizes the validity of the theory of evolution as a reasonable explanation for the physical development of the human species. The Orthodox theologian, Kallistos Ware,[60] similarly sees no contradiction between the evolutionary theory, properly understood, and Christian faith.

Christians who accept traditional Christian beliefs together with the theory of evolution are sometimes called theistic evolutionists or evolutionary creationists.[61]

Francis Collins: Genetic Scientist and Christian   4.10.3.2

Francis Collins, a distinguished American scientist with a PhD in physical chemistry, has worked as a medical doctor and research professor. He discovered several disease-causing genes and served from 1993 to 2008 as director of the National Human Genome Research Institute, an international effort to map the sequence of human DNA. In 2009, President Obama appointed him director of the US National Institutes of Health.

Collins was not raised in a religious household and during his college years, slipped into agnosticism. At the time, he viewed religious beliefs as based on only emotion, superstition, or the blind following of authority. Facing the suffering and death of others routinely in his work as a doctor, Collins was forced to think seriously about the deeper meaning of life for the first time. Studying the writings of C. S. Lewis, Collins realized that the Christian faith is not rooted solely in emotion and blind obedience to authority but can be rationally justified. After wrestling with lingering doubts and hesitations, Collins eventually became a Christian.

His 2006 book, *The Language of God: A Scientist Presents Evidence for Belief*, was a best seller. In 2007, Collins founded the BioLogos Foundation, a group of evangelical Christians dedicated to showing the compatibility of biblical faith and the theory of evolution. In 2009, Pope Benedict XVI appointed Collins to the Pontifical Academy of Sciences.

---

60. Metropolitan Kallistos Ware discusses faith and science, particularly evolution, in a video accessible at *www.youtube.com/watch?v=jSVPZykCRyQ* (time: 0:06:12).

61. See Peters and Hewlett, *God and Evolution*, 53–7; *see also the article,* "How is BioLogos different from Evolutionism, Intelligent Design, and Creationism?" accessible at *http://biologos.org/questions/biologos-id-creationism*.

Distinguishing Evolution from Evolutionism 4.10.3.3

One must be careful, however, to distinguish between evolution as (1) a scientific theory of physical development and (2) a philosophical worldview espoused by certain neo-Darwinist thinkers such as Richard Dawkins and Daniel Dennett. Their materialist worldview can be labeled *evolutionism*. The Catholic tradition accepts the validity of the former but clearly rejects the latter.

Consider two basic claims made by neo-Darwinists:

1. Evolution through natural selection of random genetic mutations is a satisfactory explanation for all forms and manifestations of life on Earth.

2. Because life is a product of random mutations, it can have no deeper or higher purpose. As Oxford chemistry professor Peter Atkins states, "Humanity should accept that science has swept away any justification for belief in the universe having a meaning or purpose."[62]

Notice that the first claim deals with observable facts that are open to scientific verification. The second, however, is a metaphysical claim that is not open to scientific verification. Following are critiques of both claims:

Critique of Evolutionism: The Origin of Life 4.10.3.4

Can the theory of evolution, defined as natural selection of random genetic mutations, fully explain all forms of life? For the sake of the argument, it will be assumed that this theory does adequately explain physical changes in living organisms. Even granted this point, however, evolution still cannot adequately answer two specific puzzles.

1. The origin of life itself.

2. The development of specifically human characteristics such as self-consciousness.

First, how did life itself come into being? In other words, how does nature go from nonliving to living? One popular theory is that, at some point three to four billion years ago, life arose when chemicals combined spontaneously from a "primordial soup," perhaps catalyzed by lightning. Scientists can analyze the chemical components of animate material but cannot explain how life arises from these chemical components—as is obvious from their inability to produce life, even when all the necessary chemical components are assembled.

Obviously, the very first life form cannot have arisen from the process of natural selection because there was nothing to select. Furthermore, although the first life form must have been a relatively simple, single-celled organism, it must also have been complex enough to replicate its own DNA, but according to

---

62. Quoted in Christopher Schönborn, *Chance or Purpose: Creation, Evolution, and a Rational Faith* (San Francisco: Ignatius Press, 2007), 28.

Darwinian theory, such complexity can only be reached as the result of a process of evolution. So how can a relatively complex, DNA-replicating organism have been produced spontaneously from nonorganic materials? Neo-Darwinians have proposed several speculative theories, but none has proved convincing.[63]

If the theory of evolution cannot explain the origins of life, could an evolutionist admit the possibility that a transcendent cause—God—created the first life form? Dawkins quickly dismisses the possibility: "But of course any God capable of intelligently designing something as complex as the DNA/protein-replicating machine must have been at least as complex and organized as that machine itself."[64] In other words, if God was complex enough to create the first single-celled life form, how can one explain how God himself originated? Again Dawkins's strictly materialist worldview is apparent: He does not consider the possible existence of a transcendent Creator who would not be subject to the laws of evolution, because he assumes, based on unprovable materialist presuppositions, that nonmaterial reality does not exist.

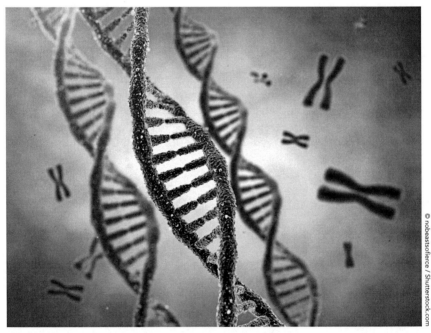

This is an image of double-helical DNA molecules and chromosomes. DNA carries the genetic instructions in all forms of life. From a materialist perspective, DNA, like everything else, developed from chance, random causes. From a traditional Christian perspective, the intelligible information stored in DNA is yet another indication that the universe was created by an intelligent mind.

63. See Dawkins, *Blind Watchmaker*, 197–237.
64. Ibid., 200.

Critique of Evolutionism: The Transition to Human Life
4.10.3.5

The second point at which Neo-Darwinian evolution is unconvincing is precisely the transition from the lower animal to the human. Granted that the human body evolved from lower life forms, the theory of evolution through natural selection is simply inadequate to explain the rise of distinctly human characteristics: a high level of intelligence, self-awareness and self-reflection, moral conscience, free will, and even a sense of the beautiful or the transcendent.

There can be no doubt that evolution through natural selection was *involved* in the development of all of these distinctly human characteristics. The brain, the physical basis of intelligence, has evolved. The Christian worldview is open to recognizing the physical and even evolutionary basis (brain, neurons, nerves) for intelligence and consciousness, but it simply insists that this physical and evolutionary basis cannot be the whole explanation. The materialist-evolutionist view, in contrast, insists that intelligence, conscience, and self-awareness are *nothing more* than their material basis.

However, the human is something more. A characteristic distinction of the human is self-transcendence—the ability of self-awareness, to think about one's thinking, to stand outside of oneself. As noted earlier, the idea that a succession of chance genetic mutations would determine a person to think, "This thought is nothing more than the result of a succession of chance genetic mutations," is self-contradictory (sec. 2.4.2). Humans have the freedom to know that they are not determined completely by evolution. In Barr's words, "Spiritual powers of intellect, rationality, and freedom cannot be accounted for by mere biology."[65]

Critique of Evolutionism: Different Levels of Causation
4.10.3.6

The theologian John Haught shows that Dawkins and others are confusing different levels of explanation when they argue that Darwin's scientific theory has replaced the belief in God as the creator. Haught uses the analogy of a page in a book to illustrate his point:

1. Level 1 cause: The page exists because a printing press stamped letters in black ink onto white paper.

2. Level 2 cause: The page exists because an author is trying to communicate ideas.

Notice that both explanations can be true; one does not rule out the other. Analogously, Darwin's theory can explain human life at a basic physical level.

---

65. Stephen Barr, "The Design of Evolution," *First Things* (October 1995), accessible at *www.firstthings.com/article.php3?id_article=238*.

However, Dawkins and others incorrectly assume that this lower-level explanation rules out a higher-level explanation. Just as one cannot determine an author's intention from examining the chemistry of how the ink bonds with paper, so too examining life at the level of natural selection can reveal nothing about whether a creator intended to create life through that process.[66]

Seeing God's Hand in Evolution? 4.10.3.7

Christoph Schönborn, a theologian and cardinal of the Catholic Church, accepts the theory that life evolved due to natural selection of genetic mutations. However, if one observes the development of life on Earth as a whole, Schönborn argues, a clear, purposeful pattern is evident to any unbiased observer. The mechanism of natural selection, random from the scientific point of view, was enough "to give rise to an upward sweep of evolution resulting in human beings."[67] In other words, one can see an overall pattern or direction in apparently random evolutionary changes.

Catholic economist E. F. Schumacher (1911–1977) presents a similar model of this purposeful progression in nature.[68] He identifies four "Levels of Being": minerals, plants, animals, humans. Each level is *qualitatively* different from the preceding level, distinguished from that previous level by a unique "power."

Specifically, plants are distinguished from minerals by the mysterious power of life—mysterious because humans can destroy life but cannot create it. Animals are distinguished from plants by the mysterious power of consciousness—mysterious in the sense that it is again beyond human power to create or even describe it accurately. It can be recognized because animals can be knocked unconscious, while plants cannot. Finally, humans are distinguished from animals by the even more mysterious quality of "self-consciousness"—the ability to consider one's thinking or actions.

For Schumacher, as well as Schönborn, it is clear that life has progressed in a definite pattern: As one moves up from mineral to plant to animal to human, one moves from passivity to activity, from necessity to freedom. One sees progress toward ever-greater intelligence, responsibility, and meaning.[69]

Is it possible to see God's purpose in this pattern of progress? Did God design the universe in such a way that it is oriented toward this goal of becoming ever freer, ever more responsible? These characteristics are distinctively human, part of the image of God with which humans alone were created according to Genesis (1:26–28).

---

66. John F. Haught, *Making Sense of Evolution: Darwin, God, and the Drama of Life* (Louisville, KY: Westminster John Knox Press, 2010): 23–25. Schönborn ("The Designs of Science") makes a similar point.

67. Schönborn, "The Designs of Science."

68. E. F. Schumacher, *A Guide for the Perplexed* (New York: Harper & Row, 1977), 15–38.

69. See also John F. Haught, *Responses to 101 Questions on God and Evolution* (Mahwah, NJ: Paulist Press, 2001), 109–11.

Could this be the meaning of such biblical passages as Romans 8, which states that "all creation [nature] is groaning in labor pains even until now" (8:22) and that at the culmination of all history, "creation [nature] itself would be set free from slavery to corruption and share in the glorious freedom of the children of God" (8:21)? Is it possible, then, that God uses the mechanism of evolution at a lower level of causation in order to fulfill the higher level purpose of the universe evolving toward a likeness like that of its creator?

Chapter 10 applies these suggestions in exploring Jesus Christ, understood by Christians to be God the Son in human form. Thus the theory of evolution, without the materialist presuppositions attached to it by neo-Darwinism, can be understood as consistent with traditional Christian doctrines. Just as all things are created through the Word, so all things at some level are striving back toward that goal.

John F. Haught argues further that specific Christian belief that God is love is consistent with evolutionary theory. The God of love does not coercively force his will on others. Through the contingency and apparent randomness of Darwinian evolution, God gives the universe freedom to evolve in surprising and dramatic ways[70]

Toward a Catholic Understanding of Science and Faith   4.11

This section summarizes some principles describing the Catholic tradition's understanding of the proper relationship between scientific thought and Christian faith.

1. Scientific and religious thought should not be kept in completely separate realms, a solution adopted by fideism or NOMA. They should be in dialogue and allowed to influence one another.

2. At the same time, science and religion each have their own separate realms of expertise and their own autonomy. "Each should possess its own principles, its pattern of procedures, its diversities of interpretation and its own conclusions."[71] The mistake of Galileo's judges was to make a judgment outside of their realm of competence.

3. Theological truth and scientific truth can never contradict one another. If they do seem to contradict, it is because either the scientists (e.g., through materialist presuppositions) or the theologians (e.g., through a faulty biblical hermeneutic) have strayed out of their realm of competence.

---

70. Haught, *God and Evolution*, 113–14.

71. John Paul II, "Letter to Reverend George V. Coyne."

4. Theologians can learn from scientific thought. John Paul II wrote, "Science can purify religion from error and superstition."[72] Science, for example, corrected the religious belief that the sun revolved around Earth. Theologians must remain current with scientific thought and be willing to adjust their teaching in light of scientifically provable information.

5. Scientists can also learn from theologians: "Religion can purify science from idolatry and false absolutes."[73] Theologians may rightly criticize scientists who—employing rationalist, materialist, or determinist presuppositions—stray beyond their realms of competence and deny the existence of metaphysical realities.

6. Rational signs of God's purpose and design in the universe can be discerned through a reasonable interpretation of scientific evidence (e.g., the implications of the big bang theory, the rational structure of the universe, and the clear pattern of evolution toward greater intelligence, freedom, and ethical responsibility).

Questions about the Text

1. What roles do intuition and authority play in modern scientific research?

2. What are some specific examples of Christians who have made significant scientific contributions?

3. Why does Whitehead believe that modern science could only have developed among people who believed in the Judeo-Christian God?

4. What factors led to the conflict between the Church and Galileo? What lessons did John Paul II draw from this conflict?

5. What are some similarities between the big bang theory and the Christian doctrine of creation?

6. Discuss arguments for and against the cosmic argument from design. Consider especially twentieth-century discoveries of order at the molecular level.

7. What is the biological argument from design? How is the neo-Darwinist theory of evolution a challenge to this argument?

8. What are the strengths and weaknesses of the following responses to the Darwinist challenge: creationism, intelligent design, and NOMA?

9. What is the difference between the theory of evolution and the philosophy of evolutionism? What are two basic criticisms of evolutionism as a theory that tries to explain the whole of life?

---

72. Ibid.
73. Ibid.

10. Is there objective evidence that the evolution of life has an overall goal or direction? Why or why not?

11. What are some basic elements in a Catholic understanding of the relationship between faith and science?

Discussion Questions

1. Has reading this chapter changed your impression of the role of scientific research in the Middle Ages?

2. In your experience, do scientifically minded people tend to be less religious?

3. Is the argument from design personally convincing to you?

4. What are your thoughts on the debates on teaching evolution, creationism, or intelligent design in the public schools?

5

C H A P T E R

Revelation

Does God Communicate with Humans?

Transcendence and Revelation   5.1

In the Christian view, God is *transcendent*, and humans are able to sense the existence of God's transcendent power (secs. 1.3–7). God is the First Cause that transcends all other causes (secs. 3.2.3–3). Humans and all things in the world are limited: God, by definition, is unlimited.

If it is true that God is beyond human ability to comprehend, how can people know anything about God? Would not statements about God be pure speculation and not true knowledge?

Knowledge about God, in the Christian view, would be impossible *unless* the transcendent God chooses to reveal that knowledge to humans. Christians believe God has indeed revealed such knowledge.

This chapter begins with a brief overview of the Christian concept of revelation. In keeping with the book's focus on the harmony between faith and reason, the chapter follows the overview of revelation with an exploration of certain reasonable questions about Christian revelation, together with the Christian responses to those questions.

The Concept of Revelation   5.2

Christian theology distinguishes between two basic types of revelation: natural, also known as "general revelation," and historical, or "special revelation."[1] Natural revelation involves God's self-revelation through creation, through nature. For example, the fact that the universe exists raises the question of how it, ultimately, began (secs. 3.3.2–3), while the order and design of the universe are signs of God as the ultimate designer (sec. 4.10). Natural revelation also includes the belief that God reveals Moral Law to all people through their conscience (sec. 1.5).

---

1. Avery Dulles, "Faith and Revelation," in *Systematic Theology: Roman Catholic Perspectives*, vol. 1, eds. F. S. Fiorenza and J. P. Galvin (Minneapolis: Fortress Press, 1991), 94.

Natural revelation is called *general* in the sense that it is open to all people at all times: All people, Christian or non-Christian, are able to know something about God through reflecting on creation and listening to the voice of conscience.

Historical revelation, in contrast, involves the belief that God has, in certain times and places, communicated more directly with people. For example, the Bible records that God spoke to Abraham, commanding him to leave his own country and go to a new land with his wife Sara. There, Abraham was to become the father of a new people, the people of Israel (Gen 12:1–3).

Special revelation, then, in the Christian view, is particularly tied to God's revelation to Israel. In forming a special relationship, a "covenant" with Israel, God continually revealed himself and his will to this people, especially through the Law given to Moses and through the messages of various prophets.

The ultimate revelation in the Christian view, however, was given in Jesus Christ, when God the Son became a human. God came down to the human level, so-to-speak, to reveal himself. As the Letter to the Hebrews puts it, "In times past, God spoke in partial and various ways to our ancestors through the prophets; in these last days, he spoke to us through a son" (Heb 1:1–2).

The historical revelation to Israel is recorded in the first part of Christian Bible, known as the Old Testament. The revelation of Jesus Christ is recorded in the second part, the New Testament. For this reason, Scripture holds a special authority, as Aquinas writes, "For our faith rests upon the revelation made to the apostles [close followers of Jesus] and to the prophets, who wrote the canonical books [Scripture], and not on the revelations (if any such there are) made to the other doctors [officially recognized teachers of the Church]" (*ST* 1.1.8 ad. 2).[2]

Why does God reveal himself? In the Christian understanding, the motive is essentially love. God, who exists as an eternal relationship of love between the Father, Son, and Holy Spirit (sec. 6.3), desires to share that eternal, perfect love with his creation. In the words of Vatican II's declaration on revelation, *Dei Verbum*,

> God chose to reveal Himself and to make known to us the hidden purpose of His will (see Eph. 1:9) by which through Christ, the Word made flesh, man might in the Holy Spirit have access to the Father and come to share in the divine nature (see Eph. 2:18; 2 Peter 1:4). (*DV*, no. 2)

God reveals himself so that humans can overcome their limitations and sins and share a life of perfect peace and happiness with him.

Accepting revelation,[3] then, is not a matter of blind faith. In general revelation, human reason is able to recognize a Creator and Designer behind the universe. In special revelation, people accept or believe revelation because they have reasons to trust the authority of the revealer.

---

2. Clarifications added in square brackets.

3. A video of Fr. Robert Barron discussing faith and reason in relation to revelation is accessible at *www.youtube.com/watch?v=_AiscqfMLh4* (time: 0:05:27).

Muslim Concept of Revelation   5.2.1

The Second Vatican Council teaches explicitly that Muslims worship the same God Christians worship. "[T]he plan of salvation also includes those who acknowledge the Creator. In the first place amongst these there are the Muslims, who, professing to hold the faith of Abraham, and along with us adore the one and merciful God, who on the last day will judge mankind" (LG, no. 16). Further, "They adore the one God, living and subsisting in Himself; merciful and all-powerful, the Creator of heaven and earth, who has spoken to men" (NA, no. 3).

Like Jews and Christians, Muslims believe that God has revealed himself to humans through the prophets. Islam uses the term *prophet* in a broad sense: Adam, Noah, Abraham, Jesus, and Muhummad are all called prophets. Islam recognizes that God gave revelations to the Jewish people and to the Christian people, and that these revelations are recorded in the Scriptures of the Old and New Testaments. The Qur'an, the Muslim scripture, calls both Jews and Christians "people of the Book" (see, e.g., Qur'an 2:105).

Islam, however, teaches that these earlier revelations were partial and not recorded with complete accuracy in the Old or New Testaments. According to Islam, the final and definitive revelation was God's revelation of the Qur'an to the prophet Muhammad, who lived about six hundred years after the time of Jesus.

According to Muslim tradition, the angel Gabriel gave a series of revealed messages to Muhammad over a period of more than twenty years. Muhammad memorized these revelations and taught them to his followers. In the generation after Muhammad's death, the revelations were written in what is now known as the Qur'an. The Qur'an often refers to characters and events familiar from the Bible: the creation; Adam and Eve; God's call of Abraham, and Jesus, including Jesus' birth from the virgin Mary. Muslims consider Jesus a great prophet but deny that he has a divine nature as the Son of God. The Qur'an also records a series of laws that govern all aspects of Muslim society, including marriage, inheritance, and punishment for crimes.

The traditional Muslim understanding is that the Qur'an is the direct revealed word of God. As such, the words have existed with God from all eternity—they were only revealed to Muhammad at a certain point in history. Thus there is no possibility of human error in the Qur'an. Because God's words were revealed in Arabic, any translation of the Qur'an is not considered the Qur'an but a paraphrase of the Qur'an's meaning.

The Qur'an is the sacred scripture of Islam. In the traditional Muslim view, the Qur'an has no human author—every word is directly from God. For this reason, some religious studies scholars argue that the closest analogy to the Qur'an in Christianity is not the Bible (because Christians acknowledge that the Bible has human authors) but rather Jesus himself: God's divine Word who mediates between God and humans.

An Objection to Natural Revelation: The Problem of Evil   5.3

When Christians claim that God reveals himself through the design and order in nature, aren't they overlooking some things? After all, when one observes nature, one sees not only beauty and order but also violence and disorder. One sees animals that survive by violence—killing and devouring other living creatures. One sees earthquakes that level cities and tsunamis that devastate vast areas of Earth and kill thousands. This is not to mention the untold cruelty of humans, whose history is filled with war, mass murder, sexual violence, hatred, greed, intolerance, and prejudice. Might these realities reveal a Creator who is cruel or, at best, indifferent to the sufferings of creation?

Why do evil and suffering exist? This is one of the oldest and most challenging questions people grapple with. All religious traditions have offered some answers. The following sections discuss some Christian responses.

Creation: Good or Evil?   5.3.1

It seems difficult to account for evil and suffering within a Christian worldview. On the one hand, Christians believe that God is completely good. Aquinas, for example, teaches that God is the supreme good (*ST* 1.6.2). Furthermore, Christians believe that all of creation is good. In the creation account in Genesis 1, the author repeatedly states, "God saw that it was good." The goodness of humans, said to be created in the image of God (Gen 1:26–27), is especially noteworthy. So if both the creator and the whole of creation are all good, how can evil exist?

Gnosticism, a non-Christian religious philosophy that developed early in the church's history, responded to the problem of evil by teaching that this world was created not by the true God but by a lesser, or even an evil, god. In the **Gnostic** view, the world is full of suffering and evil because its creator is flawed. This perspective, though reasonable, is deeply pessimistic. The physical world is not a reflection of God's goodness and design but the result of an inferior or evil power.

Christian belief in the devil as the source of evil may seem similar to the Gnostic view especially by those who see the devil as a god-like creature able to create things. Yet the Christian view of creation, with an all-good God creating an all-good universe, is quite different from Gnosticism. God created *all things* good in the beginning; the devil did not create anything.

Evil as a Corruption of Original Good   5.3.2

Given the Christian belief in the goodness of all creation, there is only one possible source of evil: It must have come from an original good. In other words, pure evil cannot exist; it can only be a corruption, or distortion, of an original good. Augustine writes, "And I asked what wickedness was, and I found that it was no substance, but a perversion of the will bent aside from thee, O God" (*Confessions* 7.16); Aquinas says similarly, "Therefore it must be said that by the name of evil is signified the absence of good" (*ST* 1.48.1).

Consider an example of what many people understand as pure evil: the attack on the World Trade Center on September 11, 2001. The attackers believed, in however a corrupt or distorted way, that they were doing God's will by attacking what they saw as a symbol of American greed and materialism. To put it another way: The 9-11 hijackers began with beliefs that are good in themselves—belief in a just God and belief in a call to create a just society not based on greed—and distorted these ideas into a justification for killing thousands of innocent people. This analysis shows that the attackers were not motivated by pure evil.

What about a sadistic person, though—one who finds pleasure in being cruel? Isn't that an example of pure evil? Notice how a sadist's behavior is described here: he or she gets pleasure out of being cruel. Pleasure itself is a good thing—becoming evil only when distorted. No one does evil simply for the sake of doing evil: It's always done for the sake of some benefit or twisted pleasure. If one analyzes any evil action, one finds that it is always an original good that is distorted or perverted.

These examples suggest that the possibility of evil, or the corruption of good, is associated with human free will. If people are limited to choosing only the good, they are not truly free.

Christians do speak of an evil power, often identified as Satan or the devil. Yet in the Christian view, even Satan was once good: God created him as a good angel. The Bible does not narrate this story, although passages such as Revelation 12:7– 9 provide hints of it. It does appear, however, in some ancient non-biblical Jewish accounts as well as in later classics of the Christian tradition, such as John Milton's *Paradise Lost* (see also *CCC*, no. 391). As a created angel, Satan became jealous of God's power and rebelled against him. God and his faithful angels defeated Satan and cast him and his followers out of heaven.

The Christian worldview, rooted in the sense that existence is a good, contrasts starkly with the pessimism of Gnosticism. Aquinas, reflecting the Christian perspective, claims "Goodness and being are really the same" (*ST* 1.5.1). Augustine, similarly, believes that "whatsoever is, is good" (*Confessions* 7.12). Simply to exist is good. Therefore, pure evil is a contradiction. If something exists, by that very fact alone, it is already good.

Christian thought on the origin of good and evil always returns to the belief that God is the First Cause of all things, the ultimate source of all being. The First Cause *must* be a positive force, because existence itself is good. To create is a positive act; evil can only distort or destroy. The goodness of the creator accounts for the deeply grounded Christian trust in the ultimate goodness and meaning of creation. Although suffering and evil are realities, in the end Christians see goodness as always stronger, because it is the basis of reality itself.

Why Do Bad Things Happen in Nature?   5.3.3

Understanding evil as a distortion of an original good can help explain how humans, or even angels, distort original good through their choices, but how can it explain the bad things in nature itself—the hurricanes, earthquakes, and tsunamis? How can it explain the violence, death, and destruction that seem to form a part of everyday nature: one animal feeding on another animal, the brutal rule of "survival of the fittest" guiding evolution? How can it explain that some children, seemingly at random, are struck with muscular dystrophy or that some elderly people must struggle with Parkinson's disease?

The first step in responding to such questions is to admit, humbly, that one does not have complete answers. Christopher Schönborn cautions that one "should by no means be given too hasty an answer," and the *Catechism* also advises, "No quick answer will suffice."[4]

---

4. Christoph Schönborn, *Chance or Purpose: Creation, Evolution, and a Rational Faith* (San Francisco: Ignatius Press, 2007), 93; *CCC*, no. 309.

At the same time, neither is it helpful to conclude that pain, suffering, and destruction in nature are mysteries beyond human understanding. When people are afflicted with tragedies or diseases, they spontaneously search for theological answers to help them make sense of their suffering. The following reflections explore some of the answers offered within the Christian tradition.

God Allows Natural Laws to Work   5.3.3.1

God gives humans the good gift of free will, even though God knows that humans will, at times, abuse that free will in order to do evil (sec. 7.13.1). If humans are to be truly free, it must be possible for them to choose to do evil.

In an analogous way, God also allows nature to have its own autonomy. Just as he allows humans free will, he allows nature to work according to its own laws rather than constantly intervening through miracles.

One should recognize that the laws of nature that allow destruction are the same laws that provide order. In most cases, natural laws benefit humans and other living things. They help people live in an orderly and predictable way. Humans could not survive (plant crops, build homes, and so on) if the laws of nature were not predictable. So for the most part, natural laws help humans and are, in that sense, good. However, natural laws do allow destruction: hurricanes and gentle breezes comply with the same laws of nature.

Schönborn points out that the devastating 2004 tsunami in the south Pacific was the result of a shift in continental plates. However, scientists have shown that if these plates were not mobile, life would never have evolved on Earth, as these plates are one of the preconditions for the planet's ability to maintain a stable average temperature necessary for life.[5] The natural systems of Earth are so interrelated that if God intervened to save humans or other life in one area of the system, it might have devastating effects in another area. If one tries concretely to imagine how one would make a perfect world, one quickly runs into difficulties.

Nature Is Flawed but Will Be Renewed
in the End   5.3.3.2

Nature is not as it should be, in the Christian view (*CCC*, no. 310). Violence, decay, and death were not part of God's plan from the beginning. Death, for example, was not part of God's creation: It is one of the consequences of human sin (see Rom 5:12). God's plan, rather, is reflected in the Garden of Eden (Gen 2): a time when humans, nature, and God interacted in perfect harmony.

Nature is still good, but it has limitations and imperfections and does not reflect the power and goodness of its creator perfectly. Yet in the Christian view, these limitations and imperfections will one day come to an end. The apostle Paul writes of the Christian hope that "creation itself would be set free . . . and

---

5. Ibid., 100.

share in the glorious freedom of the children of God" (Rom 8:21). At the end of history, humans, together with all creation, will return to the original perfection that God intends. As the Book of Revelation states, "there shall be no more death or mourning, wailing or pain" (21:4).

Good Comes Out of Evil and Suffering   5.3.3.3

Why, then, does God allow imperfection and suffering? Aquinas expresses a traditional response, quoting Augustine, "Since God is the highest good, he would not allow any evil to exist in his works, unless His omnipotence and goodness were such as to bring good even out of evil" (*ST* 1.2.3 ad. 1). The *Catechism* (*CCC*, no. 312) also teaches, "God in his almighty providence can bring a good from the consequences of an evil."

It is obvious that good can come out of evil. In the aftermath of a hurricane, for example, many people are motivated by compassion to help those affected by donating money or by spending time directly serving them.

Suffering in one's personal life often leads to good. Enduring an illness or other hardship may teach one to be more humble, as one recognizes personal limitations. It may teach one to be more empathetic and understanding of the sufferings of others. At another level, many goods involve suffering. Excelling at athletic or academic pursuits, for example, often requires sacrifices. "No pain, no gain," as the saying goes.

The positive significance of suffering is at the very center of the Christian message. After all, from the Christian perspective, the sufferings of Jesus on the cross brought forgiveness of sins and the possibility of complete peace and joy to all people (sec. 11.6). Following Jesus, too, inevitably involves suffering, as the Gospel of Mark makes clear when Jesus said, "Whoever wishes to come after me must deny himself, take up his cross, and follow me" (Mark 8:34).

It is easy to misinterpret this Christian teaching. It does *not* mean, for example, that God sends devastating hurricanes in order to teach people to be more humble or to give other people opportunities to volunteer. It means that suffering and imperfection are woven inextricably into the fabric of the world; and it is only by facing and working through this suffering, with God's help, that a person can attain the perfect peace and happiness that God intends for creation.[6]

Historical (Special) Revelation: Two Questions   5.4

As noted in section 5.1, the Christian concept of special revelation focuses on God's revelation to the people of Israel, and ultimately, God's revelation in Jesus Christ, the Son of God who became human as one of Israel's people.

---

6. A video of Fr. Robert Barron discussing God and the problem of evil is accessible at *www.youtube.com/watch?v=vx8ZMkWL8hw* (time: 0:09:55).

As usual, reasonable questions arise when one considers these claims of faith. Consider two of those questions: (1) Does it really make sense to say that the transcendent God "communicates," or "talks," with people? (2) Because human language is limited, isn't the idea that God would use language inadequate to describe the communication of a transcendent God?

Can God Really Communicate? Einstein's Rejection of a Personal God   5.5

Many reasonable people reject the idea that God communicates with humans. Albert Einstein, arguably one of the greatest minds of the twentieth century, believed that the universe "reveals an intelligence of such superiority that, compared with it, all the systematic thinking and acting of human beings is an utterly insignificant reflection."[7] Einstein also spoke of the "mind revealed in this world."[8] Despite this language about "intelligence" and "mind," however, Einstein's conception of God[9] was completely impersonal.

When Einstein referred to the intelligence or mind of the universe, he meant the fixed laws of nature. People could no more have a personal relationship with this universal mind than they could with the law of gravity. It makes no sense to pray to God to change an event, in Einstein's view, because the fixed laws of nature cannot change.

To think of God as a personal being, a being to whom one could pray and with whom one could have a relationship, Einstein believed, was "**anthropomorphic.**" It is a prescientific way of thinking, as when people believed Zeus caused lightning by throwing a lightning bolt. Einstein called on religious leaders to have the courage to plainly "give up the doctrine of a personal God."[10]

God's Mind and the Human Mind   5.5.1

Is the idea of a personal God really outdated? Consider Einstein's view in a little more detail.

Einstein's rejection of a personal God resulted in a deterministic and materialistic view of the universe. Fixed laws leave room for neither a personal God nor human free will. Einstein was quite explicit: "Man's actions are determined by necessity, external and internal."[11]

---

7. Albert Einstein, *Ideas and Opinions* (New York: Bonanza Books, 1954), 40.

8. Ibid., 39.

9. A video of Albert Einstein biographer Walter Isaacson discussing Einstein's concept of God is accessible at *www.youtube.com/watch?v=S7r57oCT2cU* (time: 0:05:27).

10. Ibid., 48; see also 36–47.

11. Ibid., 39.

Yet a strictly deterministic view of the universe cannot account for one's ability to think about one's own thinking (sec. 2.4.2). For all his scientific brilliance, Einstein seems not to have appreciated the point that human thought transcends deterministic causes.

One can also question Einstein's conclusions that the "mind" of the universe remains impersonal. Einstein used *mind* as a metaphor, comparing the rational structure of the universe to a human mind. But is it merely a metaphor? If the rational structure of human thoughts is due to the human mind, is it unreasonable to conclude that the rational structure of the universe is also due to a mind? At a deeper level, one must ask why the universe has a rational structure in the first place (sec. 4.10.1). For Joseph Ratzinger the answer is clear: An intellectual structure in the universe is impossible without thought. And thought is impossible without a subject to do the thinking.[12]

Atheists and theists agree that there is a rational structure to the universe, a "universal mind" as Einstein called it. To say that the universal mind is analogous to the human mind, however, is not anthropomorphic. This is not the same as giving human characteristics to inanimate forces such as wind or lightning. It is simply recognizing a profound similarity between the workings of one's own mind and the workings of the universe.

Signs of God's Personal Nature   5.5.2

In the Christian view, God reveals himself as more than just a universal mind. People have a natural drive to find a deeper meaning in life, asking such questions as: Is this the person I'm supposed to marry? Do people exist, in some way, after death? (sec. 1.4). Notice that this drive for meaning presumes that the creator of the universe is personal. Would the law of gravity care whom a person marries? C. S. Lewis, reflecting on the innate sense of right and wrong in all humans, also took this as a clue that the creator is personal (sec. 1.5). Laws of physics do not have a sense of right and wrong.

The mother experiences the birth of her child as a gift (sec. 1.6) Balthasar (sec. 3.5.5) writes of how a child intuitively knows that his or her own life, as well as all other life, is limited, and thus senses that all existence depends on unlimited Being. So the child too experiences life as a gift. It is something that child did not create; he or she feels that it is a gift.

G. K. Chesterton captures this sense:

> The test of all happiness is gratitude; and I felt grateful, though I hardly knew to whom. Children are grateful when Santa Claus puts in their stockings gifts of toys or sweets. Could I not be grateful to Santa Claus when he put in my stockings the gift of two miraculous legs? We thank

12. Joseph Ratzinger, *Introduction to Christianity* (San Francisco: Ignatius Press, 2000; orig. pub. 1968), 155.

people for birthday presents of cigars and slippers. Can I thank no one for the birthday present of birth?[13]

If life is a gift, reason suggests, there must be a Giver, a personal God who desires to give.

God's Nature: Impersonal Mind or Loving Being?   5.5.3

Joseph Ratzinger notes that many strictly scientific thinkers find it absurd to think that the absolute mind of the universe should be concerned with the fate of humans—an insignificant species on an insignificant planet in an obscure solar system within an ordinary galaxy, lost in the immensity of the cosmos.

However, Ratzinger asks: Why do people assume that it is somehow "greater" if the consciousness of the transcendent being is unconcerned with life on the tiny speck of the universe called Earth? Would it not be "greater," or more "divine," if, in fact, there were a place of concern within that universal mind for insignificant humanity?[14]

Ratzinger points out further how the scientific mind of an Einstein assumes that "the absolute spirit cannot be emotion and feeling but only pure cosmic mathematics."[15] But, this thinking again has a hidden assumption:

> We unthinkingly assume that pure thought is greater than love, while the message of the Gospel, and the Christian picture of God contained in it, corrects philosophy and lets us know that love is higher than mere thought.[16]

Ratzinger summed up the contrast between the "God of the philosophers" that Einstein accepted and the God of biblical faith as follows:

1. The abstract God of the philosophers is *"essentially self-centered,"* thought simply contemplating itself. In contrast, the God of faith is "basically defined by the category of relationship."[17] In other words, the God of faith is other-centered, oriented toward relationship with others.

2. The philosophical God is *"pure thought*: he is based on the notion that thought and thought alone is divine." In contrast: "The God of faith, as thought, is also love. His image is based on the conviction that to love is divine."[18]

---

13. Chesterton, *Orthodoxy*, 50.

14. Ratzinger, *Introduction to Christianity*, 145–46.

15. Ibid.

16. Ibid., 147.

17. Ibid. Emphasis original.

18. Ibid., 147–48. Emphasis original.

Revelation and Language's Limitations   5.6

While the Christian tradition thinks of God as a personal God, this does not imply that Christians should think of God as a human person. In fact, the tradition agrees with Einstein that humans must resist the temptation to anthropomorphize God—to create God in the image of the human. In speaking of God, one must always keep in mind the possibilities and limitations of human language and ideas. The following sections explore the relationship between limited language and the unlimited, eternal source of all being.

The Necessity of Human Language   5.6.1

The first point to clarify is that even if human language is limited, it is the only option. Even if a person believes that God reveals things through nature and conscience, the meaning of that revelation must be expressed in human words. People who see a rainbow as a sign from God, for example, inevitably use language to think about its possible meaning, even if not expressing thoughts aloud.

The Bible records that God revealed himself to Moses at the burning bush (Exod 3). If Moses wished to communicate that revelation to others, his only option was to use language. All revelation must pass through the medium of human language.

God Can Be Known Only through Creation   5.6.2

Because in the Christian view, humans are limited and God is unlimited, people cannot describe God fully or directly. According to the *Catechism of the Catholic Church*, "Since our knowledge about God is limited, our language about him is equally so. We can name God only by taking creatures as our starting point, and in accordance with our limited human ways of knowing and thinking" (*CCC*, no. 40).

Creatures can be the starting point because God's creation reveals the Creator: "All creatures bear a certain resemblance to God, most especially man, created in the image and likeness of God. The manifold perfections of creatures—their truth, their goodness, their beauty all reflect the infinite perfection of their Creator" (*CCC*, no. 41).

Note the similarity to Balthasar's approach (sec. 3.5.5): The goodness, truth, and beauty of this world point toward their Creator. Because evil can only be a corruption of an originally good creation (sec. 5.3.2), the evil in the world reveals nothing about God.

True Knowledge about God through Analogies   5.6.3

Aquinas teaches, "For we cannot grasp what God is, but only what He is not and how other things are related to Him" (*SCG* 1.30). In other words, humans cannot know the "essence of God"—God's nature in itself (*ST* 1.12.4). The Orthodox Christian tradition agrees that one cannot know the essence of God, but only God's "energies"—God's acts of power in the world.[19]

While one can know God *indirectly* through God's creation, one must remember that "'between Creator and creature no similitude can be expressed without implying an even greater dissimilitude'" (*CCC*, no. 43). Aquinas also notes that the analogy between God and his creature moves in only one direction: "a creature can be spoken of as in some sort like God; but not that God is like a creature" (*ST* 1.4.3 ad. 4).

As Aquinas phrased it, one can only know "what God is not." This way of speaking about God by discussing what he is not is known as the **apophatic approach**—the way of negation. Orthodox Bishop Kallistos Ware explains,

> To point at this *mysterium tremendum*, we need to use negative as well as affirmative statements, saying what God is *not* rather than what he is. . . . If we say that he is good or just, we must at once add that his goodness or justice are not to be measured by our human standards. If we say that he exists we must qualify this immediately by adding that he is not one existent object among many, that in his case the word "exist" bears a unique significance. . . . Having made an assertion about God, we must pass beyond it: the statement is not untrue, yet neither it nor any other form of words can contain the fullness of the transcendent God.[20]

Nevertheless, human language "really does attain to God himself" (*CCC*, no. 43). This is a crucial point. If language did not reach God himself, then people would be forced to conclude that theological knowledge is not true knowledge but only blind faith or unfounded opinion.

In the Catholic view, one can have true knowledge about God because the human being is analogous to God's being. Humans *have* being, but God *is* being.[21] There is a connection between God and humans.

For example, people can understand much about human creativity and intelligence. Because God, as the First Cause of all being, is the perfection of these characteristics, people can glimpse God's perfect creativity and intelligence. Similarly, people are capable of experiencing love and kindness. Because God is the unlimited source of love and kindness, people can develop a true, if limited, knowledge of God's love and kindness.

---

19. See Kallistos Ware, *The Orthodox Way* (Crestwood, NY: St. Vladimir's Seminary Press, 1995), 21–23.

20. Ibid., 14. Emphasis original.

21. Peter Kreeft, *A Summa of the* Summa: *The Essential Philosophical Passages of Saint Thomas Aquinas'* Summa Theologica (San Francisco: Ignatius Press, 1990), 90, no. 38. This theological concept of the "analogy of being" is translated in a well-known Latin phrase as the *analogia entis*.

Aquinas writes, "So when we say, 'God is good,' the meaning is not, 'God is the cause of goodness,' or, 'God is not evil;' but the meaning is, 'Whatever good we attribute to creatures, pre-exists in God,' and in a more excellent and higher way" (*ST* 1.13.2).

For Aquinas, it can be true to say "that man is wise," and "God is wise." The meaning of the word *wise* in these two phrases is not identical, because there is a qualitative difference between Creator and created human; but neither is it completely different. Rather, "it must be said that these names are said of God and creatures in an analogous sense, i.e., according to proportion" (*ST* 1.13.5).

Dangers of Anthropomorphism   5.6.4

Scripture often portrays God in **anthropomorphic** ways. Consider this passage from Psalms 7:12–14:

> God is a just judge, powerful and patient . . .
>
> If one does not repent,
>
> God sharpens his sword,
>
> strings and readies the bow,
>
> Prepares his deadly shafts.

Already in ancient times, Christian commentators on Scripture were aware that these anthropomorphisms should not be taken literally. Commenting on the Psalms passage, John Chrysostom (ca. 347–407 CE) admits that he cannot believe that there are truly bows, arrows, and instruments for sharpening swords in heaven. One must take from these words "ideas appropriate to God." However, if the reader must do this with physical things, then he must also do the same with concepts such as God's "anger and wrath."[22]

Augustine, too, taught that any passages describing God with physical attributes must be taken figuratively, but so too must any passages that attribute changeable human emotions to God: "he who thinks of God as now forgetting and now remembering, or anything of the same kind, is none the less in error." So too are those who think scriptural statements such as "I the Lord, your God, am a jealous God" (Exod 20:5), or "I regret that I made [man]" (Gen 6:7) should be taken literally (*On the Trinity* 1.1.1); see also Aquinas's comment (*ST* 1.3.2 ad.2): "God's punishment is metaphorically spoken of as His anger."

In the Christian view, the danger of anthropomorphism is that it sets God on a human level, making him no different than humans. God would then be seen as a God who loses his temper, makes mistakes, acts selfishly, or changes his

---

22. Quoted in Ronald E. Heine, *Reading the Old Testament with the Ancient Church: Exploring the Formation of Early Christian Thought*, Evangelical Ressourcement (Grand Rapids, MI: Baker Academic, 2007), 148.

mind as people do. Such a human-like God could not be the eternal Creator of the universe, nor a God in whom people would put their faith and trust.

Is God Male or Female? 5.6.5

Traditional Christian language about God is male-centered: The Bible consistently refers to God using the male pronoun *he,* and the Trinity is traditionally described as "Father, Son, and Holy Spirit." Christian believers might thus conclude that God is male. The *Catechism* addresses the issue thus:

> In no way is God in man's image. He is neither man nor woman. God is pure spirit in which there is no place for the difference between the sexes. But the respective "perfections" of man and woman reflect something of the infinite perfection of God: those of a mother and those of a father and husband. (*CCC,* no. 370)

If God is an eternal spirit, it follows that God cannot be male or female, as these terms refer to limited human characteristics. If women as well as men reflect the infinite perfections of God, as Christians believe, it follows that it is appropriate to use both female and male analogies to describe God.

The Bible occasionally uses feminine images to speak of God. In speeches in the Book of Isaiah, for example, God compares himself to a mother: "I cry out like a woman in labor" (42:14); "Can a mother forget her infant . . . ? I will never forget you" (49:15); "As a mother comforts her child, so I will comfort you" (66:13).

Non-biblical Christian writings employ female images as well. Theologian Clement of Alexandria (ca. 150–ca. 215 CE) writes, "For to those babes who seek the Word, the Father's breasts of love supply milk" (*The Instructor* 1.6). The Syriac author Aphrahat, early fourth century, speaks of the believer's love for "God his Father and the Holy Spirit his Mother," and the English visionary Julian of Norwich (ca. 1342—ca. 1416) writes, "God rejoices that he is our Father, and God rejoices that he is our Mother."[23]

All of these descriptions are only analogies; God's nature is beyond male and female. Yet one must use analogies and symbols, and if God is to be pictured as a person capable of loving relationships, which is consistent with Christian belief in a personal, loving God, the analogies must necessarily be male or female.

Some feminist thinkers have called for abandoning the traditional language of Father, Son, and Spirit in Christian worship in favor of a gender-neutral formula such as Creator, Redeemer, and Sanctifier. There are, however, good reasons to think that such language would distort the understanding of God's Trinitarian nature (sec. 6.23.1). Ware's thoughts on retaining the traditional male symbols are also worth noting:

---

23. Quoted in Ware, *Orthodox Way,* 34.

We cannot prove arguments why this should be so, yet it remains a fact of our Christian experience that God has set his seal upon certain symbols and not upon others . . . Like the symbols in myth, literature, and art, our religious symbols reach deep into the hidden roots of our being, and cannot be altered without momentous consequences. If, for example, we were to start saying, "Our Mother who art in heaven," instead of "Our Father," we should not merely be adjusting an incidental piece of imagery, but replacing Christianity with a new kind of religion. A Mother Goddess is not the Lord of the Christian Church.[24]

Julian of Norwich's
Revelations of Divine Love   5.7

Are there revelations from God not recorded in the Bible? The Christian tradition recognizes such revelations, but doesn't accord them the same authority as scriptural revelations.

In her writings, the mystic Julian of Norwich (ca. 1343–ca. 1416) states that Christ showed her a series of sixteen visions, or "showings," over a two-day period in 1373. She wrote them down immediately, and years later wrote a theological commentary to accompany them. Her book is called *Showings* or *Revelations of Divine Love*.

Julian was an anchoress, a person who chose to follow a solitary life dedicated to prayer, meditation, and study; her work shows that she was well educated theologically. Her reputation for holiness and learning drew many visitors who sought her advice.

The *Showings* include visions of, and lessons about, Christ's suffering and death, the Trinity, Jesus' mother Mary, sin, salvation, and prayer.

In the first vision, Christ tells Julian that a small object, the size of a nut that she holds in her hand, represents the universe. Julian wonders why it doesn't fall into nothingness, as it is so little. The Lord answers, "It lasts, and shall last, because God loves it. All things have their being by the love of God" (*Showings* chapter 5).

The thirteenth vision is a profound reflection on sin and salvation. Julian wonders, "Why did God allow sin in the world, since he desires only good for people?" Christ answers her, "It is necessary that there should be sin, but all shall be well, and all shall be well, and all manner of things shall be well" (*Showings* chapter 27). Yet Julian is not

Continued

---

24. Ibid.

> ### Julian of Norwich's *Revelations* Continued
>
> satisfied, she reflects further on all the sorrow caused by sin and how unrepentant sinners will be condemned to eternal punishment in hell, as the Church teaches. It seems to her impossible that "all things shall be well." Christ answers, "That which is impossible to you is not impossible to me: I shall save my word in all things and I shall make all things well" (*Showings* chapter 32).
>
> The *Catechism of the Catholic Church* (no. 313) cites this passage of *Showings* in its discussion of how, in his providence, God can bring good even out of evil. Hans Urs von Balthasar refers to Julian in support of his belief that it is possible for a Christian to hope that, in the end, all people will be saved.[25]
>
> Julian refers several times to Christ, using the images of a mother: "The mother may nurse her child with milk, but our precious Mother, Jesus, may feed us with himself, and does, with great care and tenderness, with the Blessed Sacrament that is precious food of my life, and with all the sacraments he sustains us very mercifully and graciously" (*Showings* chapter 60).
>
> God's love is primary for Julian. Reflecting later on the meaning of the "showings," the Lord tells her his meaning, "Love was his meaning. Who showed it to you? Love. What did he show you? Love. Why did he show it to you? For Love. . . . Thus I was taught that Love was our Lord's meaning" (*Showings*, chapter 86).

God Speaks as a Human   5.8

This discussion, so far, has noted the limitations of human language and knowledge in speaking and thinking about God. Yet Balthasar makes the important point that God seems not to see this as a limitation, because God chose to become human as his ultimate revelation.

> God in his freedom decided to become man, chose his creature's mode of expression in order to reveal the hidden things of his divinity, and resolved to pour out the abyss of his riches into that other abyss of emptiness and indigence, in order to find his glory in the shame of the cross and in the descent to hell.[26]

---

25. Balthasar, *Dare We Hope that All Men Be Saved?* (San Francisco: Ignatius, 1988), 101–2.

26. Balthasar, "God Speaks as Man," in *Explorations in Theology, I: The Word Made Flesh* (San Francisco: Ignatius Press, 1989), 85.

This is the Christian paradox. The eternal, almighty, and unlimited God reveals himself most clearly not through a sign of power but in the limitations of a weak, despised, crucified human. Thus God is revealed as a complete love that is willing to give up life itself for the sake of the beloved. God's willingness to communicate through limited human language is just one aspect of God's self-giving love.

Revelation in Supernatural Events (Miracles)   5.9

In the Christian view, God reveals himself not only in words but also in actions. Vatican II's *Dei Verbum* teaches that God reveals through "deeds and words" and spoke of "the deeds wrought by God in the history of salvation" (*DV*, no. 2). Prominent among these "deeds" are supernatural events: Moses splits the Red Sea and the Israelites walk across the dry ground; God rains down manna from heaven to feed the Israelites; Jesus walks on water, miraculously feeds thousands of people with only a few loaves of bread and fish, heals the sick, casts out demons from possessed people, and raises the dead. The key supernatural event in Christianity is Jesus' Resurrection from the dead.

These supernatural stories raise some reasonable questions. Perhaps the most fundamental: Is it still possible for a person in today's world of science and advanced technology to believe in supernatural events? The German biblical scholar, Rudolf Bultmann, believed that the answer was clearly no.

> It is impossible to use electric light and the wireless [radio] and to avail ourselves of modern medical and surgical discoveries, and at the same time to believe in the New Testament world of spirits and miracles.[27]

To address this issue, it's good to begin by clearly defining the terms.

Defining a Miracle   5.10

In the following discussion, the term *miracle* is used narrowly to describe a supernatural event. A miracle is an event, such as raising a person from the dead, that can never be explained by a natural cause, no matter how far the scientific understanding of nature develops. Its cause, by definition, is beyond nature—the literal meaning of the word *supernatural*.

C. S. Lewis defines a miracle as "an interference with Nature by supernatural power."[28] John Henry Newman defines it as "an event inconsistent with the

---

27. Rudolf Bultmann, et al., *Kerygma and Myth: A Theological Debate*, ed. H. W. Bartsch (New York: Harper & Row, 1961), 5.

28. C. S. Lewis, *Miracles* (New York: Macmillan, 1960), 5.

constitution of nature."[29] Aquinas wrote, "A miracle properly so called is when something is done outside the order of nature" (*ST* 1.110.4). The Christian tradition, then, understands a miracle as an event, directly caused by God, outside of the normal laws of nature.

Miracles and Worldviews   5.11

Are events not caused by natural causes possible? Lewis rightly points out that the answer cannot be based on evidence from the senses or from historical evidence, because people's worldviews will determine how they interpret this sense data or historical evidence.[30]

Consider an example. Ruth had a "near-death" experience. As she was on the operating table, her heart stopped. During that time, she remembers seeing a tunnel of light and having a great sense of peace come over her. She interprets her experience as a supernatural event—an experience of a world beyond nature. Her interpretation is consistent with Ruth's worldview, as she is a Christian.

Ruth's friend Roger believes that the physical world—nature—is the only reality. Because his worldview is closed to the transcendent, he must find a natural explanation for Ruth's experience. He has read that people who are near death often see images of light because neurons in the brain fire at a great rate during the dying process. Looking at it psychologically, he knows that Ruth is a strong Christian believer who has been taught all her life about heaven as a place of peace and light, and so he is not surprised that she would picture heaven that way in her experience.

In the same way, one's worldview will determine one's interpretation of miracles in Scripture. A rationalist or materialist will rule out the possibility that Jesus could have healed a blind person by laying his hands on his eyes (Mark 8:25); a reader with a worldview open to the transcendent must leave open the possibility.

As argued earlier, rationalist, materialist worldviews are not more reasonable than a Christian worldview. The materialist simply asserts that material existence is the only reality. The assertion cannot be proven, because if a transcendent world does exist, by definition it could not be measured (sec. 2.4.2). Those who accept the supernatural do so not on blind faith, but have reasons for thinking that a transcendent world exists: signs of the transcendent in daily life (secs. 1.4–7); the First Cause argument (secs. 3.2.1–3); the Argument from Design (sec. 4.10).

Within the Christian worldview, the possibility of miracles makes sense. God created the world and all the natural laws within it. Because he is the creator of the laws of nature, they do not bind him. God is free to cause an event by his direct, supernatural power.

---

29. John Henry Newman, *Two Essays on Biblical and on Ecclesiastical Miracles* (Westminster, MD: Christian Classics, 1969), 4.

30. Lewis, *Miracles*, 3–4.

Since God created the natural world and its laws as good (sec. 5.3.1), Christians view God as normally working through nature. A supernatural event, by definition, is unusual, out-of-the ordinary. It is a sign that this visible world is not the only reality.

Symbolic Language and the Supernatural 5.12

C. S. Lewis argues that a person can accept that supernatural events occur without necessarily accepting the ancient worldviews that Scripture uses to describe those events. For example, the New Testament often describes Jesus as one who is seated at God's right hand in heaven (Heb 8:1).

In ancient times, many people may well have believed that Jesus was sitting on a literal throne up in the sky. For Lewis, Christians today recognize that this is a symbolic way of describing a transcendent event: Jesus exists with God in a transcendent realm, sharing his divine power and rule. The interpreter must distinguish between the essential beliefs about the transcendent and the cultural way in which those beliefs are expressed.

Questions about the Text

1. What is the difference between natural revelation and historical revelation? What is the ultimate purpose of revelation?

2. Compare the Gnostic and Christian view on the question of why evil exists.

3. According to Aquinas, why does God allow evil to exist?

4. Why did Einstein reject the belief in a personal God?

5. Discuss Christian reasons for believing that God is personal, not an impersonal mind.

6. In the Christian view, why can God only be known through creation?

7. Why does the Catholic tradition teach that knowledge of God can be expressed only through analogies?

8. For Aquinas, what is the relationship between these two statements: "God is wise" and "A good parent is wise"?

9. Give an example of an anthropomorphic statement about God. Why might an anthropomorphic view distort the Christian understanding of God?

10. According to traditional Christianity, is God male, female, or neither? Explain.

11. Discuss the different perspectives on whether Christians should continue to use traditional male-centered language and images in thinking about and worshipping God.

12. Define a miracle, according to traditional Christian thought. Explain the relationship between one's worldview and one's interpretation of biblical accounts of miraculous events.

Discussion Questions

1. Would you identify any of your own experiences as a revelation from God?
2. How do you answer the question of why evil and suffering exist in this world?
3. Was Einstein consistent in accepting a "universal mind," but rejecting a personal God? Why or why not?
4. Are your own images of God male, female, or neither?
5. In your own experience, are most people open to the possibility of a miracle? Why or why not?

The Trinity

The Trinity: A Reasonable Belief?   6.1

The traditional Christian belief that God is a Trinity can be summarized briefly: God is three persons in one divine nature. These three persons are traditionally named Father, Son, and Holy Spirit.

What does this mean? Does it make logical sense? And even if it is reasonable, does it make any practical difference to a Christian?

Indeed, many respected critics have denied that the doctrine of the Trinity makes sense. Thomas Jefferson wrote in 1813, "It is too late in the day for men of sincerity to pretend they believe in the Platonic mysticisms that three are one, and one is three; and yet the one is not three, and the three are not one."[1]

Judaism and Islam, both monotheistic religions like Christianity, do not accept the idea of a triune God. The Muslim tradition, in particular, has been critical of the doctrine, believing that it is inconsistent with the fundamental belief in one God. Even some groups that aim to follow Jesus Christ, such as Unitarians and Jehovah Witnesses, reject the doctrine. Jehovah Witnesses, for example, believe that the Trinitarian understanding of God contradicts Christian Scripture, which never directly refers to God as a Trinity. Despite these challenges, it is possible to defend the doctrine of the Trinity as a reasonable belief.

Mystery and Reason   6.2

While the Catholic tradition insists that God's existence can be known through natural reason alone (*CCC*, no. 36), the tradition also teaches that the specific belief that God is a Trinity of three persons cannot be known by natural reason—it can only be known through special revelation (*CCC*, no. 237). The

---

1. Quoted in Stephen Prothero, *American Jesus: How the Son of God Became a National Icon* (New York: Farrar, Straus, and Giroux, 2003), 22.

Catholic tradition teaches that, even in heaven, humans will not fully understand the Trinity.

In Catholic theology, the doctrine of the Trinity is a "mystery of the faith." The term *mystery*, however, does *not* mean it cannot be grasped, at least to some extent, by reason. Theologically, *mystery* simply refers to an insight about God's nature that cannot be reached by reason alone: It must be revealed in order to be known (*CCC*, no. 237). However, once revealed and accepted on faith, reason can work with faith to attain a deeper understanding.

Although it is probably fair to say the typical modern Christian does not spend much time thinking about the Trinity, the belief has been an essential teaching of the Church for centuries and has remained at the heart of the Church's prayer and worship. For example, baptism is administered "in the name of the Father, Son, and Holy Spirit," and many prayers end with that phrase. In fact, the *Catechism of the Catholic Church* teaches that the Trinity is the most important truth of the faith: "It is the most fundamental and essential teaching in the 'hierarchy of the truths of faith'" (*CCC*, no. 234).

What Is the Trinity?   6.3

Before exploring the importance of the doctrine of the Trinity for Christians, consider the following points, essential for understanding the doctrine:

1. **The Trinity is one God.** Christians believe there is only one God. The unity or "oneness" of God is expressed in various philosophical terms—God has one single divine "nature," "substance," or "essence" (*CCC*, no. 252). Each of the persons of the Trinity, Father, Son, and Spirit, is "God whole and entire." The Fourth Lateran Council (1215) teaches, "Each of the persons is that supreme reality, viz., the divine substance, essence or nature" (*CCC*, no. 253).

2. **The divine persons are truly distinct from one another.** The names *Father*, *Son*, and *Spirit* are not simply identical and interchangeable—they represent true distinctions within God's nature. In other words, the Father is not the Son or the Holy Spirit; the Son is not the Father or the Holy Spirit, the Holy Spirit is not the Father or the Son (*CCC*, no. 254). Further, *Father*, *Son*, and *Spirit* refer not simply to "characteristics" or "roles" of God—each person has a distinct, subsistent existence within the divine unity. Theologians

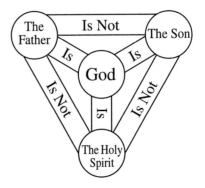

have used the technical term *person* (Latin: *persona*; Greek: *prosōpon* or *hypostasis*) to distinguish between the three (e.g., *CCC*, no. 252). Specifically, the three persons are distinct in their origin: "It is the Father who generates, the Son who is begotten, and the Holy Spirit who proceeds" (*CCC*, no. 254). The meaning of that last sentence will be explored further in this chapter.

3. **The divine persons are in relation to one another.** Although the divine persons are distinct, they do not exist independently of one another: Father, Son, and Holy Spirit have always existed in relation to one another. God's nature is Trinitarian; God has always been Father, Son, and Holy Spirit (*CCC*, no. 255).

The previous description of the Trinity does not occur in the Bible. The specialized language describing the Trinity was developed in the fourth century and expressed in various creeds issued by Church councils of that time. These creeds were the end product of much thinking, discussion, and debate among Christian theologians from New Testament times until the fourth century.

The development of Trinitarian belief includes the following decisive milestones:

1. The creed developed by the Council of Nicaea (325 CE) taught that the Son is of the same nature (Greek: *homoousios*; Latin: *consubstantialis*) with the Father.

2. The teaching of the Alexandrian theologian and later bishop Athanasius (ca. 296–373 CE), defended the understanding articulated at Nicaea.

3. The Cappadocian theologians, named after their home region in modern-day Turkey—Gregory of Nyssa (ca. 330–ca. 395 CE), Basil of Caesarea (ca. 330–379 CE), and Gregory of Nazianzus (ca. 330–ca. 390 CE)— developed and defended the classic terminology of the Trinity as the relationship of the three persons (Greek: *hypostasis*) who share the one divine substance (Greek: *ousia*).

4. The creed approved by the Council of Constantinople (381 CE) restated the creed developed at Nicaea with some alterations, the most significant of which was a clearer emphasis on the divinity of the Holy Spirit. This creed, known as the Nicene-Constantinopolitan Creed or simply the Nicene Creed,[2] is in use in Orthodox, Catholic, Anglican, and many Protestant communities to this day.

---

2. The Nicene Creed is accessible at *www.usccb.org/beliefs-and-teachings/what-we-believe/index .cfm.*

Unity, Plurality, and Ultimate Reality   6.4

Recall that theology tackles the "big questions" of life, including the nature of ultimate reality. What is truly real? What is the deepest nature of reality?

Humans experience this world not as a unified whole but as a *plurality*, an endless variety of things. People are divided on the basis of gender, ethnicity, beliefs, and other characteristics. Within the nonhuman world, there is a wondrous variety: oceans, deserts, glaciers, starfish, stars, molecules, and galaxies. However, is there something behind all this variety, a deeper reality that holds them all together and enables people to make sense of the universe and find meaning in life?

Religions and philosophers have always sought that deeper unity, which is the ultimate source of all variety. Consider a teaching from an ancient Hindu text:

> In the beginning there was Existence alone—One only, without a second. He, the One, thought to himself: Let me be many, let me grow forth. Thus out of himself he projected the universe, and having projected out of himself the universe, he entered into every being.[3]

The Greek philosopher Plotinus (ca. 205–270 CE) taught, "The One is all things and not a single one of them."[4]

The *Tao-te ching*, the ancient Chinese Taoist scripture, teaches,

> There is a thing confusedly formed, born before heaven and earth. Silent and void, it stands alone and does not change, goes round and does not weary. It is capable of being the mother of the world.[5]

Ancient Greek philosophers sought the unity of all things by identifying the one single element that forms the basis for all reality. Thales claimed it was water, Anaximenes argued for air.[6] Though science is much more sophisticated today, scientists still search for a single Grand Unified Theory that will explain all of reality. Einstein believed that this scientific goal was essentially a religious desire: he labeled the desire "to experience the universe as a single significant whole" as "cosmic religious feeling."[7] Balthasar's reflections on the relationship

---

3. *Chandogya Upanishad*, quoted in Mary Pat Fisher and John Kelsay, *Living Religions*, 6th ed. (Upper Saddle River, NJ: Prentice-Hall, 2005), 75.

4. Plotinus, *Enneads* 5.2.1, in *Plotinus*, trans. A. H. Armstrong (Cambridge, MA: Harvard University Press; London: Heinemann, 1984), 5:59.

5. Quoted in Fisher and Kelsay, *Living Religions*, 181.

6. Frederick Copleston, *A History of Philosophy, Vol. 1: Greece and Rome* (Garden City, NY: Image Books, 1962), 38–44.

7. Albert Einstein, *Ideas and Opinions* (New York: Bonanza Books, 1954), 38.

between finite being (the variety of things people experience) and infinite Being (the single source of this variety) (sec. 3.5.4) are simply another way to express this common human search for the one ultimate reality that grounds this changeable world.

What is the relationship between unity and plurality, between the one and the many? If reality began as a unity, why does it now appear as a plurality? As Plotinus asked, "How then do all things come from the One, which is simple and has in it no diverse variety, or any sort of doubleness?"[8] Is the plurality humans experience now truly real, or is it just an illusion that will pass away once humans are able to know ultimate reality?

The question of the one and the many is not simply a matter of speculation. The limited, fragmented world is often understood as the source of suffering and sin; salvation is, thus, defined as overcoming this fragmented world. In Hindu thought, for example, the ultimate goal of life may be understood as "liberation from the limitations of space, time, and matter through realization of the immortal Absolute."[9]

Seeking to understand the Christian doctrine of the Trinity, then, is not simply a matter of speculation by theologians. It can be seen as one way to satisfy the universal human desire to understand the deepest meaning, the ultimate reality of the world. The Trinitarian view, briefly, is that ultimate reality is not simply unity, nor is it plurality. In the Christian view, the ultimate unity (God) is in its own nature also a plurality (Father, Son, and Spirit). This rather abstract point is the basis for the more practical Christian claim that God, the ultimate source of all reality, is a relationship of love between the three persons of the Trinity.

Trinity: A Unique Way of Understanding Ultimate Unity

6.5

The doctrine of the Trinity answers questions about whether reality is primarily one or many, marked by unity or plurality, by going beyond both options. Ultimate reality is a one formed through a unity of many.

According to the New Testament, "God is love" (1 John 4:16). Far from being just a sentimental slogan on a greeting card, this biblical phrase is, according to Christian thought, a philosophically justifiable summary of ultimate reality. Within the oneness of ultimate reality is a plurality: The three persons of the Trinity are united as one in a relationship of love.[10]

---

8. *Ennead*, 5.2.1.

9. Fisher and Kelsay, *Living Religions*, 75.

10. A video of Fr. Robert Barron discussing the Trinity is accessible at *https://www.youtube.com/watch?v=hMI4rA4cuiM* (time: 0:02:24).

Peter Kreeft explains how the doctrine of the Trinity does not diminish the oneness of God:

> Far from God's Trinity lessening His unity, it increases it; for the oneness of love, which is the glue that holds that Trinity together, is a closer and more perfect union than the one of mere quantitative, arithmetical oneness.[11]

Joseph Ratzinger, later Pope Benedict XVI, agrees:

> To him who believes in God as triune, the highest unity is not the unity of inflexible monotony. The model of unity or oneness toward which one should strive is consequently not the indivisibility of the atom, the smallest unity, which cannot be divided up any further; the authentic acme of unity is the unity created by love. The multi-unity that grows in love is a more radical, truer unity than the unity of the "atom."[12]

One can extend Ratzinger's analogy by considering recent advances in scientific understanding. In ancient Greek philosophy, the *atom*, a word that literally means "that which cannot be cut," was conceived as the smallest bit of matter that could not be divided further and so was absolutely "one." Modern physics, however, has shown that the atom is not a simply a unity but is, in fact, composed of relationships among electrons, protons, and neutrons. Nor are any of these smaller particles a true unity as they are each composed of subatomic particles. At the atomic and subatomic levels, then, reality is not a static one but, rather, a dynamic unity of particles in relationship. At another level, Einstein's theory of relativity shows that space, time, and matter are not separate realities but an integrated whole. Physicist and theologian John Polkinghorne writes,

> The old-fashioned atomism that pictured isolated particles rattling around in the otherwise empty container of space has long been replaced by General Relativity's integrated account of space, time and matter, understood to be combined in a single package deal. . . . The physical world looks more and more like a universe that would be the fitting creation of a trinitarian God, the One whose deepest reality is relational.[13]

---

11. Peter Kreeft, *A Summa of the* Summa: *The Essential Philosophical Passages of Saint Thomas Aquinas' Summa Theologica* (San Francisco: Ignatius Press, 1990), 112, no. 75.

12. Joseph Ratzinger, *Introduction to Christianity* (San Francisco: Ignatius Press, 2000; orig. pub. 1968), 179.

13. Polkinghorne, *Quantum Physics and Theology: An Unexpected Kinship* (New Haven, CT: Yale University Press, 2007), 103–4.

Trinity, Salvation, and the Individual Person   6.6

Many religions see salvation as the overcoming of fragmented existence, and uniting oneself with ultimate reality. In Eastern traditions such as Hinduism and Buddhism, this liberation implies that an individual loses his or her individuality in the Absolute, as a drop of water is immersed in the ocean. The Christian Trinitarian view, however, is different. Because ultimate reality is a unity based on a harmonious plurality, salvation also involves this dynamic of the one and the many. In other words, in the Christian view of salvation, people remain themselves even as they become closely united to God. Salvation involves, then, "the entry of God's creatures into the perfect unity of the Blessed Trinity" (*CCC*, no. 260). People share in the relationship of love among the Father, Son, and Holy Spirit, while still remaining distinct persons in their own right.

This Trinitarian vision of salvation can be seen in Jesus' prayer before his death, as recorded in the Gospel of John. Here Jesus speaks of his followers participating in the unity that he and the Father already shared before the creation of the universe:

> I pray not only for them, but also for those who will believe in me through their word, so that they may all be one, as you, Father, are in me and I in you, that they also may be in us, that the world may believe that you sent me. And I have given them the glory you gave me, so that they may be one, as we are one, I in them and you in me, that they may be brought to perfection as one, that the world may know that you sent me, and that you loved them even as you loved me. (John 17:20–23)

Trinity—God as Three Persons: Avoiding Confusions   6.7

To say that God is three persons can lead to confusion, in two ways especially. First, this understanding might suggest God is composed of three human persons. This, however, is inconsistent with the Christian tradition's insistence that God is beyond human limitations (sec. 5.6.4). Second, the concept of three persons might suggest that Christians really believe in three gods. This cannot be true, however, as Christians are monotheists. Why then do Christians continue to use the potentially confusing term *persons* in their discussion of the Trinitarian God?

One fundamental reason is the Christian belief that God reveals himself as intelligent and as having a concern for standards of right and wrong, characteristics that show him to be personal (sec. 5.5.1). The theologian Catherine LaCugna (1952–1997) comments that the term *person*—if accepted properly as an analogy—still has the advantage of implying that Father, Son, and Holy Spirit are more appropriately compared to human persons capable of relationships with others than with impersonal powers or functions.[14]

A second reason concerns the deeper meaning of the term *person*. Strictly at the human level, what is the difference between an "individual" and a "person"? Consider how the related term *personality* is used. For example, one could say that Susie has a lively, bubbly personality, while Lorraine's personality is more reserved and private. *Personality*, then, means a person as she is revealed in her relationships with other people. Thomas Torrance writes, "You cannot be a person all by yourself, as a separated individual. You can be a person only along with other persons—you need interpersonal relations to be a person."[15]

People develop their personalities, their characters, largely through interactions with other people. Parents and family members influence their children in profound ways, ways in which the parents are not often explicitly aware. The attitudes, opinions, actions, likes, and dislikes of friends and acquaintances deeply shape people's attitudes and opinions. Think of how powerful peer pressure is, for example. It is impossible for people to develop their personality or character in isolation—they cannot separate who they are from the people with whom they interact.

The interpersonal character of the term *person* makes it appropriate in speaking of the Trinity. Father, Son, and Holy Spirit in the Trinity are understood not as independent entities but, rather, on the basis of their relation to the other Trinitarian persons (sec. 6.3). The Father cannot be who he is without the Son and the Spirit.

The classic Christian theologians define *personhood* as relationships with others. Aquinas expresses the idea this way: "a divine person signifies a relation as subsisting" [*to subsist* means to exist in a stable way] (*ST* 1.29.4). Augustine shows how the traditional names for the first two persons of the Trinity—Father and Son—relate to the concept of person. "He is not called Father with reference to himself but only in relation to the Son; seen by himself he is simply God."[16] The very word *Father* points beyond itself toward relationship with another—either a son or a daughter. Applied to the Trinity, it means that the Father does not exist except in relationship to the Son.

Finally, the term *person* corrects a modalist way of thinking about God that was condemned by the early Church as an error. According to **Modalism,** God in his own nature is absolutely one, and only appears to humans in three

---

14. Catherine Mowry LaCugna, "The Trinitarian Mystery of God," in *Systematic Theology: Roman Catholic Perspectives*, eds. F. S. Fiorenza and J. P. Galvin (Minneapolis, MN: Fortress, 1991), 179.

15. Thomas Torrance, *The Christian Frame of Mind: Reason, Order, and Openness in Theology and Natural Science* (Colorado Springs: Helmers & Howard, 1989), 150.

16. Quoted in Ratzinger, *Introduction to Christianity*, 183.

"modes," for example, as creator, as savior, or as sanctifier. The word *person* points to the reality that Father, Son, and Spirit exist in a truly distinct, subsistent way within the Godhead; they are not simply different functions of one God (*CCC*, no. 254).

Is the Trinity a Biblically Based Doctrine? Plurality within the One God in the Old Testament 6.8

As noted previously, some movements centered on belief in Jesus Christ reject the doctrine of the Trinity, claiming that it is not biblically based. It is true that the word *Trinity* does not appear in the Bible, and that the Bible never explicitly defines God as three divine persons sharing one divine nature. The Catholic tradition, however, argues that the essential seeds for Trinitarian belief are in the Bible, and the later Trinitarian definitions are a faithful development of those seeds.

This section considers the portrayal of God in the Old Testament. While the Old Testament does not identify God as a Trinity, it does hint, in a variety of ways, at the possibility of a plurality within the unity of God.

Unity of the Transcendent God 6.8.1

In the ancient world in which the Hebrews and, later, the Jews lived, societies worshipped many different gods. By teaching that there was one God alone, Jews of the **Second Temple period**—from the **Babylonian Exile** in 587 BCE until the destruction of the Jerusalem Temple by the Romans in 70 CE—were considered quite odd. Historically speaking, there is no doubt that monotheistic belief was a gradual development: At first, although the Hebrews, at least in theory, worshipped the God of Israel alone, they recognized that other nations also had their own gods. By the time of the prophecies recorded in the second portion of the Book of Isaiah, most likely written during the sixth-century BCE Babylonian Exile, the claim is made that the God of Israel is the only God: "I am the Lord and there is no other, there is no God besides me" (45:5).

"Lord," in this quotation from Isaiah, is the English translation of the divine name in Hebrew: YHWH, sometimes written out fully as Yahweh. YHWH (Lord) is the personal name of the God of Israel, applicable only to this one God alone and not to any other god. Even when the existence of other gods was considered possible, biblical writers insisted on the unity of this one God. A classic statement of the faith of Israel, still recited by Jews today, is the *Shema*, "Hear, O Israel! The Lord is our God, the Lord alone!" [sometimes translated as "the Lord is one"] (Deut 6:4).

As Richard Bauckham argues, for Second Temple Jews two actions make the Lord unique, different from all other reality: (1) the Lord is the sole creator of all things, and (2) the Lord is the sole ruler of all things.[17]

Divine Manifestations on Earth   6.8.2

Several Old Testament passages reveal a distinction between God pictured in his eternal, invisible nature and God's visible presence on Earth. The patriarch Jacob, after wrestling all night with "a man" who refuses to tell Jacob his name,

says at the end of this encounter, "I have seen God face to face" (Gen 32:23–31). After speaking with the angel of the Lord, Sarah's servant Hagar exclaims, "Have I really seen God and remained alive?" (Gen 16:7–13). In Moses' famous encounter with the divine at the burning bush, the narrative first reports, "*An angel of the Lord* appeared to him in fire flaming out of a bush," but as Moses approaches, relates, "When the Lord saw him coming over to look at it more closely, God called out to him from the bush" (Exod 3:2–4, emphasis added).

In a similar fashion, concepts such as the "glory of the Lord" are used to indicate God's presence on Earth, yet in a way that is distinct from God in his eternal invisible nature.

This famous icon of the Trinity was painted by the Russian Orthodox artist Andrei Rublev in the early 1400s. It depicts the appearance of three mysterious visitors to Abraham and Sarah (see Gen 18)—considered by many as a manifestation of the Trinity.

By User:AnonMoos (earlier version of SVG file Sumudu Fernando) [Public domain], via Wikimedia Commons

[After the priests deposited the Ark of the Covenant within the Holy of Holies,] the cloud filled the temple of the Lord so that the priests could no longer minister because of the cloud, since the glory of the Lord had filled the house of the Lord. (1 Kgs 8:10–11).

The ancient Hebrews and Jews believed that God was one. The above passages suggest, however, that the biblical authors struggled to express the belief that God is absolutely beyond human sense and comprehension, yet appears

---

17. Richard Bauckham, *Jesus and the God of Israel: God Crucified and Other Studies on the New Testament's Christology of Divine Identity* (Grand Rapids, MI: Eerdmans, 2008), 9.

in forms comprehensible to the senses. The texts attempt to express the idea that the visible form is truly God—but at the same time is not God in his own invisible nature—but, rather, God's presence manifested as an angel, a man, or glory. Balthasar refers to this as a "dialectic of sensory manifestation": the divine appearing in ways that seem to be comprehensible to the senses and yet always transcend the senses at the same time.[18] One sees that questions about the divine unity and some distinction within that unity had already arisen in Old Testament times.

God's Wisdom   6.8.3

Similar questions arose in other contexts. When the Gospel of John says God created the world through the Word (Logos), he was drawing on an extensive Jewish theological and philosophical background (John 1:1–3; sec. 2.5.2). Proverbs 8:22–31 describes God's wisdom as working alongside him to establish the heavens and fix the foundations of the earth. The Book of Wisdom 7:25–8:1 describes God's wisdom in similar terms: "For she is a breath of the might of God . . . the spotless mirror of the power of God. . . . she spans the world from end to end mightily and governs all things well." Whether the authors of Proverbs and the Book of Wisdom thought of God's wisdom as a metaphor only or as having some kind of real, ontological, existence is debated: The key point is that a distinction is made within God's divine being.

Richard Bauckham correctly argues that passages such as these do not contradict Jewish monotheism. They show, rather, that figures such as God's Word and Wisdom "are intrinsic to the unique divine identity, as understood in Jewish monotheism. . . . It means that these Jewish writers envisage some form of real distinction within the unique identity of the one God."[19]

Divine Intermediaries   6.8.4

Second Temple Judaism also had a lively interest in what is termed "divine intermediary figures." The first-century Jewish philosopher Philo, for example, wrote of how God created the universe by using his divine Logos as the model and pattern; he even referred to the Logos as "a second god" (*Questions and Answers on Genesis* 2.62). For Philo, the Logos is clearly subordinate to God but, at the same time, is in some sense divine ("a second god") and "above" the rest of creation—a divine intermediary between heaven and Earth. Other Second Temple Jews pictured powerful angels, such as the archangel Michael, acting as intermediaries.[20]

---

18. Balthasar, *The Glory of the Lord. Vol. 6: The Old Covenant*, trans. B. McNeil and E. Leiva-Merikakis (San Francisco: Ignatius Press, 1991).

19. Bauckham, *God of Israel*, 17.

20. See Bauckham, *God of Israel*, 14–15 for examples.

Summary of the Old Testament and Second Temple View   6.8.5

Some conclusions can be drawn from this quick survey of the Old Testament and Second Temple Jewish beliefs. First, the ancient Jews believe in one God. At the same time, however, biblical writers and Second Temple philosophers also refer to some kind of plurality or distinction within the unity of God—a plurality or distinction that does not deny the unity. These distinctions are seen in two ways: (1) God's presence, visible on Earth, that is distinct but not separate from God's eternal, invisible nature, and (2) a distinction within God's own nature, labeled as *Word* or *Wisdom*, through which God creates and governs the universe. In addition, there was speculation about other powerful beings that could be considered divine in some sense but who were, ultimately, subordinate to God.

So while Second Temple Judaism clearly does not speak in a Trinitarian fashion of three distinct persons subsisting within the divine unity, it allows the possibility for the development of such a belief.

Jesus within the One Divine Identity: New Testament   6.9

The New Testament clearly, to use Richard Bauckham's terminology, includes Jesus within the divine identity of God. In other words, the New Testament does not simply identify Jesus as God the Father—they are certainly distinct—but acknowledges that the crucified and resurrected Jesus is included in God's identity as the creator and ruler of all things.[21]

Jesus Rules over All Things   6.9.1

Several New Testament texts make it clear that God the Father gives Jesus the authority to rule over all things in the universe.

- Matthew 11:27: Jesus says, "All things have been handed over to me by my Father."
- John 13:3: Jesus is said to be "fully aware that the Father had put everything into his power."
- Ephesians 1:20–22: Attributes to God, "raising him [Christ] from the dead and seating him at his right hand" and placing "him as head over all things . . ."

---

21. A conversation between Richard Bauckham and Ben Witherington regarding early Christian understanding of the inclusion of Jesus within the divine identity of God is accessible at *www.youtube.com/watch?v=Qq-IfhdXDzg* (time 0:09:14).

The Son's Role in Creation   6.9.2

Several texts assume that Jesus, as the divine Son, existed with the Father before the creation, and that the Father created all things through him.

- John 1:1–3: "In the beginning was the Word, and the Word was with God, and the Word was God. . . . All things came to be through him, and without him nothing came to be."
- Colossians 1:16–17: "In him [the Son] were created all things in heaven and on earth, the visible and the invisible . . . ; all things were created through him and for him."
- Hebrews 1:2: "[H]e spoke to us through a son, whom he made heir of all things and through whom he created the universe."

The Son's Role as Final Judge   6.9.3

A specific function included in God's rule of the universe is the final judgment of all people. In the Old Testament, God's final judgment of Earth was known as the "Day of the Lord" (e.g., Amos 5:18, Joel 2:11). Several New Testament passages show that Jesus now has that function:

- Matthew 25:31–32: "When the Son of Man comes in his glory . . . , he will sit upon his glorious throne, and all the nations will be assembled before him."
- Acts 10:42: Jesus is the " judge of the living and the dead."
- 2 Corinthians 5:10: "We must all appear before the judgment seat of Christ."

Jesus' Role in Forgiving Sins   6.9.4

Jesus is closely associated with the forgiveness of sins, both directly forgiving sins and offering forgiveness of sins through his death:

- Mark 2:5: When Jesus saw their faith, he said to the paralytic, "your sins are forgiven."
- Ephesians 1:7: "In him [Jesus] we have redemption by his blood."
- 1 Corinthians 15:3: "Christ died for our sins."

Jesus Is Given the Divine Name   6.9.5

The title *Lord* was given to Jesus to signify his rule over all things. The title Lord, *kyrios* in Greek, has a range of meanings. It can be simply a title of respect, equivalent to addressing someone as "sir" in contemporary English. More generally, however, it signifies a position of authority—one title of the Roman emperors was *kyrios*, for example. Most significant for understanding the New

Testament meaning, however, is its use as the divine name in the Old Testament. When the **Hebrew** Scriptures were translated by Greek-speaking Jews in the centuries before Jesus, a translation known as the Septuagint, they used the Greek word *kyrios* as their translation for the unique name of God: YHWH.

It is precisely this unique name, which identifies God as different from every other power, that is given to Jesus. The apostle Paul writes,

> Because of this, God greatly exalted him [Jesus]
> and bestowed on him the name
> that is above every name,
> that at the name of Jesus
> every knee should bend,
> of those in heaven and on earth and under the earth,
> and every tongue confess that
> Jesus Christ is Lord,
> to the glory of God the Father. (Phil 2:9–11)

In biblical cultures, the name of a person was not arbitrary; rather, a person's name was closely associated with the power, authority, and identity of that person.

The New Testament evidence may be summed up thus:

1. Jesus, both before and after the Incarnation, is closely associated with powers and activities that Jews of that time could only associate with the one God: creation and rule over the universe, final judgment, and authority to forgive sins. Jesus is so closely associated with God the Father that he shares the divine name: Lord.

2. Jesus, nevertheless, is not identical to the Father: The two remain clearly distinct from each other in all cases.

The evidence shows that the early Christians believed that although God is one, Jesus was included in that one divine identity.[22]

The Bible and the Holy Spirit   6.10

When one turns to the biblical references to God's spirit, one finds a similar dynamic. God's spirit is never referred to as a third divine person within the Trinity, but God's spirit is described in a way distinct, but not separate, from God himself.

---

22. A video of Fr. Robert Barron discussing evidence for the Trinity in Scripture is accessible at *www.youtube.com/watch?v=-jGS1hXxIfw&feature=endscreen* (time: 0:00:45).

References to God's spirit occur already in the creation stories. The word *spirit* in Hebrew (as in Greek) can also be translated as "wind" or "breath." Genesis records that "a mighty wind"—a phrase that can also be translated as "a wind of God" or "the spirit of God"—swept over the waters (Gen 1:2) as God created. It is the breath or spirit of God that gives life to humans: "the Lord God formed man out of the clay of the ground and blew into his nostrils the breath of life, and so man became a living being" (Gen 2:7).

In the Old Testament, God's spirit is associated with the gift of prophecy— the gift of receiving and communicating God's messages. One reads, "The spirit of God rushed upon" Saul, and he joined a band of prophets (1 Sam 10:10). The Lord took some of the spirit from Moses and gave it to the elders, and they were able to prophesy also (Num 11:25).

In the New Testament, Paul writes of the close connection between God and his spirit, "For the Spirit scrutinizes everything, even the depths of God. . . . no one knows what pertains to God except the Spirit of God" (1 Cor 2:10–11). Paul admonishes members of his church, "Do you not know that you are the temple of God, and that the Spirit of God dwells in you?" (1 Cor 3:16).

In the New Testament, the Spirit is also connected with Jesus. Mary conceived Jesus not through ordinary human means but "through the Holy Spirit" (Matt 1:20). In the Gospel of John, the Father will send the Spirit, also called the Comforter or Advocate, to Jesus' followers after Jesus has returned to the Father. Jesus tells his disciples, "The Advocate, the holy Spirit that the Father will send in my name—he will teach you everything and remind you of all that [I] told you" (John 14:26). An intriguing passage reports that when the apostle Paul and his companions wished to travel to Bithynia, the Spirit of Jesus did not allow them (Acts 16:7); also (1 Pet 1:11).

The Trinity in the New Testament   6.11

Previous sections have considered biblical passages that closely associate the Father and the Son, together with other passages that closely associate God's spirit with the Father and the Son. This section presents several other passages that associate all three. Although the New Testament does not use the word *Trinity*, these passages show an intimate relationship between Father, Son, and Spirit that foreshadow later Trinitarian doctrine.

> [Jesus speaks to his disciples]: "But when he comes, the Spirit of truth, he will guide you to all truth. He will not speak on his own, but he will speak what he hears, and will declare to you the things that are coming. He will glorify me, because he will take from what is mine and declare it to you. Everything that the Father has is mine; for this reason I told you that he will take from what is mine and declare it to you." (John 16:13–15)

The intimate connection between the workings of Father, Son, and Spirit in Paul's thought is also clear:

- Galatians 4:6: "God sent the Spirit of his Son into our hearts, crying out, 'Abba, Father!'"
- 1 Corinthians 12:4–6: "There are different kinds of spiritual gifts but the same Spirit; there are different forms of service but the same Lord; there are different workings but the same God who produces all of them in everyone."
- 2 Corinthians 13:13: "The grace of the Lord Jesus Christ and the love of God and the fellowship of the holy Spirit be with all of you." (See also Rom 8:9 and Rom 8:15–17.)

The classic foreshadowing of Trinitarian thought comes at the end of the Gospel of Matthew, when the risen Jesus instructs his disciples to baptize "in the name of the Father, and of the Son, and of the holy Spirit" (Matt 28:19). From the beginning of the Christian movement, baptism was an essential ritual for joining the Christian community. It is significant that the wording accompanying this essential ritual refers to Father, Son, and Spirit.

In the Orthodox tradition, moreover, the Gospel account of Jesus' baptism, when the Father declares from heaven, "This is my beloved Son" and the Holy Spirit descends on Jesus "like a dove," is understood as a revelation of the Trinity (Matt 3:16–17).[23]

Summary of the Biblical Data   6.12

The overview of the biblical data presented here shows a continuity between the biblical evidence and later, more technical and philosophical creedal statements about the Trinity. Both the Old Testament and New Testament are familiar with the idea of distinction within the divine unity of God, and a great variety of New Testament passages show a deep sense of the unity of Father, Son, and Spirit, even though this unity is never expressed in precise, technical language.

The Experiential Basis of the Doctrine
of the Trinity   6.13

The earliest followers of Jesus were Jews who had a deep belief in the unity of the one God. Yet their experience of Jesus (e.g., witnessing his authority to forgive sins, encountering him risen) led them to apply the divine name *Lord* to Jesus, and to include him in the one divine identity of God. At the same time,

---

23. Kallistos Ware, *The Orthodox Way*, 36. Also see "The Trinity in the New Testament," by Felix Just, SJ, accessible at *http://catholic-resources.org/Bible/Trinity.htm*.

they experienced God's presence through God's Holy Spirit (e.g., through the spiritual gifts that they believed were poured out by the Spirit on them (see 1 Cor 12:4–11). Reflecting on these experiences, Christian theologians began to develop clearer thoughts on how Jesus, the Spirit, and God the Father were related to one another.

The key point is that theologians did not invent the doctrine of the Trinity. Rather, it arose out of the practical experience of the first Christians: an experience that convinced them that the one God was present to them in the Father, the Son, and the Spirit.

The Trinity and Prayer   6.13.1

C. S. Lewis also points out how the doctrine of the Trinity is not merely theoretical but also is intimately involved in practical daily Christian prayer.

> An ordinary simple Christian kneels down to say his prayers. He is trying to get in touch with God. But if he is a Christian he knows that what is prompting him to pray is also God: God, so to speak, inside him [the Holy Spirit]. But he also knows that all his real knowledge of God comes through Christ, the Man who was God— that Christ is standing beside him, helping him to pray, praying for him. You see what is happening. God is the thing to which he is praying—the goal he is trying to reach. God is also the thing inside him which is pushing him on—the motive power. God is also the road or bridge along which he is being pushed to the goal. So that the whole threefold life of the three-personal Being is actually going on in that ordinary little bedroom where an ordinary man is saying his prayers.[24]

In the Catholic understanding, prayer to God the Father is always prayer through Jesus, who through his death and Resurrection gives humans access to the Father. "Whether our prayer is communal or personal, vocal or interior, it has access to the Father only if one prays 'in the name' of Jesus" (*CCC*, no. 2664).

The Holy Spirit is also intimately involved in prayer life. As the apostle Paul taught, "the Spirit too comes to the aid of our weakness; for we do not know how to pray as we ought, but the Spirit itself . . . intercedes for the holy ones according to God's will" (Rom 8:26–27).

Within Catholic worship, Trinitarian prayer also has a prominent place, as is indicated in section 6.13.2.

---

24. Lewis, *Mere Christianity* (orig. pub. 1952; San Francisco: HarperSanFrancisco, 2001), 163.

The Trinity and the Mass   6.13.2

The Catholic Mass is filled with references to the Trinity. As worshippers enter the church, they typically dip their fingers into holy water and make the sign of the cross in the name of the Father, Son, and Spirit. The holy water is a reminder of baptism, which is also done in the name of the Father, Son, and Holy Spirit.

Eucharistic Prayer III gives thanks to the Trinity for the gift of life, "You are indeed Holy, O Lord, and all you have created rightly gives you praise, for through your Son our Lord Jesus Christ, by the power and working of the Holy Spirit, you give life to all things and make them holy."[25]

The prayer continues with the epiclesis, the calling down of the Holy Spirit to sanctify the gifts. Again it is Trinitarian:

Therefore, O Lord, we humbly implore you: by the same Spirit graciously make holy these gifts we have brought to you for consecration, that they may become the Body and Blood of your Son our Lord Jesus Christ at whose command we celebrate these mysteries.[26]

The prayer ends a Trinitarian doxology, "Through him, and with him, and in him, O God, almighty Father, in the unity of the Holy Spirit, all glory and honor is yours, for ever and ever."[27]

Development of Doctrine   6.14

The Catholic tradition teaches that the doctrine of the Trinity developed from the experience of the earliest Christians, as expressed in the New Testament, into the more precise language of the fourth-century creeds. This key concept of **development of doctrine** has its classic expression in John Henry Newman's *An Essay on the Development of Christian Doctrine* (1845).

Newman argues that in any field of knowledge, it is natural for a complex "idea" to develop over time. Consider an example from the political realm. Most Americans take for granted that the United States was founded on the idea

---

25. From the 3rd edition of the *Roman Missal* (English Translation, 2011); comparison of the four Eucharistic prayers accessed at Felix Just, "Catholic Resources" *catholic-resources.org/ChurchDocs/RM3-EP1-4.htm*.

26. Ibid.

27. Ibid.

of democracy—the belief that all people are created equal and, therefore, have both the natural right and ability to govern themselves. Yet when the United States was first founded, few people had the right to vote and participate in the democracy. White men who did not own property, African American slaves, Native Americans, and women were excluded. As the years passed, however, the "idea" of democracy developed. It became clear to many that members of these excluded groups have the right to participate in the democratic process. The essential idea of democracy remained the same, but it was *developed* to include greater portions of the American population.

In a similar way, the doctrine of the Trinity developed over the period of centuries. From the beginning, the basic categories of unity and distinction were there. Early Christians experienced the unity of Father, Son, and Holy Spirit: They experienced God's power, love, forgiveness, and challenge through all three. At the same time, they experienced the three as distinct. It was only through the experience, reflection, and, as Christians believe, the guidance of the Holy Spirit that the classic formulation of the Trinitarian doctrine was achieved in the creeds of the Councils of Nicaea and Constantinople and in the formulations of the fourth-century Fathers. Details of this development will be given in chapter 12.

In tracing the development of the doctrine of the Trinity from New Testament times, Newman admits that the belief did not develop in a smooth and unbroken line. Quite the opposite: Newman, with characteristic boldness and intellectual honesty, points out that many theologians who lived before the Council of Nicaea (325 CE) would have rejected the teaching that God is three divine persons in one nature. Judged by the later, developed Trinitarian doctrine, Ignatius of Antioch (ca. 35–ca. 107 CE) did not adequately distinguish between the three persons; and Justin (ca. 100–ca. 165 CE) and Eusebius of Caesaria (ca. 260–ca. 340 CE) failed to recognize the Son's full equality with the Father.[28] From the beginning, Christians had experienced God's presence in the Father, Son, and Spirit, but it took a long process of theological reflection, including much debate, before the doctrine of the Trinity could be stated in full clarity in the late fourth century.

God's Nature and God in the World: The Immanent and the Economic Trinity   6.15

Many Old Testament passages (see sec. 6.8.2) distinguish between God's presence in the world ("God's glory" or "God's angel") and God's transcendent presence, or presence beyond the world. In the Orthodox tradition, a similar distinction is made between God's essence—God in his own nature, unknowable to humans— and God's energies—God's activities in the world (see sec. 5.5.3). Similarly,

---

28. John Henry Newman, *An Essay on the Development of Christian Doctrine* (Westminster, MD: Christian Classics, 1968), 15–17.

Catholic theology distinguishes between what it calls the **immanent Trinity**, God in his own nature, and the **economic Trinity**, God's action in the world.[29]

Is this a legitimate distinction? Can one really know anything about the immanent Trinity? Isn't this pure speculation about something humans cannot grasp? If people accept that God can reveal himself, shouldn't they just accept what is known of God from the economic revelation and not speculate about what God is in his own hidden nature? Some theologians have taken this approach, including, for example, the German Reformed theologian Friedrich Schleiermacher (1768–1834).[30] This approach is problematic, however, because it puts people in the position of trusting in a God whose true nature is completely hidden.

The Catholic theologian Karl Rahner takes a different approach. He insists that "the 'economic' Trinity is the 'immanent' Trinity and the 'immanent' Trinity is the 'economic' Trinity."[31] For Rahner, it is fundamental that what is revealed to humans about the relationship of the Father, the Son, and the Holy Spirit accurately reflects the truth about the relationships of Father, the Son, and the Holy Spirit within God's one nature. "God relates to us in a threefold manner, and this threefold, free, and gratuitous relation to us is not merely a copy or an analogy of the inner Trinity, but this Trinity itself, albeit as freely and gratuitously communicated."[32] In other words, when humans see the Father's earthly (economic) revelation in Jesus, humanity sees God as he truly is.

To get a better sense of the theological issues involved in comparing the "economic" and the "immanent" Trinity, section 6.16 discusses some specific traditional beliefs about how Father, Son, and Spirit are related.

Economic Trinity: The Father Sending the Son and Spirit   6.16

The New Testament frequently speaks of God the Father sending his Son and Spirit into the world.

- Galatians 4:4: "But when the fullness of time had come, God sent his Son . . ."
- John 14:26: Jesus said, "The Advocate, the holy Spirit that the Father will send in my name . . ." The Gospel of John also speaks of the Son sending the Spirit from the Father, "When the Advocate comes whom I will send you from the Father, the Spirit of truth that proceeds from the Father, . . ." (John 15:26; see also John 16:7, 20:22) (secs.11.5.4–5)

---

29. See LaCugna, 174–76.

30. See Khaled Anatolios, *Retrieving Nicaea: The Development and Meaning of Trinitarian Doctrine* (Grand Rapids, MI: Baker Academic, 2011) Kindle location 372.

31. Karl Rahner, *The Trinity* (New York: Seabury, 1974), 22. Emphasis original.

32. Ibid., 35.

Immanent Trinity: The Son's Generation and the Spirit's Procession 6.17

Does this "sending" of the Son and Spirit, revealed in Scripture, also reveal something about the relationships between Father, Son, and Holy Spirit within God's nature, within the "immanent Trinity"?

Traditional Christian theology has answered yes. In technical theological language, the Father is said to eternally generate the Son, and the Spirit is said to proceed eternally from the Father and the Son.

The procession of the Spirit within the Trinity is controversial. The Nicene Creed as prayed in Western churches today states that the Spirit "proceeds from the Father *and the Son*." Although the phrase "and the Son" is found neither in the version of the creed drafted at Nicaea in 325 CE nor in the Niceno-Constantinopolitan Creed approved in 381 CE, it reflects an ancient tradition that was confessed dogmatically by Pope Leo I in 476 CE. "And the Son" (*filioque* in Latin) was gradually added to Western liturgy between the eighth and eleventh centuries (*CCC*, no. 247); the addition was not accepted by Eastern Orthodox churches.[33]

In confessing that the Holy Spirit proceeds from only the Father, the Eastern tradition emphasizes the Father as the ultimate source of the Spirit. The Western tradition agrees that the Father is "the source and origin of the whole divinity" (*CCC*, no. 245), and also believes that the Father "is the first origin of the Spirit," though the Holy Spirit proceeds from the "single principle" of the Father with the Son. The *Catechism of the Catholic Church* concludes that Eastern and Western approaches form a "legitimate complementarity," that "provided it does not become rigid, does not affect the identity of faith in the reality of the same mystery confessed" (*CCC*, no. 248). The issue has been discussed in **ecumenical dialogues**.

Crucified Son and Suffering Father 6.18

Contemporary theologians such as Jürgen Moltmann share Rahner's concern to overcome the split between the immanent and the economic Trinity. For Moltmann, it is Jesus' death on the cross that reveals the true inner nature of God. Moltmann asserts, "The theology of the cross must be the doctrine of the Trinity and the doctrine of the Trinity must be the theology of the cross."[34]

What are the Trinitarian implications of this thesis? In other words, where is the Father when his Son is suffering and dying on the cross? For Moltmann, the only answer that makes moral sense is that the Father was suffering along

---

33. For a brief sketch of the controversy, see LaCugna, "Trinitarian Mystery," 184–86.

34. Jurgen Moltmann, *The Crucified God: The Cross of Christ as the Foundation and Criticism of Christian Theology* (orig. pub. 1974; Minneapolis, MN: Fortress Press, 1993), 241.

with the Son."[35] In fact, Jesus' death on the cross reveals that the Father suffers whenever any human suffers. Jesus reveals to humanity a compassionate God who is willing to enter the depth of human weakness and pain.

Moltmann's view challenges the traditional Christian understanding that the eternal God is unchangeable and impassible (i.e., not subject to changing emotions), expressed, for example, by Aquinas (*SCG*, 1.89: "In God there are no passions of the appetites"). For Moltmann and like-minded theologians, the belief that God is impassible is a distortion of the passionate and compassionate God of the Bible. They believe that in developing this doctrine, Christianity was too influenced by the Platonic concept of a "high god" who is a pure unchanging spirit and takes no interest in the ever-changing, suffering physical world.

To illustrate his point, Moltmann cites the heart-rending scene recorded in Auschwitz survivor Elie Wiesel's *Night*:

> The SS hanged two Jewish men and a youth in front of the whole camp. The men died quickly, but the death throes of the youth lasted for half an hour. "Where is God? Where is he?" someone asked behind me. As the youth still hung in torment in the noose after a long time, I heard the man call again, "Where is God now?" And I heard a voice in myself answer, "Where is he? He is here. He is hanging there on the gallows."[36]

Moltmann comments, "Any other answer would be blasphemy. There cannot be any other Christian answer to the question of this torment. To speak here of a God who could not suffer would be to make God a demon."[37]

Moltmann's point is passionate and moving, but is it ultimately helpful? If God is so closely identified with the suffering of the world, can he at the same time be in a position to save people from their suffering?

The Limitations of a Suffering God   6.19

Theologians such as Balthasar and David Bentley Hart reject Moltmann's view in favor of the traditional belief in God's impassibility. Following are some key reasons:

1. They both recognize that Moltmann and other modern theologians' view of a suffering God is closely tied to a view of the Trinity influenced by the German philosopher G. W. F. Hegel (1770–1831). For Hegel, God, as the

---

35. Ibid., 243.

36. Quoted in Ibid., 273–74.

37. Ibid., 274.

"Absolute Spirit" needs to interact with the world in order to fully unfold his own nature in history.[38] (This line of thinking is also evident in a modern type of theology known as process theology.) Hegel's God is no longer the transcendent source of all being, as in traditional Christian metaphysics, but depends on the world to fulfill himself.

2. Suffering is a passive emotion in which a person is affected by events outside of oneself. God, on the contrary, is pure act, and cannot be changed by events outside of himself.

3. The decisive point is that a God who is so completely tied to the fate of the world cannot be its savior. God would simply suffer along with all his creatures and be simply another part of the unending interplay of life and death, good and evil that makes up the history of the universe.

God's Eternal, Active, Self-Emptying Love   6.20

If, according to traditional Christianity, God is not subject to changeable emotions, one should by no means conclude that God is simply uncaring and detached from the world. On the contrary, traditional Christianity insists that God is a God of love, but it is not a passive emotion of love but a completely active love that cannot change due to shifting emotions. The love within the Trinity is full and perfect in itself—it does not depend on the world in order to complete its love. God's love for humans is a free act of his grace.[39]

Balthasar, like Moltmann, takes the cross as the key to understanding the doctrine of the Trinity: "The full doctrine of the Trinity can be unfolded only on the basis of a theology of the cross."[40] The cross does indeed reveal a God of love, a God-man who was willing to give up his life for the sake of others. This self-giving on the cross was only the ultimate moment of a self-emptying (in Greek: *kenosis*) that began when the Son emptied himself of his divine privileges and took on human limitations: "he emptied himself taking the form of a slave, coming in human likeness" (Phil 2:7).

Balthasar also agrees with Rahner that the *kenosis* of Jesus' life and death reveals the relationships within the immanent Trinity. The Father's eternal generation of the Son is the "foundational *kenosis*."[41] In Balthasar's understanding, when the Father "eternally begets" the Son, the Father "empties

38. Hart, "No Shadow of Turning: On Divine Impassibility," *Pro Ecclesia* 11 (2002): 189; Balthasar, *Theo-Drama, Vol. 4: The Action*. trans. Graham Harrison (San Francisco: Ignatius Press, 1995), 333.

39. Hart, "No Shadow of Turning," 197–99.

40. Balthasar, *Theo-Drama, Vol. 4: The Action*, 319.

41. Ibid., 313, 323. Balthasar here follows the Russian Orthodox theologian Sergei Bulgakov.

himself" of his divinity and hands it over entirely to his Son. This generation reveals the Father's inherent nature as self-giving love: from all eternity the Father is directed outward, sharing love and pouring out his very self for the sake of others.

The Son responds to this gift of the Father's very self with the same selfless thanksgiving and love. The Spirit is involved in this mutual self-giving, proceeding from both as the essence of love.[42]

This eternal Trinitarian love continues in the creation of the world. Creation itself is a new *kenosis*, in which the Trinity continues to give itself away as love. Again, God did not need to create, because the Triune God is already self-sufficient love in itself, but brought the world into existence simply out of an overflowing love.

In the end, it is crucially important that God does not depend on the world. Only a God who is self-sufficient love in himself is in a position to truly help a suffering world.

Analogies for the Trinity   6.21

All theological language uses analogies. In seeking to better understand an especially abstract concept, such as the Trinity, the use of analogies has understandably been common.

Recent theological discussion has focused on psychological and social analogies.[43] The psychological approach takes the individual person as its starting point; the social approach takes the relationships among people as its model. Both approaches have their strengths and limitations in attempting to describe three distinct, subsistent persons united in one nature.

A social analogy is able to emphasize the real, subsistent existence of each divine person, and to bring out, in a natural way, the understanding of the Trinity as a relationship of love. Richard of St. Victor (d. 1173) gives a well-known example. He begins with the model of two people, in a mutual relationship of love but moves on to picturing both together loving a third in harmony (*On the Trinity*, Book 3). The social model is sometimes offered as a model for how humans should relate to one another as a community of mutual love. Balthasar suggested that the model of husband, wife, and child might be the best image of the Trinity in creation. Love between husband and wife reflects God's outpouring of love to another, the child images how a third person arises naturally and fruitfully from the love of two.[44]

---

42. Ibid., Kindle locations 4854–4856.

43. Anatolios, *Retrieving Nicaea*, Kindle location 433.

44. Balthasar, *Theo-Logic, Volume 2: Truth of God*, trans. Adrian J. Walker (San Francisco: Ignatius Press, 2004), 62.

The drawback of this example is its inability to picture how three separate individuals could truly be united as one. In addition, some theologians who use the social model tend to reduce the message of Christianity to the relationships among people and neglect the transcendental aspect of the faith.[45]

The psychological model is better able to visualize a unity of three elements. A well-known example of the psychological model occurs in Augustine's *On the Trinity*. Because humans are made in the Triune God's image (Gen 1:26), Augustine believes that the Trinity must be reflected in the human. He finds the clearest expression of this image in the Trinitarian structure of the human mind. Augustine conceives of the mind as an interrelationship of memory (*memoria*), intellect (*intellectus*), and will (*voluntas*).

The strength of the analogy is that it shows how three things can share the same being or substance: memory, intellect, and will are distinct, but they share the same nature as constituting one human mind: They are not three minds. In the one act of thinking, memory, intellect, and will are all at work, just as all three persons act in any action of the Triune God. The weakness of the analogy, as Augustine admits, is that each of the three elements is not fully mind in itself, whereas in the Trinity, each person is fully God.

Augustine believes that Trinitarian structure of the mind allows humans to seek the Triune God. At the end of *On the Trinity*, Augustine prays for the strength to keep seeking God. "Let me remember you [through the memory], let me understand you [through the intellect], let me love you [through the will]. Increase these things in me until you refashion me entirely" (*On the Trinity* 15.51).

Engaging with Nicene Teaching 6.22

Engaging with past tradition is essential to the Catholic faith. The authority and importance of the Niceno-Constantinopolitan Creed holds a special place; it is the standard for the Trinitarian theology studied here.

Today Catholic theologians while accepting, in faith, the truth of this creed, do not simply repeat its teaching. Their task is to understand the faith expressed in the creed and rearticulate it in ways that speak to people today. Their work can involve a number of strategies, including studying the fourth-century context in which the Creed was written and compared the Creed to other authoritative Church teaching, especially Scripture. Finally, the theologian can apply the Creed's teaching to contemporary issues.[46]

---

45. A video of theologians Karen Kilby and Thomas O'Loughlin discussing theories of the Trinity is accessible at *www.youtube.com/watch?v=02GkSAYu-V8&list=PL60FD8649577F2389&index=4* (time: 0:13:34).

46. Two important recent attempts to study Nicene theology in its historical context and relate that theology to modern concerns are Lewis Ayres, *Nicaea and Its Legacy: An Approach to Fourth-Century Trinitarian Theology* (Oxford: Oxford University Press, 2004) and Khaled Anatolios' *Retrieving Nicaea: The Development and Meaning of Trinitarian Doctrine* (Grand Rapids, MI: Baker Academic, 2011).

In seeking to understand the classic Trinitarian theology of the fourth century, then, the theologian today seeks a "fusion of horizons"—bringing together the horizons of the fourth-century text with the twenty-first century. In the process of theological inquiry, modern theologians must be aware of their prejudgments. Lewis Ayres argues that modern theologians have failed to deal seriously with Nicene theology because of modern prejudgments that are, in fact, distorted or erroneous. Among these misleading prejudgments are

1. The modern theologian cannot accept Nicene theology, because theologians with a precritical worldview, especially a naïve approach to Scriptural interpretation, developed it.

2. Ancient Christian theology, influenced by Platonist thought, has an overly abstract and philosophical understanding of God that does not do justice to the God of Scripture.

3. Many modern Trinitarian theologies rely uncritically on a Hegelian view of the Trinity, one that assumes that the Spirit requires interaction with the world in order to fully unfold itself (sec. 6.19).[47]

While Ayres' sweeping characterizations of modern theology are exaggerated, he helps drive home the necessity for scholars to examine the presuppositions and prejudices they bring to their work.

The following section, on the Trinitarian thought of the fourth-century Cappodocian, Gregory of Nyssa, shows that modern theologians still have much to gain from a serious study of ancient theologians.

Gregory of Nyssa's "On Not Three Gods"   6.23

In "On Not Three Gods,"[48] a letter to a fellow bishop, Gregory responds to the challenge: Doesn't the teaching that three persons share one divine nature really imply a belief in three gods?

First, Gregory seeks to clarify the meaning of the term *nature*. Even in this world, the nature of a thing is a unity that cannot be divided. Human nature, for example, is a unity; when one sees Peter, James, and John, one does not say, "I see three human natures." The nature of gold is a unity; when one sees three gold coins, one does not say, "I see three golds." Analogously, the divine nature cannot be divided. It is always one; therefore, there can only be one God.

How can humans know that Father, Son, and Spirit share the same divine nature? Gregory believes people cannot know divine nature directly. In fact, they can never know the nature of anything directly. One can only know a

---

47. Ayres, *Nicaea and Its Legacy*, Kindle locations, 6207–6647.

48. Gregory of Nyssa, "On Not Three Gods," accessible at *www.ccel.org/ccel/schaff/npnf205 .viii.v.html*.

thing's inner nature through its outward manifestations—its powers, energies, and actions.

Scripture shows that Father, Son, and Spirit perform the same actions. For example, all three are described as seeing all created things—not only the visible, but also the invisible. God the Father sees (Ps 84:10): "look upon the face of your anointed), Jesus sees the inner thoughts of some scribes (Matt 9:4), and the Holy Spirit sees the secret thoughts of a man who tried to hide them from the apostle Peter (Acts 5:3). Because the three persons perform the same action, one can infer that they also share the same powers and ultimately the same nature.

Gregory, then, raises a potential objection. When one sees three people performing the same action of farming, one concludes that they are three farmers. So if Father, Son, and Spirit all perform the same divine action, doesn't that show that they are three gods?

The difference, Gregory clarifies, is that each of the farmers is engaged in a separate action of farming, whereas every action of God in creation involves all three persons. Every action "has its origin from the Father, and proceeds through the Son, and is perfected in the Holy Spirit" ("On Not Three Gods"). One sees this in the act of creation itself: The actions originate in the Father, are carried out through the power of the Son (God's Word), and are perfected through the ongoing presence of the Holy Spirit in creation.

As this brief summary shows, modern theologians still have much to learn from a study of the great fourth-century theologians. Gregory's philosophical point that people can only know the essence or nature of a thing through its powers or "energies" remains worthy of consideration. His teaching that every divine action actively involves all three members of the Trinity remains a foundational Trinitarian principle.

Is Trinitarian Language Patriarchal?   6.23.1

Feminist theologians such as Mary Daly and Rosemary Radford Ruether argue that the traditional naming of the Trinity, "Father, Son, and Spirit," lends support to patriarchal social structures that deny power to women. In Daly's famous phrase, "if God is male, then the male is God."[49] Some have, therefore, advocated replacing the terms with more inclusive descriptors, such as "Creator, Redeemer, and Sanctifier." For feminist theologian Catherine LaCugna, however, such terms

Continued

---

49. Mary Daly, *Beyond God the Father: Toward a Philosophy of Women's Liberation* (Boston: Beacon Press, 1973), 19.

Is Trinitarian Language Patriarchal? *Continued*

are inadequate. They focus exclusively on the *function* of each divine person in relation to humanity. This risks breaking the connection between the economic Trinity and the immanent Trinity and threatening the ability to know God as he truly is.[50] Such terminology is also an example of Modalism, and threatens the traditional understanding of the persons as distinct.

LaCugna further argues that the language of Father, Son, and Holy Spirit need not be understood as patriarchal. The term *Father*, need not connote a stern, authoritarian patriarch. In the traditional Trinitarian vision, it actually connotes the opposite, as it envisions God as infinite love in which the centerpiece is "God's kenotic self-revelation in Christ."[51] The Trinitarian doctrine offers a vision of God "in which there is neither hierarchy nor inequality, only relationships based on love, mutuality, self-giving and self-receiving, freedom and communion," all values compatible with theological feminism.[52]

LaCugna ends her reflections by calling for a recovery of both masculine and feminine images for the Trinity, together with a constant awareness of the limitations of each. She notes that the Christian tradition already has feminine Trinitarian images; she refers to the Eleventh Council of Toledo (675), which used the phrase "from the womb of the Father" as a synonym for "the substance of the Father."[53] (Sec. 5.6.5)

The Trinity: The Deepest Reality is Love

Trinitarian belief is not a set of contradictory statements about how three really equals one. The doctrine answers a religious and philosophical puzzle with which cultures and religions have struggled: The profound sense that reality depends ultimately on a single, unified source seems to be contradicted by humans experiencing reality as pluralistic and fragmented. The Trinitarian insight is that the ultimate source of reality is a dynamic unity that includes, within itself, a kind of plurality.

The central Trinitarian insight—that ultimate reality is not a single, static unity but a dynamic unity of relationships—has been confirmed in surprising

---

50. LaCugna, "Trinitarian Mystery," 180–82.

51. Ibid., 182.

52. Ibid., 183–84.

53. Ibid., 180–84.

ways by the insights of modern quantum physics and relativity theory. Far from being an outdated medieval relic, the Trinitarian doctrine that God is a *relationship* of persons anticipated the insights of Einstein that reality can only be described in terms of *relationships* between space, time, and elemental forces.

The doctrine of the Trinity explains that ultimate reality is based on relationships of love. For this reason, the universe and human life as its highest creation has a meaning: It was called out of nothingness to share in the divine relationship of love.

The revelation of God in Jesus Christ reveals the depth of this divine love. When Jesus willingly gave up his life on the cross, he was mirroring the eternal, self-emptying love of the Father.

This Trinitarian worldview contradicts the materialist or atheist view that sees the universe as based simply on chance events of cause and effect. The Christian alternative portrays a universe that came into being and is sustained by the self-sacrificing love of its Creator.

Questions about the Text

1. What are some common objections to the doctrine of the Trinity?
2. What are the three essential points in the Christian doctrine of the Trinity?
3. Explain how all philosophies and religions must deal in some way with the relationship between the unity and plurality (the one and the many). How does the doctrine of the Trinity describe this relationship?
4. How is the word *person* especially appropriate as a term applying to Father, Son, and Holy Spirit in the Trinity?
5. How does a Trinitarian view of reality resemble the view of reality in modern physics?
6. What are some Old Testament passages that suggest a possible plurality within the unity of the one God?
7. In what ways did early Christians include Jesus within the one divine identity?
8. What does the claim that the doctrine of the Trinity has an experiential basis mean?
9. Explain Newman's idea of the development of doctrine and show how it applies to the doctrine of the Trinity.
10. Define the terms *economic* and *immanent Trinity*. Why are theologians interested in the relationship between the two?
11. Explain the beliefs concerning the Father's generation of the Son and the Spirit's procession from the Father and the Son.
12. Explain why both Moltmann and Balthasar believe that Jesus' death on the cross is the key for understanding the Trinity. Why do Hart and Balthasar criticize Moltmann's view that God the Father suffered with Jesus?

13. Give examples of the social and psychological analogies for the Trinity. Explain the pros and cons of each.

14. According to Lewis Ayres, what are some prejudgments that modern theologians bring to their study of the fourth century?

15. Summarize Gregory of Nyssa's argument that the belief in the Trinity does not imply a belief in three gods.

16. Summarize the argument that traditional Trinitarian doctrine is oppressively patriarchal and Catherine LaCugna's responses to these arguments.

Discussion Questions

1. Can you think of references to the Trinity in art, literature, or Christian worship? Elaborate.

2. Which of the objections to the doctrine of the Trinity seems most important or persuasive to you? Why?

3. How important is the doctrine of the Trinity for the typical Christian today? Give reasons for your answer.

4. Do you agree with Moltmann or Hart on the question of whether God the Father suffers with people who are suffering?

5. Which analogies of the Trinity are best for understanding this Christian doctrine?

7

Human Nature and Human Destiny

Christian Anthropology   7.1

What exactly is a human? Is human nature essentially good and innocent, only needing to be liberated from society's oppressive rules and restrictions in order for people to be happy and healthy, as the "hippy" 1960s counterculture believed? Is human nature driven by self-centered lust and the desire for power, as Sigmund Freud believed? In line with postmodern thought, is it better to conclude that there is really no such thing as a stable human nature at all? This chapter explores the Christian answer to that age-old question and lays out the basics of a Christian view of human nature, in other words, a Christian anthropology.

In the Christian view, human nature has physical, mental, emotional, and spiritual aspects—all inseparable from one another. As discussed in chapter 2, influential rationalist and materialist worldviews either ignore or deny the spiritual aspect of human nature. From a Christian perspective, these worldviews lead to a fundamental misunderstanding of what it means to be human, because the spiritual aspect is essential. As Henri de Lubac put it, humans are naturally oriented toward a supernatural goal: unity with God.

Christian beliefs about human nature are thus inextricably linked to Christian views on the ultimate supernatural destiny of humans—specifically, what happens to people after their death and at the end of history. In the Christian worldview, one can only understand this earthly life in the larger context of the ultimate destiny of humans.

Earlier chapters laid out some fundamental principles on how the natural and the supernatural are related: Aquinas' view that (supernatural) grace perfects nature (*ST* 1.1.8 ad 2), the view that every natural good already exists in God the Creator (*ST* 1.4.2), and de Lubac's paradoxical view that human nature is naturally designed for a final destiny beyond nature. This anthropology is consistent with the point made in chapter 1: all humans have a natural instinct that the deepest meaning of this natural world actually lies beyond it in a transcendent realm.

As one begins the study of Christian anthropology, one should keep in mind that this is not simply a theoretical issue. How one thinks about the supernatural destiny of humans profoundly influences how one thinks about a variety of practical issues, including the value and dignity of individual human life.

To begin to fill out some of the details of Christian anthropology, then, one needs to start at the beginning: creation.

Christian Anthropology: Original Harmony, the Fall, and Hope for Salvation   7.2

Christians believe that God created humans as the high point of all creation. Although all things are part of God's good creation, only humans are created in the image of God. As such, only humans are given authority to rule and exercise stewardship over the rest of creation (Gen 1:26–28). Only humans—alone out of all creation—have both a natural body and a supernatural soul.

In symbolic language, the first two chapters of Genesis portray God's intentions for all humans. They are meant to live peacefully and happily—in harmony with nature, with each other, and with God. Chapter 3 of Genesis, however, records how this plan was disrupted. Humans, represented by Adam and Eve, chose to turn away from God. This turning away involves a change in human nature, a move from a state of original innocence to what Christians call a state of **fallen human nature**, in which all humans still live. In other words, although humans still naturally seek God as the source of all happiness and fulfillment, they also have a tendency to turn away from God, a self-destructive tendency that ends in selfishness, deceit, and violence. This turning away affects not only humans but also all of creation. Fallen from the original state of harmony, humans along with all creation, now struggle with harsh realities of suffering, sickness, and death.

Nevertheless, Christians believe that God does not abandon fallen humanity. God continues to communicate with humans through general and special revelation, inviting humans to return to him and, thus, return to their original life of harmony and fulfillment. The ultimate act of God's efforts to recall fallen humanity is the Incarnation, in which God's Word took on human form, reconciling the divine and the human in Jesus. Because of this action, all humans have the opportunity for what Christians call salvation—the overcoming of sin, sickness, suffering, and even death in a return to that lost, original harmony with God, one another, and nature.

Christian anthropology understands this salvation as holistic. It begins in this life and is completed in a transcendent unity with God; it involves the healing and renewal not only of the spirit but also of the resurrection and transformation of the body as well.

The Christian view of the unfolding of human destiny has three major periods:

1. Original peace and harmony among humans, nature, and God (Garden of Eden)
2. Fallen existence dominated by sin and death, yet sustained by hope for salvation (history)
3. The restoration of the original peace and harmony (Kingdom of God)

The following sections (7.3–7.4.1) take a more specific, scripturally based view of Christian anthropology.

Scriptural Anthropology: Old Testament   7.3

Within the Christian Scriptures, one can discern two basic worldviews and two distinctive anthropologies: the Semitic, found largely in the Old Testament, and the **Hellenistic**, influencing some later Old Testament and all of the New Testament books. Semitic anthropology tends to be more holistic, as the ancient Hebrews did not make a sharp distinction between the physical and spiritual, between body and soul.

Consider a quotation from Psalms: "O God, you are my God—it is you I seek! For you my body [Hebrew: *basar*] yearns; for you my soul [Hebrew: *nephesh*] thirsts" (Ps 63:2). In this passage, it is clear that the two words *basar* and *nephesh* both refer to the same person, but that person is seen from two distinct points of view.

Basar is often translated as "flesh." It refers to the whole human person but viewed from the perspective of essential human fragility. The prophet Isaiah says, "All flesh [*basar*] is grass, and all their loyalty like the flower of the field. The grass withers, the flower wilts" (Isa 40:6–7).

The basic verbal meaning of the Hebrew word *nephesh* is "to breathe." For the ancient Hebrews, breath is what distinguished a living body from a dead body, and so one basic sense of *nephesh* is the "life force" that causes a body to live. Thus, "the LORD God formed the man out of the dust of the ground and blew into his nostrils the breath of life, and the man became a living being [*nephesh*]" (Gen 2:7). As does *basar*, *nephesh* refers to human life as a whole, including what moderns would call body and spirit, but focuses on the "aliveness" of the person. The *nephesh* cannot exist apart from the body.

Scriptural Anthropology: New Testament   7.4

The clear distinction in Christian thought between physical and spiritual reality results from the influence of ancient Greek anthropology. According to Plato, for example, the soul[1] (Greek: *psyche*) is clearly distinct from the body: it is an immortal, invisible force that inhabits the physical body. For Aristotle, in contrast, body and soul, although distinct, are essentially united: the soul is the "form" of the body, the principle of its life. Aquinas, and with him mainstream Catholic thought, follows Aristotle in seeing body and soul as an essential unity.

Christianity sometimes describes humans as formed of body and spirit (Greek: *pneuma*); other times, a tripartite division is made, as in Paul's Letter to the Thessalonians: "may you entirely, spirit, soul, and body, be preserved blameless" (1 Thess 5:23). The *Catechism of the Catholic Church* does not make a sharp distinction between spirit and soul (*CCC*, no. 367).

Christian Anthropology and the Holy Spirit   7.4.1

In New Testament thought, the "spirit" of a person is distinct from God's "Holy Spirit," although there is a clear connection between the two. Paul, at times, refers to a person's spirit as a supernatural gift given to one who has become a follower of Christ: "you are not in the flesh; on the contrary, you are in the spirit, if only the Spirit of God dwells in you" (Rom 8:9). Elsewhere, Paul contrasts the spiritual (*pneumatikos*) person and the natural (*psychichos*) person (1 Cor 2:14–15).

Paul contrasts the two in this way: "our old self was crucified with him, so that our sinful body might be done away with, that we might no longer be in slavery to sin" (Rom 6:6). Similarly, Paul says, "whoever is in Christ is a new creation: the old things have passed away; behold, new things have come" (2 Cor 5:17).

According to New Testament thought, the "natural" life without God's supernatural help tends to focus on pleasure in a self-centered way. This tendency is what Paul calls "the flesh." It is only with the help of God's Spirit that a person moves beyond the realm of the flesh and into the realm of the Spirit (see 1 Cor 3:1).

Does Christianity Despise the Body?   7.5

At times, one encounters the claim that Christians think of the body, especially the pleasures of the body, as evil. Thus, the German philosopher Friedrich Nietzsche (1844–1900) mocks Christians as "hair-shirted despisers of the body."[2] Many people, including some Christians, further claim that Christian salvation consists in getting rid of the body and entering into the purely spiritual eternal realm of heaven.

It is undeniable that, historically, some strands of the Christian tradition have viewed the body negatively. The theologian Origen (ca. 185–ca. 254 CE), for example, taught that souls preexisted in the heavenly realms and were bound

---

1. An article on "Ancient Theories of Soul" is accessible at *http://plato.stanford.edu/entries/ancient-soul/*.

2. Friedrich Nietzsche, *Thus Spoke Zarathustra*, no. 3.10.2. See Walter Kaufmann, ed., *The Portable Nietzsche* (New York: Viking, 1968), 300.

to bodies as punishment for sins (*On First Principles* 1.8).[3] Nevertheless, Scripture and mainstream Christian thought celebrate and glorify the human body as good.

In order to better understand the distinctive Christian view of the body and its relationship to the soul, one must first understand the context of ancient thought out of which Christianity first arose.

The Negative View of the Body in Other Ancient Traditions   7.5.1

Some religions and philosophies of the ancient Mediterranean world in which Christianity developed did have a fundamentally negative view of the body. Platonist philosophy, for example, tended to regard the body as part of the fleeting, changing, material world and, therefore, as far less real and valuable than the eternal world of unchanging ideas. The body too is the realm of unpredictable and irrational emotions, in contrast to the stable, rational mind. In the famous dialogue, the *Phaedo* (66a), for example, Socrates teaches that the body "disturbs the soul and hinders it from attaining truth and wisdom"[4] Plato's view is one influential example of an anthropology that teaches a "mind-body" dualism[5]—a sharp distinction between the body and the mind or between the body and the soul.

As noted earlier, ancient Gnostic thought[6] takes an even more negative attitude toward the body (sec. 5.3.1). Because the physical world in which humans live is the creation of a lesser (or even an evil) god, salvation involves becoming free from the prison of the body and ascending into the purely spiritual realm.[7]

Gnostic[8] and Platonist ideas about the body have influenced some Christian writers; Origen's view (sec. 7.5) serves as an example. The following sections (secs 7.6–7.10.1), however, present mainstream traditional Christianity's more positive view of the physical body as an integral part of human nature.

Christian Respect for the Body   7.6
Essential Unity of Body and Soul   7.6.1

In the Catholic tradition, the connection between body and soul is essential to what it means to be a human. In the words of the *Catechism* (note the influence of Aristotle's language):

---

3. Origen's *On First Principles* (ca. 225) is accessible at *www.newadvent.org/fathers/0412.htm*.

4. The text of *Phaedo* 66a is accessible at *www.perseus.tufts.edu/hopper/text?doc=Perseus%3Atext %3A1999.01.0170%3Atext%3DPhaedo%3Asection%3D66a*.

5. An article discussing the mind-body problem is accessible at *http://plato.stanford.edu/entries /dualism/#HisDua*.

6. An article introducing Gnosticism is accessible at *www.iep.utm.edu/gnostic/*.

7. See D. S. Noss and B. R. Grangaard, *A History of the World's Religions*, 12th ed. (Upper Saddle River, NJ: Pearson Prentice Hall, 2008), 483–84.

8. Darrell Bock discusses Gnostic Christianity in a video accessible at *www.youtube.com /watch?v=3IoqMPdebuI* (time: 0:02:01).

The unity of soul and body is so profound that one has to consider the soul to be the "form" of the body: i.e., it is because of its spiritual soul that the body made of matter becomes a living, human body; spirit and matter, in man, are not two natures united, but rather their union forms a single nature. (*CCC*, no. 365)

God Reveals Himself through the Physical: Creation, Incarnation, and Sacraments   7.6.2

In the Christian worldview, the physical world has a great value because it is through the physical world that God reveals himself to humans. Consider the following points:

- The creation account in Genesis says repeatedly that God found his creation to be good; the human creation, body and soul, was very good (Gen 1).
- God reveals his creative power and supreme intelligence through nature—general revelation.
- God, in the Second Person of the Trinity, took on a human body to "come down to the level" of humanity. This doctrine of the Incarnation signifies the highest possible respect for the body: the human body is shown to be both capable and worthy of being united in a real way to the perfect and transcendent source of all things—God.
- According to the Catholic and many other Christian traditions, God continues to work through the physical world via the sacraments of the Church. God continues to offer supernatural grace to humans through physical means—the water of baptism, the bread and wine of the Lord's Supper, the oil of the Anointing of the Sick (see chapter 13 for a further discussion).

Finally, to offer a recent, specific example of Christian respect for the body, consider Pope John Paul II's "Theology of the Body."[9] In this teaching, the pope interprets our physical sexual nature as a sign that humans were meant to be in communion and community with one another, sharing not only words and ideas but intimately sharing our physical selves as well. One can see this as a natural development of the long tradition of Christian respect for the body.[10]

---

9. A video overview of Pope John Paul II's "Theology of the Body" is accessible at *https://www .youtube.com/watch?v=E8H5BWVZl_Y* (time: 0:09:46).

10. On the "Theology of the Body," see John Paul II, *The Theology of the Body: Human Love in the Divine Plan* (Boston: Pauline Books & Media, 1997). A more popular and accessible summary of the pope's ideas are found in Christopher West, *Theology of the Body for Beginners* (West Chester, PA: Ascension Press, 2004).

Destiny of the Body: The Resurrection 7.7

Many people today, including a number of Christians, hold a rather Platonic view of life after death. They assume that the material body is left behind to decay and only the soul, or spirit, rises up to the next world.

Such a view, however, is not actually Christian. The Christian tradition has always insisted that the body, after dying and decaying, will rise again at the end of time. As the Apostles' Creed, the ancient summary statement of Christian belief, says, "I believe in . . . the resurrection of the body." Is this a reasonable belief? Isn't it a fact that living bodies decay and disintegrate after death, and that there is no scientific proof of a dead body ever coming back to life again? Here, it seems, is a clear contradiction between faith and reason.

Is Resurrection Reasonable? 7.7.1

One must carefully consider the actual Christian teaching. Christians, including Christians in New Testament times, know that in nature dead bodies stay dead. If such an event as the resurrection of a dead body has ever occurred, it could only be as the result of an intervention in nature by a power outside of nature—a supernatural power. So the more fundamental question becomes, is it reasonable to think that a supernatural power could intervene in nature? Earlier chapters argued that there are good reasons for believing that a supernatural power does exist and could intervene in this world.

Christians do not consider God's supernatural interventions to be arbitrary. Rather, they are generally understood as signs—dramatic, miraculous interventions in the world for the purpose of revealing and shaping God's plan. Jesus' Resurrection is not understood as an isolated event. It is a sign or foreshadowing of the destiny of all humans: "But now Christ has been raised from the dead, the firstfruits of those who have fallen asleep" (1 Cor 15:20). Christ's Resurrection is a sign that God intends the complete healing—physical, mental, emotional, and spiritual—of all humans. To further understand this Christian belief, one must consider the scriptural witness in more detail.

Paul on the Resurrection of the Body 7.8

As many modern people consider the belief in the resurrection of the body to be strange or unreasonable, so too did many in ancient times. Members of Paul's church at Corinth must have had similar concerns, for they questioned Paul, "How are the dead raised? With what kind of body will they come back?" (1 Cor 15:35). It is probable that these residents of Corinth, a Greek city, were influenced by Plato's philosophy. They could understand the belief that a spiritual soul could survive death, but they were confused by the idea that a *material* body could be raised again.

When Paul speaks of a resurrected body, he is, by definition, speaking of a supernatural body—a body that exists outside of the normal workings of nature, because a strictly natural body obviously does not come back to life. Therefore, Paul answers the Corinthians in the only way that a question about a supernatural reality can be answered—by analogy (sec. 5.6.3). The resurrected body is like a seed, "a bare kernel of wheat" that is sown in the ground (1 Cor 15:37). Like a seed, the human body is "sown corruptible; it is raised incorruptible. It is sown dishonorable; it is raised glorious. It is sown weak; it is raised powerful. It is sown a natural [*psychikos*] body; it is raised a spiritual [*pneumatikos*] body" (1 Cor 15:42–44).

Paul relates his comparison between the *psychikos* and the *pneumatikos* to a comparison between Adam, representative of the "natural" human, and Christ, representative of humans who have overcome sin and death and attained the *pneumatikos* life. "Just as we have borne the image of the earthly one, we shall also bear the image of the heavenly one" (1 Cor 15:49).

The resurrected body, then, will not be a resuscitated corpse, a dead body with the principle of life (the soul) put back into it. It will be a *different kind of body*: a "spiritual body," an immortal, incorruptible body (1 Cor 15:53–54). At the same time, it is not simply a completely new body; Paul's analogy of the seed only makes sense if the spiritual body is a transformation, not a replacement, of the physical body. One can see how Paul's discussion fits the broader conception of Christian salvation—the complete healing and renewal of the "natural" human being.

The Transformed Body: The Example of Jesus' Resurrected Body 7.9

Further insight into the Christian understanding of the nature of the resurrected body is gained by considering the accounts of Jesus' Resurrection in the Gospels. Recall that Paul thought of Jesus' Resurrection as a foreshadowing of the resurrection of all people (1 Cor 15:20), so the description of Jesus' resurrected body hints at the nature of the bodies of all people in the Resurrection.

In the accounts of Jesus' Resurrection from the dead, the Gospel writers go out of their way to emphasize that Jesus' *body* rose, not just his spirit. All four Gospels report that when women came to Jesus' tomb on the first day of the week, they found the tomb empty. His body had risen. When the risen Jesus appears to his disciples, it is true that, in some aspects, he seems like a pure spirit: longtime followers do not recognize him at first (Luke 24:15–16; John 20:14), and he can appear and disappear suddenly (Luke 24:31; John 20:19).

Other passages emphasize that there is still some sort of physicality to Jesus' risen body. In Luke, his sudden appearance frightens the disciples into thinking they have seen a ghost, and Jesus reassures them, "Look at my hands and my

Caravaggio, Michelangelo Merisi da (1571-1610) / Schloss Sanssouci, Potsdam, Brandenburg, Germany / Bridgeman Images

Depicting John's account (see 20:24–29) of "doubting Thomas," the Italian artist Caravaggio faithfully captures the Gospels' emphasis on the physicality of the Risen Christ. Jesus, lacking the traditional halo or any other symbol of divinity, guides the disciple's finger to his side. Thomas and the other disciples stare with undisguised fascination as Thomas probes the wound, portrayed with a stark realism.

feet, that it is I myself. Touch me and see, because a ghost does not have flesh and bones as you can see I have" (Luke 24:39). Jesus then takes a piece of fish and eats it (Luke 24:42–43). The risen Jesus also invites the apostle Thomas, who had refused to believe that Jesus had really risen, "Put your finger here and see my hands, and bring your hand and put it into my side, and do not be unbelieving, but believe" (John 20:27).

The Gospel accounts, then, seem to be an illustration of Paul's teaching about the "spiritual body." Jesus' body retains characteristics that one thinks of as physical: the ability to eat, the ability to be touched. At the same time, his body has clearly transcended physical limitations as humans know them. It has passed into a different, supernatural plane of existence.

The doctrine of the resurrection of the body is, thus, in perfect harmony with Christian teaching on salvation. Salvation is not a completely new experience, cut off from earthly reality. It is a perfection of every earthly good. Because all aspects of the human—body, soul, and spirit—are all created as good, salvation means that the whole human person will be perfected in heaven.

Resurrection of the Body and the Renewal of Nature

7.10

Paul's Letter to the Romans shows a close connection between human salvation and the renewal of all physical creation. Paul teaches that nature will be set "free from slavery to corruption and share in the glorious freedom of the children of God" (Rom 8:21).

Describing the Resurrected Body

7.10.1

In thinking theologically about these traditional teachings concerning resurrection and the ultimate destiny of the world, one must remember the limited ability of human language and reason to express fully a supernatural reality (sec. 5.6).

The traditional Christian teaching is that there is continuity between a person's physical human body and that person's resurrection body: Christ "will change our lowly body to be like his glorious body" (CCC, no. 999). Yet the question arises: How can a dead body that is already decayed and scattered be changed into a glorious body?

The Catechism teaches that the question of exactly how the body is raised "exceeds our imagination and understanding; it is accessible only to faith" (CCC, no. 1000). Perhaps, however, an analogy can help. Even in earthly life, at the purely physical level, our bodies are in fact constantly changing. "Although people may think of their body as a fairly permanent structure, most of it is in a state of constant flux as old cells are discarded and new ones generated in their place."[11] Science shows us that even our present physical identity does not depend on retaining the exact same cells and molecules.

Theologically, then, the key principle is that there is continuity between the person's self (composed of both body and spirit) in this world and the same person (composed of a spiritual body) in the future state.

Nature, with its patterns of decay and death, is not as God intended it to be. At the end times, in the renewal of all things, however, a renewed nature will arise, along with the renewed body: "a new heaven and a new earth" (Rev 21:1). As Aquinas teaches, "Wherefore at the one same time, the world will be renewed, and man will be glorified" (ST 3.91.1 Supp.).

---

11. Nicholas Wade, "Your Body Is Younger than You Think," *New York Times* (August 2, 2005): D1.

Will People See Their Pets in Heaven?   7.10.2

Many people become quite attached to their pets and experience a great sadness when the pet passes away. What does the Christian tradition say about the possibility of seeing a beloved pet in heaven?

Aquinas answers in the negative (*ST* 91.5 *Suppl.*), because animals have only a "corruptible" nature, not an eternal soul. On the other hand, Scripture and church teaching is quite clear that nature will be renewed at the end of time (e.g., Rom 8:21). Although Aquinas taught this as well, he believed that only heavenly bodies, the elements, and humans would be renewed.

C. S. Lewis, however, speculated that tame animals may exist in some way through their relationship to their resurrected masters. They are certainly not raised in the same way that humans are, Lewis thought, but rather "part and parcel of the new heavens and the new earth."[12]

What Is the Soul?   7.11

If traditional Christianity defines the human as a unity of body and soul, a reasonable question is, What exactly is the soul? Because the human soul is a transcendent reality, one cannot define it scientifically. How does the Christian tradition, then, describe the soul?

The Catholic Church rejects the belief that souls preexist in heaven, and are later sent into bodies, a belief held by Gnostics, among others. Rather, "every spiritual soul is created immediately by God" at the moment of conception (*CCC*, no. 366). Notice how this teaching is holistic, reinforcing the belief that the soul naturally belongs with the body, as both come into existence at the same time.

In the Christian tradition, the soul is often closely associated with the image of God in which humans are created (Gen 1:26–27). Thus, Augustine comments, "Man's excellence consists in the fact that God made him to His own image by giving him an intellectual soul, which raises him above the beasts of the field" (quoted in *ST* 1.93.2).

The human soul, the "image of God" in humans, is further associated with human characteristics that set humans apart from the rest of nature: greater intelligence, moral capacity to distinguish right from wrong, power of free will, and a natural sense that there is a deeper meaning, truth, and beauty beyond this world. Thus, the *Catechism* teaches, "with his openness to truth and beauty, his sense of moral goodness, his freedom and the voice of his conscience, with his

---

12. Lewis, *The Problem of Pain* (New York: Macmillan, 1962), 138–43.

longings for the infinite and for happiness, man questions himself about God's existence. In all this he discerns signs of his spiritual soul" (*CCC*, no. 33).

Notice that the *Catechism* is careful to say that all of these characteristics are "signs" of the spiritual soul, not the soul itself. The point is important, since not all humans fully develop their abilities of free will, conscience, or their intelligence. What about babies who die at a young age, or persons who have profound mental disabilities? Should one conclude that such persons do not have souls, or are not made the image of God? No, on the contrary the Catholic tradition is clear that every person, even the weakest and least intelligent, is created with an immortal soul and in the image of God (*CCC*, no. 1702).

The Human Role in Nature   7.12

Humans and Animals   7.12.1

Christian teaching boldly and without apology places humans in the center of the universe.

> Then God said, "Let us make human beings in our own image, after our likeness. Let them have dominion over the fish of the sea, the birds of the air, the tame animals, all the wild animals, and all the creatures that crawl on the earth." (Gen 1:26)

The Christian tradition is united in claiming that all creation was made for humans. Humans are "the only creature on earth which God willed for itself (*GS*, no. 24). The second-century *Letter to Diognetus* reads, "For God loved men, and made the world for their sake" (10.2). Aquinas says, "Now animals and plants were made for the upkeep of human life" (*ST* 91.5 *Supp.*). The *Catechism of the Catholic Church* teaches, "Animals, like plants and inanimate beings, are by nature destined for the common good of past, present, and future humanity" (*CCC*, no. 2415).

To many people, this view sounds arrogant, and some might accuse traditional Christians of being "speciesists." Representative of such modern intellectual trends is English evolutionary biologist Olivia Judson:

> Many people would like to think that we men are the product of a special creation, separate from the other forms of life. I do not think this, I am happy that it is not so. I am proud to know that I am part of the tumult of nature, to know that the same forces which produced me also produced the bees, the giant fern and the microbes.[13]

---

13. Olivia Judson, "Our Place in Nature's Riotous Order," *International Herald Tribune*, January 3, 2006; cited in Christoph Schönborn, *Chance or Purpose: Creation, Evolution, and a Rational Faith* (San Francisco: Ignatius Press, 2007), 108.

Actually, the Christian tradition agrees with much of Judson's observations. Humans do share the mystery of life with bees and ferns and microbes. Christianity is in no way embarrassed by this fact. Medieval theologians such as Aquinas were not ashamed of the human link with animals: They followed Aristotle in defining humans as "rational animals." They simply insisted that, while sharing much in common with other animals, humans also transcend them in many other ways.

Humans and Animals: Key Differences 7.12.2

As noted, one line of Christian theology sees the "image of God" especially in those characteristics that make humans different from all other animals—intelligence, a sense of morality, free will, and a sense of the transcendent.

This approach does not deny that other species, such as the primates, have some sort of limited intelligence. However, it is absurd to pretend that human intelligence and animal intelligence are in the same category. Human intelligence has built incredibly complex technological systems capable of producing spacecraft that can travel to other planets. Animal "technology" can, at most, produce simple tools and shelters.

Humans need not deny, either, that animals may have some rudimentary sense of right and wrong. However, laws of instinct and conditioning still essentially bind animals. Only humans are free enough to wonder whether a certain planned action is morally right or wrong.

It is also true that human actions are morally *worse*, sometimes, than those of animals. No animal can match the sadistic, calculated cruelty of a serial killer or rapist. Ironically, such sadistic behavior is only possible because humans have the transcendent gift of free will. As Giovanni Pico della Mirandola (1463–1494) wrote, "You are just as free to distort yourself into subhuman forms as you are free, by your own choice, to be reborn into higher and divine forms."[14] Humans have the freedom to shape their character to the level of the divine or distort and corrupt it to a level below that of the animals.

Ironically, the claim that humans are not essentially different from the rest of creation is a claim *only* a human could make. A chimpanzee cannot make that claim, for a chimpanzee cannot conceive of the abstract idea of "nature" nor is a chimpanzee free enough from the bonds of instinct and conditioning to ask such a self-reflective question.

In the Christian view, God appoints humans to use their freedom and intelligence to care for nature, not to exploit or destroy it. If one denies that humans are essentially different from animals, then one denies human responsibility to care for creation properly. Can humans seriously believe monkeys or great apes

---

14. Giovanni Pico della Mirandola, *Oration on the Dignity of Man*, quoted in Schönborn, *Chance or Purpose*, 111.

should take over the human role of stewards of nature? While it is true that humans, through irresponsible, greedy, and unthinking actions, have polluted, damaged, and destroyed parts of nature, it is also true that only humans are in a position to save nature from those human-produced threats.

No contradiction exists, therefore, between a traditional Christian world-view and an environmentalist ethic that seeks to preserve and care for Earth. On the contrary, the Christian should be eager to protect the beauty and integrity of God's good creation.[15]

The Catholic Tradition and Environmentalism

7.12.3

Catholic Church leaders have been actively engaged in an effort to protect and care for nature, which God has entrusted to humans.

Pope John Paul II declared Francis of Assisi (ca. 1181–1226) the patron saint of ecology. In one well-known story, Francis preached a sermon to a flock of birds that waited patiently until he finished. In his Canticle of the Sun, Francis asks that God be praised through "Brother Sun," "Sister Moon," and "our sister Mother Earth, who sustains us and governs us and who produces varied fruits with colored flowers and herbs."[16] Today, many Catholic churches still bless pets on October 4, the feast day of Saint Francis.

Recent popes have stressed the

Church of St Francis, Montefalco, Umbria, Italy, 15th century / De Agostini Picture Library / Bridgeman Images

Saint Francis, patron saint of ecology and lover of all of God's creation, preaches a sermon to a flock of birds, exhorting them to praise and love their Creator.

connection between concern for the dignity of all humans, especially the poor, and care for the environment. In his 1990 address, "Peace

Continued

15. For an article on Francis Schaeffer and Christian environmentalism, see *www.firstthings.com/onthesquare/2013/02/recalling-francis-schaefferrsquos-christian-environmentalism*.

16. Accessible at *Catholic Online, www.catholic.org/prayers/prayer.php?p=183*.

The Catholic Tradition and Environmentalism Continued

with God the Creator, Peace with All of Creation," Pope John Paul II touched on the link between poverty and abuse of the environment and asserted that no solution to ecological problems will be found until modern society takes a serious look at its wasteful lifestyle. He declared, "Simplicity, moderation and discipline, as well as a spirit of sacrifice, must become a part of everyday life, lest all suffer the negative consequences of the careless habits of a few."

In a 2011 message to Italian students, Pope Benedict XVI declared, "Respect for the human being and respect for nature are one, but both can grow and find their right measure if we respect in the human being and in nature the Creator and his creation." During Benedict's pontificate, solar panels were installed at the Vatican and goals were established to increase the use of renewable fuels.

Pope Francis chose his name in honor of Francis of Assisi, a lover of the poor and a lover of nature. In his first homily as pope, Francis raised environmental concerns, "I would like to ask all those who have positions of responsibility in economic, political and social life, and all men and women of goodwill: let us be protectors of creation, protectors of God's plan inscribed in nature, protectors of one another and of the environment"[17] (March 19, 2013). The pope is well known for his modest lifestyle.

The Challenge of Human Freedom   7.13

The Dignity and Risks of Freedom   7.13.1

Against materialist and determinist views, Christians have always insisted that humans are not determined but truly have free will. In the Christian view, this is what gives humans their great dignity—that they are truly free to make their own decisions and shape their lives. Although God is all-powerful and could control every human action, he, in a sense, limits his own power and allows humans the dignity of being responsible for their actions.

Yet because humans are truly free, they are also free to turn away from God, the ultimate source of goodness, and turn toward evil. Human choices to

---

17. A video excerpt of Pope Francis's first homily and his words on the environment is accessible at *www.youtube.com/watch?v=xFy4sADYYOY* (time: 0:02:22). See also a video summary of an address Pope Francis delivered on World Environment Day, in which he links natural ecology and human ecology at *www.youtube.com/watch?v=ytYcVPhJNWY* (time: 0:01:56).

do evil have brought about untold suffering throughout the long centuries of human history.

Why does God allow these wrong choices, as they cause so much suffering? There is no doubt that an all-powerful God could have created humans in such a way that they would never have disobeyed him. However, in that case, God would have created mere robots—creations that could only react in ways that had been preprogrammed.

In giving humans true freedom, God ran the risk, to put it anthropomorphically, that humans would abuse that freedom and disobey him. And so humans have done. However, God must have considered the gift of freedom to be so great that it was worth the risk.

Only the ambiguous gift of freedom makes people human. Otherwise, one would merely react instinctively like animals or in a preprogrammed way like machines. On a daily basis, free choices form character: Humans become more trustworthy or untrustworthy, more courageous or less courageous, based on their choices. That same freedom gives humans the ability to love. They cannot force someone to love them; love is truly love only if it is given freely. And so God, having created humans in a free act of love, showed an even deeper love in allowing them the freedom to love or not to love him in return. Kallistos Ware writes simply, "Where there is no freedom, there can be no love."[18] C. S. Lewis adds, "Free will, though it makes evil possible, is also the only thing that makes possible any love or goodness or joy worth having."[19]

Reformation Debate on Free Will   7.13.2

The Christian tradition has not always agreed on how to reconcile several theological beliefs that can, at times, seem contradictory: that humans have free will, that humans have a fallen nature, and that God is all-powerful and all-knowing. Several of the Reformers, for example, emphasizing the essentially fallen nature of humans in contrast to the almighty power and plans of God, drew the conclusion that free will was an illusion.

In his work, *On the Bondage of the Will* (1525), Martin Luther wrote,

> For if we believe it to be true, that God fore-knows and fore-ordains all things; that He can be neither deceived nor hindered in His Prescience and Predestination; and that nothing can take place but according to His Will, (which reason herself is compelled to confess); then, even according to the testimony of reason herself, there can be no "Free-will"—in man,—in angel,—or in any creature! (No. 167).

---

18. Ware, *Orthodox Way*, 76.

19. C. S. Lewis, *Mere Christianity* (London: HarperCollins, 2001; orig. pub. 1952), 48.

The Fall so corrupted human nature that it is impossible for humans to turn toward God of their own free will—the fallen human can only choose evil. It is only through the influence of God's grace that humans can turn toward God, but humans are powerless to do anything to earn that grace or even to accept it or cooperate with it when God offers that grace to them.

The Reformer John Calvin (1509–1564) wrote similarly, "When the will is enchained as the slave of sin, it cannot make a movement toward goodness. . . . Such is the depravity of his nature, that he cannot move and act except in the direction of evil" (*Institutes* 2.3.5).

Responding to the Reformers and seeking to clarify authentic Catholic teaching, the Council of Trent's (1545–1563) *Decree Concerning Justification* sought to balance the reality of human free will with Christian doctrines on the fallen nature of humans and the necessity of God's grace for salvation.

The Council agreed that the first movement in the process must be God's grace: No one can turn toward God without God's help. Once this initial help is offered, the person is free either to turn toward God "assenting to and cooperating with" God's grace or to reject that grace. Free will, although weakened by the human fall into sin, "was by no means extinguished."[20]

Modern Lutheran-Catholic Agreement 7.13.3

Four centuries after the Reformation debates, Lutherans and Catholics are in a position to reevaluate their stances. In October 1999, the Lutheran World Federation and the Catholic Church issued a *Joint Declaration on the Doctrine of Justification*. The World Methodist Conference later officially adopted this same document.

The document concludes that "a consensus in basic truths of the doctrine of justification exists between Lutherans and Catholics" (no. 5), although the consensus still allows for differences in language and emphasis (no. 40). Both parties agree that, "By grace alone, in faith in Christ's saving work and not because of any merit on our part, we are accepted by God and receive the Holy Spirit, who renews our hearts while equipping and calling us to good works" (no. 15).

The *Declaration* also addresses the issue of free will: "When Catholics say that persons 'cooperate' in preparing for and accepting justification by consenting to God's justifying action, they see such personal consent as itself an effect of grace" (no. 20). As for Lutherans, "When they emphasize that a person can only receive (mere passive) justification, they mean thereby to exclude any possibility of contributing to one's own justification, but do not deny that believers are fully involved personally in their faith" (no. 21). Agreement on the exact relationship between free will and God's grace remains difficult to achieve, but the dialogue between the churches has shown some common ground.

---

20. Council of Trent Session VI, "Decree Concerning Justification," accessible at *www.ewtn.com /library/COUNCILS/TRENT6.htm.*

Sin   7.14

The Christian tradition teaches that humans fell away from God through sin, that fallen human nature is sinful, and that salvation involves overcoming this sinful nature. In order to grasp, rightly, Christian anthropology, one must have a clear sense of what Christians mean by *sin*.

One online dictionary defines *sin* as "1. transgression of divine law; 2. any act regarded as such a transgression, especially a willful or deliberate violation of some religious or moral principle."[21] This concept of sin, however, seems to be gradually disappearing in modern thought. Consider some factors that are contributing to this disappearance:

From a materialist or determinist point of view, this definition makes no sense—human actions are determined by forces that they cannot control, so there can be no "*willful or deliberate* violation." Although few people are strict determinists, determinist-influenced language is quite common: "It was the alcohol talking, not me." "I can't help losing my temper, that's just the way I am." "Boys will be boys." All of these expressions put the responsibility for negative actions outside of the person acting, thereby eliminating the traditional concept of sin.

Ethical relativism also rejects the reality of sin. This belief that right and wrong are determined solely by individual circumstances eliminates the belief in universal religious or moral principles. A person can't violate what doesn't exist.

As societies, especially Western societies, become more religiously pluralistic, it is increasingly difficult to agree on the specifics of a "divine law." As societies become more secular, the whole concept of "divine law" gradually loses meaning.

Despite these modern challenges, Christian anthropology maintains that the concept of sin is essential for true human dignity. God has revealed universal ethical standards, not only through the revelation recorded in Scripture but also in the natural law that is within each person's conscience. The human person has been given real knowledge of good and evil and the true freedom to choose between them. A human is not simply an animal controlled by instinct or by genetic composition; a human truly has the freedom, responsibility, and dignity to shape his or her destiny by free choices.

Sin as Turning from God to Self   7.15

The *Catechism* defines *sin* as "an offense against reason, truth, and right conscience; it is failure in genuine love for God and neighbor caused by a perverse attachment to certain goods" (*CCC*, no. 1849).

---

21. Dictionary.com is accessible at *http://dictionary.reference.com*.

The essence of virtually any moral wrong can be traced back to a focus on the self, and a failure of love—many who steal, lie, cheat, and even murder do so because they selfishly think they will get some kind of benefit from it.

"Sin is an offense against God" (*CCC*, no.1850) because God is the source of all goodness and of the natural law of right and wrong. All humans, whether they belong to a specific religion or not, have a sense of the transcendent and a sense of the moral law. As Paul says, "For what can be known about God is evident to them. . . . As a result, they have no excuse" (Rom 1:19–20). In the Christian view, even atheists or agnostics can be considered sinful if they act against what God has revealed to their conscience as right and wrong.

In refusing to submit to God and God's laws, humans rebel against God and, in essence, set themselves up as their own measure of right and wrong: They claim to be their own god.

Original Sin: Sinful Babies? 7.16

According to the *Catechism*, the Catholic Church baptizes infants in order to cleanse them from the **original sin** that they inherited from Adam and Eve (*CCC* nos. 417, 1250). For many today, this teaching is inexplicable. How can an innocent baby be sinful? How can a baby commit "an offense against reason, truth, and right conscience" (*CCC*, no. 1849) even before reaching the age of reason? Doesn't the idea that a baby inherits sin contradict the Christian principle that persons are responsible for their own sins (Ezek 18)?

Original Sin and Fallen Human Nature 7.16.1

The Catholic tradition agrees that it would be absurd to hold a baby personally accountable for sin. To sin means, at some level, to make a choice (the *Catechism* defines *sin* as an offense against *reason*) for something that human reason says is wrong. Obviously, babies do not have the mental or emotional development to make true choices.

However, think about what happens when babies begin to reach the age of reason. As they grow into toddlers, they gradually begin to make conscious choices, just as they begin to develop an understanding of right and wrong. Will a child, at some point, freely choose to do certain things that he or she knows are wrong? For example, will she choose to disobey her mother, because she enjoys seeing Mom get frustrated? Will he choose to keep some toys to himself when he knows he should share them with his younger brother?

As the child continues to develop, will she ever choose to do anything selfish? Will he ever gossip about another person who is not around to defend herself? Will she ever be jealous of another girl who is more athletic or more popular?

The answer to these questions is obvious: yes. One could easily add to the list of examples. In fact, most people would probably have to admit that they do or think something that they know is wrong (judging others without knowing their full story, telling a white lie, not keeping a commitment due to fatigue, etc.) every day.

Furthermore, truth be told, some people actually enjoy doing certain things they know are wrong. They somehow enjoy gossiping, overeating, drinking too much alcohol, watching pornography, being lazy—otherwise, why would they do these things at all?

In the face of all this evidence, the Catholic tradition reasonably concludes that *all* people *inevitably* sin when they are old enough to choose between right and wrong. If this is correct, it follows logically that sinning is part of human nature. To be more precise, the attraction toward sin, the tendency toward sin, is part of human nature. That tendency is somehow innate in humans.

Catholic tradition teaches that these negative tendencies and attractions are part of humanity's fallen, not original, nature. Everyday experience confirms this teaching. Though doing wrong is common, people typically do not experience it as normal. Unless their consciences have become hardened, they usually find their wrong actions to be shameful. A person is frustrated when he or she does wrong or tries to rationalize negative behaviors. Why would humans experience shame, guilt, frustration, or the need to rationalize unless they realize their actions are truly wrong? Deep within, people seem to know that human nature was not meant to be like this.

This fallen, negative condition of humanity is what the Catholic Church calls original sin. Original sin is simply "human nature deprived of original holiness and justice"; it is "a state and not an act" (*CCC*, no. 404).

The *Catechism* continues, "As a result of original sin, human nature is weakened in its powers; subject to ignorance, suffering, and the domination of death; and inclined to sin." (*CCC*, no. 418).

When the Catholic tradition says that a baby is born with original sin, it simply means that the baby is born with a human nature that is "wounded," weak when it comes to doing what is right, and all too inclined to give in to selfishness and personal sin when that person reaches the age of reason.

Personal experience supports the truth of this doctrine. Human history in general, with its long, unhappy record of wars, violence, racism, slavery, drug and alcohol addictions, and sexual exploitations, also supports its truth. From this perspective, G. K. Chesterton was right to conclude that far from being an unintelligible teaching, the doctrine of original sin "is the only part of Christian theology which can really be proved."[22]

To say, then, that babies "inherit" original sin from Adam and Eve does not mean that original sin is passed down like some kind of genetic disorder. Rather, it means that Adam and Eve, in their role as representatives of all humans, simply passed on *human nature* to succeeding generations—unfortunately, it was a

---

22. G. K. Chesterton, *Orthodoxy* (Peabody, MA: Hendrickson, 2006; orig. pub. 1908), 10, accessible at *www.ccel.org/ccel/chesterton/orthodoxy.v.html*.

fallen human nature. Original sin involves "the transmission of a human nature deprived of original holiness and justice" (*CCC,* no. 404).

For Catholicism, the doctrine of original sin[23] is not pessimistic; it is realistic. By honestly examining personal behaviors and motivations and looking objectively at human history, it is clear that only wishful thinking allows one to avoid the conclusion that there is something deeply flawed in human nature.

The view of original sin in other branches of Christianity, including evangelical Christianity, is similar.[24]

Hell: Missing out on Salvation   7.17

Difficulties with the Doctrine of Hell   7.17.1

As noted previously, the Christian tradition sees a close connection between life in this world and life in the transcendent realm after death. Salvation—the overcoming of sin and suffering—is a process that begins in this world and is perfected in the transcendent realm. Heaven is simply the fulfillment and completion of all that is good on Earth.

If the idea of heaven as the eternal perfection of earthly goodness is perhaps the most attractive and popular of Christian teachings, the opposite seems to be the case concerning Christian teachings about hell. Catholic theologian Peter Kreeft writes, "Hell is certainly the most unpopular of all Christian doctrines. It scandalizes almost all non-Christians."[25] One might add that the doctrine of hell—the belief that God condemns unrepentant sinners to eternal punishment—scandalizes many Christians too.

The reasons for the scandalized reaction are obvious, because the doctrine of hell seems to contradict not only basic modern values such as tolerance but also other basic Christian teachings as well. Christians are taught, for example, that God is forgiving but then taught that there is no possibility of forgiveness in hell, because the punishment is eternal.

Jesus taught his followers to love their enemies and pray for those who persecute them (Matt 5:44). However, the traditional Christian imagination of hell is filled with seemingly vindictive, even sadistic portraits of the suffering of sinners. In the classic Christian literary description of hell, the *Inferno,* Dante (1265–1321) describes some sinners tortured in a river of boiling blood, others chased eternally by ferocious dogs, others forced to lie on burning sand while fiery flakes rain down upon them (*Inferno,* canto 14).

---

23. Fr. Robert Barron explains the Catholic understanding of The Fall in a video accessible at *www.youtube.com/watch?v=n3u4kYuSTHA* (time 0:07:16).

24. See Marguerite Shuster, "The Mystery of Original Sin," *Christianity Today,* 57 (April 2013): 38, accessible at *www.christianitytoday.com/ct/2013/april/mystery-of-original-sin.html.*

25. Peter Kreeft, *Everything You Ever Wanted to Know about Heaven—but Never Dreamed of Asking* (San Francisco: Ignatius Press, 1990), 213.

The images of Scripture, while less graphic, are no less horrible. Jesus speaks of hell as a "fiery furnace, where there will be wailing and grinding of teeth" (Matt 13:42), "the eternal fire" (Matt 25:41), and "eternal punishment" (Matt 25:46). The Book of Revelation describes a "pool of fire" (Rev 20:14–15).

Christians claim that God is love, but God seems to have no love for those he punishes or allows to be punished in hell. Because Christians believe that God is just, it is understandable that those who have committed great crimes would be punished or corrected in some way, but why is the punishment eternal, with no chance for repentance?

The following sections (7.17.2–7.17.6) consider the Christian doctrine regarding hell in more detail.[26]

Describing Hell   7.17.2

First, one should recall the limitations of language. Because hell, according to Christian doctrine, is a supernatural reality, it cannot be described directly, only indirectly by using analogies (sec. 5.6.3). A teaching of the German Catholic Bishops' Conference made the point this way:

> Holy Scripture teaches us the *essence of hell* in images. When it speaks of the fire of hell, it is not to be understood in a grossly realistic sense. Much less should we think of sadistic tortures. But neither does a purely spiritual understanding do justice to the declaration in Scripture. The image expresses a reality of a much deeper nature. God in his holiness is a consuming fire for evil, deceit, hate, and violence (Isaiah 10:17). Just as heaven is God himself, won forever, so hell is God himself as eternally lost.[27]

The first point to note is that neither heaven nor hell is a physical place. One could not get to heaven by traveling in an airplane, nor could one reach hell by digging a tunnel under the earth. The tradition speaks of heaven and hell as places in an analogous way. Using more precise language, one would refer to heaven and hell as states of existence, not as places.

The images in Scripture, or other images such as those in Dante, or popular images of devils and pitchforks, need not be taken too literally. Images of fire and torture are analogies for the pain of eternally losing God. God is the source of everything good in life, and to exist apart from God in a state of hell is unimaginably painful. The pain of fire is simply an attempt to convey a realistic sense of that pain.

---

26. For further objections to the Christian doctrine of hell, see ibid., 219–25.

27. *The Church's Confession of Faith: A Catholic Catechism for Adults* (San Francisco: Ignatius Press, 1987), 346–47. Emphasis original.

Hell as Eternal Separation from God   7.17.3

In the Christian understanding, heaven may be defined simply as being with God. God is the ultimate source of goodness, truth, beauty, love—everything meaningful in life. Persons united in heaven with God experience and enjoy every conceivable goodness.

Hell, in contrast, is simply being without God. It is an existence without goodness and without meaning. Such an existence is hard to imagine, but one can, perhaps, just begin to conceive of it. Just as people can glimpse heaven in their experiences of goodness and love, so too can they glimpse hell. Whenever people experience any sort of distortion or twisting of an original good, they have some insight into what hell is like.

To experience the pain and emptiness of hell, one does not have to picture images of fire and brimstone. One has only to imagine a life that is cut off from all goodness. Instead of true friendship, there will be only relationships of fear and mistrust; instead of true love, only selfishness and self-centeredness; instead of true joy, only the twisted pleasure of cruelty; instead of true communication and sharing, only isolation; instead of hope, only a cynical despair; and instead of trust and honesty, lies and deception. This sort of existence, most truly and without exaggeration, would be hell.

When one says hell does not necessarily have devils with pitchforks, this does not mean that demons or devils do not really exist or that they are merely metaphors. The Christian tradition is quite clear that evil spirits do exist and are involved in some way in the pains of hell. They do not necessarily have horns, tails, and pitchforks, however. C. S. Lewis, in *The Screwtape Letters*, imagines the demons of hell organized in an office bureaucracy; each demon is polite and smiling on the surface but inwardly always scheming and conniving, ready to stab his or her partner in the back if it suits a purpose. Again, the essence of hell is the distortion of all good—selfishness, deceit, fear, and twisted pleasures are the only reality.

Hell as Freely Chosen   7.17.4

How, then, would a person come to be in this state without God? The answer has already been outlined earlier in this chapter. All humans have a fallen human nature, and all have a tendency toward sin and selfishness. All are born with these tendencies, yet all are free, in each individual instance, to cooperate or not to cooperate with these tendencies. According to Christian anthropology, however, people can never overcome this sinful aspect of their nature by their own power— they will always fall short and fall back into selfish, deceitful tendencies. They need to accept God's help to overcome sin; they need to accept God's grace in order to achieve that original happiness that God intended.

However, it is precisely "accepting help" that is the problem. The human situation is analogous to the observation counselors often make: the hardest step in overcoming any addiction is for persons to admit they have a problem they cannot handle on their own.

It is just so with human pride. Before persons can cooperate with the offer of God's freely given grace, they must first admit that they are too weak to overcome their sins on their own. This is precisely what is so difficult for humans—giving up the sense of control over one's life. Humans have a natural tendency to hold onto the old way of life with all of its distortions, deceits, and corruptions—under the illusion that they are still in control.

The New Testament plainly describes what is involved in this process. Jesus tells his disciples, "whoever wishes to save his life will lose it, but whoever loses his life for my sake and that of the gospel will save it" (Mark 8:35). The apostle Paul says, "our old self was crucified with him, so that our sinful body might be done away with, that we might no longer be in slavery to sin" (Rom 6:6). Accepting Christ involves a dying to one's old way of life, a crucifying of oneself; and people are naturally not eager to make such a hard decision.

In Catholic anthropology, humans are truly free to cooperate with or reject God's offer of help. By the innumerable free decisions people make in their lives, they orient their lives either toward God or away from God. They can either make a fundamental decision to humble themselves, as Christ did, and accept God's will for their lives, or they can decide to hang onto the illusion that they are in control of their lives. The one choice ultimately leads to the life with God, heaven; the other choice leads to the life without God, hell.

In this sense, God does not "send" people to hell. The Day of Judgment simply reveals the fundamental choice a person has already made. In the end, as C. S. Lewis says, there are only two kinds of people: those who say to God, "Thy will be done" and those to whom God says, "Thy will be done."[28] In other words, God respects human free will so much, that he will not force someone to be with him if that person has chosen to reject God.

In the Catholic understanding, God does not torture people in hell. God continues to love all people. It is impossible for God to stop loving, since his nature is to love. Yet those who have chosen hell do not experience his love as love. In their self-centered anger, hatred, and fear, they experience God's love as a burning pain.[29] In Dante's *Inferno*, an inscription above the gates of hell reads, "My maker was divine authority, the highest wisdom, and the primal love" (Canto 3.5–6).

Eternal Hell?   7.17.5

Why is hell eternal? Why not punish sinners for a certain amount of time or until they repent? Consider two points:

---

28. C. S. Lewis, *The Great Divorce* (New York: Macmillan, 1946), 72.

29. See Kreeft, *About Heaven*, 219.

First, the "eternity" of heaven and hell is *not* an endless amount of time; the human concept of time does not apply to transcendent reality.

Second, an essential element of true human freedom is that in order to be truly free, a human must, at some point, make a final, definitive decision either for or against God. If a person chooses to reject God but holds back, thinking, "I will always have a second chance later," then that person is not really choosing, but avoiding a final decision. God insists, so to speak, that humans exercise their freedom to choose—one way or another.

Who Is in Hell? 7.17.6

The Catholic tradition's answer to the question, "Who is in hell?" is simple: Anyone who has made the final, definitive choice against God. As the *Catechism* says, "This state of definitive self-exclusion from communion with God and the blessed is called 'hell'" (*CCC*, no. 1033).

Does anyone know, for sure, whether any particular person is in hell? Many would answer yes, listing such people as Judas, Hitler, or Stalin. Based on the idea that people cannot save themselves from sin, some Christians would say, "Anyone who has not accepted Jesus as Savior." Salvation and non-Christians will be discussed in more detail in chapter 14.

Some thinkers, such as Augustine, were convinced that most humans were destined to hell. In Augustine's view, humanity is so corrupt that all people deserve to go to hell; but God, out of his great mercy, has chosen to have mercy on a few.

A strand of Catholic thought exists, however, that is much more cautious in its assertions. Thus, the German Bishops' Conference declares "neither Holy Scripture nor the Church's Tradition of faith asserts with certainty of any man that he is actually in hell."[30]

As Balthasar shows, there are hints, both in Scripture and in Tradition, that *all* people *might* be saved.[31] Paul says, "God delivered all to disobedience, that *he might have mercy upon all*" (Rom 11:32, emphasis added). Paul's letter to Timothy asserts that God "wills everyone to be saved and to come to knowledge of the truth" (1 Tim 2:4). If God wills that all people be saved, can God's will truly be opposed? Mystics such as Mechtilde of Hackeborn (d. 1299) and Julian of Norwich (sec. 5.7) received private revelations from Christ that support the hope of universal salvation.[32]

Balthasar's thinking is also influenced by the absolute, qualitative difference between good and evil. If evil really is a corruption of good, if pure evil cannot exist, then can hell truly be eternal? The fourth-century theologian Gregory of Nyssa, taught that because evil cannot be absolute, there must be a limit to the

---

30. *Catholic Catechism for Adults*, 346.

31. Hans Urs von Balthasar, *Dare We Hope "that All Men Be Saved"?* (San Francisco: Ignatius, 1988).

32. Ibid., 98–102.

pains of hell.[33] Similarly, Balthasar notes the possible implications of Paul's train of thought in Romans: "just as through one transgression [of Adam] condemnation came upon all, so through one righteous act [of Christ] acquittal and life came to all" (Rom 5:18).[34]

Theologians such as Henri de Lubac, Karl Rahner, Joseph Ratzinger, and the Reformed theologian Karl Barth, as well as C. S. Lewis, all take seriously the possibility of universal salvation. These thinkers do not claim that all people *will* be saved—such a belief—attributed to Origen—has been officially condemned in Church teaching.[35] "Hell is always held before our eyes as *real possibility*."[36] Balthasar concludes that Christians are entitled to *hope* that each individual person might be saved, but they should in no way assume that all people definitely will be saved.[37]

Purgatory: Final Cleansing in Heaven 7.18

Another aspect of Catholic and Orthodox doctrine regarding the final destiny of humans is controversial: the teaching on purgatory. The Reformers, Luther and Calvin, for example, flatly rejected the Catholic teaching on purgatory (see, for example, Calvin's *Institutes* 3.5.6–10).

Misconceptions about Purgatory 7.18.1

Many Christians misunderstand the Catholic doctrine of purgatory to mean a third option between heaven and hell. This is not the case. The Catholic tradition agrees with the orthodox Christian tradition that there are only two options after death: life with God (heaven) or life without God (hell). To understand how purgatory fits into this two-option framework, one needs to review, briefly, the Christian view of salvation.

In Catholic anthropology, a person must cooperate with God's grace offered through Christ in order to be saved. One aspect of this cooperation is known as repentance—a genuine regret for having done wrong and a serious commitment to try, with God's help, to live a better life. To attain salvation, furthermore, a person must be cleansed of all sins. Because God is pure goodness and holiness, no one can be in God's presence unless all sins have been completely cleansed.

---

33. See ibid., 244–45.

34. Ibid., 39–40.

35. The doctrine attributed to Origen is known as the *apokatastasis*: the belief that all of creation, including the demons, would be restored. Origen's actual teaching is not clear, however.

36. *Catholic Catechism for Adults*, 346.

37. Balthasar, *Dare We Hope*, 211–21. Fr. Robert Barron addresses the question "is Hell crowded or empty" in a video accessible at *www.youtube.com/watch?v=dmsa0sg4Od4* (time 0:09:25).

Notice that even though Christians believe salvation is ultimately possible only through God's grace, a person's repentance is involved at some level. It would be absurd, for example, for a Christian to conclude, "Christ's death paid the price for all my sins, so therefore I can keep lying, cheating, committing adultery, and killing, since Christ has me covered." In Romans 6:1, Paul explicitly rejects this line of thinking.

Consider a hypothetical example. Mrs. Matthews has accepted God's offer of salvation in Christ and is saved. At her death, however, she still has certain sins on her conscience that she never fully faced. Perhaps she committed a great wrong earlier in life but never honestly faced that wrong because it was too painful to think about. Perhaps she has hurt some loved ones in ways of which she is not even aware.

The point is that all people, according to Christian anthropology, have weaknesses or faults in their lives, large or small, that they have either ignored or not completely faced. Although saved, those faults remain on people's consciences.

In the Catholic and Orthodox view, even after her death, Mrs. Matthews must go through a process, with God's help, of facing and truly repenting of those remaining wrongs and faults. Purgatory is simply this final process of cleansing before a person enters fully into God's presence. The *Catechism* expresses the teaching thus,

> All who die in God's grace and friendship, but still imperfectly purified, are indeed assured of their eternal salvation; but after death they undergo purification, so as to achieve the holiness necessary to enter the joy of heaven. (*CCC*, no. 1030)

The Catholic tradition sees purgatory not as a third place between heaven and hell but as an entryway into heaven. A soul in purgatory will eventually be fully in God's presence.

Notice again, however, the limitations of language. One speaks of "going" to heaven, hell, or purgatory as if they were physical places, but of course, they are not—they are transcendent realities, states of supernatural being rather than places.

The doctrine of purgatory implies that even in heaven those who are saved still go through progress, change, and development. They continually grow deeper in purity and holiness, growing ever deeper in their knowledge and experience of God.

Purgatory and Scripture   7.18.2

A major reason why the Reformers objected to the teaching on purgatory is that it is not found in Scripture. Admitting that the doctrine is not found explicitly in Scripture, the Catholic tradition nevertheless understands the teaching as a legitimate development of doctrine—a growth in human understanding of the scriptural teachings about salvation. Newman argued that purgatory was a logical development from earlier church teaching regarding the possibility of forgiveness of sins after baptism.[38]

The Catholic tradition has sometimes spoken of the number of "years" that a soul spends in purgatory, but such language is metaphorical. As Pope Benedict XVI taught, "It is clear that we cannot calculate the 'duration' of this transforming burning in terms of the chronological measurements of this world."[39] The pope suggested further that the doctrine of purgatory may be one way of imagining the encounter with Christ on the Day of Judgment:

> Some recent theologians are of the opinion that the fire which both burns and saves is Christ himself, the Judge and Saviour. The encounter with him is the decisive act of judgment. Before his gaze all falsehood melts away. This encounter with him, as it burns us, transforms and frees us, allowing us to become truly ourselves. (*SS*, no. 14)

The pope's understanding of purgatory[40] opens much common ground between Protestant, evangelical, and Catholic ways of thinking about salvation.[41]

A passage from one of Paul's letters, while not a direct support of purgatory, nevertheless, seems to be compatible with Benedict's teaching about purgatory. Here, Paul speaks about a purifying fire on the Day of Judgment:

> For no one can lay a foundation other than the one that is there, namely, Jesus Christ. If anyone builds on this foundation with gold, silver, precious stones, wood, hay, or straw, the work of each will come to light, for the Day [of Judgment] will disclose it. It will be *revealed with fire*, and the fire [itself] will test the quality of each one's work. If the work stands that someone built upon the foundation, that person will receive a wage. But if someone's work is burned up, that one will suffer loss; the *person will be saved, but only as through fire*. (1 Cor 3:11–15, emphasis added)

Prayers for the Dead 7.18.3

In line with their critique of purgatory, the Reformers also rejected the Catholic tradition's practice of praying for the dead.[42]

---

38. Newman, *An Essay on the Development of Christian Doctrine* (Westminster, MD: Christian Classics, 1968), 383–93 is accessible at *www.newmanreader.org/works/development/chapter9.html*.

39. Pope Benedict XVI, *Saved in Hope: Encyclical Letter* (*Spe Salvi*) (San Francisco: Ignatius Press, 2007), no. 14, accessible at *www.vatican.va/holy_father/benedict_xvi/encyclicals/documents /hf_ben-xvi_enc_20071130_spe-salvi_en.html*.

40. Pope Benedict XVI comments on Purgatory in a *romereports.com* video are accessible at *www.youtube.com/watch?v=dZDZ-dTPut0* (time 0:01:17).

41. On the possibility of reconciling traditional Protestant and Catholic views on Purgatory, see Kreeft, *About Heaven*, 61–62.

42. For example, Calvin, *Institutes* 3.5.10.

For many, the concept of praying for the dead makes no sense. In traditional Christian thought, the moment of death is definitive—a person is judged and "goes" to heaven or hell. What difference would the prayers of another person make at that point?

First, one must recall the principle that God is not confined to the human concept of chronological, sequential time. For God, all time is the present moment. Thus, a prayer said on behalf of a person who has died is not heard by God *after* the person's death. It is heard by God from all eternity and may benefit that person in the time, from a human perspective, *before* death. Pope Benedict XVI writes, "It is never too late to touch the heart of another, nor is it ever in vain."[43]

Second, the Catholic teaching is that prayers of the living can help a person through the process of Purgatory, the final cleansing of sins. In this understanding, one can say, metaphorically, that prayers can lessen a person's time in Purgatory. Just as Christians believe that the prayers of a fellow Christian can help a person through a difficult time on Earth, so the traditional doctrine teaches that prayers of those on Earth can help a person through the final cleansing.

The Catholic tradition also finds justification for this practice in the Second Book of Maccabees, when Judas Maccabeus "made atonement for the dead that they might be absolved from their sin" (2 Macc 12:46).[44]

Human Nature and Human Destiny   7.19

The Christian view of human nature and destiny cannot be summed up neatly as optimistic or pessimistic. On the one hand, it seems extremely optimistic. It claims that humans are the high point of the entire created universe and that the final destiny of humans is nothing less than absolute, unimaginable joy, contentment, peace, and love. On the other hand, it is also, in the eyes of many, deeply pessimistic. It claims that innocent babies are born with original sin and that humans are so weak and enmeshed in sin that they cannot free themselves; they must rely completely on God's help.

For Christians, however, these seemingly contradictory extremes can be reconciled. The supposed pessimism is simply an honest look at the limitations, weakness, and tendency to selfishness and corruption that lie deep in the heart of every human. The seeming optimism is based on fundamental Christian doctrines: all humans are created in the image of an all-good, all-powerful, and all-loving God, and God's planned destiny for every person is to share in the perfect peace, love, and harmony that God experiences in his triune nature.

---

43. Benedict XVI, *SS*, no. 48

44. Churches in the Protestant tradition do not accept the canonical status of 1 and 2 Maccabees.

Human Rights and the Image of God 7.19.1

The recognition of basic human rights is crucially important. Today, most nations give at least lip service to the belief that all humans have equal rights, including the right to be treated with dignity and respect. However, what is the basis of those rights and that dignity? In Christian anthropology, it is based on the transcendent nature of humans—that all humans have an immortal soul, made in the image of God. This transcendent basis for human rights is recognized even in the Declaration of Independence, that "all men are created equal, that they are endowed by their Creator with certain unalienable Rights, that among these are Life, Liberty, and the pursuit of Happiness."

If modern society loses belief in the transcendent nature of the human made in God's image, is there any other foundation on which to build the values of equality and respect for the rights of all? The systematic abuse of human rights in officially atheistic regimes, such as the former Soviet Union, is one reason to suggest that the answer is no.

Jesus Christ: the Model of Humanity 7.20

In the Christian view, Jesus Christ models what it means to be truly human. Although considered divine, the tradition insists that Jesus was still truly human in every way: "For we do not have a high priest who is unable to sympathize with our weaknesses, but one who has similarly been tested in every way, yet without sin" (Heb 4:15).

Unlike Adam, the representative of humans fallen into sin, Christ perfectly represents the human potential to give up temptations to selfishness and to live a life of obedience to God's will. Paradoxically, it is in giving up the selfish life that a person becomes free to be truly and fully human—to live a fulfilling life of love and service toward others.

From a Christian perspective, the transcendent destiny of humanity has already been fulfilled in Jesus as well. Jesus is the model of how each person will be raised from the dead; his perfected and glorified earthly body has already been raised. He is now in heaven, existing in perfect harmony and love with the Father and the Holy Spirit. In the Christian vision, the destiny of all humans is to one day join him in that harmony and love.

Questions about the Text

1. What is meant by the term *Christian anthropology*?
2. Describe each of the three major periods in the Christian theological view of history.
3. How does the Christian view of the body compare with the view of the body in Gnosticism or Platonism?
4. Explain how the Catholic understanding of creation, Incarnation, sacraments, and the resurrection of the body reflect the respect Christians have for the body and the physical world.
5. Explain the traditional Christian understanding of the resurrection of the body, especially the apostle Paul's teaching and the Resurrection appearances of Jesus.
6. Discuss ways in which the Christian tradition has described a person's soul and how that soul is different from any other created reality, including animals.
7. In the Christian view, why does God allow free will, if people abuse their free will to cause harm and suffering to others?
8. Summarize the Reformation debates about free will, as well as the main points of agreement expressed in the Lutheran-Catholic *Joint Declaration on Justification*.
9. How is *sin* defined in the Christian tradition, and what are some modern challenges to the concept of sin?
10. What is the traditional Christian understanding of original sin? Why do other religious traditions not accept this doctrine?
11. What are some challenges to the Christian doctrine of eternal punishment in hell?
12. Explain why hell can only be described using analogies.
13. Is it possible to believe that God is loving and forgiving and still believe in eternal punishment in hell?
14. Explain the basic Catholic understanding of purgatory. Why did Reformers reject this doctrine? Is it possible for Catholics and traditional Protestants to agree regarding this issue?

Discussion Questions

1. Summarize your own basic anthropology (view of human nature). How does it compare with traditional Christian anthropology?
2. What is your view of what happens to the body and soul after death? How does your view compare with the traditional Christian view?

3. Are you familiar with some accounts of "near death experiences"? How do the descriptions of the afterlife in these experiences compare with traditional Christian teaching?

4. Do you agree that the concept of sin is losing meaning in modern society? If so, what factors do you think are contributing to this decline?

5. Describe the traditional Catholic doctrine on hell and purgatory. Do you agree or disagree with it? Explain.

The Catholic View of Scripture

Inspiration and Inerrancy

What Is Scripture?   8.1

The word *scripture* (from the Latin *scripto*, "to write") simply means "writing." In religious traditions, however, the word means "holy writings" or "authoritative writings."

Virtually all religious traditions that have a written language have scriptures: writings those traditions consider holy and authoritative. Judaism has the *Tanak*: the Torah, Prophets, and Writings, which Christians call the Hebrew Scriptures or Old Testament. Islam has the Qur'an. The Hindu tradition has the Vedas. Theravada Buddhists have the Pali Canon, while the Mahayana Buddhist tradition has other scriptures, such as the Lotus Sutra. Nonliterate traditions also have something analogous to scripture in their sacred stories of the gods and spirits.

While Christian Scripture today includes both the Old Testament and New Testament, the earliest Christians had only the Jewish Scriptures. Thus all references to *Scripture* in the New Testament refer to these Jewish sacred writings. It was only through a gradual process that the Church developed and recognized a separate body of writings that would come to be called the New Testament.

Scripture within God's Revelation   8.2

The Second Vatican Council's document *Dei Verbum* (*DV*, Dogmatic Constitution on Divine Revelation) understands Scripture as part of God's overall plan of revelation. God created all things through his Word (John 1:3), and for this reason, people are able to recognize God's power and design through creation.

At the end of God's long process of special revelation to Israel, *DV* explains, the Word became human in Jesus: the ultimate revelation (John 1:14).

Dei Verbum states that Jesus gave his closest followers, the apostles, the authority to hand down his revelation to future generations. This apostolic tradition was passed along through Scripture—writings that became the New Testament—and tradition, which include practices such as the celebration of baptism and the Eucharist. As *DV* expresses it, "Sacred tradition and Sacred Scripture form one sacred deposit of the word of God" (*DV*, no. 10).

In the Catholic tradition, the phrase "Word of God" is not simply identical with the Scriptures, as it also refers to God the Son, and it refers to the entire revelation of Christ handed on through the Bible and Church tradition. Pope Benedict XVI teaches, "All this helps us to see that, while in the Church we greatly venerate the sacred Scriptures, the Christian faith is not a 'religion of the book': Christianity is the 'religion of the word of God,' not of 'a written and mute word, but of the incarnate and living Word'" (*VD*, no. 7).[1]

Scripture: Divine and Human   8.3

In the Catholic understanding, Scripture has both a divine and a human aspect. Regarding its divine element, "God is the author of Sacred Scripture. 'The divinely revealed realties, which are contained and presented in the text of Sacred Scripture, have been written down under the inspiration of the Holy Spirit.'" (*CCC*, no. 105; *DV*, no. 11). The human element is just as clear: "In Sacred Scripture, God speaks to man in a human way" (*CCC*, no. 109; *DV*, no. 12).

Scripture, both human and divine, therefore, is analogous to the Incarnation of God's Son: "Indeed the words of God, expressed in the words of men, are in every way like human language, just as the Word of the eternal Father, when he took on himself the flesh of human weakness, became like men" (*CCC*, no. 101; *DV*, no. 13).

The remainder of this chapter focuses on two central theological beliefs about Scripture in the Catholic tradition: (1) it is inspired by God, and (2) it is inerrant.

Inspiration of Scripture   8.4

Christians commonly call the Bible the "Word of God." By this, Christians do not imply that God wrote the Bible directly but that God "inspired" human authors to write. What does this belief in God's inspiration of Scripture mean in practical terms? Exploring two basic questions can clarify its meaning:

---

1. Benedict quotes from Saint Bernard of Clairvaux.

1. How did God inspire the biblical authors? Did God dictate a message word for word to the author? Did God inspire an author more indirectly, guiding the author's writing without directly selecting the words for him?

2. How did God's inspiration affect the author? When God inspires an author, does God share all divine knowledge with him or only a limited amount? Does God's inspiration remove the possibility of any human limitations or errors?

To explore the Catholic approach to these questions, this chapter will give primary attention to the Vatican II teaching on revelation, *Dei Verbum*,[2] and will draw further clarification from the Pontifical Biblical Commission's (PBC) *The Interpretation of the Bible in the Church* (1993)[3] and Pope Benedict XVI's *VD*, a response to issues raised at an international synod of bishops held in 2008 on the theme, "The Word of God in the Life and Mission of the Church." Finally, the chapter will draw insights from some other Christian traditions, as virtually all Christian traditions have reflected theologically on God's inspiration of Scripture.

Because these theological topics are rather abstract, many concrete examples from Scripture are also considered.

The Word *Church* 8.5

In any discussion of inspiration and Scripture in the Catholic tradition, one must refer frequently to the term *Church*, because Scripture and Church are inseparably linked in Catholic belief. As used in this book, Church with a capital C generally refers to the one, holy, catholic, and apostolic Church referenced in the Nicene Creed. Vatican II's *Lumen Gentium* teaches that this one Church "subsists in" the Catholic Church (*LG*, no. 8). Essentially, this means that the one Church founded by Christ exists most fully and completely in the Catholic Church. Yet this one Church is also found, though in a less complete way, in other Christian churches (e.g., the Orthodox churches) and communities (e.g., the various Protestant churches) (sec. 13.17). The meaning of the word Church as used in Catholic theology, then, has some ambiguity. It can refer specifically to the Catholic Church alone, but can also refer to the wider existence of the Church outside of the Catholic Church. The reader should be aware of this ambiguity.

---

2. Donald Senior discusses *Dei Verbum* in a video available at *www.youtube.com/watch?v=1w ZA35-JycY* (time 0:01:03).

3. The PBC is a consultative body attached to the Vatican's *Congregation for the Doctrine of the Faith*. The text is accessible at *http://catholic-resources.org/ChurchDocs/PBC_Interp.htm*.

What Is Inspiration?   8.6

The apostle Paul's letter to Timothy states, "All Scripture is inspired by God" (2 Tim 3:16). The Greek word translated as "inspired" is *theopneustos*, meaning literally "God-breathed." Similarly, the English word *inspiration* is derived from the Latin verb *inspiro*, "to breathe into."[4]

The word for *breath* in both Greek (*pneuma*) and Latin (*spiritus*) can also mean "spirit." The Christian tradition presents a metaphorical picture of God inspiring the biblical authors—breathing his Spirit into them. The tradition consistently identifies the Holy Spirit as the inspirer of the scriptural authors. *Dei Verbum* affirms that,

The books of both the Old and New Testaments in their entirety, with all their parts, are sacred and canonical because written under the inspiration of the Holy Spirit, they have God as their author and have been handed on as such to the Church herself. (*DV*, no. 11)

Rembrandt's seventeenth-century painting of an angel dictating the words to Matthew as he writes his Gospel captures a common understanding of how God inspires the authors of Scripture.

Christian art has often portrayed the Holy Spirit inspiring a biblical author by means of an angel who dictates the words of Scripture.

Inspiration and Prophecy   8.7

Early Christians closely identified the inspiration of Scripture with the gift of prophecy. A New Testament writer says,

[W]e possess the prophetic message that is altogether reliable. . . . there is no prophecy of scripture that is a matter of personal interpretation, for no prophecy ever came through human will; but rather human

---

4. It should be noted that the passage in 2 Tim 3:16–17, seen in its historical context, refers only to the Scripture of what Christians today call the Old Testament; the books of the New Testament had not yet been recognized as books of the Scripture.

beings moved by the holy Spirit spoke under the influence of God. (2 Pet 1:19–21)

Early Christian apologists tended to think of God's inspiration of a biblical author as virtually the same as God's inspiration of a prophet—the Holy Spirit giving a message to a human.[5] The Christian apologist Justin Martyr (ca. 100–ca. 165 CE) wrote, "You must not suppose that they [scriptural passages] are spoken by the inspired [writers] themselves, but by the Divine Word who moves them" (*1 Apology* 36). Similarly, the apologist Athenagoras (ca. 133–190 CE) believed the biblical authors, "lifted in ecstasy above the natural operations of their minds by the impulses of the Divine Spirit, uttered the things with which they were inspired, the Spirit making use of them as a flute-player breathes into a flute" (*A Plea for the Christians* 9).

Aquinas does not write on biblical inspiration directly but seems to understand it within the category of prophetic inspiration.[6] Scholastic theologians such as Aquinas used the different types of cause in Aristotelian logic to describe the relationship between God and the inspired author: God is the primary efficient cause, and the human author is the instrumental cause of Scripture.[7] Scholastic authors, however, had different interpretations of "instrumental cause." Some thought this meant the Spirit used an author as a writer uses a pen—there is no true human influence in the process of writing. Other scholastics sought to give more credit to an author's free cooperation with the inspiring Spirit.[8]

The Relationship of God's Spirit and the Human Author in Inspiration   8.8

This scholastic discussion raises a key question in the theology of biblical inspiration: what is the exact relationship between the human and the divine? Does the Holy Spirit dictate the very words of Scripture and the author simply copy them down? At the other extreme, is the writing a thoroughly human process in which God is the ultimate cause of the writing, because God created the author and his intellect but otherwise does not interfere with the human author?

---

5. See Bruce Vawter, *Biblical Inspiration*, Theological Resources (Philadelphia: Westminster, 1972), 20–42.

6. Aquinas discusses biblical authors under the general heading of "Prophecy" (*ST* 2–2. 171–74), accessible at *www.ccel.org/ccel/aquinas/summa.SS_Q171.html*.

7. "In prophetic revelation the prophet's mind is moved by the Holy Ghost, as an instrument that is deficient in regard to the principal agent" (ST 2–2.173.4), accessible at *www.ccel.org/ccel/aquinas/summa.SS_Q173_A4.html*.

8. See Vawter, *Biblical Inspiration*, 43–75.

Dei Verbum affirms that because they were "written under the inspiration of the Holy Spirit," all biblical books have "God as their author [Latin: *auctor*]" (*DV*, no. 11). However, this phrase need not imply that God actually wrote the words. *Auctor* can mean "literary author" but also "source" or "originator."[9]

Dei Verbum, at several points, affirms human involvement in the process of writing. God made use of the sacred writers' "powers and abilities" so that they were "true authors" (*DV*, no. 11). In Scripture, "God speaks to men in human fashion," and a central task of the biblical interpreter is to "investigate what meaning the sacred writers really intended" (*DV*, no. 12).

In the end, however, according to *Dei Verbum*, one cannot separate the human author and the Holy Spirit: the author wrote "only those things which He [God] wanted" (no. 11), the meaning that the author intended is "what God wanted to manifest by means of their word" (no. 12), and "everything asserted by the inspired authors . . . must be held to be asserted by the Holy Spirit" (no. 11).

Beyond these general statements, however, the Church gives little guidance on exactly *how* a biblical author is inspired, whether through vision, direct dictation, or indirect motivation. It does insist that any theory about inspiration must do justice both to the true divine authorship of the scriptural books and the true human authorship of those same books.

Inspiration and Concrete Examples   8.9

Fr. Raymond E. Brown (1928–1998) was a leading American Catholic biblical scholar, appointed to the Pontifical Biblical Commission in 1972 by Pope Paul VI and, again, in 1996 by Pope John Paul II. To gain a more concrete sense of how biblical inspiration actually works, Brown insists that one should not start with *a priori* assumptions but with the concrete evidence of actual biblical texts and then build theories of how inspiration works.[10] The following sections take Brown's advice.

Luke's Introduction   8.9.1

A good place to start is the Gospel of Luke in the New Testament, because Luke provides concrete information about how he wrote his account of the life, death, and Resurrection of Jesus.

Luke lived in the generation after Jesus and his first disciples and did not know Jesus directly. In his introduction, Luke tells his reader how he received his information. The following table sets down Luke's introduction along with some explanatory comments.

---

9. See Raymond F. Collins, "Inspiration," in *NJBC*, 1027–28.

10. R. E. Brown, *The Critical Meaning of the Bible* (New York: Paulist Press, 1981), 18–19.

Luke 1	Explanatory Comments
1:1: "many have undertaken to compile a narrative of the events that have been fulfilled among us, . . . "	Luke acknowledges that many people have passed down accounts about Jesus and his first followers, although Luke does not specify whether the accounts were oral or written. Most biblical scholars believe that Luke wrote approximately fifty years after the death of Jesus.
1:2: "those who were eyewitnesses from the beginning and ministers of the word have handed them down to us,"	Because Luke lived after the time of Jesus, he must rely on the accounts of eyewitnesses, who heard and saw Jesus, and on "ministers of the word," who passed down these accounts either in oral or written form. The "ministers of the word" apparently were Christians who made sure the accounts about Jesus were taught accurately.
1:3–4: "I too have decided, after investigating everything accurately anew, to write it down in an orderly sequence for you, most excellent Theophilus, so that you may realize the certainty of the teachings you have received."	Luke personally checked the accuracy of these accounts, put them in order, and used them as sources in writing his story of Jesus. He now sends his completed Gospel to a man named Theophilus, most likely a recently baptized Christian and Luke's patron—the person who supported Luke financially while he worked on his Gospel. Ancient authors often dedicated their works to patrons. Luke hopes his account will help Theophilus become more confident about the accuracy of the oral teaching about Jesus that Theophilus had already received.

Luke's introduction shows that he worked much like any historian in ancient or modern times: He gathered accounts from eyewitnesses, checked the accounts for accuracy, and arranged them in a logical or chronological sequence.

The Christian theologian accepts, on faith, the Church's teaching that, as a biblical author, Luke was inspired by the Holy Spirit. Examining Luke's statements, a theologian can draw the reasonable conclusion that inspiration by the Holy Spirit does not necessarily imply divine, word-for-word dictation. Luke never hints that the Holy Spirit whispered in his ear—rather, he says that he gathered his information in a thoroughly human manner. God's inspiration, then, must work through ordinary human practices of writing. In fact, it seems that the inspired author need not know or think of himself as "inspired" at all—Luke's account certainly gives no indication of this awareness.

Inspiration and the Use of Sources by Biblical Writers   8.9.2

Like Luke, biblical authors clearly use a variety of human sources in their compositions. In the Old Testament, Ezra quotes from a copy of a letter from the Persian king Artaxerxes (Ezra 7:12–26). The Book of Proverbs includes collections of wise sayings from various sources, including sayings from Lemuel, king of Massa (Prov 31:1). These biblical authors made use of conventional human sources just as other historians or collectors of wise sayings do.

Inspiration and Paul's Letters   8.9.3

Paul, author of many New Testament books, similarly shows little or no awareness of being directly inspired by the Holy Spirit in his writing. Rather, Paul is focused on the human business of corresponding with his fellow Christians, often writing about very mundane, practical issues: "Greet Prisca and Aquila, my co-workers" (Rom 16:3); "have a little wine for the sake of your stomach" (1 Tim 5:23); "When you come, bring the cloak I left with Carpus in Troas" (2 Tim 4:13). Again, if one accepts from Church teaching that Paul is inspired, the evidence suggests that this inspiration worked through Paul's thoughts, practical concerns, and personality.

Paul does indeed show an awareness of the Spirit's guidance in his teaching: "I think that I too have the Spirit of God" (1 Cor 7:40; see also 1 Cor 14:37). However, Paul's letters give no indication that he thought the Spirit was directly guiding his writing

Inspiration and the Prophets   8.9.4

One type of biblical writing is seemingly based on direct inspiration from God: the words of the prophets. In the book of the prophet Jeremiah, for example, Jeremiah asserts that God spoke to him directly, and then quotes God's words: "The word of the Lord came to me: 'Before I formed you in the womb I knew you, before you were born I dedicated you'" (Jer 1:5). Jeremiah then says explicitly, "Then the Lord extended his hand and touched my mouth, saying to me, 'See, I place my words in your mouth!'" (Jer 1:9). Jeremiah and other prophets also report receiving visions from God (e.g., Jer 1:11–12; Isa 1:1; Micah 1:1; Habakkuk 1:1) along with God's words.

As a rule, prophets in ancient Israel would deliver their prophecies orally. Jeremiah is told, "Stand at the gate of the house of the Lord, and proclaim this message there: 'Hear the word of the Lord, all you of Judah who enter these gates to worship the Lord'" (Jer 7:2). The prophetic words were only written down at a later stage, as the book reports, "Baruch . . . wrote down on a scroll, what Jeremiah said, all the words which the Lord had spoken to him" (Jer 36:4).

Even in the case of the prophets, then, Scripture does not give a model of completely direct inspiration. Although one may take it on faith that the prophets did receive a divine message, the recording of that message inevitably involved a human process: a scribe such as Baruch had to write down the words, and that manuscript, in turn, was copied and distributed to others. Even in the cases of direct prophetic inspiration, the words are not recorded in the Bible without a human process of dictation, writing, copying, and distribution.

Inspiration and the Ten Commandments — 8.9.5

What about the Ten Commandments recorded in Scripture, commandments that were reportedly "inscribed by God's own finger" on tablets of stone (Exod 31:18; Deut 9:10) and given to Moses? Isn't this an example of a direct message from God without human influence?

The short answer is no. Even if one accepts the historical accuracy of the biblical accounts, the stone tablets are not available for verification. Further, when one examines the biblical record, some critical questions arise, because there are actually two scriptural versions of the Ten Commandments (Exod 20:1–17; Deut 5:6–21). While several of the commandments are the same in both versions, others differ. A striking example is the commandment to keep the Sabbath (compare Exod 20:8–11 and Deut 5:12–15).

The basic commandment to keep the Sabbath is the same in both versions, but the rationale for keeping the Sabbath is completely different. If one assumes that Scripture recorded God's words exactly, one is forced to ask: Which version was the original written by God?

The Ten Commandments are part of a much larger collection of God's laws for Israel recorded in Exodus and Deuteronomy. Comparing a pattern of similarity and difference between the law codes in these books, scholars reasonably conclude that the code in Exodus 21–23 "reflects a political, social, and religious situation of Israelite society different from that reflected in the other law codes preserved in Deuteronomy (chs. 12–16) and in Leviticus (the holiness code, chs. 17–26)."[11] In other words, the way in which God's divinely inspired commandments are recorded is shaped by human political, social, and religious influences. Different authors and editors at different points in Israel's history recorded the books of Exodus and Deuteronomy.

---

11. PBC, *The Interpretation of the Bible in the Church*, I.A.4.

Inspiration and Textual Criticism   8.10

Theories about inspiration usually hold that the original author and the original writing are inspired. This belief is reflected in the influential 1978 *Chicago Statement on Biblical Inerrancy*: "WE AFFIRM that the whole of Scripture and all its parts, *down to the very words of the original*, were given by divine inspiration" (no. 6, emphasis added).[12]

One critical problem with the belief that original writings of the scriptural books are verbally inspired is that no original text of any book of the Bible is known to exist. Modern scholars possess only copies of these original writings, handwritten by ancient scribes, but no two of these copies are exactly the same. Through a process known as textual criticism, scholars study these copies in an attempt to recover the original wording.

Although scholars do not have access to the originals—known technically as autographs—modern readers can still have a great deal of confidence that they are reading accurate texts.[13] In the case of the New Testament, for example, scholars can compare nearly six thousand handwritten, ancient Greek manuscripts. This number is far more than is available for the writings of most ancient authors; typically scholars have fewer than twenty manuscripts of works by ancient Greek or Latin authors. In addition, several NT manuscripts, although fragmentary, date within 100 years of the original writings. Again this contrasts favorably with other ancient writings; the oldest manuscript of the Roman historian Tacitus, for example, dates 800 years after the original.

In most cases, the variations among New Testament manuscripts are differences of spelling and word order that do not affect the sense.

A small number of variants are more significant. For example, a majority of manuscripts include Mark 16:9–20, but the earliest Greek manuscripts lack these verses. For this and a variety of other reasons, most textual critics believe those verses were not part of Mark's original Gospel; *The Catholic Study Bible* indicates these verses by including the text in brackets.[14] Yet as the notes to *The Catholic Study Bible* indicate, this passage "has traditionally been accepted as part of the gospel and was defined as such by the Council of Trent."[15]

---

12. Nearly 300 evangelical leaders, including J. I. Packer, Francis Schaeffer, and R. C. Sproul, signed the *Chicago Statement on Biblical Inerrancy*, *www.bible-researcher.com/chicago1.html*.

13. See Daniel B. Wallace, "The Reliability of the New Testament Manuscripts," in *Understanding Scripture: An Overview of the Bible's Origin, Reliability, and Meaning*, eds. W. Grudem, C. J. Collins, and T. R. Schreiner (Wheaton, IL: Crossway, 2012), 111–20. Wallace describes his work to preserve biblical texts by photographing all known Greek New Testament manuscripts in a video accessible at *www.youtube.com/watch?v=cp1nF_GgC_0&feature=c4-overview&list=UUW-WeT-LcpA85I2edobmf41w* (time 0:03:28).

14. See Bruce M. Metzger and Bart D. Ehrman, *The Text of the New Testament: Its Transmission, Corruption, and Restoration*, 4th ed. (Oxford: Oxford University Press, 2005), 322–26.

15. *Catholic Study Bible*, eds. Donald Senior, John J. Collins, and Mary Ann Getty (New York: Oxford University Press, 2006),1432.

As discussed in the following section, historical-critical studies have shown that the Gospel of Mark is not unique. In several cases, studies show that additions were made to the original versions of biblical books before they were officially accepted as Scripture. These findings, then, seem to rule out the possibility that *only* the original (autograph) is inspired—inspiration would necessarily apply to these later additions as well.

Inspiration and Multiple Authors   8.11

In traditional discussions about inspiration, theologians assume that a single author wrote a particular biblical book. This assumption works well in some cases: Historical and literary studies support that Paul was indeed the single author of such letters as Romans and Galatians.

However, a critical evaluation of biblical books reveals that many had more than one author. This is clear, for example, at the ending of the Gospel of John, when the text states, "It is this disciple who testifies to these things and has written them, and we know that his testimony is true" (John 21:24). Who is speaking in this passage? If "this disciple," called the "disciple whom Jesus loved" (John 21:7), is the main author of the Gospel, there must be at least one other author or editor who was involved in writing the Gospel and who in 21:24 comments on the trustworthiness of the disciple's testimony.[16]

Evidence of a complex literary process in other biblical books exists as well. Notice the differences when one compares accounts of God's creation in the first two chapters of Genesis.

Genesis 1:1–2:3	Genesis 2:4–25
• God is called "God" (in Hebrew, Elohim).	• God is called "Lord God" (in Hebrew, Yahweh Elohim).
• Creation occurs in six days.	• No timeframe for creation is given.
• Fish, birds, and land animals (1:20–25) are created first, humans last (1:26–27).	• Man is formed first (2:7), before the plants (2:5) and before the animals (2:19–20).
• God creates humans in the divine image, male and female (1:27).	• Lord God forms Adam (2:7) and then later Eve from his rib (2:21–22).
• God creates things by speaking ("Let there be").	• Lord God forms things by working with his hands (2:7, 19, 22).

---

16. For a discussion of the current text of John as a revision of earlier editions, see Pheme Perkins, "John," in *Catholic Study Bible*, 412–13.

194 REASON, FAITH, AND TRADITION

One can see from this comparison why many scholars believe that there were originally two stories of creation that were combined by a later editor. Scholars have labeled these hypothetical sources the Priestly (P) source (Gen 1) and the Yahwist (J) source (Gen 2).[17]

Finally, consider what modern scholarship concludes about a composition such as the Book of Judges. Stories in Judges likely began as oral traditions passed down by various tribes. After circulating for centuries, they were gathered into two written collections: a northern (Israel) and a southern (Judah) collection. An editor (or editors) eventually united the two collections. After the Babylonian Exile (after 587 BCE), the same editors who put together the Book of Deuteronomy further edited the Book of Judges. Finally, another editor added more material, including an introduction and appendices. The entire process took some eight hundred years.[18]

Scripture and Conversion   8.12

In a famous passage in *Confessions*, Augustine describes how reading Scripture was a key to his conversion. As a young man, Augustine was attracted to the Christian faith but part of him still desired to cling to his old self-centered, pleasure-seeking way of life. One day, as he sat in a friend's garden, tormented by his own indecision, he began to weep uncontrollably. Suddenly, he heard a child's voice from a neighboring house, chanting in a singsong rhythm, "Take up and read. Take up and read." In an instant, Augustine stopped weeping, trying to remember if this chant was part of a children's song or game. He could not recall hearing it before, and he interpreted the voice as a commandment of God: "Take up the Scriptures and read the first thing that you find there."

Augustine thought back to a story he had read about St. Anthony: the great founder of monasticism had been converted to following Christ when he happened to hear the words of the Gospel, "Go, sell what you have and give to [the] poor . . . then come, follow me" (Mark 10:21).

Augustine then opened a volume of Paul's letters that was lying nearby. He read, "not in orgies and drunkenness, not in promiscuity and licentiousness, not in rivalry and jealousy. But put on the Lord Jesus Christ, and make no provision for the desires of the flesh" (Rom 13:13–14). By the time he finished reading the sentence, Augustine's mind was calm; "by a light as it were of serenity infused into my heart, all the darkness of doubt vanished away." He had made his decision (*Confessions* 9.12).

17. See Lawrence Boadt, "Genesis" in *Catholic Study Bible*, 102–3.

18. See Vawter, *Biblical Inspiration*, 104–5.

The extended process involved in writing the Book of Judges is not an isolated exception. Scholarship has shown that the Book of Isaiah, for example, is composed of different sections that were written over a period of centuries.[19] This historical-critical evidence seems to call for a more social concept of biblical inspiration; inspiration must apply not only to single authors, but also to a group of authors or editors, or perhaps a "school," composing some inspired books of Scripture over a period of centuries.[20] James Barr, Old Testament scholar and minister of the Church of Scotland, writes,

> If there is inspiration at all, then it must extend over the entire process of production that has led to the final text. Inspiration therefore must attach not to a small number of exceptional persons . . . it must extend over a larger number of anonymous persons . . . it must be considered to belong more to the community as a whole.[21]

The PBC's 2014 statement, *The Inspiration and Truth of Sacred Scripture*, concurs: "The prophetic charism was certainly active in these anonymous redactors" (no. 143).

Inerrancy and Inspiration   8.13

Pope Benedict and the 2008 bishops' synod noted a close connection "between the theme of inspiration and that *of the truth of the Scriptures.*"[22] Thus Christians have traditionally linked God's inspiration with **inerrancy**, meaning "incapable of making a mistake." As applied to Scripture, *inerrancy* refers to the belief that God protected the biblical authors from making errors.

Many writers, both Catholic and non-Catholic, have assumed that inspiration and inerrancy logically cannot be separated. If God, who is perfect, inspired an author to write, then it follows that the author's writing must also be perfect—inerrant, or without mistakes.

Theological theories of inerrancy are closely tied with issues of the authority or trustworthiness of Scripture. If there are mistakes in Scripture, how can it be trusted? The issue of the trustworthiness of Scripture is critical, because as Aquinas writes, "our faith rests upon the revelation made to the apostles and prophets, who wrote the canonical books" (*ST* 1.1.8). One wants to be sure that the foundation is solid.

---

19. See Richard J. Clifford" in *Catholic Study Bible*, 280–81.

20. For "social theories" of inspiration, see Collins, "Inspiration," in *NJBC*, 1032.

21. Quoted in ibid.

22. Benedict XVI, *VD*, no. 19, is accessible at *www.vatican.va/holy_father/benedict_xvi /apost_exhortations/documents/hf_ben-xvi_exh_20100930_verbum-domini_en.html.*

Strict Inerrancy, Limited Inerrancy, and the Nature of Truth

8.13.1

The *Chicago Statement* affirms, "Scripture, having been given by divine inspiration, is infallible, so that, far from misleading us, it is true and reliable in all the matters it addresses" (art. 11). The scope of this inerrancy is clearly expressed in the introduction to the statement: "Scripture is without error or fault in all its teaching, no less in what it states about God's acts in creation, about the events of world history, and about its own literary origins under God, than in its witness to God's saving grace in individual lives" (art. 4). Scripture has no errors regarding any topic, including how the world was created and historical events. One can refer to this view that the Bible has no mistake of any kind as *strict inerrancy*.

Strict inerrancy has been a traditional doctrine of the Catholic Church. Aquinas quotes Augustine, "Only those books of Scripture which are called canonical have I learned to hold in such honor as to believe their authors have not erred in any way in writing them" (*ST* 1.1.8 ad. 2). Pope Leo XIII's encyclical *Providentissimus Deus* (1893) also taught that the belief in inspiration is incompatible with a belief in any error (nos. 20–21). Pope Pius XII's encyclical *Divino Afflante Spiritu* (no. 1), reiterated Pope Leo's teaching. Furthermore, both popes rejected the suggestion that the inerrancy of Scripture is limited to matters of faith and morals; they believed that all statements of the Bible (including historical statements) are inerrant.

Dei Verbum, however, is more cautious in its discussion of inerrancy. Because the authors were inspired by the Holy Spirit, the document explains, the biblical books teach "solidly, faithfully and without error that truth which God wanted put into sacred writings for the sake of salvation" (*DV*, no. 11).

Dei Verbum's teaching has been interpreted in different ways. Some Catholic interpreters maintain the traditional view, that Scripture has no error of any kind, since any kind of error is incompatible with the belief that God inspired the Scriptures.[23] Other Catholic scholars understand the wording of *Dei Verbum* to have placed a limitation on the truth that Scripture teaches "without error." The truth that is "without error" is the truth that is recorded "for the sake of our salvation." This interpretation leaves open the possibility that other biblical information that is not necessary for salvation (for example, historical details or descriptions of nature) could contain errors.[24] This second view is sometimes labeled as limited inerrancy, the belief that only the truths necessary for salvation are to be considered inerrant.[25]

---

23. For example, Brian W. Harrison, "Does Vatican Council II Allow for Errors in Sacred Scripture?" *Living Tradition: Organ of the Roman Theological Forum* (2010) is accessible at *www.rtforum .org/lt/lt145-6.html.*

24. For a discussion of these points, see Collins, "Inspiration,"1030.

25. On this interpretation, see Joseph Fitzmyer, *The Interpretation of Scripture: In Defense of the Historical-Critical Method* (New York: Paulist Press, 2008), 8.

The Pontifical Biblical Commission's 2014 document, *The Inspiration and Truth of Sacred Scripture*, supports this second approach. It clarifies that *Dei Verbum* should not be understood to mean that biblical truth "concerns only those parts of the Sacred Book that are necessary for faith and morality, to the exclusion of other parts" (no. 63). Rather, since all of scripture is inspired, then all of scripture must be true. The key is determine the nature of this truth.

After an extensive overview of biblical evidence, the PBC concludes, "the truth which the Bible wishes to communicate to us regards God himself and his plan of salvation for human beings" (no. 104). Specifically, "it is undeniable that *Dei Verbum*, with the expression "the truth . . . for the sake for our salvation" (no. 11),[26] restricts biblical truth to divine revelation which concerns God himself and the salvation of the human race" (105). Benedict XVI affirmed the essential connection between inspiration and truth but stated that "one must acknowledge the need today for a fuller and more adequate study of these realities" [i.e., of inspiration and truth] (*VD*, no. 19).

The PBS's *Inspiration and Truth* responds to Benedict's challenge. The following sections also seek to contribute to this task.

The Differing Truths of Differing Genres   8.14

Because the Scriptures were written by human authors, a major task of interpretation is to understand the intention of the human author: "in order to see clearly what God wanted to communicate to us, [the interpreter] should carefully investigate what meaning the sacred writers really intended" (*DV*, no. 12). An important step toward this goal is to determine the literary form of a biblical text. This is because knowing the literary form (e.g., history, poetry, prophesy) helps the interpreter grasp the meaning intended by the sacred author. The interpreter must further study how the author used "contemporary literary forms in accordance with the situation of his own time and culture" (*DV*, no. 12).

Most Christians would agree that Jesus' parables are not meant as literal historical facts: Jesus told stories to illustrate points. Thus in Jesus' story of the son who wastes his father's inheritance but eventually repents and is forgiven (Luke 15:11–32), few would insist that the details of the story must be literally true. The truth of Jesus' parable, therefore, is not a historical truth but an ethical lesson on repentance and forgiveness.

The Parable Genre of Jonah   8.14.1

What about the story related in the Book of Jonah? If one reads the book literally, it presents Jonah as a prophet every bit as historical as Jeremiah: "The word of the Lord came to Jonah" (Jon 1:1).

---

26. Harrison, "Errors in Sacred Scripture?" *Living Tradition*, accessible at *www.rtforum.org/lt /lt145-6.html.*

However, as one reads the story, one finds several unbelievable details. A "great fish" swallows Jonah, and he remains in its belly for three days (Jon 2:1). In the main action of the story, Jonah preaches to the people of Nineveh for one day, and they repent and believe God's message (3:5). How is this possible, historically speaking? The Assyrian people of Nineveh believed in their own gods, and no doubt, the vast majority had never even heard of the God of Israel. How could they have been converted by one sermon? On an even more basic level, how would the Assyrian-speaking people even have understood the Hebrew-speaking Jonah?

Some would answer these historical-critical questions by relying on faith. If one accepts that God can perform miracles, why can't one say God sent a miraculous fish and caused the Ninevites to understand Jonah and believe miraculously in the God of Israel instead of their own gods? However, notice that the author of Jonah never presents the events as miracles. He simply narrates the events in a straightforward manner.

The key is for the modern interpreter to understand the literary genre of Jonah. The author of Jonah did not intend to present a historical report about a prophet. Ancient Israelite readers would have recognized the exaggerated and wildly improbable elements of the story—they would have known, for example, that the Assyrians were the bitter enemies of Israel and had not the remotest interest in worshipping Israel's God.

The literary genre of Jonah, therefore, is not history but parable.[27] It is, in fact, intended to be humorous in its portrayal of a string of implausible events, starting with a prophet who hears the word of the Lord but instead of preaching it, as prophets are supposed to do, tries to escape from the Lord by sailing away in a ship![28]

As a parable, Jonah is a story intended to teach a lesson. It was intended to point out, in an entertaining way, that the God of Israel is concerned not only with the salvation of the people of Israel but also with the salvation of non-Jews, including the salvation of Israel's historical enemies, the Assyrians.

Job as a Didactic Story 8.14.2

The Book of Job raises critical questions—not so much historical or scientific questions as theological and ethical ones. In the first chapter, God essentially makes a bet with Satan to see whether Job will remain faithful to God, allowing Satan to test Job—a test that includes killing all of Job's children, destroying all his wealth, and afflicting him with a terrible skin disease (Job 1). Are people really to believe that a loving God would make such cruel deals with Satan?

On these ethical grounds alone, people have good reason to question whether Job is literally true. Augustine (354–430 CE) developed this principle of biblical interpretation: "Whatever there is in the word of God that cannot,

---

27. John J. Collins "Jonah," in *Catholic Study Bible*, 357. See also PBC, *Inspiration and Truth*, no. 110.
28. Ibid.

when taken literally, be referred either to purity of life or soundness of doctrine, you may set down as figurative."[29]

Another clue that the story is not meant to be historical is its almost complete lack of specific references to historical time and place. The only locater is the very general beginning sentence: "In the land of Uz there was a blameless and upright man named Job" (Job 1:1).

One can reasonably conclude that Job is meant as a didactic story. The biblical scholar Dianne Bergant calls the first and concluding chapters "a prose folktale" to which poetic dialogues have been added.[30] The clear purpose of the opening scenes involving God and Satan, along with the additional speeches and dialogue, is to deal, in a dramatic manner, with the question of why good people suffer. In order to dramatize the issue, the author or authors develop a story of a good man, Job, who suffers terrible tragedies.

The truth of Job is not a historical, literal truth. Its truth emerges in its wrestling with answers to the age-old question of why bad things happen to good people and in its conclusion that a person should continue to trust God even when answers to such questions are beyond human understanding (Job 38).

Cultural Limitations on Scriptural Truth   8.15

Previous examples (secs. 8.9.1–5) show that inspired authors work and think very much as any human author does; they are true human authors (*DV*, no. 11), and to be human is to be part of a particular human culture. The biblical authors lived in ancient Hebrew, Jewish, and Hellenistic cultures. The biblical evidence suggests that God's inspiration did not release them from the moral and intellectual limitations of those cultures. The following sections consider some specific examples.

Cultural Limitations on Scientific Knowledge   8.15.1

The biblical authors lived and wrote in a time before modern science. It is hardly surprising, then, that they thought that the sun literally moved across the sky, as this passage from the book of Joshua demonstrates: "Joshua prayed . . . : Sun, stand still at Gibeon, Moon, in the valley of Aijalon! The sun stood still, the moon stayed. . . . The sun halted halfway across the heavens; not for an entire day did it press on" (Jos 10:12–13).

Pope Leo XIII, in his 1893 encyclical *Providentissimus Deus* (On the Study of Holy Scripture), also recognized the scientific limitations of the biblical authors. He explains that in Scripture, the Holy Spirit does not intend to teach scientific knowledge but uses "terms which were commonly used at the time," or

---

29. Augustine, *On Christian Doctrine*, 3.14, is accessible at *www.ccel.org/ccel/augustine/doctrine .xi_2.html*.

30. Dianne Bergant, "Job," in *Catholic Study Bible*, 237.

describes things as they appear to the senses, so that God's message was put in the way "men could understand and were accustomed to" (no. 18). Thus when Joshua describes the sun as moving across the sky, this is not a scientific statement but a description of what humans apparently observe.

In the Catholic view, it is a mistake to regard the creation accounts in Genesis as scientific reports. The biblical authors were not intending to teach science but were using ordinary language or describing common-sense understandings of things to express theological points.

When Genesis reports that God created the universe in six days and rested on the seventh, this also is not intended as a scientific statement. Rather, the author seems to have used the literary framework of creation in six days to tell the creation story to an ancient Israelite audience (who also worked for six days and rested on the seventh) in a way in which they could relate. The PBC notes that the six-day framework "intends to communicate . . . that there exit an order and purpose in creation" (*Inspiration and Truth*, no. 67).

The creation stories convey profound theological messages, teaching humans essential truths: the all-powerful, all-good God, not the "lesser" god of the Gnostics, created all things good in the beginning; in particular, he created humans in his own divine image. Interpreters can, and have, written literally hundreds of volumes delving deeper into the theological messages of the creation stories. It is important not to miss the theological messages of Genesis by misreading[31] it and assuming it has a scientific purpose.

Cultural Limitations on Ethical Values   8.15.2

Although certainly ethical evil exists still today, many would agree that the human race as a whole has made ethical progress over the centuries. The modern world, for the most part, has gained a better understanding of the dignity and equality of all people, for example. This enlarged understanding has led us to such ethical advances as the abolition of slavery and increased opportunities for women.

Because the biblical authors wrote as members of ancient cultures, they shared many of the ethical limitations of their cultures. To take just one example: The biblical authors shared in the ancient world's general acceptance of the institution of slavery as natural and normal—a view accepted by the great philosophers Plato and Aristotle, for instance. The great patriarchs of Hebrew history, such as Abraham (Gen 12:16), Isaac (Gen 24:35), and Jacob (Gen 32:6), all owned slaves. One of the Ten Commandments presupposes ownership of slaves (see Exod 20:10). Even in the New Testament, slavery is seen as normal: Paul's Letter to the Ephesians advises, "Slaves, be obedient to your human masters" (Eph 6:5), and Paul himself sent a runaway slave back to his master (Phil

---

31. Fr. Robert Barron comments on the misreading of Genesis in a video accessible at *www .youtube.com/watch?v=UVsbVAVSssc* (time 0:07:41).

1:15–16). It is true that Paul insists that masters should treat their slaves well (e.g., Eph 6:9), but neither Paul nor any other biblical writer challenges slavery as an institution.

That biblical texts suggest slavery is morally acceptable by no means implies that they are to be interpreted to mean that God views slavery as good. As Pope Benedict XVI explains,

> God's plan is manifested *progressively* and it is accomplished slowly, *in successive stages* and despite human resistance. God chose a people and patiently worked to guide and educate them. Revelation is suited to the cultural and moral level of distant times and thus describes facts and customs, such as cheating and trickery, and acts of violence and massacre, without explicitly denouncing the immorality of such things. This can be explained by the historical context. (*VD*, no. 42; emphasis original)

In other words, in the Catholic view, God works with people at their time and place, gradually educating them. References to slavery as normal reflect the human culture of the author's time, not God's intention.

Although the people of the biblical age were not ready to hear or understand the message that slavery is intrinsically evil, the seeds of that idea had already been planted in passages such as Gen 1:26 (all people are created in God's image) or Gal 2:28 (all are one in Christ Jesus). These seeds would bear fruit later, for example, when a series of papal protests against slavery culminated in Pope Gregory XVI's proclamation forbidding Catholics from engaging in slavery or the slave trade (in the 1839 encyclical *In Supremo Apostolatus*).

Development in Understanding Truth within the Bible
8.16

Within Scripture there is a dynamic process of reinterpretation.[32] The process occurs even within single books. Historical-critical studies have shown that books such as Isaiah grew and developed over centuries as new material was added to reinterpret and update the old in the light of new experiences of the people of Israel. At the time of the Babylonian Exile, the prophecies of "Deutero-Isaiah" were added to the centuries-old oracles of the original prophet Isaiah.[33] Following are some examples of development in belief:[34]

---

32. See the Pontifical Biblical Commission's *The Interpretation of the Bible in the Church* in *The Scripture Documents: An Anthology of Official Catholic Teachings*, ed. D. P. Béchard (Collegeville, MN: Liturgical, 2002), 284–89.

33. Richard J. Clifford, "Isaiah," in *Catholic Study Bible*, 280.

34. See "Rereadings," in Pontifical Biblical Commission, *Interpretation of the Bible in the Church*, III.A.1, accessible at *http://catholic-resources.org/ChurchDocs/PBC_Interp3.htm*.

Development in the View of the Afterlife   8.16.1

The early Hebrews believed that all the dead, good and bad, exist in a shadowy sort of way in Sheol (see Gen 37:35; Ps 9:18); in later passages, the belief in the resurrection of the dead and reward and punishment in heaven and hell appears (for example, Dan 12:2; Matt 25:31–46).

From the Old Testament to the New Testament   8.16.2

From a Christian perspective, a central movement or development in the Bible is from the Old Testament that reflects God's covenant relationship with the people of Israel—expressed especially in the Mosaic Law—to the New Testament that reflects God's new covenant relationship with people through Jesus Christ. The New Testament authors often refer to the Old Testament scriptures, seeing the fulfillment of these scriptures in the life, death, and Resurrection of Jesus.[35]

Traditionally, Christians have understood the development from the old covenant to the new in two ways:

1. The Mosaic laws, especially ritual laws, foreshadow later Christian beliefs or practices; for example, animal sacrifices foreshadow Christ's ultimate sacrifice of offering his life on the cross. The Letter to the Hebrews states, "He [Jesus] has no need, as did the high priests, to offer sacrifice day after day, first for his own sins and then for those of the people; he did that once for all when he offered himself" (Heb 7:27).

2. The Mosaic covenant prepared for the coming of the Messiah Jesus. Its deepest meaning would be fulfilled in Jesus, as he taught in Matthew, "Do not think that I have come to abolish the law or the prophets. I have come not to abolish but to fulfill." (Matt 5:17). Jesus also speaks of a "new covenant in my blood" (Luke 22:20).

That the Jewish people do not accept Jesus as the fulfillment of their Scriptures does not imply that Jews and Christians must be in a hostile relationship. Vatican II teaches, "Although the Church is the new people of God, the Jews should not be presented as rejected or accursed by God, as if this followed from the Holy Scriptures" (*NA*, no. 4). Pope Benedict XVI teaches similarly that differences between Jews and Christians "by no means implies mutual hostility. The example of Saint Paul (cf. Rom 9–11) shows, on the contrary, that "'an attitude of respect, esteem and love for the Jewish people is the only truly Christian attitude in the present situation, which is a mysterious part of God's wholly positive plan'" (*VD*, no. 43).[36]

---

35. See PBC, *Bible in the Church*, III.A.2; and Pope Benedict XVI, *VD*, no. 40–41.

36. Benedict quotes the 2001 PBC document, *The Jewish People and their Sacred Scriptures in the Christian Bible*, no. 87, accessible at *www.vatican.va/roman_curia/congregations/cfaith/pcb_documents /rc_con_cfaith_doc_20020212_popolo-ebraico_en.html*.

Truth as Dynamic Tension 8.16.3

Consider a few other developments within Scripture. Many of these developments are a result of a "dialogue" taking place on particular issues between authors who are separated by time and cultural perspective. Yet when the community, either of Israel or of the Church, places these divergent writings into the same collection of Scripture, fresh, dynamic insights often arise from the encounter.

Group Punishment and
Individual Responsibility 8.16.3.1

Sometimes the partial insights of an earlier time were challenged or complemented in later writings. Consider one of the Ten Commandments:

> For I, the Lord, your God, am a jealous God, inflicting punishment for their ancestors' wickedness on the children of those who hate me, down to the third and fourth generations. (Exod 20:5).

The Book of Ezekiel states,

> Only the one who sins shall die. The son shall not be charged with the guilt of his father, nor shall the father be charged with the guilt of his son. Justice belongs to the just, and wickedness to the wicked. (Ezek 18:20).

At the verbal level, the two statements flatly contradict each other: Exodus says that God punishes the children for their fathers' sins, and Ezekiel says God does not. Such a comparison involves a static concept of truth. Applying the idea of development within the biblical tradition, one can see that both passages express *partial* truths that must be held in tension to attain a fuller sense of the truth.

From the viewpoint of cultural anthropology, one can say that the cultural values evident in the Exodus passage emphasize the value of the social group over the individual; a person in such a culture would have a "group-oriented personality."[37] This perspective, common in ancient Mediterranean cultures, saw children not so much as independent persons in their own right but as family members who received their identity from the family as a whole. From this perspective, it would be natural to speak of the child being punished for the sins of the father.

One must also consider the anthropomorphic language of the Exodus passage. It is clear that God does not punish people for their sins, much less their parents' sins, in the same way that humans would punish. In fact, one could argue

---

37. See Bruce J. Malina, *The New Testament World: Insights from Cultural Anthropology*, rev. ed. (Louisville, KY: Westminster/John Knox, 1993), 65–73. See also the discussion on the value of the cultural anthropology approach in PBC, *Bible in the Church*, I.D.2.

that *punishment* is a misleading term. To say that "God punishes" can be understood as an anthropomorphic way of saying that human sin results in destructive consequences, which harm both sinners and their families (sec. 5.6.4). God's discipline, justice, and love are all involved in these negative consequences in ways that are not easy for humans to discern.

The Ezekiel passage, written at the time of the Babylonian Exile, centuries after the Exodus account, marks a development from the group-oriented perspective. By Ezekiel's time, the Jewish culture was able to view the individual more as an independent person responsible for his or her own actions.

One sees a development in ideas, but the partial truth of the earlier insight is still valid. If one were to consider the truth of both passages, one might say that together they provide a more holistic view of a person. Each person is ultimately responsible for his or her own actions, as Ezekiel saw. However, no person is an island—each individual is influenced profoundly, often in unconscious ways, by others around him or her, especially close friends and family—a truth to which the Exodus passage still witnesses today.

Are the Good Always Rewarded and the Bad Always Punished in this World?   8.16.3.2

Some passages present a black-and-white view that righteous people are always rewarded and the wicked are always punished:

[The righteous person] is like a tree
planted near streams of water,
that yields its fruit in season;
Its leaves never wither;
whatever he does prospers.
But not so are the wicked, not so!
They are like chaff driven by the wind. (Ps 1:3–4)

The book of Job passionately disputes this view as too simplistic. As Job complains, "Why do the wicked keep on living, grow old, become mighty in power?" (21:7). Against his friends' assumptions that his sufferings must be the result of his sins against God, Job insists on his innocence.

Both views contain truth, and the biblical reader is challenged to see how they relate. Wickedness always has some negative consequences, even if it only harms the wicked person's conscience and soul, and good behavior always has an intrinsic reward; yet Job is right to insist that the realities of life are too complex to be conveyed by simply asserting that God rewards the good and punishes the wicked in this life.

By the time of the later Old Testament writings, the concept of reward and punishment in the next world added a deeper dimension to these questions.

The Relationship of Faith, Action, and Salvation 8.16.3.3

Paul's Letter to the Romans says, "For we consider that a person is justified by faith apart from works of the law" (Rom 3:28). The Letter of James seems to flatly contradict Paul, "See how a person is justified by works and not by faith alone" (Jas 2:24).

As one studies the passages further, however, the tensions lessen. One finds that Paul refers specifically to following the Law, whereas James was referring to good actions in general. Taking insights from both, one might come to understand that true faith is always expressed through actions. Thus the truth of the whole of scripture is dynamic, as the PBC's *Interpretation of the Bible in the Church* sees,

> Granted that tensions can exist in the relationship between various texts of Sacred Scripture, interpretation must necessarily show a certain pluralism. No single interpretation can exhaust the meaning of the whole, which is a symphony of many voices." (III.A.3)

A recent method of reading the Bible as a whole—putting together different perspectives into a holistic vision—has been labeled "the canonical approach," with **canon** meaning the official collection of books understood as Scripture.[38] In truth, however, the **canonical** approach has been a fundamental method of interpreting Scripture from the beginning of Christianity. As *Dei Verbum* put it, "no less serious attention must be given to the content and unity of the whole of Scripture if the meaning of the sacred texts is to be correctly worked out" (*DV*, no. 13; see also *CCC*, no. 112).

Truth and Error in the Bible 8.17

In understanding truth and the trustworthiness of the Bible, then, one must pay special attention to the literary form in which a truth is expressed and to the cultural limitations of the authors. In addition to these considerations, it is clear that the Bible also contains what can only be called factual errors.

Consider the following example concerning the story of David and Goliath. The books of 1 and 2 Samuel and 1 Chronicles, whose authors intend to report historical events rather than didactic stories or parables, present conflicting versions of Goliath's death.

1. 1 Samuel reports that David killed the Philistine "Goliath of Gath" whose javelin shaft "was like a weaver's beam" (1 Sam 17:4–50, esp. 17:7).

2. A later account, however, states that a man named Elhanan killed Goliath: "There was another battle with the Philistines, in Gob, and Elhanan, son of

---

38. See *Interpretation of the Bible in the Church*, no. I.C.1.

Jair from Bethlehem, killed Goliath of Gath, whose spear shaft was like a weaver's beam" (2 Sam 21:19).

3. The author of 1 Chronicles, who used the books of Samuel as a source, saw the discrepancy and tried to smooth it out: "There was another battle with the Philistines, and Elhanan, the son of Jair, slew Lahmi, the brother of Goliath of Gath, whose spear shaft was like a weaver's beam" (1 Chron 20:5).

All three accounts cannot be historically accurate. Concerning the first two accounts, either David killed Goliath, or Elhanan did. One could possibly argue that two men were named "Goliath of Gath," both of whom owned a spear "like a weaver's beam," but this would be a stretch. It seems that two different versions of the same event exist. The author of Chronicles saw the historical problem and apparently tried to solve it by saying that Elhanan killed the brother of Goliath, not Goliath himself. It's unclear whether the author of Chronicles had additional information or simply changed the account so it would no longer be a contradiction.

Any theory of inspiration, therefore, must take into account that the biblical authors were not only limited in their understanding of truth but also plainly made errors in details.

The PBC's *Inspiration and Truth* is remarkably frank in this regard (no. 144). It acknowledges that many have questioned Scripture's reliability and claims to its divine origin due to "inaccuracies and contradictions of a geographical, historical, and scientific nature, which are rather frequent in the Bible." Yet, paradoxically, it is precisely through these weaknesses that the saving truth of Scripture is manifested: "in this very human weakness, the glory of the divine Word nonetheless shines through" (no. 149).

Inspiration, Error, and the Incarnation 8.17.1

Dei Verbum, as noted, draws an analogy between the Bible and the Incarnation, "For the words of God, expressed in human language, have been made like human discourse, just as the word of the eternal Father, when He took to Himself the flesh of human weakness, was in every way made like men" (no. 13). For Christians, the Bible has a divine aspect, but one must take seriously the "weakness" of the human aspect. This chapter has shown that Scripture reflects human limitations, at a cultural and ethical level. There seems to be no reason why the limitations might not also include the possibility of error in nonessential details. Just as Jesus took on all the weaknesses of human nature while still remaining God, so too, Scripture can reflect human weakness while still remaining the Word of God.[39]

---

39. In its discussion on fundamentalism, the PBC's *Interpretation of the Bible in the Church*, connects a certain type of fundamentalism with a failure to take the Incarnation seriously, "The basic problem with fundamentalist interpretation of this kind is that, refusing to take into account the historical nature of biblical revelation, it makes itself incapable of accepting the full truth of the Incarnation itself (I.F).

Toward a Communal Model of Inspiration 8.18

Having completed a discussion on inerrancy, one can return to the question of inspiration to draw some conclusions.

Traditional Christian views of biblical inspiration have been based on the paradigm of the Holy Spirit inspiring a single prophet to write a book, thus ensuring that God's word is recorded without any serious errors, or with no errors at all, if one follows strict inerrancy. In light of historical and critical study of how the biblical books were written, however, such a model is no longer adequate. Building on other theological beliefs from within the Catholic tradition, one can consider how the traditional model of inspiration might be adapted to reflect the more communal nature of biblical authorship.

Communal View of Inspiration: Israel and the Church 8.18.1

While Paul's Letter to the Galatians, for example, is the product of one author at one point in time, the authorship of many other biblical books is better understood as a process, sometimes involving multiple authors and editors, that lasted for centuries (sec. 8.11).

It seems appropriate to speak of the inspiration of the *community* in which oral and written traditions were passed down: the Old Testament took shape in the community of Israel, the New Testament in the community of the Church. This suggestion does not imply some vague notion that every member of the community was inspired in some way but, rather, the reasonable theological insight that the God who gathers people together as a community of faith also guides that community in its vital task of finding written expression of its fundamental beliefs and tasks in Scripture.

This idea of a more communal concept of inspiration is not new. It is one aspect of the Catholic understanding of the close relationship between Scripture, Church, and Tradition: Scripture cannot be properly understood apart from the believing community that recognizes, collects, and interprets the books that are themselves produced within the community. Thus *Dei Verbum* teaches, "sacred tradition, Sacred Scripture and the teaching authority of the Church . . . are so linked and joined together that one cannot stand without the others" (*DV*, no. 10).

The Canonization of Scripture 8.18.2

The books of the Bible are known as a canon. The Greek word *kanon* originally meant a measuring tool; metaphorically, then, it could be understood as a standard or rule by which more abstract ideas are evaluated. As applied to the Bible, *canon* refers to the authoritative list of books that, according to the faith community—Israel or the Church—meets the standard of correct belief. Christians consider all books of the canon, by definition, to be inspired by the Holy Spirit.

The main process of canonization as it applies to New Testament writings can be summarized briefly. Jesus himself did not write, and his earliest followers preached his message orally. The early Church did have a Scripture, but it was the Scriptures of Israel that Christians today call the Old Testament. For the specific beliefs about who Jesus was, the early church communities relied on oral traditions about Jesus that had been passed down from Jesus' closest disciples, also known as apostles.

An example of this "apostolic tradition" is found in Paul's letter to his church in Corinth. "For I handed on to you [orally] as of first importance what I also received [orally]: that Christ died for our sins in accordance with the Scriptures [the Old Testament]; that he was buried; that he was raised on the third day" (1 Cor 15:3–4). One sees here the standard fundamental beliefs about Jesus. When writings such as Paul's letters or the Gospels appeared, their truth was measured against the standard of this oral apostolic tradition.

These early writings were penned by believers for church members. Paul's letters are written to churches or to church leaders and were typically read aloud when the members were gathered. As discussed, the Gospel of Luke was written for Theophilus, to deepen his understanding and assurance about the oral teaching he had already received from his church. It was hardly meant for Theophilus alone, however. It must have been read aloud in Theophilus's community and copied for reading elsewhere.

Over time, then, a body of writings came to be accepted within the Church community as canonical—writings that were considered to witness faithfully to the originally oral apostolic tradition. Such writings were read aloud in Christian worship (see Col 4:16; Rev 1:3). The authors of these writings, apostles or followers of the apostles, were considered to have been inspired by the Holy Spirit.

At first, **canonization**[40] was an informal process—certain writings, such as Paul's letters, or the Gospel of Matthew, were given a prominent place in church teaching and worship because of their apostolic origin or their agreement with apostolic teaching. By the late second century, a collection of Paul's letters, and the Gospels of Matthew, Mark, Luke, and John were widely accepted in orthodox Christian churches as canonical.

The canonical status of certain books, such as the Book of Revelation, was debated. In these instances, churches considered a further criterion: whether certain books were accepted by other orthodox churches, especially the great churches known to have apostolic origins, such as in Antioch and Rome.

---

40. Michael J. Kruger comments on the development of the New Testament canon in a video accessible at *www.youtube.com/watch?v=zoEBEXlXuaO* (time: 0:02:55).

The exact list of twenty-seven books that are now part of the New Testament canon does not appear until the later fourth century (367, Athanasius's *Festal Letter* 39). Catholic theologians have made it clear that the Church does not have the authority to *grant* inspiration to a particular writing after the fact. It only has the authority to *recognize officially*, at a later date, that a particular writing was inspired by the Holy Spirit.[41]

An analogous process took place in which the community of Israel also recognized and accepted certain writings that formed its scriptural canon. As the PBC commented, "In this way, these texts ceased to be merely the expression of a particular author's inspiration; they became the common property of the whole people of God."[42]

Canonization and Inspiration   8.18.3

In the Catholic Christian view, the communities of faith, Israel and the Church, had the authority to recognize and accept which books would be considered inspired and canonical. Long before official pronouncements by bishops or Jewish leaders designated certain books as canonical, faith communities exercised authority to guide the process of writing texts and identifying some as sacred.

Biblical scholar Bruce Vawter concludes, "Inspiration should be thought of primarily as one of the qualities bestowed upon the community of faith by the Spirit of God that has called it into being."[43] Individuals, such as Jeremiah or Luke, are of course inspired; but they are inspired as members of a faith community.

Karl Rahner speaks of the inspired writing of Scripture as a "constitutive element" of the Church. In other words, the Christian Church was in a certain sense not fully established until the inspired Scripture was written and recognized.[44] In the process of writing and later canonizing Scripture, the Church expresses its own self-understanding in a more objective way and produces a concrete, visible standard or canon that the later generations of Christians can follow. In Scripture, "the apostolic Church interprets itself for later ages."[45]

A Dynamic View of Truth   8.19

Traditional models of inspiration tended to give little credit to the human author of scripture. Justin cautioned, "You must not suppose that they [scriptural

---

41. Collins, "Inspiration," in *NJBC*, 1029.

42. PBC, "Church in the World," III.B.1

43. Vawter, *Biblical Inspiration*, 158.

44. Karl Rahner, *Inspiration in the Bible*, Quaestiones Disputatae (New York: Herder and Herder, 1961), 47–50.

45. Karl Rahner, "Scripture and Tradition," in *Theological Investigations* (London: Darton, Longman & Todd; New York: Seabury Press, 1974), 6:102.

passages] are spoken by the inspired [writers] themselves, but by the Divine Word who moves them" (*1 Apology* 36); Athenagoras used the analogy of the Spirit speaking through an author "as a flute player breathes into a flute" (*A Plea for the Christians* 9) (sec. 8.7)

While accepting that God inspired the author, more recent literary, critical, and historical studies of Scripture have shown that the writing of Scripture was very much a *human* process. The writing often involved not a single author, but many authors and editors composing over lengthy periods. Human culture influenced, shaped, and at times limited the way in which divine truths were expressed.

Due to these human limitations, the interpreter must recognize that the truth expressed in certain passages is often partial and must be understood in the light of Scripture as a whole. One can see the understanding of truth developing and deepening as later authors reinterpreted earlier traditions. As Pope Benedict teaches, "God's plan is manifested *progressively* and it is accomplished slowly, *in successive stages*" (*VD*, no. 42; emphasis original).

Questions about the Text

1. In the Catholic tradition, why does the term *Word of God* mean more than just *Scripture*?
2. In the Catholic tradition, in what sense does Scripture have both a divine and a human aspect?
3. What is the basic meaning of the theological belief that Scripture is inspired by the Holy Spirit?
4. Explain the difference between a direct and an indirect model of how the Spirit inspires a biblical author.
5. Compare the statements of Luke and Jeremiah about how their books were written. How would a theory of inspiration be applied to each of these authors?
6. Explain why the Bible has two different versions of the Ten Commandments.
7. Describe some of the evidence for the conclusion that many biblical books have multiple authors and editors. How would this evidence affect a theory of inspiration?
8. Explain the doctrine of biblical inerrancy and show how it is related to doctrines of biblical inspiration. Explain the difference between strict and limited inerrancy and provide some criticisms of each view.
9. Describe how the truth of a parable is different from the truth of a historical narrative.

10. What are some examples of how the scientific understanding of the biblical authors was limited? How would this insight have applied to the Galileo affair?

11. Since all biblical writings accept slavery as a natural institution of society, does this imply that God, who inspired the Bible, also accepts slavery? Why or why not?

12. In what ways do Christians see a development from Old Testament beliefs to New Testament beliefs?

13. Summarize one of the examples in section 8.16.3. What does the concept of "truth as dynamic tension" mean?

14. Identify two biblical passages that appear to contradict one another. Is there a way of explaining the relationship of these passages without concluding that at least one must be an error?

15. Explain the concept of a "communal model of inspiration." Discuss the evidence that causes some people to support such a model.

16. Briefly describe the process of the canonization of the New Testament books. How is this process related to a "communal model of inspiration"?

Discussion Questions

1. Are you familiar with non-Christian religions that have sacred writings? If so, do they have concepts similar to the Christian doctrines of inspiration or inerrancy? Explain.

2. Are you familiar with the views of specific Christian churches regarding the doctrines of inspiration or the inerrancy of the Bible? If so, discuss how their views relate to the views presented in this chapter.

3. From a Christian perspective, would a belief in God's inspiration of Scripture always imply a correlative belief in some kind of inerrancy?

4. In your view, is it possible for any human writing to be completely without error? Why or why not?

5. Do you agree that there is a difference between a "dynamic" view of truth and a "static" view of truth?

6. Does an individual or a communal model of inspiration make more sense to you? Explain.

9

CHAPTER

Understanding the Bible

God's Word in Human Words 9.1

Chapter 8 considered, from the Catholic perspective, the basic Christian belief that the biblical authors are inspired by the Holy Spirit. It showed how scriptural evidence leads to the theological conclusion that **inspiration** does not remove all of the human authors' limitations of knowledge and cultural perspective. As guided by the Spirit, they remain very much human authors, with human skills and knowledge, and human limitations.

Vatican II's *Dei Verbum* acknowledges that both the human and divine factors must be considered when interpreting Scripture. "[S]ince God speaks in Sacred Scripture through men in human fashion, the interpreter of Sacred Scripture, in order to see clearly what God wanted to communicate to us, should carefully investigate what meaning the sacred writers really intended." Yet at the same time, the divine element of scripture cannot be neglected, "Scripture must be read and interpreted in the sacred spirit in which it was written" (*DV*, no. 12).

To gain a deeper understanding of Scripture, then, a reader must consider the historical and cultural context of a biblical author, because these conditions have a profound influence on how any human thinks and writes. To get a good sense of this context, the biblical scholar may legitimately use any of the historical and critical tools that are used to study ancient human writing. At the same time, however, the interpreter must keep in mind the unique status of these writings as the divine Word of God.

The following sections consider two topics:

1. Approaches to understanding the human authors of the Bible. These approaches focus especially on understanding the ancient text within its original historical and cultural context.
2. Approaches to understanding the Bible theologically, as God's message to the Christian community that is still relevant today.

In the Catholic understanding, while these two general approaches can be distinguished from each other, they can never really be separated.

The Historical-Critical Method 9.2

In Scripture studies, the umbrella term for the approaches focusing on understanding the human author in his cultural and historical contexts is the **historical-critical method**.

The term itself is somewhat misleading, because it suggests there is *one* clearly defined historical-critical method. This is not the case. Rather, the method involves several ways of approaching the text, including textual criticism, source criticism, and redaction criticism. Yet it is useful to retain the label, *historical-critical method*, because all of these individual methods share basic characteristics.

Essentially, the historical-critical method "studies the biblical text in the same fashion as it would study any other ancient text and comments upon it as an expression of human discourse" (PBC, *Interpretation of the Bible in the Church*, I.A.2).[1] In other words, the method studies the biblical text as a human product and does not consider the theological question of how the Holy Spirit may have been involved in the writing.

The term *historical* means that the interpreter works to clarify the historical context in which the biblical writing occurred. The term *critical* does not mean taking a hostile or suspicious approach to the text but signifies using methods that, as far as possible, apply objective criteria to the study of texts.

A consideration of some specific historical-critical approaches follows, together with a discussion of their importance for a proper understanding of the human authors of Scripture.

Textual Criticism 9.2.1

As noted in section 8.10, no original manuscript of any biblical book is still in existence, and scholars must, therefore, compare the numerous copies of biblical manuscripts in an effort to determine the original text. As noted, this critical process allows modern readers to read authors such as Paul or Matthew with a great degree of confidence that they are reading the author's original words.

Consider just one example to illustrate why textual criticism is necessary as a first step in understanding biblical books: the text of the New Testament's

---

1. For a fuller description of the historical-critical method, especially as it is used in scriptural studies, see Joseph A. Fitzmyer, *The Interpretation of Scripture: In Defense of the Historical-Critical Method* (New York: Paulist Press, 2008), 63–66.

First Letter of John (1 John 5:7–8). All of the earliest Greek manuscripts read, "So there are three that testify, the Spirit, the water, and the blood, and the three are of one accord." In some later manuscripts, however, the following words were added after the word *testify*, "the Father, the Word, and the Holy Spirit: and these three are one. And there are three that bear witness to earth." The great majority of textual scholars believe that these words were not in the original text, because out of thousands of Greek manuscripts, they appear in only a handful of medieval manuscripts. The additional words probably began as a comment written by scribes in the margin of an early manuscript—this was common practice in ancient and medieval times—and was later copied into the text.[2]

Text-critical study, then, ensures that modern translations are based on extensive manuscript evidence and that they have clearly identified the few cases (e.g., 1 John 5:7–8) in which there have been significant additions to the original text.

Source Criticism (Literary Criticism) 9.2.2

Many biblical authors use sources in their work, both oral and written (secs. 8.9.1–2). To better understand the actual writings, as well as to answer critical questions about the reliability and trustworthiness of the biblical authors, one needs to have a good sense of the sources they used. For example, when writing a historical account, did the author have access to eyewitness accounts or was the author relying on secondhand information? The effort to identify an author's sources is known as source criticism or literary criticism.

Chapter 8 pointed out the value of source criticism. Source criticism helps the interpreter explain why there are two different versions of the Ten Commandments, for example. Historical-critical study gives a more accurate sense of how the law codes of ancient Hebrew society were drawn up in different historical and cultural circumstances and how those differing circumstances are reflected in the different emphases of the law codes themselves.

Source criticism is essential for the understanding of the Gospels. Consider the following comparison of three versions of Jesus' parable comparing the **kingdom of God** with a mustard seed.

---

2. See Bruce M. Metzger and Bart D. Ehrman, *The Text of the New Testament: Its Transmission, Corruption, and Restoration*, 4th ed. (Oxford: Oxford University Press, 2005), 146–48. Some modern translations, which are based on later manuscripts (such as the New King James version), still include these additional words. Most modern editions (for example, the New International Version, or the New American Bible) following the judgment of most textual scholars, do not include these additional words.

Matthew 13:31–32	Mark 4:30–32	Luke 13:18–19
He proposed another parable to them. "The kingdom of heaven	He said, "To what shall we compare the kingdom of God, or what parable can we use for it?	Then he said, "What is the kingdom of God like? To what can I compare it?
is like a mustard seed that a person took and sowed in a field. It is the smallest of all the seeds, yet when	It is like a mustard seed that, when it is sown in the ground, is the smallest of all the seeds on the earth.	It is like a mustard seed that a person took and planted in the garden.
full-grown it is the largest of plants. It becomes a large bush,	But once it is sown, it springs up and becomes the largest of plants and puts forth large branches,	When it was fully grown, it became a large bush
and the 'birds of the sky come and dwell in its branches.'"	so that the birds of the sky can dwell in its shade."	and 'the birds of the sky dwelt in its branches.'"

All three authors are reporting the same parable: Jesus comparing the kingdom of God with a mustard seed that, when planted and fully grown, becomes a place for birds to nest. Yet just as clearly, Jesus' exact parable was not recorded word-for-word as it was given, because there are differences when the three versions are compared.

This raises the historical-critical question: Why are the three versions so similar, while at the same time recording different details and language? Clearly, if one could explain how the Gospels are related to one another on a literary level, one would be in a better position to understand how they were written and how well they reflect the original words of Jesus himself.

The most widely accepted source-critical solution among scholars is the so-called Two-Source Hypothesis. According to this theory, Mark was the first written of the Gospels, and Matthew and Luke used two main sources in writing their own Gospels: Mark itself and a written collection of Jesus' sayings (labeled "Q" by scholars).

Matthew and Luke's use of Mark's basic account explains the similarity between the three, while certain editorial changes made by Matthew and Luke—as when Matthew writes "kingdom of heaven" for Mark's "kingdom of God"—accounts for the differences.

Two-Source Theory

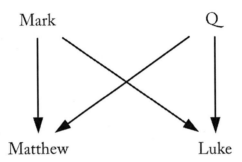

Some type of source criticism[3] is essential if one is to understand how the Gospels are related to one another, thus shedding light on how the Gospel authors worked.

In addition to textual and source criticism, the historical-critical method includes related methods such as genre criticism, determining the particular literary genres of writings, and redaction criticism, the study of how editors used and adapted their sources (PBC, *Interpretation of the Bible in the Church*, I.A.3).

Cultural Context   9.3

A correct understanding of cultural context is crucial for understanding the Bible. For example, to interpret Paul's teaching that women should wear head coverings in the church at Corinth (1 Cor 11:3–16), one needs to know the cultural expectations regarding women's dress at that time, as well as the cultural significance and symbolism of head coverings. When the Letter of James instructs a sick person to call the elders of the church to pray and anoint him with olive oil (Jas 5:14), one needs to understand the meaning of anointing and the significance of olive oil in the ancient world. When one reads that Jesus cast out a "mute and deaf spirit" (Mark 9:25), it helps if the interpreter is familiar with ancient beliefs about spirits and causes of illness. To understand why a pig is "unclean" and not fit for food (Lev 11:6–7), one needs to have a sense of what *unclean* meant in ancient Hebrew culture and why a pig was considered unclean.

---

3. A presentation of the Gospels of Matthew, Mark, Luke, and John (*Revised Standard Version*) set side-by-side can be found at *http://sites.utoronto.ca/religion/synopsis/meta-4g.htm*.

An uncritical reading of Scripture, uninformed about the cultural background, can be misleading and harmful (sec. 8.14). Such a reading, for example, could lead to the assumption that Genesis 1–2 should be understood as a scientific account. Alternatively, it could lead to the assumption that God still favors slavery, as the Bible accepts slavery as a normal institution of society. Southern slave holders before the Civil War did, in fact, interpret the Bible in this way, arguing that passages such as Genesis 9:25, "Cursed be Canaan! The lowest of slaves shall he be to his brothers," proved that God had decreed that the black race would always be slaves.[4]

To shed light on the cultural background of the Bible, studies from the disciplines of sociology and cultural anthropology are helpful.[5] To cite just one example, the anthropologist Mary Douglas'[6] work shows how purity laws in Leviticus (e.g., determining which animals are "clean" and which are "unclean" in Leviticus 11) reflect a cultural view in which wholeness and integrity is associated with holiness. Animals are classed into certain groups: Those that fit into clearly defined boundaries are "clean," (e.g., fish with both fins and scales) while borderline cases are considered unclean (e.g., water creatures that have scales but no fins [Lev 11]).[7]

Related Approaches to Studying Scripture as Written by Humans   9.4

The PBC's *Interpretation of the Bible in the Church* also describes and analyzes other methods and approaches to understanding Scripture as a product of human authors. Literary approaches, such as rhetorical and narrative analysis, allow the interpreter to appreciate better the literary art with which biblical books were composed (*Bible in the Church*, I.B.1–2).

Contextual approaches pay particular attention to how readers' worldviews shape their interpretation of the biblical text, as well as how their reading of the Bible affects their daily actions (*Bible in the Church*, I.D.1–2). The liberationist approaches the text from the perspective of the poor and oppressed, with a view toward achieving liberation for these groups. A feminist view takes a similar approach from the perspective of women. The PBC acknowledges the values of both approaches for providing a deeper understanding of certain aspects of the

---

4. See Stephen R. Haynes, *Noah's Curse: The Biblical Justification of American Slavery* (Oxford: Oxford University Press, 2002).

5. PBC, *Interpretation of the Bible in the Church*, I.D. 1–2.

6. See Mary Douglas, "The Abominations of Leviticus," *Purity and Danger: An Analysis of the Concepts of Pollution and Taboo* (London: Routledge and Kegan Paul, 1966), 41–57 is accessible at *http://fontes.lstc.edu/~rklein/Documents/douglas.htm*.

7. Douglas' classic work is *Purity and Danger: An Analysis of the Concepts of Pollution and Taboo*, 2nd ed. (London: Routledge, 2002).

biblical text but also warns that they can be too one-sided and, in some cases, use methodologies that are incompatible with Christianity (e.g., the use of a Marxist class analysis by certain liberationist approaches).

Catholic Acceptance of the Historical-Critical Approach 9.5

The PBC's *Interpretation of the Bible in the Church* calls the historical-critical method "indispensable" for gaining a deeper understanding of the human aspect of the biblical texts.

> The historical-critical method is the indispensable method for the scientific study of the meaning of ancient texts. Holy Scripture, inasmuch as it is the "Word of God in human language," has been composed by human authors in all its various parts and in all the sources that lie behind them. Because of this, its proper understanding not only admits the use of this method but actually requires it. (I.A)

Pope Benedict supports this judgment, linking it to the doctrine of the Incarnation:

> Before all else, we need to acknowledge the benefits that historical-critical exegesis and other recently-developed methods of textual analysis have brought to the life of the Church. For the Catholic understanding of sacred Scripture, attention to such methods is indispensable, linked as it is to the realism of the Incarnation: "This necessity is a consequence of the Christian principle formulated in the Gospel of John 1:14: *Verbum caro factum est*. The historical fact is a constitutive dimension of the Christian faith. The history of salvation is not mythology, but a true history, and it should thus be studied with the methods of serious historical research." (*VD*, no. 32)[8]

In other words, the events at the center of the Christian faith, involving the Son of God becoming human, are actual events that took place in history and, such, can legitimately be studied by historical approaches.

Limitations of the Historical Critical Method 9.6

While the Catholic tradition accepts the value of the historical-critical and related human-centered approaches to the Bible, it also insists that they are not adequate in themselves for understanding Scripture as the word of God.

---

8. A video overview of Pope Benedict XVI's *VD* by romereports.com is accessible at *www.you tube.com/watch?v=wMaBxDHDheY* (time: 0:01:47).

(*VD*, no. 35) The Christian reader must always keep in mind the limitations of the historical-critical and related methods and balance them with a theological approach. Following are some general cautions:

1. Various studies have shown how those who first developed the historical-critical method were deeply committed to a secular worldview that denied God's influence in the world.[9]

2. The historical-critical method is often portrayed as scientific and neutral, when in fact it is impossible to take a purely neutral approach to Scripture. All interpreters approach texts with prejudgments (sec. 1.10).

3. The historical-critical method, when used by itself, can often be combined with what Pope Benedict called "a positivistic and *secularized hermeneutic*" (*VD*, no. 35; emphasis original). Such a rationalistic way of reading Scripture rejects the possibility of God intervening in human history. Any event can only have a natural explanation, and so any supernatural cause of an event is ruled out. Such a hermeneutic naturally casts doubt on central Christian claims such as the Resurrection of Jesus.

4. The historical-critical method is sometimes portrayed as the only legitimate approach to understanding Scripture; scriptural interpretation before modern times is dismissed as precritical or naïve. The Catholic tradition insists, however, that much can still be learned from a study of how Scripture was interpreted in the 2000 years of Christian history, especially in the early centuries.

5. If Scripture is read only in a historical-critical way, it is read as "a text belonging only to the past." It is studied as literature or history but does not speak to the faithful today as the Word of God[10] (*VD*, no. 35).

Combining the Historical-Critical and Theological Approaches 9.7

Despite these cautions, the Catholic tradition insists that a historical-critical approach to Scripture is legitimate and, in fact, necessary. The Christian interpreter should use the historical-critical method then but in a way that (1) involves a critical awareness of its limitations and that (2) balances the method with theological approaches.

---

9. For example, Scott W. Hahn and Benjamin Wiker, *Politicizing the Bible: The Roots of Historical Criticism and the Secularization of Scripture 1300–1700* (New York: Crossroad, 2013). See also Luke Timothy Johnson and William Kurz, *The Future of Catholic Biblical Scholarship* (Grand Rapids, MI: Eerdmans, 2003), 15–17.

10. A video presentation by Fr. Robert Barron on Pope Benedict XVI and how to read the Bible is accessible at *www.youtube.com/watch?v=Ha5flTRTZWY* (time: 0:07:40).

Pope Benedict teaches that in "applying methods of historical analysis, no criteria should be adopted which would rule out in advance God's self-disclosure in human history" (*VD*, n. 36). Evangelical authors Paul Eddy and Greg Boyd make a similar point in their discussion of a critical study of the New Testament. They advocate an **open historical-critical method,** in other words, one that does not reject from the start any possibility of a supernatural event. Such an approach, Eddy and Boyd clarify, does not accept all supernatural accounts uncritically. It remains critical in the sense that, all other things being equal, it prefers a plausible, naturalistic explanation to a supernatural one for any given event. However, this approach is open to considering a supernatural explanation if no plausible naturalistic ones are available.[11]

The Historical-Critical Method and the Traditional Interpretation of Scripture 9.8

A Catholic approach, then, sees no inconsistency in combining historical-critical and traditional Christian theological approaches. Pope Benedict and the bishops recommend paying renewed attention to the scriptural approach of the Fathers of the Church (*VD*, no. 37). The following sections consider how a traditional approach to understanding Scripture can harmonize with a historical-critical analysis.

The Four Senses of Scripture 9.8.1

From ancient times, the Christian interpretive tradition has spoken of two senses of Scripture: the literal or historical, and spiritual. The spiritual sense has been divided into the allegorical, moral, and anagogical senses (see *CCC*, no. 115 and Thomas Aquinas *ST* 1.1.10).[12]

The literal or historical sense is essentially the meaning intended by the words of Scripture. As stated in the *Catechism*, "The literal sense is the meaning conveyed by the words of Scripture" (no. 116). Thus the literal sense in a historical account (e.g., 1 and 2 Kgs) is to the events in Israelite history. However, an author's use of figurative language is also part of the literal sense, because the author intended this figurative meaning. For example, when Scripture refers to God's mighty arm, the literal sense is God's power (*ST* 1.1.10 ad 3).

The spiritual sense of Scripture is based on the doctrine that the events described in Scripture are signs pointing toward another reality.

1. **Allegorical sense.** When scripture speaks of the Israelites crossing the Red Sea, it refers literally to an event in history. This event has a further

---

11. Paul R. Eddy and Gregory A. Boyd, *The Jesus Legend: A Case for the Historical Reliability of the Synoptic Jesus Tradition* (Grand Rapids, MI: Baker Academic, 2007), 82–90.

12. See Henri de Lubac, *Medieval Exegesis*, vol.1, *The Four Senses of Scripture* (Grand Rapids, MI: Eerdmans/Edinburgh: T & T Clark, 1998).

allegorical sense as a sign or type of Christ's victory and of Christian baptism (*CCC*, no. 117). Scripture refers, in a literal way, to the laws of Moses as laws given to the Israelites in history, but the laws also have an allegorical sense (*ST* 1.1.10). For example, laws commanding the sacrifice of animals foreshadow Christ's offering his life on the cross (for example, Heb 10:1–18).

2. **Moral sense.** When Scripture refers to certain events in history, those events can be models of ethical behavior for future generations. In the words of the *Catechism*, "the events reported in Scripture ought to lead us to act justly" (*CCC*, no. 117). As Aquinas says, "whatever our Head (Christ) has done is a type of what we ought to do." (*ST* 1.1.10). For example, when Jesus washes the feet of his disciples, he tells them, "I have given you a model to follow, so that as I have done for you, you should also do." (John 13:15).

3. **Anagogical sense.** The events recorded in Scripture can also have an anagogical meaning—one that points toward fulfillment at the end of time. The *Catechism* states, "We can view realities and events in terms of their eternal significance, leading us toward our true homeland: thus the Church on earth is a sign of the heavenly Jerusalem" (*CCC*, no. 117).

The Literal Sense and the Historical-Critical Method

9.8.2

The historical-critical method is important for recovering the literal sense. The *Catechism* states that the literal sense is "discovered by exegesis, following the rules of sound interpretation" (*CCC*, no. 116). In his 1943 encyclical *Divino afflante Spiritu* (*On the Promotion of Biblical Studies*), Pope Pius XII—although he did not refer specifically to the historical-critical method—explicitly stated that historical and critical techniques are necessary for recovering the literal sense:

> What is the literal sense of a passage is not always as obvious in the speeches and writings of the ancient authors of the East, as it is in the works of our own time. For what they wished to express is not to be determined by the rules of grammar and philology alone, nor solely by the context; the interpreter must, as it were, go back wholly in spirit to those remote centuries of the East and with the aid of history, archaeology, ethnology, and other sciences accurately determine what modes of writing, so to speak, the authors of that ancient period would be likely to use, and in fact did use.[13]

---

13. Pope Pius XII, Encyclical Letter *On the Promotion of Biblical Studies* (*Divino afflante Spiritu*), no. 35, in Béchard, *Scripture Documents*, 128.

The proper use of the historical-critical method enhances an interpreter's ability to recover a sense of the author's original intention: the literal sense, in traditional terms.

The Spiritual Sense   9.8.3

The spiritual sense of Scripture, in the Catholic tradition, is not simply an arbitrary meaning placed on a text by the believer's imagination. Aquinas insists that the spiritual sense "is based on the literal, and presupposes it" (*ST* 1.1.10). The *Catechism* teaches the same: "All other senses of Sacred Scripture are based on literal" (*CCC*, no. 116).

Notice the further similarities shared by the allegorical, the moral, and the anagogical:

1. All agree that the events recorded in Scripture have a deeper meaning— they point beyond themselves to another reality.
2. All offer a way of relating the literal, historical sense to the contemporary life of the interpreter. A historical-critical approach would study the literal sense of a saying of Jesus, while the spiritual sense would ask how that saying applies to the life of the believer today or in the future.

Combining the Interpretation of the Literal and Spiritual Senses   9.8.4

Following is an example that illustrates questions one might ask when interpreting the literal and the spiritual senses—specifically the moral sense—of Scripture: Jesus' saying in Matthew 5:39: "When someone strikes you on (your) right cheek, turn the other one to him as well."

Literal sense	Spiritual (moral) sense
Was this saying originally meant to be taken literally or metaphorically? How does this version in Matthew compare with the version in Luke 6:29? How does the historical and political context (a Jewish population occupied by the vastly more powerful Roman Empire) affect the literal meaning? In its context, was Jesus simply giving practical advice so that the Jews would not be crushed by the overwhelming power of the Romans?	How does a Christian apply this command in today's world? How can a Christian learn to react nonviolently when confronted with hate or violence? Does it imply that a Christian should literally never use violence, even in personal self-defense or in defending one's country from foreign attack?

An Ancient Allegorical Reading 9.8.5

The Song of Songs has long puzzled readers of Scripture. It is a poem celebrating the passionate desires of two lovers and is filled with suggestive sexual imagery:

- "Let him kiss me with kisses of his mouth, for your love is better than wine" (Song 1:1).
- "Your breasts are like two fawns, twins of a gazelle, feeding among the lilies" (Song 4:5).

God's name is never mentioned nor are any religious topics discussed. Why is this book in Scripture?

Patristic and medieval interpreters, following ancient Jewish practice, read it allegorically. In his *Commentary on the Song of Songs*, Origen, for example, recognizes that in its literal sense, it is a marriage song for a couple about to be wed. At the allegorical level, however, Origen understood it as a dialogue between the soul and Christ, the Word of God, or between the Church and Christ.

The sexual desire is an allegory for the soul's love of the Word of God. Each "kiss" of the Word of God is a pure teaching or spiritual insight that the soul receives from the Word.

This allegory is not the only connection made between the male-female relationship and the human-divine relationship in the Bible. The Old Testament prophets often use the image of the Lord as a faithful husband and Israel as his unfaithful wife (e.g., Hos 1–2). Paul also makes this intriguing connection:

"For this reason a man shall leave [his] father and [his] mother and be joined to his wife, and the two shall become one flesh." This is a great mystery, but I speak in reference to Christ and the church (Eph 5:31–32).

Interpreting the Bible: Reading Theologically 9.9

To read the Bible in its spiritual sense is to read it theologically, which means understanding it as God's word addressing people today. The *Catechism*, in a summary of *Dei Verbum*'s teaching, offers three guidelines for grasping the spiritual sense:

1. Be especially attentive "to the content and unity of the whole of Scripture."
2. Read the Scripture within "the living Tradition of the whole Church."
3. Be attentive to the "analogy of faith" (*CCC*, nos. 112–14).

The following sections consider each point in more depth.

Guideline 1: The Content and Unity of Scripture   9.9.1

At one level, this means interpreting Scripture as a whole rather than focusing on individual passages (sec. 8.15). At a deeper level, however, this unity is found in Jesus Christ: "Scripture is a unity by reason of the unity of God's plan, of which Christ Jesus is the center and the heart" (*CCC*, no. 112); "the person of Christ gives unity to all the 'Scriptures'" (*VD*, no 39).

Jesus is understood as a unifier because of the central Christian belief that the Word (Logos) of God, who became human in Jesus, is the ultimate source of the meaning of human life and indeed of the whole universe. God created all things through his Word (John 1:3); thus all things have their meaning through the Word. The deepest meaning of human life and love was revealed when God the Son became human, "emptied himself," and offered his life for the sake of sinful humanity.

Jesus Christ is the hermeneutical key to Scripture because he is the hermeneutical key to understanding the entire universe.

Guideline 2: Reading Scripture within the Tradition of Church   9.9.2

In the Catholic view, the theological meaning of Scripture can be properly understood only when it is read within the living tradition of the whole Church. This claim has several implications; two will be highlighted here: (1) only members of the Church can provide a proper interpretation, and (2) the traditional teaching of the Church should guide interpretation.[14]

In US culture, which values highly individual autonomy and freedom of choice, these claims are countercultural. The value of individual autonomy suggests that each person's interpretation is valid. By comparison, the Catholic approach may appear close-minded and authoritarian. Such a conclusion, however, isn't warranted. To grasp a deeper sense of the Catholic perspective, the following points should be considered.

Prejudgments, Tradition, and Understanding the Bible   9.9.2.1

The PBC reiterates Gadamer's point that purely objective, scientifically precise interpretations of ancient texts simply do not exist (PBC II.A.1; see also

---

14. One should clarify that nonchurch members can indeed have good insight into historical-critical aspects of the text, but that theological interpretation requires different approaches.

sec. 1.10). Rather, a person inevitably reads a text with certain prejudgments and approaches a text from within a certain tradition. The Catholic claim simply makes explicit its conviction that interpretation should come from within the Catholic tradition.

Granted that everyone comes to interpretation from the standpoint of a certain tradition, however, raises a question: why should the Catholic tradition be preferred over any other? The following sections consider the Catholic answer to this question.

Interpreting the Scripture within the Church 9.9.2.2

The very concept of "scripture" presupposes an organized community of faith (sec. 8.1). *Scripture* means "holy writing"—but "holy" for whom? The Qur'an is scripture for Muslims, the Tanak is scripture for Jews, the Vedas are scripture for Hindus, and the Bible, both Old and New Testaments, is scripture for Christians.

Scripture is formed by a community. As noted earlier (secs. 8.18.1–2), it was the community of faith, either Israel or the Church, that officially recognized a particular writing as inspired by God and as Scripture. The Bible, as a collection of books, only came into existence because the communities of Israel and the early Church formed their canons. It is through the Church's Tradition that the full canon of the Old and New Testaments was known (*DV*, no. 8).

Historical-critical investigations have shown that one can go further in this understanding: the very books themselves are the products of a faith community. The Book of Isaiah, for example, was put together over a period of centuries under the guidance of the faith community.

It stands to reason, then, that the community that produced the Scriptures would be in the best position to guide their interpretation.

Reading Scripture within Church Tradition 9.9.2.3

How, specifically, would a person read Scripture within Church tradition? A few examples can be given:

1. By being aware of how the great church leaders and theologians of the past have read Scripture

2. By hearing Scripture and reflecting on its meaning as it is proclaimed at Mass and interpreted in homilies

3. By being aware of the great spiritual traditions of reading scripture, such as *lectio divina*

4. By being aware of the official teaching of the church expressed by the **Magisterium,** composed of the bishops and pope, who have been entrusted with the task of authentic interpretation

Listening Prayerfully to God's Word: *Lectio Divina* 9.9.2.4

Lectio divina, developed originally by monks, is an ancient practice of reading Scripture prayerfully. After a time of quieting one's distracted thoughts, the *lectio divina* traditionally consists of four parts:

1. *Lectio* (reading): Read a short passage slowly.

2. *Meditatio* (reflection): Reflect on the passage, seeking to know how God is speaking through it.

3. *Oratio* (prayer): Pray to God based on the thoughts and feelings that arise from the Scripture reading.

4. *Contemplatio* (contemplation): Consider how God is calling one to change and to conform one's life more closely with Christ. Many contemporary methods of *lectio divina* include a fifth step—*actio* (action), during which a person takes actions in relation to step 4's call to change.

Guideline 3: Be Attentive to the Analogy of Faith 9.9.3

The *Catechism* defines the "analogy of faith" as "the coherence of the truths of faith among themselves and within the whole plan of Revelation" (*CCC*, no. 114). This definition corresponds well with interpretation of Scripture according to the four senses—both hold a holistic understanding of the faith and of Scripture.

The faith of Christians is incarnational: it centers on the belief that God the Son truly became human in a certain time and place. This claim is both historical and theological. The concern with the historical truth of Christianity corresponds well with historical-critical approaches that attend to the literal sense of the text.

Christians find the meaning of all history in Jesus Christ. This aspect of the faith corresponds well with an allegorical approach, which sees certain events as signs pointing toward Jesus. The Christian faith is deeply concerned with goodness, truth, and meaning in this world, which corresponds to an ethical interpretation of Scripture. At the same time, Christianity insists that the full meaning and fulfillment of humanity cannot be found in this world but, rather, lies in the transcendent destiny of all humanity.

Scripture and Tradition 9.10

The Church's relationship with Scripture is closely tied to Tradition. Scripture and Tradition, though distinct, are so closely related that neither can stand alone (*DV*, no. 10). To grasp this point more fully, one must understand the Catholic meaning of tradition.

The word *tradition* (see sec. 1.10) can have a broad meaning: the phrases "the Jewish tradition" or "the Christian tradition" can be synonymous with Judaism as a whole or Christianity as a whole. This broad sense of tradition, covering all essential Christian beliefs and practices, may also be called the *gospel* or the *deposit of faith* (*CCC*, no. 84).

In Catholic theology, Tradition (note the capital *T*) is distinct from Scripture. "This living transmission [that is, the passing down of the Christian faith], accomplished in the Holy Spirit, is called Tradition, since it is distinct from Sacred Scripture, though closely connected to it" (*CCC*, no. 78).[15] The entire deposit of faith, then, has been passed down in "two distinct modes of transmission": Tradition and Scripture[16] (*CCC*, no. 81). An essential Catholic claim is that the deposit of faith—the essential Christian beliefs and practices—is not found completely and explicitly in Scripture. Here, the Catholic tradition differs from Christian traditions that hold that Scripture alone contains all essential Christian beliefs and practices.

The following sections consider why the Catholic Church makes this distinction between Scripture and Tradition and at the same time attempt to clarify further the meaning of Tradition itself.

Tradition Apart from Scripture 9.11

Apostolic Tradition before the New Testament 9.11.1

The earliest followers of Jesus passed down the deposit of faith before the New Testament books were written (sec. 8.18.2). The apostles and their close associates passed down the essential Christian teachings through oral preaching and instruction—only later did the idea of creating a written deposit of faith, a scripture, emerge. The earliest Christians did not have the New Testament as a source for their beliefs and practices. The oral tradition of the apostles, regarded as a trustworthy interpretation of Jesus' identity and significance, gave rise to written Scriptures.

---

15. See also Yves Congar, *The Meaning of Tradition*, The Twentieth Century Encyclopedia of Catholicism, vol. 3 (New York: Hawthorne Books, 1964), 10.

16. A video report on Pope Francis's speech to the members of the Pontifical Biblical Commission in 2013 during which he addressed the unbreakable unity of Scripture and Tradition is accessible at *www.youtube.com/watch?v=eIBAnHDBIEk* (time 0:00:40).

The New Testament is filled with witnesses to oral tradition. Paul refers to the essential teachings he had passed on to the Corinthians, "For I handed on to you as of first importance what I also received" (1 Cor 15:3).

In numerous other passages, Paul and other New Testament authors refer to these oral teachings.

- I praise you because you remember me in everything and hold fast to the traditions, just as I handed them on to you. (1 Cor 11:2)

- For you know what instructions we gave you through the Lord Jesus. (1 Thess 4:2)

- [S]tand firm and hold fast to the traditions that you were taught, either by an oral statement or by a letter of ours. (2 Thess 2:15)

This apostolic tradition was not composed of oral teachings alone but also of firmly established practices that later tradition called sacraments. Paul's letters (the earliest of the New Testament writings) show that baptism (Rom 6:3; 1 Cor 1:14) and the Lord's Supper (1 Cor 11:23–34) were firmly established practices in the churches already in Paul's time.

Theologian Yves Congar points out that nowhere in the New Testament is there a systematic teaching about the practice and significance of the Lord's Supper in the early churches. Various questions are left unanswered. Should children receive the Lord's Supper? Who should distribute the Lord's Supper? What prayers should be said during the ceremony? Paul offers a few remarks about the Supper but this is only because the Corinthians had raised specific issues for him to address (1 Cor 10:16–22, 11:17–34).

Congar's point is that the New Testament writings, especially Paul's letters, were never meant to give a systematic overview of Christian belief and practice. They were written to address specific issues that arose in specific churches. Paul's writings, and other New Testament texts, presuppose that a more systematic instruction had already been given orally in pre-baptismal teaching. Therefore, one cannot expect to find the full apostolic tradition in the Scriptures.[17]

The New Testament references to oral tradition are not haphazard and occasional. When Paul says, "For I handed on to you as of first importance what I also received" (1 Cor 15:3), he is using technical terms that refer to precise, systematic teaching and reception of the traditions of the Christian faith.

Finally, one should note that Scripture does not claim to be the only basis of Christian teaching. In a passage referenced previously (2 Thess 2:15), Paul admonishes his community to hold fast to his teachings, expressed both in his letters *and in oral traditions*. Scripture shows that it is not self-sufficient for Christian faith.[18] As *Dei Verbum* teaches, the Church "does not derive her certainty about

---

17. Congar, *Meaning of Tradition*, 37, 96–98.

18. Ibid., 36–37.

all revealed truths from the holy Scriptures alone" (*DV*, no. 9 quoted in *CCC*, no. 82). The apostolic tradition before the New Testament shows that, in theory, it is possible to live and transmit the Christian life even without Scripture.[19]

Further Examples of Tradition Apart from Scripture

9.11.2

Today, Christians no longer have direct access to the apostolic oral traditions not recorded in Scripture. They do have indirect access, however, in the continuing Tradition passed down since apostolic times. Following are some examples of beliefs and practices that have been transmitted through non-scriptural Tradition.

1. **Canonization of Scripture.** The process of recognizing which writings should be accepted as part of the canon necessarily stands outside of Scripture itself (sec. 8.18.2). Only a non-scriptural authority can determine the canon of Scripture.

   In this sense, Scripture cannot be the only source of authoritative teaching for a Christian. The New Testament does not explain how the books of the New Testament were chosen. The collection presupposes the authority of the Church to recognize the inspiration of certain writings.

2. **Sunday worship.** The first Christians, as Jews, celebrated the Sabbath on Saturday. The tradition of Christians worshiping together on Sunday in honor of Jesus' Resurrection rather than Saturday is neither commanded nor justified in Scripture, though there seem to be allusions to this practice in 1 Cor 16:2 and Rev 1:10. In fact, the tradition of weekly worship itself is not described, explained, or commanded in the New Testament.

   Similarly, there are no systematic instructions on how a worship service should be structured (e.g., order of scriptural readings, homilies, Lord's Supper), only occasional references to practices that had already been established through the oral tradition (e.g., 1 Cor 11–14).

3. **Infant baptism.** The New Testament has no direct teaching on whether infants should be baptized. It explicitly describes only the baptism of adults. However, accounts sometimes refer to the baptism of whole households and families (see Acts 16:15 and 33), which would have included infants and other children. Yet despite the lack of explicit scriptural evidence, infant baptism is accepted by the Roman Catholic Church, the Orthodox churches, the Anglican Church, and the main churches of the Reformation—Lutheran and Reformed. Infant baptism is rejected by traditions that have their roots in the Anabaptist movement, a radical branch of the Reformation.[20]

---

19. Ibid., 22–23, 95.

20. Ibid., 36–47, 96–105.

4. **Authority of the creeds.** The process of writing brief, systematic summaries of the main Christian beliefs lies outside of Scripture. Catholics regard creeds such as the Apostles' Creed and the Nicene-Constantinopolitan Creed as authoritative guides to Christian belief.

5. **Living experience of the Church.** Tradition includes the living experience of the Church through the centuries: the teachings of the great theologians (e.g., Augustine, Aquinas, Gregory of Nyssa, Luther, and Calvin); various liturgies and prayers; the sacraments; sacred music (e.g., Gregorian chant,[21] Bach's Masses, Handel's *Messiah*, contemporary Christian music); great religious art (e.g., icons[22] of the Orthodox tradition, Michelangelo's paintings in the Sistine Chapel,[23] medieval cathedrals); and Church symbols (the crucifix, the act of making the sign of the cross). All of these and many more are powerful, essential mediums by which the faith has been passed down outside of Scripture.[24]

Congar compares this living sense of Tradition to the process of education. A child receives an ethical education, learning right from wrong, not so much from direct instruction as through a living process of daily experience, learning especially from the examples of parents or other loved ones.[25] So too through Tradition, the Church passes down the faith through such varied means as art, music, worship, and social interactions, as well as instruction.

What is passed down in the Tradition is Christianity, in all of its lived experience—an experience so rich and mysterious that it can never be fully expressed in writings.

Tradition Interprets Scripture: The Magisterium   9.12

One crucial role of Tradition as distinct from Scripture is to provide Christians with an accurate interpretation of Scripture. Every Christian community recognizes some type of authority that guides its approach to Scripture. As noted, many Christians accept the creeds as a guideline to what is most important in Scripture. The Lutheran tradition recognizes, in addition to the ancient creeds, statements such as the Augsburg Confession, the Smalcald Articles, and Luther's

---

21. A video presenting an example of Gregorian chant, recorded at the Cistercian Abby Stift Heiligendreuz, is accessible at *www.youtube.com/watch?v=UiRpXsWIZK4&feature=c4-overview-vl&list=PL95785929AE116C08* (time: 0:03:44).

22. A video showing an example of an icon, the Mother of God of Vladimir, is accessible at *www.youtube.com/watch?v=4d2D-WLyAO8* (time: 0:01:23).

23. A video report by CNN on the 500th anniversary of the completion of the Sistine Chapel's ceiling is accessible at *www.youtube.com/watch?v=Fwl640Yc6JM* (time: 0:03:09).

24. Ibid., 14–18.

25. Ibid., 26–27.

small and large catechisms as authoritative guides. The Reformed tradition recognizes the Westminster Confession. Many non-denominational churches have official statements of belief. Every Christian community recognizes authoritative pastors or teachers, past or present, that are seen as reliable interpreters of Scripture.

Religious traditions have been providing authoritative interpretations of their sacred texts throughout history. Orthodox Jews consult not only the Tanak but also the traditional rabbinic teachings preserved in the Mishnah and Talmud. Traditional Muslims base beliefs and practice not on the Qur'an alone but also on the Hadith (traditions of Muhummad) and the guidance of the Ulama (community of religious scholars).

In the Roman Catholic tradition, the Magisterium, the official teaching office of the Church comprised of the bishops in union with the pope, is entrusted with the task of interpreting Scripture: "The task of . . . authentically interpreting the word of God, whether written or handed on, has been entrusted exclusively to the living teaching office of the Church" (*DV*, no. 10).

In the Catholic view, it is essential to have a definitive authority in order to resolve the inevitable theological disputes that arise in the life of the Church. In the Arian controversy, for example, both orthodox theologians who believed that the Son was equal to the Father and Arian theologians who believed that the Son was less than the Father, found support in Scripture. It was only when the Magisterium spoke through councils and creeds, using non-scriptural, philosophical language to add precision to its teaching, that the conflicts were resolved.

Dei Verbum is careful to qualify this authority when it adds, "This teaching office is not above the word of God, but serves it" (no. 10). The Magisterium is not the source of divine truths, the Church teaches; its task is to clarify and explain the divine truths that have already been revealed.

The Church Interprets Scripture: Further Examples   9.12.1

In placing different books together into a single canon, a religious community already has begun the process of interpretation. Israel's community of faith decided the Exodus statement of sons being punished for their fathers' sins must be interpreted together with Ezekiel's insistence on individual responsibility (sec. 8.16.3).[26] The Church determined that Paul's insight that people are "justified by faith apart from works of the law" (Rom 3:28) must be balanced with the assertion of James that people are "justified by works and not by faith alone" (Jas 2:24; sec. 8.16.3.3).

---

26. There is much scholarly debate about the precise limits of the Jewish canon in the time of Jesus. Certainly, however, the Torah of Moses (the first five books) and the writings of prophets such as Ezekiel were accepted as scriptural.

232 REASON, FAITH, AND TRADITION

Many early Christian writers express the idea that Church leaders have the authority to interpret Scripture. Irenaeus writes that presbyters of the Church "expound the Scriptures to us without danger" (*Against Heresies* 4.36.5). Origen insists, "The key to the Scriptures must be received from the tradition of the Church, as from the Lord himself."[27] "I should not believe the gospel" Augustine writes "except as moved by the authority of the Catholic Church" (*Against the Epistle of Manichaeus* 5.6).

Recent Developments on the Relationship of Scripture and Tradition 9.13

Many of the Reformers' disagreements with the Roman Catholic Church were rooted in their belief that Church teaching went beyond Scripture. They taught that scripture alone (*sola scriptura* in Latin) is the basis of Christian belief. The Roman Catholic Church responded by insisting that both Scripture and Tradition are necessary in order to pass down the entirety of the faith.

In recent decades, however, this sharp dichotomy has softened, as many Protestant and Evangelical churches are recovering a sense of the importance of Tradition, and Catholic theologians are recovering a sense of the centrality of Scripture within the traditional Catholic understanding of the relationship of Scripture and Tradition. In addition, ecumenical dialogues between Catholics and other Christian traditions have helped to clarify the theological meaning of Tradition.

Tradition and Traditions 9.13.1

One important clarification is that Catholic theology distinguishes between unchanging Tradition (capital *T*) and traditions that are subject to change (lowercase *t*).[28] *Tradition* (capital *T*) is an expression of a central belief of the faith, while *traditions* (lowercase *t*) are expressions of Catholic practice or belief that are relevant only in certain times and cultures and thus subject to change.

The Roman Catholic Church, for example, as a result of the renewal associated with the Second Vatican Council, changed centuries-old traditions, such as obligatory fasting from meat every Friday and celebrating Mass in Latin. The phrase "sacred Tradition," however, as it is used in *Dei Verbum*, refers to essential teachings and practices that are not subject to change, for example, the clarification given to the doctrine of the Trinity by the councils of Nicaea and Constantinople.

This same distinction was made in a 1963 statement on Scripture, Tradition, and Traditions of the Faith and Order Commission of the World Council of Churches, a broad-range alliance of more than three hundred Christian churches, including Orthodox and Protestant churches. "We can speak of the Christian

---

27. Quoted in Congar, *Meaning of Tradition*, 83.

28. Ibid., 46–47.

Tradition (with a capital *T*), whose content is God's revelation and self-giving in Christ, present in the life of the Church" (no. 46).[29] The statement uses the word *traditions* (lowercase *t*), to refer to the "diversity of forms of expression" in the Christian Tradition, and "also what we call confessional traditions, for instance, the Lutheran tradition or the Reformed tradition" (no. 39).

The Faith and Order statement speaks of a living Christian Tradition, in a sense very similar to that of Congar:

> We exist as Christians by the Tradition of the Gospel (the *paradosis* of the *kerygma*) testified in Scripture, transmitted in and by the Church through the power of the Holy Spirit. Tradition taken in this sense is actualized in the preaching of the Word, in the administration of the sacraments and worship, in Christian teaching and theology, and in mission and witness to Christ by the lives of the members of the Church. What is transmitted in the process of tradition is the Christian faith, not only as a sum of tenets, but as a living reality transmitted through the operation of the Holy Spirit. (no. 46–47)

In this broad sense, then, Tradition includes Scripture.

Evangelical and Protestant Recovery of Tradition
9.13.2

The 1963 Faith and Order report does not hold a strict *sola scriptura* position: "The very fact that Tradition precedes the Scriptures points to the significance of tradition" (no. 42). The report also concurs with *Dei Verbum*'s teaching that Scripture must be interpreted within the context of Church Tradition:

> The Tradition in its written form, as Holy Scripture (comprising both the Old and the New Testament), has to be interpreted by the Church in ever new situations. Such interpretation of the Tradition is to be found in the crystallization of tradition in the creeds, the liturgical forms of the sacraments and other forms of worship, and also in the preaching of the Word and in theological expositions of the Church's doctrine. (no. 50)

Many Protestant and Evangelical writers are becoming aware of the value of interpreting Scripture not solely as individuals but also as self-conscious members of a two-thousand-year-old tradition.[30] The Faith and Order report asks, "Should we not study more the Fathers of all periods of the Church and

---

29. "Scripture, Tradition and Traditions," in *The Fourth World Conference on Faith and Order, Montreal, 1963*, eds. P. C. Rodger and L. Vischer (London: SCM Press, 1964), 50–61. The text of the statement is also accessible at *www.andrews.edu/~fortind/Scripture-Tradition-traditions.htm*.

30. See references in Congar, *Meaning of Tradition*, 89–90.

their interpretations of Scripture in the light of our ecumenical task?" (no. 55). Representative of this renewed interest are a number of ongoing series published by traditionally Evangelical presses. Baker Academic, for example, publishes the Evangelical Ressourcement series, a series "grounded in the belief that there is a wealth of theological, exegetical, and spiritual resources from the patristic era that is relevant for the Christian church today and into the future."[31]

Two other Evangelical series, the Ancient Christian Commentary on Scripture (InterVarsity Press) and The Church's Bible (Eerdmans) have adopted the ancient Christian *catena* method for reading Scripture. In this method, passages from biblical books are followed by exegetical comments drawn from the influential early Christian theologians such as Irenaeus, Tertullian, and Augustine.

A Renewed Catholic Sense of the Centrality of Scripture 9.13.3

As discussed, the Catholic tradition recognizes that both Scripture and Tradition are essential to the expression of the Christian faith (secs. 9.10–12). At the same time, the Catholic tradition has always recognized that Scripture has a unique authority.

The Centrality of Scripture in Earliest Christianity 9.13.3.1

Even before the canonization process that resulted in the New Testament began, the earliest followers of Jesus had Scriptures: the Scriptures of Israel. In fact, it is not an exaggeration to say that the essence of Christian theology was— and is—an interpretation of the Jewish Scriptures in light of Jesus Christ. Recall that Paul reminds the Corinthian church that his basic teachings tell of events that unfolded in accordance with the Scriptures (see 1 Cor 15:3–4).

Paul emphasizes that the Jewish Scriptures are in harmony with the basic Christian beliefs about Jesus: Paul regards them as prophecies of later events.

Scripture as the Primary Authority for Christian Faith 9.13.3.2

Henri de Lubac writes of a pre-Reformation consensus that, in a sense, "all of revelation is contained in Scripture" and in the interpretation of Scripture, "all of theological science is encompassed."[32] Aquinas teaches that Scripture is the foundation of the Christian faith: "For our faith rests upon the revelation made to the apostles and prophets who wrote the canonical books" (*ST* 1.1.8 ad. 2). Aquinas recognizes other theological authorities, especially the teachings of the

---

31. See *http://bakerpublishinggroup.com/books/evangelicals-and-tradition/227551*.

32. De Lubac, *Medieval Exegesis*, 24.

popes and the Church Councils, but believes that the authority of Scripture is primary. According to one strand of Catholic theology, then, one can say, "Scripture contained, in one way or another, all the truths necessary for salvation."[33]

Congar writes that, for a Catholic, "the holy Scriptures have an absolute authority which Tradition has not. Scripture is the supreme authority to which all other authorities would be subjected."[34] Rahner even speaks of a "Catholic *sola scriptura*" principle. Rahner argues that the saving truths of the Catholic faith are all based on Scripture alone—but based on Scripture as it has been recognized and interpreted by the Church and its Magisterium. Such interpretation, for Rahner, includes the principle of the "development of doctrine"—that, in some cases, Scripture contains the seeds of truths that were later developed within Church Tradition.[35]

The Inseparability of Tradition and Scripture 9.14

Dei Verbum is careful to say that Tradition and Scripture are not two separate sources of God's revelation. They "form one sacred deposit of the word of God" (no. 10). The two "are bound closely together, and communicate one with the other"; "both of them, flowing out from the same divine wellspring, come together in some fashion to form one thing and move towards the same goal. . . . Both Scripture and Tradition must be accepted and honored with equal sentiments of devotion and reverence" (*DV*, no. 9 quoted in *CCC*, nos. 80, 82).

Congar writes, "No article of the Church's belief is held on the authority of Scripture independently of Tradition, and none on the authority of Tradition independently of Scripture."[36] Scripture is the primary witness to the Christian faith. However, Scripture cannot be separated from Tradition and from the teachings of the Magisterium that interpret it. *Dei Verbum* sees all three as intimately cooperating in order to achieve the ultimate purpose of the salvation of humanity:

> [S]acred tradition, Sacred Scripture and the teaching authority of the [Church] . . . are so linked and joined together that one cannot stand without the others, and that all together and each in its own way under the action of the one Holy Spirit contribute effectively to the salvation of souls (no. 10).

---

33. Congar, *Meaning of Tradition*, 44. Other Catholic theologians believed that an "objective or material imperfection" in the Scriptures needed to be supplemented by nonscriptural traditions.

34. Ibid., 94–95.

35. Rahner, "Scripture and Tradition," in *Theological Investigations* (London: Darton, Longman & Todd; New York: Seabury Press), 6:107– 8.

36. Congar, *Meaning of Tradition*, 45.

Development of Doctrine   9.15

Essential to the Catholic understanding of the relationship between Scripture and Tradition, as Rahner noted, is the principle of "development of doctrine." Chapter six considered a classic example of this Catholic principle: the gradual development of Trinitarian doctrine from its scriptural roots (sec. 6.14). The key point is that although the precise definition of the Trinity as one divine nature in three subsistent persons is not in the Bible, the foundation for that belief is clearly there. Over time the Church developed its understanding of truths about the Trinitarian nature of God that appeared in Scripture only in an embryonic form.

A basic principle of the faith communities of Israel and the Church is that Scripture should be updated and applied to new circumstances. In particular, a crisis in the life of the community, such as the Babylonian Exile, can spark the need to reinterpret Scripture to fit a new situation (sec. 8.16). In their application to new situations, however, scriptural ideas develop and deepen.

Jesus himself, in the Gospel of John, further supports this theory of development in understanding. He says to his disciples, "I have much more to tell you, but you cannot bear it now. But when he comes, the Spirit of truth, he will guide you to all truth" (John 16:12–13).

The following discussion briefly applies the concept of the development of doctrine to Catholic teaching about the sacraments.

Sacraments   9.15.1

Today the Catholic Church teaches that there are seven sacraments (*CCC*, no. 1113), but the teaching that there are precisely seven did not arise until centuries after New Testament times. As Raymond Brown points out, the New Testament does not use the term *sacrament* at all and, in fact, has no general term to discuss rituals such as baptism and the Lord's Supper.[37] The *Catechism* thus explicitly refers to a process of development with regard to sacraments: "Thus the Church has *discerned over the centuries* that among liturgical celebrations there are seven that are, in the strict sense of the term, sacraments instituted by the Lord" (*CCC*, no. 1117; emphasis added).

However, how can one be sure that the later Catholic doctrine on the seven sacraments is a legitimate development of New Testament teachings and not a corruption of them, as the Reformers believed?

Newman discusses seven "notes" or characteristics of any development that shows it to be a true development and not a corruption.[38] He discusses the development of Catholic sacramental theology under the heading of logical development—one idea leading logically and naturally to the next.

---

37. Brown, *Biblical Exegesis*, 33–34.

38. For an overview of the seven notes, see Newman, *Development of Doctrine*, 169–206, accessible at *http://www.newmanreader.org/Works/development/chapter5.html*.

Newman begins with his conviction that "the Incarnation is the central aspect of Christianity" and that the sacramental system is a logical development of this central aspect.[39] The Incarnation expresses the central Christian belief that the physical world has such dignity and worth that God the Son is able to take on physical form in Jesus Christ (sec. 7.6.2). The sacramental teaching that God's grace can be communicated through the physical agents of water (in baptism), bread and wine (in the Lord's Supper), or olive oil (in baptism, Confirmation, Ordination, and the Anointing of the Sick) flows logically from this central idea.

Newman also describes how the sacrament of Penance developed from the sacrament of baptism. The New Testament is clear that a person's sins are washed away in baptism (e.g., Acts 2:38; Col 2:12). However, what about sins that are committed after baptism? They cannot be cleansed by another baptism, since baptism is given only once (e.g., Eph 4:5).

This question caused great controversy in the early church. Since the answer was unclear, some persons attracted to Christianity delayed receiving baptism until they were on their deathbed to ensure that they would commit no other sins after baptism. Gradually, however, the Church developed the sacrament of Penance as an official means by which the Church could administer God's grace of forgiveness even for sins committed after baptism.[40]

The sacrament of penance, not explicitly described in Scripture, then, developed from the practice of baptism, which is recognized explicitly in Scripture.[41]

Reading Scripture within the Tradition 9.16

In the Roman Catholic tradition, a valid interpretation of Scripture requires paying attention to its two inseparable aspects: the human and the divine. Proper understanding of the human author of a scriptural book involves interpreting that author's intention within his historical and cultural context, and thus requires the application of a variety of historical-critical and literary tools to the text.

The use of the historical-critical and related methods alone, however, cannot lead to a proper theological understanding of Scripture. These methods, focused on understanding the human author, must be supplemented by approaches that read the text theologically and attempt to recover its spiritual sense—that is, how it applies to the church community today.

To understand Scripture theologically, one must also read particular passages within Scripture as a whole and within Church Tradition. Church Tradition, especially its teaching authority, the Magisterium, serves as a guide to

---

39. Ibid., 36, 325.

40. Newman, *Development of Doctrine*, 60–63; 384–88.

41. Scriptural passages such as John 20:22–23 and Matthew 16:19 and 18:18 also support the general theology behind the sacrament of penance, specifically, the Church's authority to forgive sins.

interpretation. Just as Tradition was the guide that first discerned the specific books of the scriptural canon, the Tradition also guides the faithful in a legitimate understanding of and even development of scriptural teaching.

In the Catholic vision, Scripture and Tradition are inseparable. In its widest sense, Tradition is simply the passing down of the Christian faith from generation to generation in all of its fullness: the official teachings, the sacraments, the art and literature, the daily religious experience of the faithful. Scripture is a unique, privileged, and essential expression of that Tradition.

It is a hopeful sign of future Christian unity that understanding of the relationship between Scripture and Tradition among Catholic and other Christian communities is converging, as churches with roots in the Reformation recover a sense of the importance of Tradition and Catholics recover a sense of the centrality of Scripture within the Tradition.

Questions about the Text

1. What did *Dei Verbum* mean by saying that Scripture should be interpreted with both its human and divine aspects in mind?

2. What is the historical-critical method? Define textual, source, and redaction criticism, and give examples.

3. What are some reasons why a modern reader should be aware of the cultural background of Scripture?

4. What are some of the limitations of the historical-critical approach to Scripture, especially if it is used by itself? Describe the alternative concept of an open historical-critical method.

5. Explain the traditional "four senses of Scripture" and how the "literal sense" of Scripture can be grasped with a historical-critical approach.

6. Explain the *Catechism*'s three guidelines for interpreting Scripture theologically.

7. In Catholic thought, define the Magisterium, explain its functions, and explain why it is necessary.

8. How is the Church's role in defining the canon of Scripture related to the Church's claim that its Magisterium should guide the theological interpretation of Scripture?

9. What is the basic meaning of "Tradition" (capital *T*) in Catholic theology? How is *Tradition* distinguished from *traditions* (lowercase *t*)?

10. Why do Catholics say that the entirety of their faith is not found in Scripture? Name some specific references to non-scriptural oral traditions in Scripture itself.

11. Name some specific beliefs or practices held generally by Christian churches that are not in Scripture.

12. Why does every religion that has a scripture also have an official authority to provide correct interpretation?

13. In what ways have modern Protestant and Evangelical churches recovered a sense of the importance of Tradition?

14. What does Rahner mean by a Catholic *sola scriptura*?

15. How does *Dei Verbum* sum up the relationship between Scripture, Tradition, and Magisterium?

16. In what sense is Scripture the primary authority of Catholics?

17. Explain how Newman saw the sacramental system as a logical development of the Incarnation.

Discussion Questions

1. Does a person need to know the historical and cultural context of Scripture in order to interpret it theologically? Why or why not?

2. Discuss some nontheological examples of how a text requires interpretation by a reliable interpretive tradition. (Think of the US Constitution or other codes of law or interpretations of classic literary texts such as those by Shakespeare.)

3. Reflect on another institution, such as a college or sports team. Does this organization have a certain Tradition that never changes alongside traditions that are open to change?

4. What are your experiences or knowledge of the relationship between Scripture and Tradition in Christianity?

The Historical Jesus, Part I

Is the Christian Jesus the Real Jesus?   10.1

Is the real Jesus—the actual person who lived two thousand years ago in the Galilean village of Nazareth—the same as the Jesus portrayed in the New Testament or Nicene Creed? Alternatively, has the theological agenda of early Christianity so distorted this portrayal that the real Jesus, the Jesus of history, is no longer recognizable? This question, raised already in the first Christian centuries, has become more insistent since the time of the Enlightenment.

This chapter considers the issues involved in the "quest for the historical Jesus," together with the closely related question of the historical accuracy of the Gospels. From a Catholic theological viewpoint, the quest is indeed legitimate and is compatible with traditional Christian views. Just as Catholic tradition accepts the legitimacy of the historical-critical method as one approach to the Scriptures, so too, the tradition has a place for historical study of Jesus in its overall theological vision.

Dividing the Historical Jesus from the Christ of Faith   10.1.1

"Two thousand years later, the Christ of Paul's creation has utterly subsumed the Jesus of history."[1] This quotation, from Reza Aslan's[2] 2013 best-selling book *Zealot: The Life and Times of Jesus of Nazareth*,[3] sums up a widespread claim found in both scholarly and popular writings—that there is a radical difference between who Jesus actually was, "the historical Jesus," and Jesus as he is portrayed in the New Testament and Nicene Creed, "the Christ of faith."

---

1. Reza Aslan, *Zealot: The Life and Times of Jesus of Nazareth* (New York: Random House, 2013).

2. A video recording of a PBS *NewsHour* interview of Reza Aslan is accessible at *www.youtube .com/watch?v=YKc2kjgo7dU* (time 0:06:01).

3. Fr. Robert Barron comments on Aslan's *Zealot* in a video accessible at *www.youtube.com /watch?v=YtvXbEMkiCY* (time 10:09).

In Aslan's view, the **historical Jesus** never claimed to be divine. The historical Jesus did indeed claim to be the Messiah, but he saw himself as a strictly this-worldly Messiah, a king who would establish the kingdom of God on Earth. This kingdom was also strictly this-worldly—it would be established by driving out the Roman forces that occupied Israel and overthrowing the priestly aristocracy and the Temple system in Jerusalem.

It was only after Jesus' death, Aslan argues, that people who did not know the historical Jesus created the myth that Jesus was God, the Son, who had come down to Earth in human form. The myth was officially recognized by state-sponsored councils such as Nicaea and has been the belief of Christians ever since.

Aslan is not alone in his claims. Following are just a few examples of contemporary challenges to the traditional Christian portrait of Jesus found in the Gospels.

- According to New Testament scholar John Dominic Crossan, Jesus preached a radical vision of a this-worldly kingdom of God in which all people were equal, but he never claimed to be the savior. Christians later invented stories of Jesus' bodily resurrection.[4]
- According to early Christian scholar Bart Ehrman, Jesus was an apocalyptic prophet who preached God's imminent judgment but did not consider himself divine in any sense. "The idea that Jesus was divine was a later Christian invention, one found, among our Gospels, only in John."[5]
- Aslan and Ehrman write that the Gospels are not eyewitness accounts of Jesus. Rather, they are documents of faith, written decades after Jesus' life by people who did not know Jesus.[6]

The challenge to traditional Christianity is clear: these scholars insist that the historical Jesus is radically different from traditional Christian claims.

Reasons for the Quest for the Historical Jesus   10.2

The traditional Catholic belief that faith and reason are in harmony cannot ignore this reasonable challenge from scholars of history. Following are some reasons why traditional Christians take interest in scholarly debate about the historical Jesus.

---

4. John Dominic Crossan, *The Historical Jesus: The Life of a Mediterranean Jewish Peasant* (San Francisco: HarperSanFrancisco, 1991).

5. Bart D. Ehrman, *Jesus Interrupted: Revealing the Hidden Contradictions in the Bible (And Why We Don't Know About Them)*, (New York: Harper Collins e-books, 2009), PDF e-book, 249.

6. Ehrman, *Jesus Interrupted*, 143–44; Aslan, *Zealot*, xxvi.

Christianity Makes Historical Claims   10.2.1

A central theological claim of Christianity is that Jesus Christ, in his existence on Earth two thousand years ago, was fully divine and fully human. The first part of this claim is not open to scientific or historical investigation: one cannot prove or disprove the claim about Jesus' divinity in scientific or historical fashion, because its subject matter is transcendent. Jesus' human activities, on the other hand, are open to historical investigation. Christianity's claims are very specific: Jesus of Nazareth lived at a specific time, born around 3 BCE and died around 30 CE, and in a specific place, the provinces of Galilee and Judea in the eastern Roman Empire, and that he did and said specific things that are publicly recorded, primarily in the Gospels. The accuracy of these documents is also open to historical investigation, as the documents make not only theological claims about Jesus but also historical claims.

If it can be proven on a historical level that the actual Jesus of Nazareth was radically different from the historical and theological portrait of him given in the Gospels, this would indeed *disprove* the truth of Christianity. If Christianity makes historical claims that can be proven fundamentally wrong, then the Christian faith is not true.

Historical Questions about the Gospels   10.2.2

The historical circumstances in which the Gospels were written raise legitimate questions about the reliability of the Gospels. Consider the following examples:

1. **Differences between the Gospels.** As noted in section 9.2.2, a comparison of the same story in Matthew, Mark, and Luke shows a pattern of both similarity and difference. When one compares these accounts with those in the Gospel of John, the differences are greater still. These differences force the reader to ask the historical question: What is the reason for these differences, and what do these differences say about the historical accuracy of the Gospels?

2. **Possible changes during the oral tradition.** It is a historical fact that Jesus' teachings and the stories about Jesus were passed down orally before they were written in the Gospels. According to the most widely accepted historical-critical scholarly theory, the Gospel of Mark was the first of the Gospels, written approximately 65–70 CE. As Jesus died around the year 30 CE, the Jesus tradition was passed down primarily by oral tradition for a period of 35 to 40 years. To what extent were Jesus traditions lost, changed, distorted, or reinterpreted during this time?

3. **Translation.** Jesus spoke Aramaic; the Gospels are written in Greek. How accurately was the material translated?

4. **Supernatural events.** The Gospels report numerous supernatural events: Jesus miraculously cures illnesses, casts out demonic spirits from people, walks on water, and even raises people from the dead. This material raises the fundamental issue of worldview: Are supernatural events possible? If they are not, then clearly the Gospels are not historically reliable documents.

Does History Matter?   10.3

Some Christians, such as Roman Catholic author Luke Timothy Johnson, have denied that the historical Jesus is relevant for faith.[7] Johnson criticizes the approach of historians who dissect New Testament documents for historical information, because these documents were not intended to provide such information. For Johnson, the "real Jesus" cannot refer to a historical reconstruction by scholars but only to contemporary Christians' claims of encountering the real Jesus in religious experiences and convictions that are based on the New Testament. Because it is based on private religious experience, the Christian claim to encounter the real Jesus is not open to historical challenge, though it is open to religious, theological, or moral challenges.[8]

Johnson correctly points out the limitations of historical research into the Gospels and the tendency of many scholars to claim more than they can know, as responsible historians, about the history of earliest Christianity.[9] He is also correct to say that the Christian faith cannot be based on the results of a historical-critical investigation of Jesus. The object of the Church's worship in the Catholic view can only be Jesus as made known through Scripture and Tradition, including the sacraments, liturgy, and the interpretation of Scripture as found in the creeds. Theologian Avery Dulles agrees, "But in no case does the method [i.e., historical method] provide a religiously adequate portrait, one that can take the place of Jesus Christ as proclaimed by the Church and received in faith."[10]

Nevertheless, Johnson's criticism tends to border on fideism (sec. 2.6). As has been stressed throughout this book, the Catholic tradition insists that faith and reason cannot be separated, and so, one should by no means conclude that historical research is irrelevant to Christian faith. Just as the Catholic tradition rejects a nonoverlapping magisterial (NOMA) response that would partition faith and science into separate and mutually exclusive realms

---

7. Johnson, *The Real Jesus: The Misguided Quest for the Historical Jesus and the Truth of the Traditional Gospels* (San Francisco: HarperSanFrancisco, 1996).

8. Ibid., 167.

9. Ibid., 81–104.

10. Avery Dulles, *The Craft of Theology: From Symbol to System* (New York: Crossroad, 1995), 224.

(sec. 4.10.2.4), so too the tradition rejects separating history and faith into separate realms.

Dei Verbum explicitly recognizes the importance of the historical trustworthiness of the Gospels, affirming that

> . . . the four Gospels just named, whose historical character the Church unhesitatingly asserts, faithfully hand on what Jesus Christ, while living among men, really did and taught for their eternal salvation. (*DV*, no. 19)

Because the Church upholds the historicity of the Gospels, the Church should also be able to provide reasonable answers to those who question it. As Aquinas wrote, the Christian tradition cannot *prove* the truth of an article of faith to a skeptic, but it can answer the skeptic's claims that a particular article of faith is illogical or unreasonable (*ST* 1.1.8). When critics attack traditional beliefs about Jesus from a historical perspective, the Christian should be able to demonstrate that Christian beliefs are at least historically plausible.

A Brief History of the Quest for the Historical Jesus 10.4

Any discussion of the historical Jesus should consider the gains and limitations of previous scholarly research into this topic.

The "First Quest"[11] had its immediate roots in the Enlightenment. Using historical-critical methods, often combined with a rationalist worldview, these researchers rejected the Gospel portraits of Jesus and offered their own reconstruction of his life. Hermann Samuel Reimarus (1694–1768) is usually identified as the pioneer of this movement; other well-known products of the quest included books on the life of Jesus by David Strauss (1835) and Ernest Renan (1863).[12] In his well-known critique of this initial quest, however, Albert Schweitzer showed how the allegedly historical lives of Jesus were not really historical at all—each author portrayed Jesus in a way that reflected his subjective interests. For example, liberal Christians who understood Christianity primarily as an ethical religion portrayed Jesus primarily as an ethical teacher.[13]

---

11. A video presenting N. T. Wright commenting on the quests for the historical Jesus is accessible at *www.youtube.com/watch?v=bm4iOlRCLMI* (time 0:03:25).

12. For a history of the various stages of the so-called quest for the historical Jesus, see N. T. Wright, *Jesus and the Victory of God* (Minneapolis: Fortress, 1996), 13–124.

13. Schweitzer, *The Quest of the Historical Jesus* (Minneapolis: Fortress, 2001; Originally published 1906; rev. 1913).

For the next fifty years, there was little interest in further historical Jesus research.[14] Biblical scholars such as Rudolf Bultmann argued that the Gospels portraits of Jesus were so heavily influenced by the theological agenda of the early Church that it was now virtually impossible to recover the historical Jesus behind these portraits. On a theological level, Bultmann added, the quest was unnecessary, because faith depends on accepting the New Testament proclamations about Jesus, not the results of historical investigation.

A "Second Quest" for the historical Jesus, however, began in the 1950s, led by biblical scholars such as Bultmann's students Ernst Käsemann and Günther Bornkamm. These scholars insisted that the quest was legitimate, because it is important for faith to show a connection between the New Testament proclamation and the actual Jesus of history. A third phase, sometimes called the "Third Quest," began in the 1970s and continues to this day."[15] Chapter 11 discusses this "Third Quest" in detail.

The following sections consider a specifically Catholic response to the quest, beginning with the fundamental question of the historical reliability of the Gospels.

Catholic Responses to Historical Challenges: Recognizing How the Tradition Was Passed Down

10.5

As noted, Vatican II's *Dei Verbum* (no. 19) explicitly recognizes the importance of the historical trustworthiness of the Gospels. To respond to critical challenges to the historicity of the Gospels, it is essential to develop a concrete view of how the actual traditions about Jesus were passed down. A 1964 publication of the Pontifical Biblical Commission (PBC), *Instruction Concerning the Historical Truth of the Gospels*[16] does just this, referring to three stages in which accounts of Jesus' sayings and actions (no. VI.2) were passed down:

1. **Jesus' public ministry.** Jesus preached and taught his apostles and larger crowds (no. VII; generally dated 27–30 CE).

2. **Apostolic preaching.** After Jesus' death and Resurrection, his apostles preached and taught about him, primary by oral tradition (no. VIII; generally dated 30–70 CE).

3. **The writing of the four Gospels.** (no. IX; generally dated 70–100 CE).

---

14. A video presenting Darrell Bock commenting on the quests for the historical Jesus is accessible at *www.youtube.com/watch?v=gX2IL4F5B6U* (time 0:04:37).

15. See N. T. Wright, *Jesus and the Victory of God* (Minneapolis: Fortress, 1996), 83–124.

16. The text of the PBC's *Instruction Concerning the Historical Truth of the Gospels* is accessible at *http://catholic-resources.org/ChurchDocs/PBC_HistTruthFitzmyer.htm* - PBCText.

246 REASON, FAITH, AND TRADITION

In the following sections, each stage is discussed, with details provided from contemporary historical scholarship.

Stage 1: Jesus and His Disciples   10.5.1

The *Instruction* states, "Christ our Lord joined to Himself chosen disciples, who followed Him from the beginning, saw His deeds, heard His words, and in this way were equipped to be witnesses of His life and doctrine" (no. VII). The *Instruction*, here, makes the historically well-supported point that Jesus deliberately chose twelve close companions who lived with him from the beginning of his public ministry and who were eyewitnesses of his life and teaching (see Mark 3:13–19 par.).[17] They would have heard Jesus' teaching repeatedly over the course of the three years of his public ministry.

Even the most skeptical reconstructions of the historical Jesus acknowledge that he was a Jewish teacher (*rabbi* in Hebrew); the ancient Jewish historian Josephus also noted the title (*Antiquities* 18.3).[18] This simple fact correlates well with the view of the disciples as reliable witnesses.[19] Jewish teachers in Jesus' time had disciples; the primary meaning of the Greek word translated as "disciple," *mathetes*, is "learner" or "student." The specific function of the disciples was to carefully preserve and pass on the teachings of and stories about the master.[20]

Jesus taught his disciples in ways that would fix his teachings in their memories. He taught in short, well-crafted sayings and parables, using familiar examples, so that his teaching could be remembered easily and accurately.[21] Consider the following examples:

- "Blessed are the merciful, for they will be shown mercy" (Matt 5:7).
- "The kingdom of heaven is like a mustard seed that a person took and sowed in a field" (Matt 13:31).
- "The kingdom of heaven is like yeast that a woman took and mixed with three measures of wheat flour until the whole batch was leavened" (Matt 13:33).

---

17. The abbreviation *par.* indicates that a parallel version of this passage is found in one or more of the other canonical Gospels.

18. The text of Josephus's *Antiquities* is accessible at *www.gutenberg.org/files/2848/2848-h/2848-h.htm#link182HCH0003*.

19. On the importance of Jesus as a teacher and the subsequent reliability of the Gospels, see Rainer Riesner, "From the Messianic Jesus to the Gospels of Jesus Christ" in *Handbook for the Study of the Historical Jesus, Volume 1: How to Study the Historical Jesus*, ed. T. Holmén and S. E. Porter (Leiden: Brill, 2011), 405–46; and S. Byrskog, "The Transmission of the Jesus Tradition," in *Handbook for the Study of the Historical Jesus, Volume 2: The Study of Jesus*, 1465–94.

20. See Birger Gerhardsson, *The Reliability of the Gospel Tradition* (Peabody, MA: Hendrickson, 2001), 7–9; Riesner, "Messianic Teacher, 420–22; Byrskog, "Jesus Tradition," 1476–77.

21. Riesner, "Messianic Teacher," 417–20.

Because his disciples regarded Jesus as an authoritative teacher, it stands to reason that from the start, they were concerned about preserving his words as faithfully as possible.[22]

The Gospels, moreover, also report that Jesus taught his disciples privately, clarifying the deeper meaning of his public teaching (see Mark 4:1–20 par. and 10:1–12 par.). Jesus sent the disciples out on their own to preach the message of the coming kingdom of God to the Galilean villages (see Mark 6:7–13). The disciples, at that point, very plausibly began making collections of Jesus' sayings, either oral or written, to help in their preaching.[23]

There were, in addition to the Twelve, numerous other eyewitnesses of Jesus' teaching and actions. Richard Bauckham[24] has argued that when the Gospels mention an incidental name in a narrative (for example, the mention of Simon of Cyrene and his son in Mark 15:21), they are referring to the eyewitness who passed down that account.[25]

Stage 2: The Oral Tradition of the Disciples   10.5.2

Much New Testament scholarship, influenced by a scholarly method known as form-criticism (a variation of source criticism) works with a model in which Jesus traditions were passed down anonymously by early Christian "communities," and were subject to change due to the particular needs of those communities.[26] New Testament scholar Bart Ehrman compares the oral tradition to the "telephone game," in which traditions were passed down "not as disinterested news stories reported by eyewitnesses but as propaganda meant to convert people to faith, told by people who had heard them fifth-or sixth-or nineteenth-hand."[27]

Evidence of Careful, Systematic Passing Down of Traditions   10.5.2.1

The evidence of the New Testament, however, paints a different picture. Section 9.11.1 describes how traditions in the early church were passed down in a careful, systematic fashion, as one sees in Paul's reminder to his congregation, "I handed on to you as of first importance what I also received: that Christ died for our sins . . . was buried . . . was raised on the third day"

---

22. Ibid., 414–416; Gerhardsson, *The Reliability of the Gospel Tradition*, 27–29; Byrskog, "Jesus Tradition," 1479.

23. Riesner, "Messianic Teacher," 422–23; Byrskog, "Jesus Tradition," 1476–77.

24. A video presenting Richard Bauckham discussing *Jesus and the Eyewitnesses* is accessible at *www.youtube.com/watch?v=292NTf1cCNw* (time 0:10:28).

25. Bauckham, *Jesus and the Eyewitnesses*, 47– 55.

26. For an overview of form-critical assumptions, see PBC, *Interpretation of the Bible in the Church*, I.A; Eddy and Boyd, *Jesus Legend*, 239–41; Bauckham, *Jesus and the Eyewitnesses*, 241–46.

27. Ehrman, *Jesus Interrupted*, 146–47.

(1 Cor 15:3–4).[28] Paul did not know Jesus during Jesus' life on Earth, and so he most likely received this tradition from Jesus' disciples.[29]

What does it mean, concretely, for Paul to "hand down" a tradition to his church? New Testament scholar Birger Gerhardsson, drawing on his knowledge of similar transmission of tradition in later rabbinic circles, clarifies what the process must have been:

> Either the apostle has passed the text on in a written form which the congregation then has at its disposal, or he has presented the text orally, and impressed it upon them in such a way that the congregation (or, more precisely, one of its leaders) knows it by heart. To "hand over" a text is not the same as to recite it once. It rather means that the text is presented to the hearers in such a way that they "received" it and possess it.[30]

After handing down a tradition with fixed wording, a teacher such as Paul might then have added some interpretive comments, as Paul seems to have done in 1 Cor 15:6.[31]

Luke also insists that those who were "eyewitnesses from the beginning and ministers of the word" handed down the Jesus material. Bauckham[32] writes that the process of passing down traditions about Jesus technically not be called *oral tradition*[33]—usually referring to the passing down of traditions beyond one generation—but *oral history*—the passing down of traditions within the lifetime of eyewitnesses.[34]

The Twelve, the Jerusalem Church, and the Authoritative Handing Down of Tradition   10.5.2.2

Jesus' twelve disciples were the central eyewitnesses to what Jesus said and did. After Jesus' death, the New Testament records that the Twelve, along with James, brother of the Lord, became leaders of the first church in Jerusalem (see Acts 6:2; Gal 2:9). Bauckham agrees with Gerhardsson that "we should certainly expect them [the Twelve] to have been authoritative transmitters of the

---

28. On 1 Cor 15:3–4 as an example of Paul carefully receiving and passing on an apostolic tradition, see Gerhardsson, *Memory and Manuscript*, 295–300.

29. In his Letter to the Galatians, Paul reports meeting with the apostle Peter (Cephas is the Aramaic version of Peter's name) (1:18). See also Gerhardsson, *Memory and Manuscript*, 296–298.

30. Gerhardsson, *Gospel Tradition*, 22. See also Riesner, "Messianic Teacher," 429–31; Byrskog, "Jesus Tradition," 1482–83.

31. Gerhardsson, *Memory and Manuscript*, 299–300; *Gospel Tradition*, 21–22.

32. A video presenting Richard Bauckham discussing the Gospels as eyewitness testimony is accessible at *www.youtube.com/watch?v=XL01T4mVBf8*.

33. For more on oral tradition see video presentation by Darrell Bock accessible at *www.youtube.com/watch?v=--Qy3VcbwGE* (time 0:05:33).

34. Bauckham, *Jesus and the Eyewitnesses*, 30–38.

traditions of Jesus and to have had something like an official status for their formulation of those traditions."[35] In other words, the Twelve would have had a key role in collecting, authenticating, organizing, and interpreting the various sayings, stories, and teachings about Jesus.

The Twelve would have had assistance in this task. The Jerusalem community was bilingual, composed of both Greek- and Aramaic-speaking believers (see Acts 6:1); the community also included "a large group of priests" (Acts 6:7) as well as Pharisees (Acts 15:5). It is doubtless in the Jerusalem church that the Jesus' tradition was translated from Aramaic into Greek.[36]

The Jerusalem church did not produce a full, written Gospel. However, as Gerhardsson has shown, the church must have worked intensively with the early traditions about Jesus. Traditions were arranged either in writing or memorized in oral texts so that they could be passed down accurately to other communities. The Jerusalem community had an authoritative status as the original source of the Jesus traditions; even Paul, who emphasizes his independence as an apostle, acknowledged the authority of the Jerusalem church to approve his teaching (see Gal 2:2).[37]

Outside the Jerusalem church, authoritative individuals handed on the Jesus traditions. The New Testament often refers to "teachers" (Acts 13:1; Rom 12:7; 1 Cor 12:28–29; Eph 4:11; Heb 5:12; Jas 3:1) in the various churches who would have taught the traditions; Luke refers to "ministers of the word" (Luke 1:2).[38] Presbyters, or elders, appointed by the apostles also played a role in handing on tradition and teaching (see Acts 14:23; 1 Tim 4:13–14; Titus 1:5–9).

Written Notes and Oral Tradition 10.5.2.3

The view that the oral stage of passing down Jesus tradition was completely oral is inaccurate. Some of the Twelve were surely able to write, most obviously Matthew, the tax collector (Matt 10:3). Gerhardsson has shown the important role that written notes played in the rabbinic oral tradition. By analogy, there is no reason to doubt that unofficial written collections of Jesus' sayings and key points of the tradition were written by the early Christian preachers for use in their preaching and teaching, even during the lifetime of Jesus.[39]

The PBC, then, is correct to say that some skeptical scholars "make light of the authority of the apostles as witnesses to Christ, and of their task and influence in the primitive community, extolling rather the creative power of that community" (no. V.1). The evidence shows that the oral tradition was a careful, systematic process of handing down eyewitness's accounts of Jesus' sayings and actions.

---

35. Ibid., 94.

36. Riesner, "Messianic Teacher," 439–40.

37. See Gerhardsson, *Memory and Manuscript*, 220–61, 274–80.

38. See Eddy and Boyd, *Jesus Legend*, 264–66.

39. See Gerhardsson, *Gospel Tradition*, 1–13; Eddy and Boyd, *Jesus Legend*, 241–52; Riesner, "Messianic Teacher," 433–34.

The Written Gospels   10.5.3

Dei Verbum notes that the four Gospels are not necessarily the direct writings of the apostles. Rather, the Gospels are of apostolic origin. "For what the Apostles preached in fulfillment of the commission of Christ, afterwards they themselves and apostolic men, under the inspiration of the divine Spirit, handed on to us in writing: the foundation of faith, namely, the fourfold Gospel, according to Matthew, Mark, Luke and John" (*DV*, no. 18). Luke and Mark were not among the twelve apostles. As noted in section 8.11, the Gospel of John gives clear evidence that it is not the work of one author (John 21:24).

The Evangelists and Their Symbols   10.5.3.1

In Christian art, one often sees each of the four evangelists associated with a particular symbol.

One widespread approach associates Matthew with a human or angel, Mark with a lion, Luke with a calf or ox, and John with an eagle. These associations seem to be based on John's vision of the "four living creatures" around God's throne in Revelation 4:7 "The first creature resembled a lion, the second was like a calf, the third had a face like that of a human being, and the fourth looked like an eagle in flight." This vision in turn connects with visions of the prophet Ezekiel (1:1–11; 10:14). Irenaeus (*Against Heresies* 3.11.8) associates the winged lion with John, because of that Gospel's glorious teaching in John 1:1–3: "In the beginning was the Word, and the Word was with God, and the Word was God . . ." The calf alludes to the priestly nature of Luke's Gospel because calves are

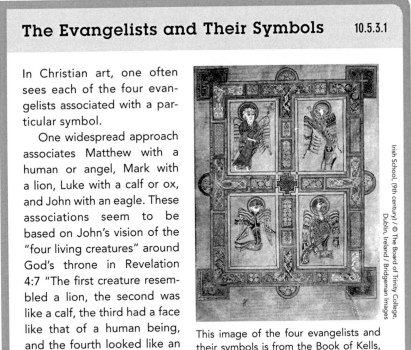

Irish School, (9th century) / © The Board of Trinity College, Dublin, Ireland / Bridgeman Images

This image of the four evangelists and their symbols is from the Book of Kells, an illuminated manuscript of the four Gospels dated ca. 800 CE and housed at Trinity College in Dublin. Each figure is portrayed with wings.

Continued

> ### The Evangelists and Their Symbols *Continued*
>
> offered as sacrifices. In addition, the first human to speak in Luke is the priest Zechariah (1:18). The human is associated with Matthew, because his Gospel begins with the genealogy of Jesus' human ancestry and, throughout, portrays Jesus as a humble and meek man. The eagle is associated with Mark, because his Gospel begins with a prophecy coming down from on high (1:2). Augustine (*Harmony of the Gospels* 1.6.9) prefers to link the lion to Matthew, the man to Mark, the calf to Luke, and the eagle to John. Jerome (*Preface to Commentary on Matthew*) witnesses to the most common associations mentioned above.

Nevertheless, a strong case can be made that all four Gospels draw directly on apostolic eyewitnesses and tradition. Traditionally, Mark is associated with the apostle Peter. Papias[40] (ca. 60–130 CE), a bishop of Hierapolis in Asia Minor, calls Mark an interpreter of Peter who wrote down accurately, although not in order, what he heard from Peter concerning the words and actions of Jesus; Irenaeus (*Against Heresies* 3.1.1) also knows this tradition.[41] Luke states that he draws on eyewitness accounts (1:2); the apostles certainly would have been among these eyewitnesses.[42] John asserts that his Gospel is based on the eyewitness testimony of Jesus' disciple (21:24).

The reliability of the four canonical Gospels as faithful witnesses to Jesus was firmly established by the mid- to late-second century. As Irenaeus, around 180 CE, writes, "It is not possible that the Gospels can be either more or fewer in number than they are. For since there are four zones of the world in which we live, and four principal winds . . . it is fitting that she should have four pillars" (*Against Heresies* 3.11.8).

Flexibility in the Tradition   10.6

The PBC's *Instruction*, while arguing for the historical accuracy of the Gospels, does not claim that they are *verbatim* accounts. The apostles of Jesus took "into account in their method of preaching the circumstances in which their listeners

---

40. Papias's account is quoted by the ancient church historian Eusebius (*Ecclesiastical History* 3.39.15) accessible at *www.ccel.org/ccel/schaff/npnf201.iii.viii.xxxix.html*.

41. For more on this tradition see video presenting Martin Hengel accessible at *www.youtube .com/watch?v=BD403cPOu2A* (time 0:08:24).

42. Bauckham, *Jesus and the Eyewitnesses*, 123.

252 REASON, FAITH, AND TRADITION

found themselves" and "interpreted His words and deeds according to the needs of their listeners" (no. VIII). *Dei Verbum* agrees that the Gospel writers did not simply write down, word-for-word, the testimony of eyewitnesses but engaged in a process of "selecting some things from the many which had been handed on by word of mouth or in writing, reducing some of them to a synthesis, explaining some things in view of the situation of their churches and preserving the form of proclamation but always in such fashion that they told us the honest truth about Jesus" (no. 19).

As a concrete example of how the Gospel writers recorded tradition "in view of the situation of their churches" (*DV*, no. 19), one can compare two versions of Jesus' teaching on divorce: Matthew 19:1–12 and Mark 10:1–12. Both accounts preserve essentially the same teachings, with Jesus using a quotation from Genesis 2:24 ("That is why a man leaves his father and mother and clings to his wife, and the two of them become one body") to show that divorce and remarriage contradict God's original plan: "what God has joined together, no human being must separate" (Matt 19:6; Mark 10:9). However, Matthew's and Mark's versions of Jesus' further explanation of the teaching differ:

[W]hoever divorces his wife (unless the marriage is unlawful) and marries another commits adultery. (Matt 19:9)

Whoever divorces his wife and marries another commits adultery against her; and if she divorces her husband and marries another, she commits adultery. (Mark 10:11–12)

Notice two differences. First, Matthew applies the teaching only to the case of a man divorcing his wife. This is most likely Jesus' original teaching, because in first-century Jewish society, women had little or no right to initiate a divorce against their husbands. Mark, who most scholars agree was writing for a Greco-Roman audience (many think his Gospel was written in Rome), adjusts Jesus' teaching to include the possibility of a woman initiating the divorce, because such a scenario was plausible in Greco-Roman society.

Notice, too, that Matthew includes an exception to Jesus' teaching: "unless the marriage is unlawful."[43] While it is possible that Matthew is using another version of Jesus' teaching, it is more likely that Matthew added this phrase to adjust Jesus' teaching to the needs of his audience because only Matthew has this exception; versions of Jesus' teaching on divorce in Luke 16:18, Mark 10:1–12, and 1 Corinthians 7:10 do not.

Why did Matthew apparently add this phrase? In early Christianity, many Gentiles joined the Christian communities, and some were married to relatives; those marriages were in violation of the rules in the Torah (for example, the

---

43. In Greek, the literal wording of the "exception" clause is "except in cases of porneia"—*porneia* was a general term for a sexual sin. This exception clause can be translated in different ways: the NIV, for example, translates "except for marital unfaithfulness."

rules in Lev 18:6 –18). Such marriages would have been considered a kind of sexual sin and unlawful. It seems that Matthew adjusted Jesus' basic teaching on divorce to apply to a situation that did not exist in Jesus' lifetime.[44]

This example of Jesus' teaching supports Gerhardsson's view that the Jesus tradition was passed down in fixed sayings that allowed for flexible interpretation.

Remembering with Fuller Understanding   10.7

The PBC writes further,

> On the other hand, there is no reason to deny that the apostles passed on to their listeners what was really said and done by the Lord with that fuller understanding which they enjoyed, having been instructed by the glorious events of the Christ and taught by the light of the Spirit of Truth. (no. VIII)

The PBC cites some texts from the Gospel of John that suggest that the events of the Resurrection influenced the disciples' memories of historical events. When Jesus entered Jerusalem riding on a donkey, for example, John comments that the disciples did not understand, but "when Jesus had been glorified they remembered that these things were written about him and that they had done this for him" (John 12:16; cf. 2:22).

The point was reiterated in *Dei Verbum* (no. 19): "Indeed, after the Ascension of the Lord the Apostles handed on to their hearers what He had said and done. This they did with that clearer understanding which they enjoyed after they had been instructed by the glorious events of Christ's life and taught by the light of the Spirit of truth."

Consider the following example of how that "fuller understanding" might have been expressed. In John 6:22–59, the evangelist records an exchange between a crowd and Jesus at the village of Capernaum in Galilee. Several indications show that this is not a strictly historical record.

First, Jesus makes explicit claims about himself that are not found in the Synoptic Gospels: "I am the bread of life; whoever comes to me will never hunger" (6:35); "To everyone who sees the Son and believes in him may have eternal life" (6:40); "Everyone eats my flesh and drinks my blood has eternal life, and I will raise him up on the last day" (6:54). If Jesus clearly said such significant things about himself in his public teaching, why do the other Gospels not record them?

Second, Jesus' words are in the form of a lengthy discourse, not in the short sayings that characterize the Synoptic Gospels and that, as Gerhardsson has shown, were characteristic of the historical Jesus.

---

44. See the notes to Matthew 5:31–32 in *The Catholic Study Bible New American Bible*, 2nd ed. (Oxford: Oxford University Press, 2006).

Third, the narrative refers to the crowd as "[t]he Jews" (6:41, 52). Jesus tells the crowd, "Your ancestors ate the manna in the desert" (6:49), instead of "our ancestors," setting himself apart from "the Jews." Historically, Jesus was of course a Jew, his followers were all Jews, and the crowds to whom he spoke would have been almost exclusively Jewish. John's narrative, then, is written decades after the death of Jesus, from a perspective in which there was indeed a sharp distinction between "the Jews" and Jesus' followers, now known as "Christians." Such a sharp distinction would have been incomprehensible for the historical Jesus.

Fourth, it seems clear that references to eating the body and drinking the blood of Jesus are influenced by later reflection on the Christian practice of the Lord's Supper. It is historically incomprehensible that Jesus would have publicly discussed the intimate meaning of the Last Supper with a crowd long before the actual Last Supper with his disciples had taken place. In the Synoptic Gospels, the words, "This is my body, which will be given for you; do this in memory of me" (Luke 22:19) are given to the Twelve disciples only shortly before his death.

John, then, is not writing strict history, in the sense of recording events as they actually occurred. Later perspectives color his portrait of Jesus, as the Gospel (12:16) plainly states. The unique character of John has long been recognized; Clement of Alexandria wrote that "John, perceiving that the external facts had been made plain in the Gospel [of Mark], being urged by his friends, and inspired by the Spirit, composed a spiritual Gospel" (quoted in Eusebius's *Ecclesiastical History* 6.14.7). Clement's remarks seem to be a fair assessment of John's writing: John is not concerned so much with chronological order or strict historical accuracy, as with bringing out the full spiritual meaning of Jesus' life and actions. Writing with full knowledge of Jesus' words at the Last Supper and of the early Christian practice of sharing the Lord's Supper, John places a theological interpretation of the Lord's Supper on Jesus' lips at a time and place, when, historically speaking, Jesus certainly did not say them.

Scripture and History: Ancient Jewish Perspectives   10.8

As *Dei Verbum* (no. 12) recognizes, to understand ancient authors, one must be aware of the literary forms they used. Later Jewish authors employed what Second Temple Jewish scholar Devorah Dimant calls the "compositional" use of Scripture, in which "biblical elements are woven into the work without external formal markers."[45] The author of Tobit models his title character on the earlier biblical character of Job. The author deliberately reuses details from Job's

---

45. Devorah Dimant, "Use and Interpretation of Mikra in the Apocrypha and Pseudepigrapha," in *Mikra: Text, Translation, Reading and Interpretation of the Hebrew Bible in Ancient Judaism and Early Christianity*, ed. M. J. Mulder; (repr. Peabody, MA: Hendrickson, 2004), 382.

life—his prosperity, his loss of possessions, his nagging wife, his prayer asking to die—in his portrait of Tobit (see Tobit 1–3).[46]

Dimant suggests that this same process occurs in historical narration. In 1 Maccabees, she shows that the description of how Judas Maccabeus was denied safe passage through the city of Ephron during the rebellion against the Greek ruler Antiochus Epiphanes (1 Macc 5:48) is modeled on an account in Numbers 20–21 in which the Israelites were denied safe passage through Edom and the land of the Amorites. Dimant suggests that the words of Judas are a conflated quotation of Numbers 21:22, Deuteronomy 2:26–29, and Judges 11:19 three versions of the Israelites' request for safe passage to King Sihon of the Amorites. By employing this technique, "the author of 1 Maccabees implies that Judas was enacting the patterns of biblical history."[47]

The interpreter of the Gospels, then, should be open to the possibility that the Gospel writers often wrote in this same way—weaving the paradigms, patterns, and even details of Scripture into their telling of the story of Jesus. From a historical-critical perspective, one must distinguish between events that are clearly historical and events that may reflect a compositional use of Scripture—weaving in Scripture as part of composing a narrative.

Compositional Uses of Scripture and the Passion Narratives　　10.8.1

The use of scripture, both in direct citations and in allusions, is prevalent in the passion narratives. For example, in his account of Jesus' crucifixion, Mark reports that the Roman soldiers "divided his garments by casting lots" (Mark 15:24 par.). This appears to be an allusion to Psalm 22:19: "They divide my garments among them; for my clothing they cast lots." The Gospel of John expands the narrative of this incident and ends it with a quotation of Psalm 22:19, prefaced with "in order that the passage of scripture might be fulfilled" (John 19:24).

Did early Christians make up this scene, based on Psalm 22:19? Alternatively, are the Gospels recording an event that truly did fulfill prophecy? It is historically certain that Jesus was crucified. A further historical fact is that victims of crucifixion were generally crucified naked and so the dividing of Jesus' clothes is historically plausible. Brown suggests that the original tradition of Jesus' crucifixion that was passed down included "the customary stripping of the prisoner but doing so in the language of a psalm about the suffering just one."[48] In other words, the Gospel writers employed a compositional use of Scripture to fill out some historical details.

---

46. Dimant, "Mikra in the Apocrypha," 418.

47. Ibid., 407.

48. Raymond E. Brown, *The Death of the Messiah: From Gethsemane to the Grave*, 2 vols., Anchor Bible Reference Library (New York: Doubleday, 1994), 2:954.

Jesus' last words from the cross, *"Eloi, Eloi, lema sabachthani?"* ("My God, my God, why have you forsaken me?" Mark 15:34) is a quotation of Psalm 22:2. For Crossan, this is simply another example of "prophecy historicized"—the Gospel writer using details to fill out the narrative for which he had no historical information.

Yet such a conclusion would be too hasty. Historically, there were certainly witnesses to the crucifixion—primarily women who followed Jesus (e.g., Mark 15:40)—who would have heard Jesus' last words. Jesus, as a Jewish teacher, would have been very familiar with the Psalms and may well have used their wording in his final lament.

The final word, then, must be one of caution. The critical reader must be aware that ancient Jewish writers made a compositional use of Scripture even in their historical writing. The Gospel writers certainly use this technique as well, and in a few cases, they have introduced details into their scriptural accounts that are historically improbable.[49] However, in the great majority of cases, they seem to have used it simply as a technique to describe actual historical events.

Sources for Historical Jesus Research   10.9

The previous discussion has shown that, from a Catholic perspective, the search for the historical Jesus is a legitimate one. There are solid reasons for thinking that there is a distinction between the Christ of faith and the Jesus of history within the Gospels. The challenge of the Catholic interpreter, then, is to show—against the claims that there is a radical difference between them—that there is an essential continuity between the Jesus of history and the Christ of faith.

Section 10.5 provided solid reasons for seeing the Gospels as based on eye-witness testimonies, while section 10.6 cautioned that they should not be seen as *verbatim* reports of Jesus' life. The historical Jesus scholar must ask a further question: Are there other documents that can also give access to the historical Jesus? For the historian, this is an important question, as the Gospels were written by followers of Jesus and in the eyes of skeptical observers, will always be open to the suspicion that they are religious propaganda and not history.

Non-Christian Sources for the Historical Jesus   10.9.1

There is little early, non-Christian evidence for Jesus' life. The little evidence[50] there is allows historians to be confident that Jesus certainly did exist as a

---

49. This seems to have been especially the case in compositions outside of Jesus' public ministry, such as the infancy narratives in Matthew 1–2 and Luke 1–2. The events in Matthew 2, for example, are historically improbable and seem to be modeled on events in the life of Moses. For details, see Brown, *Birth of the Messiah*, 188–229.

50. N. T. Wright discusses evidence for Jesus' existence in a video accessible at *www.youtube.com /watch?v=eeu0ezo7HfA* (time 0:00:53).

historical person.[51] Jesus is mentioned briefly by ancient non-Christian sources that were either indifferent or hostile to the Christian movement and are more likely to serve as "objective" historical witnesses. For example, the Jewish historian Josephus, born shortly after Jesus' death, calls Jesus a "wise man," a "doer of startling deeds," and a "teacher" (*Antiquities* 18.3.3). The Roman historian Tacitus (ca. 57–ca. 118 CE), describing the persecution of Christians by Nero, adds, "Christus, the founder of the name, had undergone the death penalty in the reign of Tiberius, by sentence of the procurator Pontius Pilatus" (*Annals* 15.44). Pliny the Younger (ca. 61–112 CE), a Roman official in Asia Minor, writes of Christians in his district who sang hymns "to Christ as to a god" (*Letter* 10.96).[52]

Noncanonical Christian Sources for the Historical Jesus
10.9.2

In addition to four Gospels, there are also early Christian writings that were not accepted into the Christian canon. Do these documents provide some insight into the historical Jesus?

Some contemporary scholars argue that they do. Leading historical Jesus scholar John Dominic Crossan, for example, argues that use of noncanonical sources allows people to recover a more accurate picture of who Jesus really was. Relying on hypothetical early versions of the *Gospel of Thomas*, which he dates to within twenty years of Jesus' death, and "Q," a hypothetical collection of Jesus' sayings that many scholars believe Matthew and Luke used as a source, Crossan, and others—especially a group of scholars known as the Jesus Seminar—argue that the historical Jesus was essentially a wise man who taught a radical form of social equality.[53] Beliefs that Jesus was the Messiah, the Son of God, the Savior, that he rose from the dead, and other "apocalyptic" ideas are all later developments that have little to do with the actual Jesus of history, these scholars argue.[54] The earliest Christian communities that composed *Thomas* and Q thought of Jesus as a human teacher only and did not believe in his atoning death or Resurrection.

Crossan and the Jesus Seminar's work, then, is a direct challenge to traditional Christian views of Jesus. The introduction to the Jesus Seminar's *The Five*

---

51. See Samuel Byrskog, "The Historicity of Jesus: How Do We Know that Jesus Existed?" in *Handbook for the Study of the Historical Jesus, Vol. 3: The Historical Jesus*, eds. T. Holmén and S. E. Porter (Leiden: Brill, 2011), 2183–2212.

52. For a discussion of these sources, see John P. Meier, *A Marginal Jew: Rethinking the Historical Jesus, Vol. 1: The Roots of the Problem and the Person* (New York: Doubleday, 1991), 56–92; and Eddy and Boyd, *Jesus Legend*, 165–99.

53. On the dating of these documents, see John Dominic Crossan, *The Historical Jesus: The Life of a Mediterranean Jewish Peasant* (San Francisco: HarperSanFrancisco, 1991), 427–29.

54. See Wright's critical summary of their work in *Victory of God*, 29–65.

Gospels, for example, argues that it was only through the efforts of critical scholars beginning in the Enlightenment that "the discrepancy between the Jesus of history and the Christ of faith emerged from under the smothering cloud of the historic creeds."[55]

Scholars such as N. T. Wright have shown, however, that the challenges of the Jesus Seminar and Crossan can be answered on a historical basis. Wright notes that the arguments of these scholars are built on a series of shaky hypotheses.

First, because there is no textual evidence for earlier versions, they must hypothesize that there were earlier "layers" of both the *Gospel of Thomas* and Q that included only the non-apocalyptic wisdom sayings of Jesus. It is especially questionable to hypothesize layers in Q, as Q itself is a hypothetical source.

Second, these scholars make the unwarranted assumption that these earlier versions of Q and *Thomas* represent the comprehensive theological view of entire Christian communities. Simply because these hypothetical communities read a hypothetical collection of Jesus' sayings that do not refer to Jesus' atoning death or Resurrection does not imply that readers of these documents had no such theological beliefs; they may well have had other writings or oral traditions that did refer to these beliefs.[56]

Thomas is not the only noncanonical gospel known from early Christianity. Other writings, such as the *Gospel of the Hebrews* and the *Gospel of the Ebionites*, which are both preserved only in fragmentary form, come from Jewish-Christian sources, followers of Jesus who still kept the Torah. Scholars have also published fragmentary copies of *The Gospel of Peter*, the *Gospel of Mary*, and the *Gospel of Judas*. In several scholarly and popular works, these gospels have been used as evidence that, from the beginning, the Christian movement was quite diversified, with a variety of interpretations of Jesus. Only much later did orthodox Christianity emerge as the "winner," with political support of emperors such as Constantine, marginalizing these other views of Jesus.

Claims based on these gospels, however, lack historical credibility. These gospels date from the second century, after the composition of the canonical Gospels, and often show dependence on those Gospels.[57]

Works such as the *Judas* and *Thomas* gospels show a Gnostic influence. The *Gospel of Thomas*, a collection of 114 sayings attributed to Jesus, may indeed have versions of Jesus' sayings that can be traced back to the historical Jesus. Other sayings, however, are clearly later and reflect Gnostic influence, such as saying

---

55. Robert W. Funk, Roy W. Hoover, and the Jesus Seminar, *The Five Gospels: The Search for the Authentic Words of Jesus* (New York: Macmillan, Polebridge Press, 1993), 7.

56. See Wright, *Victory of God*, 40–44.

57. For discussion on dating of these and other noncanonical documents, see Craig A. Evans, *Fabricating Jesus: How Modern Scholars Distort the Gospels* (Downer's Grove, Ill.: InterVarsity Press, 2006), 52–99.

113, "Woe to the flesh that depends on the soul! Woe to the soul that depends on the flesh!" *Thomas* ends with an exchange between Jesus and Simon Peter that reflects an ancient association of maleness with spirit:

> Simon Peter said to them: "Let Mary go away from us, for women are not worthy of life." Jesus said: "Lo, I shall lead her, so that I may make her a male, that she too may become a living spirit resembling you males. For every woman who makes herself a male will enter the kingdom of heaven." (Saying no. 114)

The noncanonical gospels,[58] then, contribute little to human understanding of the actual historical Jesus. Although they demonstrate that Jesus was understood in diverse ways in the ancient world, especially in a Gnostic direction, the canonical Gospels are the only credible sources on which to base a portrait of the historical Jesus.[59]

The New Testament outside of the Gospels and the Historical Jesus 10.9.3

While the rest of the New Testament outside of the Gospels is about Jesus, it offers very little information about the historical Jesus. Paul's primary focus in his letters is the theological meaning of Jesus' death and Resurrection. On the few occasions when he does refer to the historical Jesus (e.g., 1 Cor 7:10–11 on Jesus' teaching on divorce or 1 Cor 11:23–26 on Jesus' words and actions at the Last Supper), he gives valuable insights; but he simply gives too little material on which to build a historical portrait. The other New Testament letters also have few references to the historical Jesus. The Book of Revelation describes visions of the risen Jesus but gives no information on the earthly Jesus.

In the end, then, any portrait of the historical Jesus must rely primarily on the information in the canonical Gospels.[60] As discussed, the historian has good reason to accept the basic reliability of the Gospel accounts (sec. 10.5) but also reasons to be cautious about possible errors in passing down the Jesus traditions (see sec. 10.2.2) and about later theological interpretations that may have obscured the actual historical Jesus (sec. 10.6–8). To distinguish between (1) material that definitely goes back to the historical Jesus and (2) material that reflects later interpretations of the Church, scholars have developed several historical criteria, known as "criteria of authenticity."

---

58. A video presenting Craig Evans arguing against attempts to recover the historical Jesus by using noncanonical sources is accessible at *www.youtube.com/watch?v=HIwV__gW5v4* (time 22:51).

59. For this conclusion, see Meier, *Marginal Jew*, 139–41; and Evans, *Fabricating Jesus*, 52–99.

60. See Meier, *Marginal Jew*, 140–41.

Criteria of Authenticity and the Historical Jesus   10.10

The debate over "criteria of authenticity" has been a long one in historical Jesus research.[61] The following three criteria are widely used.

1. **Multiple attestation.** If a tradition about Jesus is found in only one source (e.g., only in the Gospel of John), it is less historically secure. If a Jesus tradition is found in several independent sources, it can more securely be traced back to Jesus. For example, Jesus' teaching about divorce is found not only in the Gospels (Mark 10:1–2 par.) but also in Paul (1 Cor 7:10–11), making it more likely to go back to Jesus himself.

2. **Embarrassment.** If a tradition is recorded that does not fit well with later orthodox teaching about Jesus, it is likely to be historically authentic. The reasoning is that the later church would not make up a tradition that would be embarrassing to its theology. An example is that all four Gospels record John the Baptist baptizing Jesus. This tradition is difficult for the later church to explain, because it seems to give John the Baptist more authority than Jesus. The only reason to record it, then, is because it actually happened.

3. **Dissimilarity.** This is a controversial criterion. Essentially, it compares Jesus to (1) the beliefs of Second Temple Judaism and (2) the beliefs of the early Church. The idea is that if a Jesus tradition is dissimilar to both, then it must go back to Jesus himself. While this criteria can be helpful in authenticating certain sayings, it can also be misused. Some historical Jesus scholars, for example, have used it to arrive at very skeptical results: they judge the majority of Gospel traditions to be inventions of the early Church or products of Jesus' Jewish culture. Such conclusions, however, are not historically credible. It stands to reason that much of what Jesus said and did would be in continuity with both Second Temple Judaism and the early Church.

While the criteria of authenticity can be helpful in some cases, Third Quest scholars such as N. T. Wright tend to see them as having limited value, as will be discussed in chapter 11.

Worldview and the Historical Jesus   10.11

As noted previously, one's view about the possibility of supernatural events affects how one thinks about the reliability of the Gospels. An interpreter who denies the possibility of the supernatural will, therefore, reject the authenticity of the Gospel reports of Jesus' miraculous healings and similar supernatural events.

---

61. See Evans, *Fabricating Jesus*, 46–51.

In light of Pope Benedict's warnings about a dualism that completely separates the historical-critical and the theological approaches to scripture (*VD*, no. 35), it seems that a Catholic approach to the historical Jesus should, at a minimum, leave open the possibility of the supernatural.

This openness can take different forms. Scholars Paul Eddy and Greg Boyd advocate an open historical–critical method—an approach to history that first seeks natural causes to events but is open to supernatural explanations if all natural explanations are inadequate (sec. 9.7).

The Catholic historical Jesus scholar John P. Meier takes a more cautious attitude. In his understanding, the search for the historical Jesus involves "the Jesus whom we can 'recover' and examine by using the scientific tools of modern historical research."[62] Historical tools, Meier insists, cannot determine whether supernatural events actually occur, because this is a philosophical question. As a historical Jesus scholar, however, Meier believes he can investigate more modest question, such as (1) were the *reports* of Jesus' miracles invented by the early church, or do they go back to the time of the historical Jesus; (2) did the historical Jesus perform startling actions that he and his followers claimed to be miracles; (3) how did Jesus and his followers interpret these startling acts?[63]

Following detailed investigations of Gospel reports of Jesus' exorcisms, healings, and raising the dead using his strictly defined historical approach, Meier finds a portrait of

> [a] 1st–century Palestinian Jew who performed startling actions that both he and at least some of his audience judged to be miraculous deeds of power. To Jesus' mind these acts—including what he claimed to be acts of raising the dead—both proclaimed and actualized, however imperfectly, the kingdom of God promised by the prophets.[64]

The next chapter considers in detail how the portrait gained from a historical investigation of Jesus compares with the theological view of Jesus passed down by the tradition.

Questions about the Text

1. What are the reasons for seeing a difference between the Jesus of history and the Christ of faith?

---

62. Meier, "Basic Methodology in the Quest for the Historical Jesus," in *Handbook for the Study of the Historical Jesus, Vol. 1: How to Study the Historical Jesus*, eds. T. Holmén and S. E. Porter (Leiden: Brill, 2011), 296.

63. Meier, *A Marginal Jew: Rethinking the Historical Jesus, Vol. 2: Mentor, Message, and Miracles.* (New York: Doubleday, 1994), 517.

64. Ibid., 837.

262 REASON, FAITH, AND TRADITION

2. What does the term *historical Jesus* mean?

3. Name some reasons why the Gospels may not be reliable as historical documents.

4. Why do some Christians believe that the quest for the historical Jesus is not relevant for a person's faith, while others do?

5. What are the three main phases of the quest for this historical Jesus?

6. According to the Pontifical Biblical Commission, what are the three stages in which the Gospel traditions about Jesus were passed down?

7. How does Jesus being a teacher and his disciples students affect the historical reliability of the Gospels?

8. Describe the form-critical model of how Jesus' traditions were passed down, contrasting this model with the eyewitness model presented in this chapter.

9. Describe some of the evidence that Jesus' traditions were passed down carefully and systematically.

10. What role did the twelve apostles play in handing down the Jesus traditions?

11. What exactly does it mean to say that the four Gospels are of apostolic origin?

12. What factors account for the differences between Matt 19:9 and Mark 10:11–12?

13. Discuss reasons for thinking that John 6:22–59 is not a strictly historical account. What factors influenced how it was written?

14. What is the compositional use of Scripture?

15. Describe some of the ancient non-Christian accounts of Jesus.

16. Summarize the main points of the current scholarly debate over whether noncanonical sources such as the gospels of Thomas and Peter can be used as evidence of the historical Jesus.

17. Summarize the historical reliability of the canonical Gospels.

18. Explain some of the criteria of authenticity applied by historical Jesus scholars to the Gospels in order to distinguish the historical Jesus from later elaborations of the early Church.

Discussion Questions

1. In your view, how reliable are the canonical Gospels as historical records?

2. In your view, is there a difference between the Jesus of history and the Christ of faith? If so, how much of a difference?

3. Were you familiar with any of the noncanonical writings mentioned in this chapter?

The Historical Jesus, Part II

The Quest for the Historical Jesus and Traditional Theology

This chapter considers the relationship between the quest for the historical Jesus and traditional Christian theological beliefs about Jesus. This quest is important from a theological point of view because

1. Christianity makes historical claims,[1] and these should be open to historical investigation.

2. The quest for the historical Jesus is an invitation to non-Christians to consider the significance of Jesus. If one considers the Gospels as documents of faith to be read only by convinced believers, there would be no reason for a non-Christian to consider them.

3. Christians believe that God's Son became truly and fully human in the Incarnation. A historical investigation aids the believer in coming to a deeper understanding of Jesus' humanity.

4. The Catholic tradition, in particular, insists that faith and reason are compatible. If this is true, then a historical investigation should be able to show that there are no fundamental discrepancies between the historical Jesus and the Jesus proclaimed in the New Testament and by the Church in the Creeds. In particular, the defender of a traditional view of Jesus should be able to answer, on a historical basis, challenges by those who claim that the portrait of Jesus in the Gospels is a fundamental distortion of the historical Jesus.

---

1. N. T. Wright comments on the relationship between history and Christian faith in a video accessible at *www.youtube.com/watch?v=ksAE061_CsM* (time: 0:01:09).

This chapter, then, compares the key results of the Third Quest for the historical Jesus with traditional Christian theological beliefs, compares the key results of the Third Quest for the historical Jesus with the following theological beliefs:

1. Did the historical Jesus really think that he was the Messiah, the chosen one sent by God to establish the kingdom of God on Earth?
2. Did the historical Jesus really think his death would somehow make **atonement** for the sins of other people?
3. Did the historical Jesus really rise from the dead?

The Third Quest Approach to the Historical Jesus

11.2

Historical Jesus scholar N. T. Wright lists some of the fundamental questions asked and approaches taken by Third Quest historians.[2]

1. How does Jesus fit into first-century Judaism? Often even orthodox Christians picture Jesus as a divine person who is "above" any particular time and place. Third Quest historians study how first-century Judaism shaped Jesus' worldview and actions.
2. What were Jesus' aims in the context of first-century Judaism? An aim is the fundamental direction of a person's life, shaped by a particular worldview. When historians study the aims of a historical person, they do not claim to understand the inner psychology of that person but attempt to uncover a consistent pattern in the person's words and actions.[3]
3. Why was Jesus executed? Even the most skeptical historical scholars agree that Jesus was executed. Understanding the historical reasons behind this event sheds light on his life as a whole.
4. How and why did the early Church begin? It is historically certain that Jesus lived and died as an ethnic and religious Jew but the movement he began developed into the religion of Christianity. Was it one of Jesus' aims to begin a new religion? Or are later figures, such as Paul, the true founders of the Christian religion?"[4]

Wright, then, with other Third Questers, wishes to move beyond the "criteria of authenticity" (sec. 10.10) and establish a portrait of Jesus that makes sense of him as a first-century Jew.

---

2. N. T. Wright, *Jesus and the Victory of God* (Minneapolis: Fortress, 1996), 89–116.

3. Ibid., 110–12; see also Ben F. Meyer, *The Aims of Jesus* (San Jose, CA: Pickwick Publications, 2002; orig. pub. London: SCM, 1979), 76–81.

4. Wright, *Victory of God*, 117.

Locating Jesus within First-Century Judaism

11.3

To understand Jesus within his first-century Jewish context, a common beginning point is the attempt to understand, historically, what Jesus meant when he preached about the kingdom of God.[5] The kingdom of God is a central theme in Jesus' teaching in the Gospels, beginning with his first words recorded in Mark's Gospel, considered the earliest Gospel by many scholars: "This is the time of fulfillment. The kingdom of God is at hand. Repent, and believe in the gospel" (Mark 1:15).

In first-century Judaism, beliefs about the kingdom are closely tied to beliefs about the messiah; the following sections discuss both terms.

Ancient Jewish Understanding of the Kingdom of God and the Messiah

11.4

On the surface, the meaning of the *kingdom of God*, also named the *kingdom of heaven* in Matthew, is clear enough: it is a place or condition where God, as king, rules. Many modern Christians assume the kingdom is the same as heaven. While there is evidence for this identification in the Gospels, there is also evidence of other meanings. Four main points emerge:

1. **The kingdom is a transcendent reality (heaven).** Jesus taught, "And if your eye causes you to sin, pluck it out. Better for you to enter into the kingdom of God with one eye than with two eyes to be thrown into Gehenna [hell]" (Mark 9:47).

2. **God's kingdom will be established on Earth in the near future.** Jesus taught his disciples to pray to the heavenly Father, "Your kingdom come, your will be done, on earth as in heaven" (Matt 6:10). Jesus seems to have believed that the kingdom would come very soon: he says that the kingdom is "at hand" (Mark 1:15); and asserts that some in the crowd before him "will not taste death until . . . the kingdom of God has come in power" (Mark 9:1).

3. **A few sayings suggest that the kingdom has already come.** Jesus says, "if it is by the Spirit of God that I drive out demons, then the kingdom of God has come upon you" (Matt 12:28).

4. **The kingdom is associated with the eschatological judgment.** Jesus compares the kingdom of heaven with a field that has both wheat and weeds. He explains that at the final judgment angels will throw evildoers and those who cause others to sin "into the fiery furnace" (Matt 13:42).

---

5. See Wright, *Victory of God*, 198–243; E. P. Sanders, *The Historical Figure of Jesus* (London: Penguin, 1993), 169–204.

The phrase, "already, but not yet" is sometimes used as a summary of Jewish expectations regarding the kingdom. In other words, the kingdom is, in a sense, already present through Jesus' actions (point 3), but it has not come fully (point 2).

In historical Jesus scholarship, there is a debate between those who see Jesus' message about the kingdom as "**eschatological**"—events or language involving final judgment—and those, such as John Dominic Crossan, who see it more as a "wisdom" teaching about current political and social realities (sec. 10.9.2).

The Third Quest understands Jesus within the eschatological framework, without denying that he was also concerned about current social and political issues. E. P. Sanders points out that the Gospels begin with John the Baptist warning about God's imminent judgment, that Jesus' earliest followers expected him to return soon to establish the kingdom, and that Paul, in the earliest New Testament document, also expects Jesus will return within his lifetime to gather his followers up to heaven (1 Thess 4:14–17). "It is almost impossible to explain these historical facts on the assumption that Jesus himself did not expect the imminent end or transformation of the present world order. He thought that in the new age God (or his viceroy) would reign supreme, without opposition."[6]

The Kingdom in Jewish Context   11.4.1

First-century Jews thought of the kingdom as the fulfillment of history—the end of the age when God's reign of complete justice and peace would be established on Earth. In the "new age" of the kingdom, God would restore the twelve tribes of Israel, who had been scattered in exile, to their homeland.

When Israel is restored, the world will be judged—the righteous will receive their reward and the wicked will be punished. Gentile nations will either be destroyed or submit themselves to God's rule. In Isaiah's vision of the eschatological age, he sees the Gentile nations coming to Jerusalem to worship God in the Temple (Isa 2:2–3). He describes the universal peace of this time:

> They shall beat their swords into plowshares
> and their spears into pruning hooks;
> One nation shall not raise the sword against another,
> nor shall they train for war again. (Isa 2:4)

The peace and harmony would be so complete that even nature would be taken up into it:

> Then the wolf shall be a guest of the lamb,
> and the leopard shall lie down with the young goat;
> The calf and the young lion shall browse together,
> with a little child to guide them. (Isa 11:6)

---

6. Sanders, *Historical Figure of Jesus*, 183.

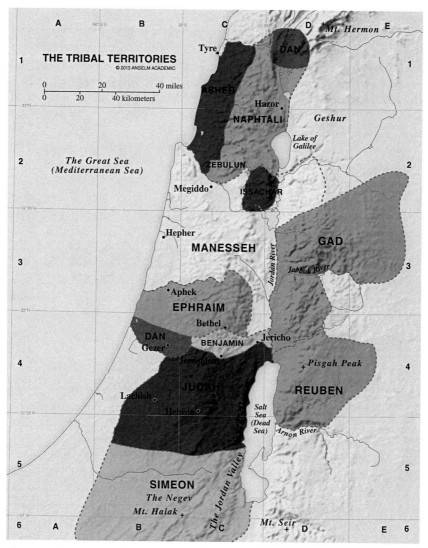

This map of ancient Israel shows the territories of the twelve tribes.

The Kingdom and the Messiah   11.4.2

Second Temple Jews commonly believed that God would act through a human intermediary to establish the eschatological kingdom on Earth. This person, usually identified as a royal descendant of King David, was often called the messiah—in Hebrew *maschiach*.

    Within first-century Judaism, there was no one, fixed concept of the messiah.[7] The term literally means "one who is anointed," referring to the ancient Israelite

7. See Wright, *People of God*, 307–20.

custom of anointing a king, priest, or prophet with olive oil as part of the ritual establishing that person in his office. The term came to have a more metaphorical meaning of one who has been chosen by God. The community at Qumran that produced the Dead Sea Scrolls, for example, believed in two eschatological messiahs: a priestly messiah and a royal messiah.[8] The term does not necessarily imply divine status—the messiah might simply be a human through whom God works. The Greek translation of *messiah*, "anointed one," is *Christos*, from which the English *Christ* derives.

According to ancient Hebrew belief, a major role of Israel's king was to establish God's values of peace and justice in society: "You love justice and hate wrongdoing; therefore God . . . has anointed you with the oil of gladness" (Ps 45:8). The future messiah would have this same task, only this time it would be a worldwide establishment of justice: "he shall judge the poor with justice, and decide fairly for the land's afflicted" (Isa 11:4).

The historical reality never matched this ideal, however. Many Israelite kings were weak and corrupt and worshipped other gods. The Davidic kingship in fact ended with the Babylonian conquest of Jerusalem in 587 BCE. The Jewish people of Jesus' time, however, had not lost the hope that one day God would again anoint a messianic king who would defeat the forces of evil and establish the perfect reign of peace and justice on Earth.

The Son of Man and the Eschatological Age   11.4.3

Ancient Judaism did not always associate this ideal future age specifically with a Davidic king. A figure known as the Son of Man was also understood as playing a key role in bringing about the eschatological kingdom of God. In a vision in the book of Daniel, a mysterious figure, described as "one like a son of man" appears before God's heavenly throne, where he "received dominion, splendor, and kingship; all nations, peoples and tongues will serve him" (7:14). In Second Temple writings such as *4 Ezra 13* and the *Similitudes (Parables) of Enoch* (part of a larger work known as *1 Enoch*), this Son of Man is associated with the Messiah and given divine qualities. This Son of Man has a heavenly origin and will carry out God's eschatological judgment. He is shown seated on God's throne (1 *Enoch* 62:5 and 69:29).[9]

This Enochic Son of Man, moreover, seems to be identified with the human Enoch (see Gen 5:21–24), who is raised up into heavenly glory as the eschatological judge (1 *Enoch* 71:14 and 69:27).[10] This Son of Man in the

---

8. See James C. VanderKam, *The Dead Sea Scrolls Today*, 2nd ed. (Grand Rapids, MI: Eerdmans, 2010), 145–46.

9. On these Second Temple interpretation of Daniel's "one like the son of man," see John J. Collins, "The Son of Man in Ancient Judaism," in *Handbook for the Study of the Historical Jesus: Vol. 2: The Study of Jesus*, eds. T. Holmén and S. E. Porter (Leiden: Brill, 2011), 1545–1568.

10. On the complex relationship between the Son of Man and the human Enoch, see John J. Collins, *The Scepter and the Star: Messianism in Light of the Dead Sea Scrolls*, 2nd. ed. (Grand Rapids, MI: Eerdmans, 2010), 178–81.

Similitudes seems to parallel many of the later Christian beliefs about Jesus—a human with a divine origin who, after his death, is raised up to heaven as an eschatological judge.

To sum up, many Second Temple Jews had a strong sense that the eschatological kingdom of God would soon be established on Earth. God's Messiah, an ideal king at times associated with the mysterious eschatological judge known as the Son of Man, would bring in that kingdom. It is against this background that one must understand the historical Jesus.

Did Jesus Think He Was the Messiah?   11.4.4

According to scholars such as Rudolf Bultmann, Jesus never claimed to be the Messiah; the Church gave him that role by after his Resurrection.[11] Scholars, such as Crossan, also reject the idea that Jesus thought in these eschatological terms (sec. 10.9.2). In contrast, members of the Third Quest insist that Jesus' words and actions are most plausibly understood in this eschatological, messianic framework.

Several historical considerations support the Third Quest approach:

1. In the earliest dated writings of the New Testament, Paul's letters, Paul refers so constantly and naturally to "Jesus Christ" (i.e., "Jesus the Messiah") that the title *Messiah* seems almost part of Jesus' name. It is hard to explain how this title could have become so firmly established so soon after Jesus' death unless it had been used by Jesus' followers within his lifetime.

2. Jesus' identity as the Messiah was so firmly established that even early non-Christian authors referred to Jesus as "Christ": e.g., the Jewish historian Josephus, writing ca. 93–94 CE (*Antiquities* 20.9.1); the Roman historian Tacitus, writing ca. 117 (*Annals* 15.44); the Roman historian Suetonius writing ca. 120 (*Life of Claudius* 25.4); and Pliny the Younger, writing ca. 112 (*Letter* 10.96).[12]

3. The Gospels record that Jesus was crucified as "King of the Jews" (Mark 15:26 par.). (The inscription on many crucifixes, *INRI*, is Latin for *Iesous Nazarani Rex Ioudorum*: "Jesus Christ, King of the Jews.") It is historically probable that the Romans executed Jesus because his claim to be a messianic king was seen as a threat to their rule or to the rule of Roman clients such as King Herod. Jesus' proclamation of the kingdom of God had political implications: To proclaim that God is the true king could easily be understood as a threat to Caesar's kingship.

---

11. See the discussion in Meyer, *Aims of Jesus*, 177.

12. For a discussion of these sources, see Meier, *Marginal Jew*, 56–92; Eddy and Boyd, *Jesus Legend*, 165–99.

4. If Jesus had not been thought of as the Messiah before his death and Resurrection, it is virtually impossible that he would have been called Messiah after these events. The belief that Jesus rose from the dead could not have convinced anyone that Jesus was the Messiah if they had not believed it previously. There is no evidence that first-century CE Jews expected the Messiah to rise from the dead.[13]

Jesus' Actions, the Kingdom, and the Messiah   11.5

Admittedly, the Synoptic Gospels portray Jesus as secretive about his identity as the Messiah. In a scene regarded by many scholars as the literary center of the Gospel of Mark, Peter responds to Jesus' question, "Who do you say that I am?" with, "You are the Messiah." Jesus then warns the disciples not to tell anyone (Mark 8:29–30).

Much has been written about the possible reasons for this "messianic secret." If one thinks about the question in its historical context, however, the reason for Jesus' reticence seems clear: it would have been highly dangerous, even suicidal, for a popular first-century religious leader to claim to be the true king or Messiah of Israel. Neither the Jewish nor the Roman rulers would have hesitated to respond violently to such a perceived threat to their authority. The Jewish ruler Herod Antipas, for example, executed John the Baptist, according to E. P. Sanders, "in part because he proclaimed the coming judgment," and a Roman procurator killed a certain Theudas, a self-proclaimed prophet who claimed that he would divide the Jordan River, an action signalling the start of the messianic age (see Acts 5:36).[14]

Historically speaking, then, it is highly likely that if Jesus did indeed regard himself as the Messiah, he would have kept his claim quiet to avoid immediate arrest or execution.

The Actions of the Messiah: the Kingdom of God as Defeat of Evil Spiritual Powers   11.5.1

Members of the Third Quest have shown that Jesus' self-understanding as the Messiah of Israel can be discerned not only in his words but also in his actions.

Sanders concludes that the many references to exorcism in the Synoptics "makes it extremely likely that Jesus actually had a reputation as an exorcist."[15]

---

13. On these points, see Wright, *Victory of God*, 487–88; Martin Hengel, *The Atonement: The Origins of the Doctrine in the New Testament* (Philadelphia: Fortress, 1981), 41, 49; Meyer, *Aims of Jesus*, 175–79.

14. See Sanders, *Historical Figure of Jesus*, 29–30.

15. Ibid., 149. Sanders lists the evidence from the Synoptics (149–50); interestingly, John does not record any exorcisms.

Jesus seems to have understood his power to perform exorcisms as a sign that the kingdom of God was being established through him (see Matt 12:28). Historical Jesus scholar John Meier also concludes that Jesus believed that his "startling actions," understood as exorcisms, healings, and raising people from the dead, "both proclaimed and actualized, however imperfectly, the kingdom of God promised by the prophets."[16]

A quick look at various New Testament passages demonstrates the ancient Jewish conviction that evil spirits dominate the world. The Gospel of John refers to the devil as the ruler of this world (12:31; cf. 14:30; 16:11). Paul calls the devil the "god of this age" (2 Cor 4:4) and characterizes the current time as the "present evil age" (Gal 1:4). Such ruling demonic forces would need to be defeated for God's kingdom to be established.

Ancient Jewish culture understood illness and demon possession as manifestations of the power of evil in the world. At times, illness is said to be caused by demons: Jesus explains that a crippled woman had been "bound" by Satan "for eighteen years" (Luke 13:10–16). In other cases, illness is associated with sin: when four men bring a paralyzed man to Jesus for physical healing, Jesus' first response is, "Child, your sins are forgiven" (Mark 2:5). Jesus does deny that a tragedy, such as a falling tower killing a group of people, was a direct result of their sins, but at the same time, he makes it clear that suffering and death are inevitable consequences of sin and evil: "If you do not repent, you will all perish as they did!" (Luke 13:1–5).

When Jesus heals a person or casts out a demon, it was understood as an assault on the demonic dominance of the world and the beginning of the establishment of the kingdom of God on Earth. When Jesus' disciples report that even the demons are subject to them because of Jesus' name (authority), Jesus responds, "I have observed Satan fall like lightning from the sky" (Luke 10:18). According to Scripture, Jesus believed[17] that through his messianic actions of healing and exorcism, God's kingdom had come to Earth.

The Kingdom of God and the New Israel   11.5.2

According to the Gospels, Jesus chose twelve men (Mark 3:13–19; see also 1 Cor 15:5) to be his closest followers. For an ancient Jew, the number twelve is not arbitrary. It symbolizes the twelve tribes of Israel, the totality of the chosen people. Jesus' action signifies the beginning of the eschatological age: the gathering of the twelve scattered tribes (sec. 11.4.1).

Choosing twelve disciples was a sign that Jesus was renewing Israel. Jesus the Messiah began to establish the kingdom through his preaching, exorcisms,

---

16. John P. Meier, *A Marginal Jew: Rethinking the Historical Jesus, Vol. 2: Mentor, Message, and Miracles.* (New York: Doubleday, 1994), 837.

17. N. T. Wright discusses whether Jesus thought he was the Messiah in a video accessible at *www.youtube.com/watch?v=QQJTF_XAiL0* (time 0:01:44).

and healings; he gave authority to his disciples to accomplish these same actions. Mark relates how Jesus called the Twelve and sent them out in pairs. "[T]hey went off and preached repentance. They drove out many demons, and they anointed with oil many who were sick and cured them" (Mark 6:7–13).[18]

In the eschatological age, the disciples would share in ruling the kingdom: "You who have followed me, in the new age, when the Son of Man is seated on his throne of glory, will yourselves sit on twelve thrones, judging the twelve tribes of Israel" (Matt 19:28).

The Authority of the Messianic Teacher   11.5.3

The role of Jesus as a teacher is essential in establishing the reliability of the Gospel tradition (sec. 10.5.1) and in understanding Jesus' aims as the teacher of the new law of the kingdom of God.

The Third Quest emphasizes how the Law (Torah) and its interpretation was central in Second Temple Judaism. To be a teacher in Second Temple Judaism is to teach and interpret the Law. As John Meier writes, "the historical Jesus was the halackhic Jesus"—*halakhah* being the technical term for a rabbi's authoritative ruling on an issue of Torah interpretation.[19]

An important collection of Jesus' teaching on the Torah is found in Matthew (5:17–48), part of the so-called Sermon on the Mount. Jesus first presents a teaching of the Torah (or an interpretation of the Torah common in his time) and then presents his own teaching. For example, he says, "You shall not commit adultery," quoting from the Ten Commandments. He then gives his own interpretation, *"But I say to you*, everyone who looks at a woman with lust has already committed adultery with her in his heart" (Matt 5:27–28; emphasis added).

When Jesus says, "Do not think that I have come to abolish the law or the prophets. I have come not to abolish but to fulfill" (5:17), he was not throwing out the law, but was claiming that in his interpretation, given in the eschatological age, he was fulfilling the law's true meaning.

Continued

18. On the historicity and significance of Jesus' choosing of twelve disciples, see John P. Meier, *A Marginal Jew: Rethinking the Historical Jesus, Vol. 3: Companions and Competitors* (New York: Doubleday, 2001), 125–62.

19. Meier, *A Marginal Jew: Rethinking the Historical Jesus, Vol. 4: Law and Love* (New Haven, CT: Yale University Press, 2009), 1.

The Authority of the Messianic Teacher Continued

What is striking about this and similar passages is that Jesus gives his interpretation by his own authority. He does not refer to other teachers or authorities that give similar teaching as support for his position (a common practice of other ancient Jewish teachers); he simply states his interpretation.

The people of Jesus' time recognized that he taught with more than ordinary authority. Matthew explains that "the crowds were astonished at his teaching, for he taught them as one having authority, and not as their scribes" (Matt 7:28–29). As the Messiah, the Chosen One of God who was establishing the kingdom, Jesus had full authority to interpret the Torah.

Jesus' claims are extraordinary as he is claiming to have the authority to interpret God's Law in radically new ways and, in some cases, to change commandments of the Law. In Jesus' mind, his authority to interpret and even change Torah could only have been connected with his authority as the Messiah whose task is to establish the kingdom on Earth. Jesus' teaching was the eschatological Torah, the new law of the kingdom of God. Jesus taught as if he had unquestioned authority as God's representative.[20]

Jesus' Relationship with the Father   11.5.4

Jesus' supreme self-assurance as God's representative to establish the kingdom of God on Earth is clearly founded on Jesus' sense of a close relationship with God the Father. The following passages illustrate this relationship:

- "All things have been handed over to me by my Father. No one knows the Son except the Father, and no one knows the Father except the Son and anyone to whom the Son wishes to reveal him" (Matt 11:27).
- "Everyone who acknowledges me before others I will acknowledge before my heavenly Father. But whoever denies me before others, I will deny before my heavenly Father" (Matt 10:32–33).

Jesus' sense of an intimate relationship with the Father is often expressed in terms of being "sent" [by God].

- "To the other towns also I must proclaim the good news of the kingdom of God, because for this purpose I have been sent" (Luke 4:43).

---

20. Ben Witherington discusses the question "was Jesus telling the truth when he claimed to be God?" in a video accessible at *www.youtube.com/watch?v=D8BcUkZhc5Q* (time 0:05:17).

- "I was sent only to the lost sheep of the house of Israel" (Matt 15:24).

Other sayings illustrate the same consciousness of being sent by God but are expressed in terms of "coming":

- "I have come not to abolish but to fulfill" (Matt 5:17).
- "For the Son of Man has come to seek and to save what was lost" (Luke 19:10).[21]

The theme of the Father sending the Son is expressed more directly in the Gospel of John: "[T]he Father has sent me" (John 5:36); "This is the work of God, that you believe in the one he sent" (John 6:29).[22]

Theological Implications of the Father "Sending" the Son   11.5.5

In comparison with the Synoptic Gospels, the Jesus portrayed in the Gospel of John makes unusually explicit claims about his equality with the Father, including the assertion, "The Father and I are one" (John 10:30). Many historical Jesus scholars, therefore, conclude such Johannine statements come not from the historical Jesus but are later theological developments of the early Church.

Yet when one considers Jesus' self-understanding, attested in the Synoptics, as being "sent" by the Father, the differences between John and the other three evangelists is not as great as they first appear. All four Gospels present Jesus as claiming to be sent by God the Father to establish the eschatological kingdom. As the Messiah, he understood himself as the central actor in a drama that would determine the destiny of the entire Earth.

Balthasar shows how Jesus' sense of his mission as one sent by God provides the link between the historical understanding of Jesus and traditional Christological beliefs. The Father sending Jesus into the world parallels the eternal procession of the Son from the Father, in keeping with the thesis that the economic Trinity reflects the immanent Trinity (secs. 6.15–6.16). As the Son eternally comes forth (eternally begotten) from the Father within the Trinity, the Father sends the Son into the world.

Just as there is a profound unity between Son and Father within the immanent Trinity, so too is there a profound unity between the Father and the incarnate Jesus. Balthasar does not claim that Jesus "remembered," in a human way, his time with the Father before the creation of the world. Rather, one can say that Jesus' total confidence that the Father has given him the divine mission of establishing the kingdom is analogous to the eternal Son's complete love

---

21. On the "sent" and "coming" sayings, see also Meyer, *Aims of Jesus*, 166–68.

22. See this point in Hans Urs von Balthasar, *Theo-Drama: Theological Dramatic Theory*, vol. 3, *The Dramatis Personae: The Persons in Christ* (San Francisco: Ignatius Press, 1992), 152.

and acceptance of the Father within the Trinity. In this sense, "Jesus' certainty regarding the universality and finality of his mission suffices to allow us to take everything said in the Prologue of the St. John's Gospel [in the beginning was the Word, and the Word was with God] and trace it back to his earthly consciousness."[23] The historical Jesus' profound sense of oneness with the Father who had sent him is a reflection of the eternal Trinitarian oneness.

Jesus and the Eschatological Temple   11.5.6

Many historical Jesus scholars agree that Jesus' action at the Jerusalem Temple is key in understanding his intentions. The Gospel accounts report that Jesus drove out people buying and selling and overturned the tables of the money changers (Mark 11:15–17 par.). Although a common interpretation is that Jesus was protesting economic exploitation or corruption in the Temple, his intention seems to have gone much deeper.

The symbolic significance of the Temple in Second Temple Judaism is hard to overestimate. In Jewish understanding, the Temple was nothing less than the sacred site at which the divine met the earthly.[24] The Temple was built on the "cosmic rock" that held together and gave meaning to the universe; the rabbis speculated that this very spot was

> the site of creation, of Paradise and the tree of life, source of the rivers of the world, proof against the Deluge. Here was the altar on which Abraham was ready to sacrifice Isaac; here, too, was the altar of Melchizedek; here, the house and the throne of God and the destined locale of the judgment of the world.[25]

In the eschatological vision delivered to his disciples, Jesus had predicted that the Temple would be destroyed (Mark 13:1–2); at his trial he was accused of threatening to destroy the Temple (Mark 14:58). Noting these hints, Meyer, Sanders, and Wright all conclude that Jesus' action at the Temple was intended not merely as a sign that the practices in the Temple should be reformed but also as a sign of the Temple's imminent destruction. Jesus' intention makes sense within ancient Jewish eschatological expectations: In the new age of the Messiah, the Temple would be destroyed so that a new and better one could be rebuilt.[26]

---

23. Balthasar, *Persons in Christ*, 255.

24. In his discussion on the significance of Jesus' Temple action, Sanders says, "Some readers may think that I have made too much of the issue. I think that it is almost impossible to make too much of the Temple in first-century Jewish Palestine" (*Historical Figure of Jesus*, 262).

25. Meyer, *Aims of Jesus*, 185–86.

26. Sanders, *Historical Figure of Jesus*, 254–62.

The Eschatological Temple and Jesus' Community
11.5.7

Meyer offers evidence that Jesus intended to replace the Temple with the community of his followers, centered on the Twelve.

Second Temple Judaism connected the Messiah with a new, eschatological Temple. A prophecy about a descendant of King David, "He it is who shall build a house for my name. And I will make his royal throne firm forever" (2 Sam 7:13), was interpreted by many to mean that the Messiah would build an eschatological Temple.[27]

For Meyer, Jesus' response to Peter's confession that he, Jesus, was the Messiah (Matt 16:16) is a key to Jesus' intention. Jesus says, "[Y]ou are Peter, and upon this rock I will build my church" (Matt 16:18). Jesus here plays on the name *Peter*. In Greek, *Petros* is related to the word *petra*, meaning solid rock. Peter's name in Aramaic, *Cephas*, or *Kephas*, is related to the word *kepha*, equivalent to the Greek *petra*.

When Jesus refers to Peter as his rock, he is tapping into the cosmic imagery of the Temple. Meyer explains,

> The text's operative presupposition is that the task of "the Messiah, Son of the living God" (Matt 16:16) is precisely to build the eschatological temple. Here temple is translated by "church," the community of restored Israel, or rather by "my church," for the restored community of Israel is messianic.[28]

The basic meaning of the Greek word *ekklesia*, translated as "church" here, does not correspond exactly to modern ideas of a Christian church. However, ancient and modern meanings both point to a people "called out" (the literal meaning of the Greek word) to form a community. Jesus thought of the community of his disciples, led by the twelve, as the restored Israel, the beginning point of the kingdom of God.

This passage is also fundamental to the Catholic understanding of Peter as the first head of the church founded by Jesus (sec. 13.8).

Did Jesus Think He Would Die for the Sins of the World?
11.6

A fundamental Christian theological belief is found in a tradition handed down to the apostle Paul, that "Christ died for our sins" (1 Cor 15:3). Similarly, in the Gospel of John, John the Baptist describes Jesus as the one "who takes away the sin of the world" (John 1:29).

---

27. Meyer, *Aims of Jesus*, 179–80.

28. Ibid., 186.

At first glance, such statements seem like a later theological interpretation of the historical Jesus' death. It seems unlikely that a first-century Jew could have believed that his death would affect the sins of the rest of humanity. The following sections, however, show that such a belief is plausible. One must approach this historical question, as with all Third Quest thinking, by placing Jesus firmly within the worldview of first-century Judaism.

Forgiveness of Sin and the Kingdom of God   11.6.1

The modern concept of sin is much more individualistic than that of the ancient Jews. The scriptural concept of sin is a dynamic tension between a group, or "corporate" sense of sin, as well as an individual responsibility for sin (sec. 8.16.3.1). From a biblical view, one must try to hold onto the truth of both perspectives.

Contrary to some modern interpretations, first-century Jews did not believe that they could "earn" God's forgiveness by their good deeds. As authors such as Sanders and Wright have shown, the whole concept of sin and forgiveness was inseparable from the belief that the individual was part of the community of Israel that had a covenant with God. A person was saved by remaining faithful as an individual to this covenant made with the group.[29]

From the eschatological perspective of Jesus, then, forgiveness of sin was tied to the *renewed* covenant that God would make with Israel in the last days. As the prophet Jeremiah prophesied,

> [D]ays are coming . . . when I will make a new covenant. . . . I will be their God, and they shall be my people. . . . For *I will forgive their iniquity and no longer remember their sin.* (Jer 31:31–34; emphasis added).

Wright sums up, "Forgiveness of sin is another way of saying 'return from exile': the eschatological gathering of the twelve tribes."[30]

If Jesus understood himself as the Messiah who would restore Israel, it follows that he would expect to play a key role in this eschatological forgiveness of sins.

Dying for the Sins of Others   11.6.2

The belief that Jesus died for the sins of others is connected, theologically, with the concept of making atonement for sins. The theological meaning of atonement will be discussed in the next chapter; only the historical question is considered here. Historically, did the belief that one person could die for the sake of the sins of another make sense in ancient worldviews?

---

29. See Wright, *Victory of God*, 268–74; and E. P. Sanders, *Paul and Palestinian Judaism: A Comparison of Patterns of Religion* (Philadelphia: Fortress, 1977), 236; 426–28.

30. Wright, *Victory of God*, 268.

The answer is yes. The Roman poet Lucan, a contemporary of the apostle Paul, records the speech of the statesman Cato: "May I alone, receive in death the wounds of all the war! Thus may the people be redeemed, and thus Rome for her guilt pay the atonement due" (*Pharsalia* 2.304–9).[31]

More relevant for the ancient Jewish context of Jesus are examples taken from *Fourth Maccabees*, composed around the time of Jesus' death in the middle of the first century CE. The work describes the Jewish resistance to the Hellenistic king Antiochus IV Epiphanes' attempt to force the Jews to convert to Greek religion. The author narrates how the aged priest Eleazar is tortured to death for refusing to eat pork. Just before dying, Eleazar proclaims,

> You know, O God, that when I might have been saved, I am slain for the sake of the law by tortures of fire. Be merciful to your people, and be satisfied with the punishment of me on their account. Let my blood be a purification for them, and take my life in recompense for theirs (4 Macc 6:27– 29).[32]

In his reflections on the death of Eleazar and other martyrs for the Jewish faith, the author concludes, "For they became the ransom to the sin of the nation; and the Divine Providence saved Israel, aforetime afflicted, by the blood of those pious ones, and the propitiatory death" (4 Macc 17:22).

Further examples of one person atoning for the sins of another are found in Scripture itself. In Isaiah, the "Servant" of God atones for the sins of the people: "he was pierced for our sins, crushed for our iniquity. He bore the punishment that makes us whole, by his wounds we were healed" (Isa 53:5).

Jewish tradition, then, provides several clear examples of the belief that one person's suffering or death could atone for the sins of the people. If Jesus understood himself as the Messiah, the royal representative of his people, he could well have imagined the possibility of suffering or dying on behalf of his people.[33] Historically, it is likely that Jesus was influenced by the example of the Servant of the Lord in Isaiah—a figure who, like the Messiah, is especially chosen by God (Isa 42:1) and who, like the Messiah, represents his people Israel. The Second Temple writing *1 Enoch* had already identified Isaiah's Servant with the Messiah (sec. 11.4.3).

Did Jesus Know He Would Die?   11.6.3

The Gospels portray Jesus as predicting his death and Resurrection. Directly after narrating Peter's confession of Jesus as the Messiah and Jesus' warning not to tell anyone, Mark adds, "He began to teach them that the Son of Man must suffer greatly, and be rejected by the elders, the chief priests, and the scribes, and be killed, and rise after three days" (Mark 8:31 par.).

31. *Pharsalia*, 2.304–9; quoted in Hengel, *The Atonement*, 23–24.

32. The language of the translation has been modernized. See Lancelot C. Brenton, *Septuagint with Apocrypha: Greek and English* (Peabody, MA: Hendrickson, 1986, orig. pub. 1851).

33. For these examples and further discussion, see Wright, *Victory of God*, 579–91.

Is this a classic case of what Crossan calls prophecy historicized? Writing years after Jesus' death, has Mark added these prophecies to embellish the supernatural nature of his main character, Jesus?

Again, the question can best be answered historically. Jesus led a messianic movement that proclaimed the kingdom of God. In other words, he implicitly proclaimed a challenge to the ruling authorities, both Jewish and Roman. During his public ministry, the Gospels show Jesus playing down the revolutionary implications of his movement, warning his disciples not to tell anyone that he was the Messiah (e.g., Mark 8:30 par.).

At a certain point, however, it seems clear that Jesus intended to provoke a confrontation. For the celebration of Passover, Jesus traveled from his home base of Galilee to Jerusalem, center of Jewish priestly power and Roman military and political authority and—most importantly—the site of the Temple. He entered Jerusalem as a messianic king (in fulfillment of Zech 9:9; see Mark 11:1–11 par.) and performed an action that symbolized the destruction of the Temple (sec. 11.5.6). He was claiming, if still symbolically, that he was the messianic king sent by God to destroy the current Temple and rebuild it with an eschatological one.

Jesus would have known that by radically challenging the authority of either Jewish or Roman authorities he was virtually assuring himself of a death sentence. He was well aware of what happened to prophets such as John the Baptist (notice Jesus' reaction to the news of the Baptist's death in Matt 14:13) and Theudas who challenged the authorities.

Jesus' words to his disciples at the Last Supper,[34] then, make historical sense, if one draws together the threads discussed in this chapter. Breaking the bread, Jesus said, "this is my body." After drinking from the cup, Jesus said, "This is my blood . . . , which will be shed for many" (Mark 14:22–24 par.).

In speaking of the covenant, Jesus refers to the coming of the kingdom and Israel's renewed covenant with God. He adds, "I shall not drink again the fruit of the vine until the day when I drink it new in the kingdom of God" (Mark 14:25). The breaking of the bread and the drinking of the wine are completely consistent with Jesus' practice of performing symbolic actions. Both bread and wine were rich symbols in first-century Judaism—both were dietary staples and symbols of life; both were associated with the Temple and with sacrifice. The two as a meal symbolized the eschatological banquet in the kingdom of God.

At the practical, human level of knowledge, Jesus knew that because of his more direct challenge to the religious and political authorities, his death was imminent. Given first-century Jewish thought on the atoning death of martyrs, Jesus' self-understanding[35] as the Messiah, representative of Israel, and his likely identification of himself with the Servant of the Lord, Jesus very reasonably

---

34. N. T. Wright discusses the historicity of the Last Supper in a video accessible at *www.youtube.com/watch?v=9qCotTdUnn8* (time 0:02:40).

35. N. T. Wright discusses Jesus' understanding of the meaning of his death in a video accessible at *www.youtube.com/watch?v=5WdKpnMq9Lo* (time 0:01:13).

believed that he was laying down his life as a sacrifice for the sins of his people, the renewed Israel.[36] Historical Jesus scholar John Meier concludes that with his words and breaking of the bread, Jesus wishes to communicate to his disciples that "he goes to his death, giving his flesh, his whole self, his very life, even unto suffering and death, to bring about the restoration of Israel in the end time. The one person willingly surrenders himself to death to give life to the many."[37]

In Second Temple thought, the fate of the whole world was associated with the fate of Israel in the eschatological age (sec. 11.4.1). In this sense, it is no exaggeration to say that Jesus thought of his death as a sacrifice for the sins of the world—a perfectly understandable claim in the context of first-century Jewish eschatology.[38]

Finally, one must note that the earliest Jesus traditions in the New Testament are those that were passed down to the apostle Paul from Jesus' first disciples (sec. 10.5.2.1). These traditions interpret Jesus' death as an atonement for sin: "Christ died for our sins" (1 Cor 15:3); "Jesus on the night he was handed over, took bread, and after he had given thanks, broke it, and said, 'This is my body that is for you'" (1 Cor 11:23–24). The theological interpretation of Jesus' death as atoning cannot then be considered a later theological development; it is demonstrably the earliest interpretation available to the historian.

Therefore, the best historical conclusion is that Jesus thought of his death as atonement[39] for sin and taught this to his disciples. If Jesus did not think of his death in these terms, it is difficult to explain how this belief became so firmly established among his followers at such an early date.

Did Jesus Expect to Rise on the Third Day?   11.6.4

If, considering Jesus in his ancient Jewish context, it is plausible that he understood his own death as a sacrifice for renewed Israel, what can one say about the historicity of the Gospel prophecies that Jesus would "rise on the third day"? Once again, this at first sounds suspiciously like a later belief of the church placed back into the mouth of the historical Jesus as a prophecy.

Consider one of these prophecies, mentioned in section 11.6.3, that the Son of Man would suffer death and rise from the dead after three days (see Mark 8:31 par.). One key to interpreting this passage is to identify exactly what Jesus meant by the title Son of Man.

---

36. On the previous points, see Hengel, *The Atonement*, 65–75; Wright, *Victory of God*, 540–611; Meyer, *Aims of Jesus*, 216–19.

37. John P. Meier, "The Eucharist at the Last Supper: Did It Happen?" *Theology Digest* 42 (1995): 349.

38. Meyer, *Aims of Jesus*, 217–18.

39. N. T. Wright discusses reasons for Jesus' death in a video accessible at *www.youtube.com /watch?v=gVxs51WwdxE* (time: 0:02:04).

Some Second Temple writings use the title "Son of Man" to refer to the Messiah who would be raised up to God's throne to serve as the eschatological judge after his death (sec. 11.4.3). Scholars such as Bart Ehrman believe that the historical Jesus did not think of himself as the eschatological Son of Man, because in several Synoptic accounts, Jesus speaks of the Son of Man in the third person.[40] Meyer and Wright, however, argue that such passages are connected with Jesus' reluctance to publicly identify his role as Messiah or Son of Man.[41] It is only near the end of his life, at his trial before the high priest Caiaphas, that Jesus openly claims these titles.

Following is Mark's account of Jesus' response to Caiaphas's question whether he is the Messiah:

> "I am; and 'you will see the Son of Man seated at the right hand of the Power and coming with the clouds of heaven.'" (Mark 14:61–62; Mark writes *Power* as a substitute for *Lord*)

Jesus' answer is a conflation of two Old Testament texts, "I saw coming with the clouds of heaven, One like a son of man" (Dan 7:13), and "The Lord says to my lord 'Sit at my right hand'" (Ps 110:1).

Jesus' vision, then, is of a time after his death when he would be raised to heaven and enthroned with God, an honor indicating God's vindication of Jesus as the Messiah, the true representative of Israel.[42] Although Jesus the Messiah had been defeated and killed by his enemies, the defeat was not a lasting one, for God had raised him from the dead to share in God's rule and judgment of the world.

This belief is consistent with Jesus' overall eschatological and apocalyptic outlook and with his self-identification as the Son of Man.[43]

Finally, the phrase "on the third day" does not necessarily refer to three calendar days. Biblically, it can mean "a short time." The prophet Hosea, however, records the people's hope, "on the third day he will raise us up" (Hos 6:2).[44]

Alternatively, it is also possible that Jesus originally predicted that God would vindicate him after his death but that the Gospel writers who were influenced by their own knowledge that Jesus had been resurrected on the third day added to Jesus' prediction the detail of "after three days."

In any case, Jesus' belief, in the context of Second Temple eschatological thought, that he would be raised up to share in God's power and judgment is entirely plausible, as the traditions in the *Similitudes* of *1 Enoch* show (sec. 11.4.3).

---

40. Ehrman, *Jesus Interrupted*, 159.

41. Meyer, *Aims of Jesus*, 202–9; Wright, *Victory of God*, 510–19.

42. Wright, *Victory of God*, 524–28; Meyer, *Aims of Jesus*, 209.

43. N. T. Wright discusses the significance of Jesus declaring himself as the Son of Man in a video accessible at *www.youtube.com/watch?v=WXQbBhNSkHs* (time 0:04:19).

44. See other references in Meyer, *Aims of Jesus*, 182.

Did Jesus Really Rise from the Dead?   11.7

Finally, to consider the theological belief in Jesus' Resurrection from the view-point of historical Jesus study, two preliminary issues must be addressed:

- Clarification of what is precisely meant by the claim that "Jesus rose from the dead."
- Demonstration that a supernatural event such as Jesus' Resurrection can actually be studied historically.

Defining Resurrection   11.7.1

Not only do scholars disagree about *whether* Jesus rose from the dead, they also disagree on *what* the claim entails.

In his definition of "Easter faith," John Dominic Crossan writes that Jesus' physical resurrection was not essential to early Christian belief:

> Jesus' presence was still experienced as empowerment. . . . It started among those first followers of Jesus in Lower Galilee long before his death, and precisely because it was faith as empowerment rather than faith as domination, it could survive and, in fact, negate the execution of Jesus himself. . . . An empty tomb or a risen body susceptible to food and touch were dramatic ways of expressing that faith.[45]

The first followers of Jesus did not claim that he physically rose from the dead—they were only claiming that they still experienced Jesus' presence even after his death. It was only later Christians who invented stories about the empty tomb or Jesus' risen body appearing to believers.

Other scholars trace the Resurrection back to visionary or psychological experiences of Jesus' followers.[46] When first-century Christians spoke of Jesus' Resurrection, they were perhaps only referring to visions of Jesus, or a subjective sense that Jesus was still alive and present in some way in their community. Alternatively, they may have thought of Jesus' Resurrection as Jesus' spirit rising to heaven, in a manner similar to New Testament scholar Luke Timothy Johnson's definition of Resurrection: "the passage of the human Jesus into the power of God."[47]

Historical Jesus scholar N. T. Wright,[48] however, rightly insists that historians must pay close attention to the words that the earliest followers of Jesus used

---

45. John Dominic Crossan, *Who Killed Jesus? Exposing the Roots of Anti-Semitism in the Gospel Story of the Death of Jesus* (San Francisco: HarperSanFrancisco, 1995), 209–10.

46. See the discussion in N. T. Wright, *The Resurrection of the Son of God* (Minneapolis: Fortress, 2003), 20; Johnson, *Real Jesus*, 137.

47. Luke Timothy Johnson, *The Real Jesus: The Misguided Quest for the Historical Jesus and the Truth of the Traditional Gospels* (San Francisco: HarperSanFrancisco, 1996), 136.

48. N. T. Wright discusses whether Jesus rose from the dead in a video accessible at *www.youtube.com/watch?v=zVhgAiGihoA* (0:06:11).

in making their claims about Jesus and then seek to understand the meaning of these claims within a first-century Jewish context. When early Christians speak of Jesus' Resurrection, they use such Greek words as *anastasis* ("rising"), *anistēmi* ("to raise or rise up"), and *egeirō* ("to raise"). For example, "God raised (*egeiro*) him from the dead" (Acts 3:15). The reference, then, is *not* to a person entering a spiritual afterlife or to a subjective experience of Christ's presence or of a vision of the risen Jesus. Rather, the language plainly refers to a person coming back to some kind of physical life after a period of being dead.[49]

At the same time, early Christian records clearly claim that Jesus was not simply a resuscitated corpse, a dead body come back to normal human life as, for example, is said to have happened in the case of Lazarus (John 11). Both the Gospel stories of Jesus' risen body and Paul's description (a "spiritual body"; 1 Cor 15:44) show that Christians are *not* speaking of a spirit, ghost, or vision, on the one hand, or of a corpse come back to life on the other but of a deceased person raised to a transformed, bodily type of life after a period of being dead (secs. 7.8–9).

Resurrection in the Context of Ancient Belief   11.7.2

This Christian belief in the resurrection of the body shows both similarities to and differences from other ancient beliefs. Wright summarizes the major points:

1. The belief in a resurrection of the body differentiated Jewish belief from Greco-Roman belief. In general, Greco-Roman ideas pictured some kind of shadowy post-death existence in places such as Hades, the Isles of the Blessed, or Tartarus. The Platonic tradition emphasized the immortality of the soul. These traditions did not envision anything like a renewed physical body in the afterlife.

2. Ancient Jewish tradition held a variety of beliefs. Sadducees rejected the belief in resurrection; the Jewish philosopher Philo believed in continued existence of the soul without a body; the author of 2 Maccabees plainly believed in a bodily resurrection, as did the Pharisees.

3. The early Christian view of resurrection, however, differed even from those Jews who accepted bodily resurrection, in two ways:

    a. The Jewish view was that there would be a general resurrection of the dead on the eschatological Day of Judgment. In contrast, the early followers of Jesus insisted that Jesus had *already* risen into the eschatological renewal of his physical body. They understood Jesus as a kind of prototype for the eschatological resurrection of his followers in the last days (1 Cor 15:20).

    b. The resurrected body was described as a transformed physical body (a "spiritual body").

---

49. Wright, *Resurrection*, 31.

Can the Resurrection Be Studied Historically?   11.7.3

Luke Timothy Johnson rejects the idea that Jesus' death can be studied as an event in history. Starting from his definition of Jesus' Resurrection as "the passage of the human Jesus into the power of God," Johnson concludes that because Jesus "is no longer defined by time and space," the event lies beyond "history's limited mode of knowing." "The Christian claim concerning the Resurrection in the strong sense is simply *not* historical." The only sense in which it can be considered historical is "as an experience and claim of human beings, then and today, that organizes their lives and generates their activities."[50]

However, Johnson's definition of resurrection is at odds with the early Christian understanding of resurrection as the raising of a physically transformed body. The early Christians made two claims about Jesus' Resurrection that are open to historical investigation: (1) Jesus' tomb was empty, and (2) Jesus appeared to many eyewitnesses in a transformed bodily state. These two historical claims can be checked using the usual historical tools.

History and Jesus' Resurrection   11.7.4

Wright agrees that, in the strictest sense, the actual moment of Jesus' Resurrection cannot be studied historically. No one claims to have witnessed the moment when Jesus, allegedly, rose up and walked out of the tomb.[51]

What can be studied, however, are the early Christian beliefs and accounts about Jesus' Resurrection, and the historical plausibility of the Christian claims. To study these claims about a supernatural event, however, one must at least be open to the possibility of a supernatural explanation—an openness that is not at all unreasonable (secs. 5.11 and 9.7).

Claims about the Empty Tomb   11.7.4.1

Consider first the Gospel accounts claiming that Jesus' tomb was found empty. In assessing this claim, one is faced with two general options: (a) the accounts are historically accurate, or (b) early Christians made up the accounts.[52] If option (b) is accepted, however, several historical difficulties arise.

---

50. Johnson, *Real Jesus*, 136.

51. The noncanonical *Gospel of Peter* does record that the Roman soldiers and Jewish elders saw three men emerge from the tomb (apparently Christ and two angels) followed by a cross. This is an account from the second century and not part of "mainstream" Christian beliefs (sec. 10.9.2).

52. To be thorough, one would first need to discuss the historical credibility of the Gospel accounts that Jesus was buried in a private tomb, which some scholars have indeed challenged. For a historical defense of their credibility, see P. R. Eddy, "Response [to W. L. Craig's "John Dominic Crossan on the Resurrection of Jesus"] in *The Resurrection: An Interdisciplinary Symposium on the Resurrection of Jesus*, eds. S. T. Davis, D. Kendall, and G. O'Collins (New York: Oxford University Press, 1997), 272–85.

1. Historically speaking, there is no plausible reason for Jesus' followers to fabricate a story that Jesus had risen bodily from the tomb. As noted, ancient Greco-Roman society and many first-century Jews did not believe in a bodily resurrection. Those groups (like the Pharisees) who did believe in bodily resurrection, believed in a general eschatological resurrection and not in a single individual resurrection. There is, moreover, no evidence that any first-century Jewish group thought the Messiah, in particular, would rise from the dead, much less that he would rise as an individual before the general eschatological resurrection.

2. All four Gospels indicate that women were the main witnesses to the empty tomb (Mark 16:1–8 par.). If the accounts were fabricated to persuade people that Jesus had risen from the dead, why would the followers of Jesus have invented women witnesses? In ancient Jewish society, "women were simply not acceptable as legal witnesses."[53] If the stories had been made up, the fabricators would certainly have invented reliable male witnesses to add credibility to their claims.

It is inconceivable, from a historical point of view, that the earliest followers of Jesus would have invented a story that made no sense within any first-century worldview and then supported it by fabricating women eyewitnesses. The only option left, then, is option (a)—eyewitnesses really did find Jesus' tomb empty.

The Resurrection Appearances of Jesus   11.7.4.2

Consider the other claim concerning Jesus' Resurrection: the appearances of the risen Jesus in a transformed body. In this case, the options are more complex: (a) the accounts record actual historical events; (b) the accounts were fabricated by the early Church; or (c) the followers of Jesus experienced some kind of visions or hallucinations of Jesus that they believed were real appearances of the risen Jesus.

Option (c) is highly implausible, because the Gospel accounts are designed to rule out the explanation that these events were merely visions or appearances of Jesus' spirit. Luke records Jesus telling his disciples, "Touch me and see, because a ghost does not have flesh and bones as you can see I have" (Luke 24:39). The risen Jesus invites "doubting Thomas" to touch his wounded hands and side (John 20:24–29).

The second-century orthodox Christian tradition is also remarkably unified in its insistence that Jesus was raised in a transformed body, ruling out the possibility that the appearances were regarded as visions. Only Gnostic-influenced second-century texts reinterpret *resurrection* as referring to a purely spiritual future life.[54] Only the first two options remain: the encounters with the risen

---

53. Wright, *Resurrection*, 607.

54. See the evidence in ibid., 480–552.

Jesus in his transformed body are either (a) historical accounts of actual events, or (b) fabrications of the early Christians. Once again, option (b) raises serious historical problems. If the early followers of Jesus had intended to persuade others that Jesus had risen from the dead by inventing resurrection stories, they did a remarkably poor job.

First, as discussed earlier (sec. 11.7.4.1), the claim that Jesus' body was a transformed physical body fits into no first-century worldview. Second, if the appearance accounts were supposed to persuade unbelievers that Jesus had risen, one would expect stories about a glorious figure in blinding white robes instead of the strange Gospel descriptions in which Jesus is not recognized at first, (Luke 24:13–35 John 20:15), still bears the marks of his crucifixion (John 20:27), and eats fish (Luke 24:42–43).

The historical problems with option (b) are so serious that unless one had already ruled out, *a priori*, the possibility of a supernatural explanation, one would have to consider option (a) as the more likely alternative.

The explanation that best fits the available evidence in the Gospels is that Jesus' tomb was found empty and that Jesus actually appeared to many witnesses in a transformed bodily form. All alternative explanations create hypothetical scenarios that fit badly within the historical context of first-century Judaism and cannot adequately explain the origin of early Christian belief in the Resurrection.[55]

The Jesus of History and the Jesus of Tradition   11.8

A major purpose of many of the original questers for the historical Jesus was to demonstrate the discrepancy between the actual Jesus of history and the portrait of Jesus found in the Gospels and in the Church. It is ironic, then, that many of the results of the Third Quest for the historical Jesus support the plausibility of traditional Christological beliefs.

Within the context of first-century Jewish eschatology, solid historical evidence supports the conclusion that Jesus believed he was God's Messiah, whose work was to establish the eschatological reign of God on Earth. The Gospel reports that Jesus believed that his death would atone for the sins of his people and, by extension, the sins of the world, and that God would raise him in vindication, are historically plausible within a Second Temple Jewish worldview. Finally, the historical implausibility of any natural explanation of early Christian claims that the crucified Jesus was raised from the dead in a transformed physical body forces an objective historian (provided he or she has not ruled out supernatural explanations *a priori*) to consider the possibility that early Christians' reports of the empty tomb and appearances of the resurrected Jesus are historically credible.

---

55. N. T. Wright discusses Jesus' Resurrection in a video accessible at *www.youtube.com/watch?v=Fki5wq48fpc* (time 0:10:20).

The efforts of the Third Quest are a decisive vindication of the Catholic and Christian principle that reason (in this case a reasoned study of history) can never contradict faith. On the contrary, the use of a historical-critical approach lends convincing support to traditional belief. To the extent that the Third Quest has allowed believers to gain a more concrete sense of Jesus as a first-century Jew, historical study can deepen a believer's understanding of the Incarnation.

Questions about the Text

1. Summarize some theological reasons in defense of the historical quest for Jesus.

2. What are some questions asked and approaches taken by the Third Quest for the historical Jesus?

3. How was the kingdom of God understood in first-century Judaism? What was the role of Israel in that kingdom? What was the role of the royal Messiah in establishing the kingdom? What does the term *eschatological* mean in scholarly discussion of this topic?

4. What is the historical evidence that Jesus considered himself the Messiah?

5. How do Jesus' exorcisms and healings fit within the first-century Jewish understanding of God's kingdom?

6. How does Jesus' selection of twelve disciples fit into the first-century Jewish view of the kingdom?

7. In what way is Jesus' teaching on interpreting the Torah connected with his role as the Messiah?

8. How does Balthasar relate the relationship between the Father and the Son within the Trinity to the relationship between the Father and the historical Jesus?

9. How do members of the Third Quest interpret Jesus' action at the Temple? How does this action fit into first-century Jewish eschatological expectations of the Messiah and the Temple?

10. In what ways is it historically plausible that Jesus thought his death would atone for the sins of the world? Consider especially Jesus' self-consciousness as the Messiah and first-century Jewish concepts of eschatological salvation.

11. How do early Christian beliefs about Jesus' Resurrection compare with ancient Greco-Roman and Jewish views of life after death?

12. What is the historical evidence for and against Christian claims that Jesus' tomb was found empty? What is the historical evidence for and against Christian claims that Jesus appeared to his followers in a transformed physical body?

Discussion Questions

1. What are your beliefs about what will happen in the "last days" when history ends? How do your ideas compare to ancient Jewish beliefs about the kingdom of God?

2. Are you familiar with any beliefs about a Messiah or other type of savior who will come in the last days? How do these beliefs compare with ancient Jewish beliefs about the Messiah or the Son of Man?

3. Do you agree that studying the historical Jesus can help make theological beliefs, such as the belief that Jesus died for the sins of all people, seem more plausible?

4. Do you agree with Wright that claims about whether Jesus rose from the dead can be studied historically? Why or why not?

Christology

The Christian View of Jesus Christ 12.1

This chapter considers a specific field of study within Christian theology known as **Christology**: the theological understanding of Jesus Christ within Christian faith. As Jesus Christ is central to the faith, so too is Christology to Christian theology.

The following sections begin the study with a consideration of perhaps the central Christian belief about Jesus: the Incarnation.

The Incarnation 12.2

Shock and Offense I: The Particularity of Jesus 12.2.1

Make no mistake. The Christian understanding of Jesus is a shock and an offense to millions of people. For millions more, it is incomprehensible.

The traditional Christian belief is that one human, Jesus, who lived two thousand years ago in a remote village in the region of Galilee in the eastern Roman Empire, is the key to understanding God's plan for the universe. Christians claim nothing less than that the salvation and happiness of every person who has ever lived depends on Jesus. This claim focuses on the particularity of Jesus: This particular man, who lived at a particular place and time, is the Savior of the world.

Many are understandably shocked and puzzled by this claim. How can it be that, of the billions of people who have lived, *one person* would have this central role? Given the thousands or even millions of religious teachers and leaders over the centuries, isn't it unbelievably arrogant to assume that only one would be the key to bring people back to a saving relationship with God? Anyone who is not shocked and even offended by this Christian teaching probably has not understood it.

Why do Christians make a claim that seems so unbelievable or unacceptable to many?

The Logic of Jesus' Particularity   12.2.2

Recall some basic points from earlier chapters. Chapter 1 indicated that all humans desire the transcendent, even if they do not explicitly articulate that desire. The desire is expressed through frustration with human limitations, striving for meaning in life, hoping for existence beyond death, and so on. Likewise, all cultures have developed religions that seek to connect humans with the transcendent world of God or the gods.

However, humans are frustrated in their striving for God. To use Christian vocabulary, humans are caught in sin and cannot save themselves from it. Sin separates them from God, the source of truth, love, and meaning. Humans cannot overcome this separation on their own.

The logic of the Incarnation is this: When the Second Person of the Trinity humbled himself to become human, humans were given the opportunity to overcome sin and reconnect with God. Jesus is unique, different from every other human, in that he was both divine and human. God and humanity truly met in him. In Jesus, the great gap between human and divine is overcome.

Why, in the Christian view, is the separation between the human and the divine overcome only in this one individual? Theoretically, the great chasm between the human and divine might have been bridged in another way.

According to Christianity, for reconciliation and salvation to occur it is essential that the human and the divine come into contact. It is necessary that Jesus be both God and human. However, to be human means to suffer, doubt, worry, laugh, love—and one can only do these things *as an individual*, in one particular period, culture, and sex. There is no such thing as a *generic* human. So if God were to come concretely into contact with humanity, it would need to be through an individual person, in one culture, one time in history.

This is the logic behind the Christian teaching that God has humbled himself to meet humans at their own level of experience and understanding. In Jesus,[1] God has entered into human history—not abstractly or theoretically, but in the flesh.

Shock and Offense II: The Humility of God   12.2.3

Besides the scandal of the Incarnation's particularity—that the Savior of humanity lived at only one certain place and time—the view of God implicit in the Incarnation also scandalizes many. Christianity claims that the ultimate power of the universe, the eternally perfect source of all being, became a limited

---

1. Robert Barron explains the Catholic understanding of who Jesus is in a video accessible at *www.youtube.com/watch?v=4Y4xacvLUXo* (time 0:06:36).

human—not merely that God *appeared* as a human or that God *revealed* himself through the words of the human Jesus but that God *became* human.

For many this makes no sense. The concept is a scandal for Islam, for example, which holds that God, in his transcendent power and greatness, is absolutely different from all created things. For a Muslim, it reveals great confusion, if not blasphemy, to say God could become human. Even the Christian language about Jesus as God's Son is unacceptable, as this seems to conflict with the belief that there is only one Divine being, completely separate from all other created reality. As the Qur'an, the holy book of the Islam, says,

> The Messiah, Jesus son of Mary, was only a messenger of Allah. . . . So believe in Allah and His messengers, and say not "Three"—Cease! (it is) better for you!—Allah is only One God. Far is it removed from His Transcendent Majesty that He should have a son. (Qur'an 4:171)

This belief that God would or could humble himself is central to the uniqueness of Christianity. The divine Son, the Second Person of the Trinity, "emptied himself, taking the form of a slave, coming in human likeness" (Phil 2:7). The self-emptying was carried out to the final degree: God the Son died as a despised criminal on a cross. The apostle Paul recognized that outsiders regarded this central Christian teaching as foolishness or madness, "we proclaim Christ crucified, a stumbling block to Jews and foolishness to Gentiles" (1 Cor 1:23).

In the end, however, this central doctrine of Christianity cannot be a logical contradiction, foolishness, or madness. It has its own logic to it: a logic of love. The Christian claim is that God's essential nature is not transcendence and omnipotence but love—the mutual love of the persons of the Trinity. God's love for humans allows him, through Jesus, to humble his divinity in order to come into real contact with humans.

Development of Doctrine: True God and True Man   12.2.4

The central idea that God became human in Jesus, though present in Christianity from the beginning, went through a long period of development during which its various implications were worked out and expressed more clearly. This is not surprising: As just noted, the idea that the unlimited Divine became human in Jesus of Nazareth runs counter to human expectations on many levels. It took many years of reflection and debate to clarify the meaning of this unique event (see secs. 6.14 and 9.15 on the development of doctrine).

In Paul's letters, the earliest documents of the New Testament, Paul thinks of Jesus as Divine in the fullest sense of the word (sec. 6:9), including him in the divine identity as Lord of the universe who shares the divine name. At the same time, Paul's and Jesus' earliest followers, regarded Jesus as fully human: "Born of a woman, born under the law" (Gal 4:4), Jesus truly died and was buried (1 Cor 15:3–4).

Yet this starting point, established by the experience and faith of the earliest Christians, raises a host of theological questions. The questions fall into two broad categories:

1. **What is the relationship between God the Father and Jesus?** If one believes Jesus is fully divine, doesn't that imply that Jesus is God, just as the Father is God? If both are God, aren't they exactly the same? Yet if they are exactly the same, why does the Bible describe them as distinct from each other? On the other hand, if they are truly distinct from each other, doesn't that imply that they are two Gods?

2. **How are Jesus' humanity and divinity related to each other?** The earliest Christians experienced Jesus as both human and divine. How can one person be both, as these are opposite qualities? Divinity has all knowledge, for example, while the knowledge of humanity is limited. Did Jesus know all things because he was divine? Or did he not know all things because he was human?

These Christological issues are complex. It is not surprising that it took the Church decades, and even centuries, of discussion, debate, and clarification to work out its Christology. The following sections consider some of the major signposts on that road of development.

Christology and Greek Philosophy   12.3

A crucial choice made by early Christian theologians was to use the categories of Greek philosophy to guide them through the complex issues concerning the relationship between Father and Son. This choice is already evident in the Gospel of John when John describes their relationship using the word *Word*, or *Logos*, which is a key term in Greek philosophy (secs. 2.5.2 and 6.8.3). The Son, John proclaims, is the Logos of the Father.

John's language, in turn, drew on an earlier Jewish tradition, seen in such writers as Philo of Alexandria[2] (ca. 20 BCE–40 CE), of reflecting on the Scriptures through the lens of Greek philosophy. This Christian and Jewish belief in the compatibility of philosophy and faith is one element of a deeper belief in the compatibility of faith and reason. In the second century, writers such as Justin Martyr (ca. 100–ca. 165 CE) continued this philosophical-theological tradition.

Justin the Philosopher and Logos Christology   12.3.1

The works of Justin Martyr are one signpost on the road of Christological development. Historians of Christianity place Justin among a group of second-century-CE writers, including Aristides, Theophilus, and Athenagoras, who are known as apologists. These authors wrote works, called apologies, which

---

2. An overview of Philo of Alexandria and his work is available at *www.iep.utm.edu/philo/*.

used rational arguments to present and defend Christian beliefs to the wider Greco-Roman culture. Such a task was especially urgent at times when Christians were persecuted by Roman authorities for their beliefs. Justin, for example, wrote his *First Apology* to the Emperor Antoninus Pius; his second is addressed to the Roman Senate.

Justin was born to pagan parents and converted to Christianity when he was about thirty years old. Wearing the traditional philosopher's cloak, he wrote and taught as a philosopher. In his youth, Justin studied Stoic, Aristotelian, Pythagorean, and Platonist philosophies. After his conversion, he taught the Christian faith at Ephesus and, later, at Rome where he opened a Christian school. He, along with some of his disciples, was executed at Rome when they refused to sacrifice to the gods.

Justin's *Second Apology* expounds his Logos Christology, a blend of Greek philosophical ideas and Christian faith. Stoic philosophers taught that the order and regular laws apparent in nature are the result of the divine Logos (reason, word, law) that pervades and orders all of reality. Human reason is a reflection of this universal Logos. Middle Platonist philosophers thought of the Logos as a sort of intermediary between the highest God and the world. Justin, following a long line of Jewish and Christian thinkers, applies these ideas to his Christology.

Justin taught that the Logos was God's mind and reason, through which God created and gave order to the world. It was this Logos that became human in Jesus. Even before Jesus' incarnation, humans had access to the Logos, because God had implanted seeds of it in all people (2 *Apol.* 8). Through the seeds of the Logos, philosophers, such as the Stoics and Platonists, could glimpse part of God's divine truth (e.g., 2 *Apol.* 13). In fact, Justin refers to philosophers such as Socrates and Heraclitus as Christians, even though they lived long before Jesus, because they lived "by the Logos" (1 *Apol.* 46).

However, only when the Logos became human in Jesus was the full divine truth revealed.

Justin maintained both the unity and distinctiveness of the Son in relation to the Father. As God's Logos, the very reason and mind of God, the Son obviously has the closest possible relationship with the Father. Yet the Logos is clearly distinct from the Father. In fact, Justin placed the Son a little lower than the Father, saying, Christians "hold him in the second place" after God the Father (*1 Apol.* 13). As Christological understanding developed, Justin's teaching would be seen by later Christians as inadequate.

Does Logos Christology Corrupt the Original Christian Message?   12.3.2

Some Christians have claimed that Justin's blending of pagan philosophy and Christian faith amounts to a betrayal of the original Christian message. According to these critics, the originally pure, simple gospel of love preached by the Jewish

Jesus was corrupted by later Christians, like Justin, who complicated the message by superimposing Greek philosophical ideas on Jesus' simple teaching.[3]

This narrative is false and misleading on many levels. Several points can be made:

1. One cannot sharply divide Jewish and Greek influences in earliest Christianity. By the time of Jesus' birth, Palestinian Judaism had been deeply influenced by Greek culture and philosophy for more than three centuries—since the conquest of Palestine by Alexander the Great (d. 323 BCE) and its subsequent rule by Hellenistic kings. The Hellenistic influence on ancient Jews who lived outside of Palestine was even more pervasive: The example of Philo has already been noted.

2. Because of the large number of Greek-speaking Jews, the Old Testament had already been translated from Hebrew to Greek by the time of Jesus. It is, in fact, primarily the Greek version of the Old Testament, known as the **Septuagint**, that the earliest Christians, such as the apostle Paul, quoted in their writings.

3. Greek philosophical influence is already clear in the New Testament, most obviously in the prologue to the Gospel of John (John 1:1–3).

For these and other reasons, Pope Benedict argues that there is, in fact, an intrinsic relationship between the Christian message and Greek philosophy. "The encounter between the Biblical message and Greek thought," he writes, "did not happen by chance."[4] Benedict sees a deep relationship between (1) the Old Testament prophetic movement that declares that the Lord is the only God and that all other gods are false idols, and (2) the movement of Greek philosophy (e.g., in Plato) that finds only one ultimate power of the universe and declares that the mythological stories of the gods (in which the gods had anthropomorphic characteristics) are unworthy of the divine.[5]

The Unity and Distinctiveness of Father and Son: Search for a Christological Balance   12.4

As noted, Christian theology strove to remain faithful to two key Christological insights: (1) the Son is equal to the Father in his divinity; yet (2) the Son is distinct from the Father. It is difficult to do justice to both of these insights. In

---

3. The great historian of early Christianity, Adolph von Harnack, popularized one form of this line of thought.

4. Pope Benedict XVI, "Faith, Reason, and the University: Memories and Reflections," (2006), is accessible at *www.vatican.va/holy_father/benedict_xvi/speeches/2006/september/documents /hf_ben-xvi_spe_20060912_university-regensburg_en.html.*

5. Joseph Cardinal Ratzinger, *Introduction to Christianity* (San Francisco: Ignatius Press, 2004), 137–43.

the history of early Christian theology, one can trace two basic errors, Modalism and **subordinationism**, that resulted when one side of the balance was given too much weight.

Modalism: Overemphasizing the Unity   12.4.1

One erroneous Christian tendency overemphasized the unity within God. This tendency, known as Modalism, also known as Modalist Monarchianism, was especially prevalent in the third century. The Modalists feared that a clear distinction between Father and Son implied a belief in two Gods. They taught that there are no permanent distinctions within the oneness of God. Rather, the one God exists in different, temporary "modes" or "activities." The theologian Praxeas reportedly taught that the entire Godhead took on the mode of the Savior in his incarnation, implying that both Father and Son suffered on the cross.

Subordinationism: Overemphasizing the Distinctiveness   12.4.2

The opposite Christological error is to overemphasize the distinctiveness of the Son. This tendency could result in subordinationism, or subordinating the nature of the Son to the divine nature of the Father. There is a tendency toward subordinationism, for example, in the thought of the great third-century theologian Origen.

In the following sections, a particular form of subordinationist thought is considered: the so-called Arian controversy of the fourth century. Arian thought ignited a complex debate that involved not only bishops and theologians but also political figures, including Roman emperors.

Theologically, the key outcome of the Arian controversy is that it allowed the Church to find the right language with which to clarify its core beliefs that the Son is both fully equal to the Father yet distinct from him. The debate also clarifies why these theological beliefs matter—because they are closely tied to articulating how humans are saved from sin and death.

The Arian Controversy   12.5

Arius (d. 336 CE) was an Alexandrian priest whose teaching sparked the controversy. In the following decades, so-called Arian theologians developed distinctive theological approaches. The Arians agreed, however, that although the Son was the Savior whose death atoned for sins, he was, nevertheless, clearly subordinate to God the Father. According to Arius, God the Father created the Son as his first act of creation and then created the rest of the universe through the Son.

The Arians were able to point to many scriptural texts to support their position. They were especially fond of passages concerning the human Jesus found in the Synoptic Gospels: "But of that day or hour [i.e., the time of the coming of the Son of Man in glory], no one knows, neither the angels in heaven, nor the Son, but only the Father" (Mark 13:32), or Jesus' answer to the rich man, "Why do you call me good? No one is good but God alone" (Mark 10:18). From John, they favored 14:28, "the Father is greater than I."

The Arians argued that the Son was subordinate to the Father not only when he was incarnate as a human but also before and after his incarnation. Their main motivation was to protect the oneness of God. They believed that if the Son's divinity was equal to the Father's, then this in effect meant a belief in two Gods.

Orthodox opponents of the Arians responded with their own biblical proof-texts. The great Arian opponent, Bishop Athanasius of Alexandria (ca. 296–373 CE), cited passages showing that the Son and the Father shared the same "being," including Heb 1:3: The Son "is the refulgence of his [God's] glory, the very imprint of his being." Athanasius was especially fond of Jesus' words in the Gospel of John, "The Father and I are one" (10:30), and, "Whoever has seen me has seen the Father" (14:9). Athanasius insisted that many of the Arian Scriptural proof-texts applied to the human nature of Jesus, not to his divinity.

Do Theological Debates Really Matter? 12.5.1

Before discussing how the controversy was resolved, a basic question should be addressed: Does it really matter if the Son is equal to the Father, or if he is slightly less than the Father? After all, the Arians believed that Jesus was divine, in a sense, and that he had become human and suffered and died so that human sins could be forgiven. They believed Jesus rose from the dead, ascended into heaven, and is seated at the right hand of the Father. Doesn't that make them fully orthodox Christians?

Athanasius insisted that more was at stake than an abstract dispute among theologians. In fact, the stakes are the highest possible:

1. If the Arians are right, then Christians do not really know God.
2. If the Arians are right, then Christians are not really saved.

Do Christians Really Know God? 12.5.1.1

The first issue involves revelation. Because the eternal, invisible, omniscient, and omnipotent God is so far beyond human comprehension, humans can only know God if God reveals himself (sec. 5.1).

Christianity teaches that God reveals himself most fully in his Son Jesus Christ. However, if the Son is not equal to the Father, if he does not share God's essential nature, then the Son cannot fully reveal the Father. If the Son is less than the Father, if he is only one of the Father's creations, as the Arians insisted, then followers of the Son do not truly know God the Father.

Are Christians Really Saved?   12.5.1.2

For Athanasius, the entire logic of Christian salvation is that God and humanity meet in Jesus Christ. To link God and humans, the savior must be *truly* God and *truly* human. If the Son is a creature (i.e., created by God), he could not have linked God and humans, for a creature does not have the power to join creatures to God (*Discourses against the Arians* 2.69). "Therefore He was not man, and then became God, but He was God, and then became man, and that to deify us" (*Discourses against the Arians* 1.39). By *deify*, Athanasius meant the process of salvation: humans becoming completely cleansed of all sin so they might share God's divine life.

If Arius was right, then Christians are not saved from their sins and cannot enter heaven.

Answering the Arians: Linguistic Precision   12.5.2

Scripture alone could not settle the Arian controversy, because both sides claimed they could prove their position from Scripture.

Part of the problem was that the scriptural terms used in the debate, such as *Father* and *Son*, were too ambiguous. The Arians insisted it is only logical that the Father must exist before his Son. How can a son be born at the same time as his father? The orthodox countered that the Arians were thinking of the Father and Son within the human categories of father and son. The relationship of father and son, when applied to God, should be understood as an analogy.

The father-son analogy is used to suggest the close relationship between the divine Father and Son. If the divine Father is eternal, then his divine Son must also be eternal, because divinity is eternal. The Son must have been with the Father from all eternity, because the eternal God could not be called "Father" if the Son had not been there from the beginning.

When Christian bishops drew up a creed[6] at the Council of Nicaea[7] in 325 CE in an attempt to settle the Arian controversy, they wished to avoid ambiguity and, so went beyond scripturally based terms such as *Father* and *Son*.

They described the Son's relationship with the Father with a philosophically precise term: *homoousious*, which is usually translated in English as "one in being." (The prefix *homo* means "the same," while the root word *ousia* means "being"; the Latin translation is "*consubstantial*"). *Ousia*, a term common in Greek philosophy, means the substance of a certain thing—that which makes a thing what it is and not something else. So the point was that Father and Son share the same divine nature: that divine essence that makes the Father God is also shared by the Son (see *CCC*, nos. 200, 465).

---

6. The text of the Nicene Creed is accessible at *www.usccb.org/beliefs-and-teachings/what-we-believe/index.cfm.*

7. A video presentation by Charles Gutenson on the Council of Nicaea is accessible at *www.youtube.com/watch?v=NxrugLwUYKE* (time 0:07:06).

Aquinas, acknowledging that some words used in the Church's official declarations are not biblical, insists that "the urgency of confuting heretics made it necessary to find new words to express the ancient faith about God" (*ST* 1.29.3 ad. 1).

To further clarify the relationship, the bishops included the phrase, "begotten, not made." This clarified, against Arius's position, that the Son was not made or created by God but was "eternally begotten." The Son's being has come forth from the being of the Father from all eternity.

Answering the Arians: Trinitarian Analogies 12.5.3

In addition to using precise philosophical language, the Nicene Creed also employed analogy to clarify the relationship between Father and Son. In describing the relationship of Father and Son, the Creed reads, "God from God, Light from Light, true God from true God."

In the phrase "Light from Light," God the Father, the ultimate source of all things, is compared to the sun. The Son is compared to the rays of light streaming forth from the sun. The rays of sunlight are distinct from the sun, but at the same time, they share the very essence of the sun—they are sunlight. The analogy shows how something can be both unified with, yet distinct from, something else.

The analogy also addresses the issue of time. As soon as our sun came into existence, rays of sunlight began to stream forth. There was no interval of time, not even a fraction of a second, between the beginning of the sun and the first rays of sunlight. In the same way, there is absolutely no interval of time between the existence of the Father and the existence of the Son. Both are eternal. From all eternity, the Son has been streaming forth from the source of the Father: "true God" coming forth from "true God."

Did the Council of Nicaea Invent Christian Orthodoxy? 12.5.4

A popular modern myth is that orthodox Christian theology, especially the belief in the divinity of Christ, was invented at the Council of Nicaea. According to this myth, early Christianity had a variety of views of Jesus. Wishing to promote one view to unify the Roman Empire, the Emperor Constantine gathered a group of bishops at Nicaea. The bishops voted to adopt the belief in Jesus' divinity; afterward, all other Christian views of Jesus that disagreed with the Nicene statement were violently suppressed with state power. One influential version of the myth is found in Dan Brown's novel, *The Da Vinci Code*.[8]

---

8. See Brown, *The Da Vinci Code*, Second Anchor Books Mass Market Edition (New York: Anchor Books, 2009).

The following points should help clarify the historical facts:[9]

1. Followers of Jesus believed in his divinity centuries before the Council, arguably from the time of the first disciples (sec. 6.9).
2. The emperor Constantine did, in fact, call the Council, which was attended by some 300 bishops from across the empire, was present at the Council, and enforced the Council's decrees, including banishing Arius. Constantine, a Christian, was interested in promoting unity within the Church.
3. It is true that Roman emperors were involved in Church politics after Constantine, but they were hardly unfailing supporters of the orthodox position. The emperor Valens (364–378 CE), for example, was an Arian supporter who banished the orthodox Gregory of Nyssa and made sure that an Arian bishop took over in Alexandria after Athanasius's death.
4. The Council of Nicaea did not settle Christological debate once and for all. On the contrary, various groups were dissatisfied with the creed's wording, and over the next fifty years, a series of councils were held and many alternative creeds were written. It was only at the Council of Constantinople in 381 CE that the Nicene Creed was officially approved, but only with additions that emphasized belief in the divinity of the Holy Spirit. This is the text of the Nicene Creed read in churches today, more properly called the Niceno-Constantinopolitan Creed.[10]

The Relationship between the Human and the Divine in Jesus　　12.6

Theological debates in the fourth century focused on the relationship between Father and Son, culminating in the official teaching of the Niceno-Constantinopolitan Creed. However, another thorny theological problem remained. If Jesus was truly God and truly human, how exactly are these two natures related? How exactly did the divine and the human interact in Jesus?

The Council in Chalcedon (451 CE) clarified the relationship in theologically precise language: in Jesus are "two natures without confusion, change, division, or separation" (*CCC*, no. 467). Like the debates over the Son's relationship with the Father, however, this definition came only at the end of a long process of debate. Along the way, there were three challenges to the definition that would eventually be given at Chalcedon: (1) challenges to Jesus' true humanity, (2) challenges to Jesus' true divinity, (3) erroneous views on how the divine and human are related in Jesus.

---

9. See Lewis Ayres, *Nicaea and Its Legacy: An Approach to Fourth-Century Trinitarian Theology* (Oxford: Oxford University Press, 2004), 85–92.

10. A video presentation by Charles Gutenson on the Niceno-Constantinopolitan Creed is available at *www.youtube.com/watch?v=8ElvBgWAJC0* (time 0:08:50).

Challenges to the True Humanity and the True Divinity   12.6.1

At a very early stage in Christian history, some Christians were teaching that Jesus was not truly human. One sees traces of this belief already within the New Testament, "This is how you can know the Spirit of God: every spirit that acknowledges Jesus Christ come in the flesh belongs to God" (1 John 4:2). The author apparently is objecting to groups who teach that Jesus was a spirit who did not truly take on human form and limitations.

On the opposite end of the theological spectrum are groups that denied the full divinity of Jesus. In the late second-to-third century, the so-called Adoptionist or, more properly, the Dynamic Monarchiasm theologians taught that Jesus was an ordinary human. Due to his great piety, God "adopted" Jesus as his divine Son at Jesus' baptism.[11]

How Are Jesus' Human and Divine Nature Related?   12.6.2

In the course of the fourth and fifth centuries, many different models of understanding the relationship between the human and divine in Jesus emerged and were debated. Three of these—Nestorianism, Monophysitism, and Apollinarism—were rejected as errors as the Church clarified the orthodox understanding.

The Nestorian Controversy: Separating the Human and Divine   12.6.2.1

Nestorian beliefs about Jesus were associated with Nestorius (ca. 351 CE–ca. 451 CE), Patriarch of Constantinople.[12] Nestorians accepted that Jesus had both a human and divine nature but believed that the two were essentially separate, united only by the will of the human Jesus. Their position implied that there were two persons in Jesus: human and divine.

For the Nestorians, Mary could be called the mother of the human Jesus but could not be called Mother of God because it is absurd to think a human woman could be the mother of the uncreated source of the universe.

In answering the Nestorians, Cyril, Bishop of Alexandria, and the Council of Ephesus (431 CE) insisted Jesus must be thought of as *one* person: the human nature and the divine nature are united to one another in an essential way. In

---

11. The second- and third-century Adoptionists should be distinguished from another form of Adoptionism that was taught in eighth-century Spain.

12. There is a scholarly debate on what Nestorius actually taught; see "Nestorius," *Oxford Dictionary of the Christian Church*, 3rd ed., eds. F. L. Cross and E. A. Livingstone (Oxford: Oxford University Press, 2005), 1145–46.

technical theological terms, this is known as the **hypostatic union**: the divine Son of God "assumed" human nature and "made it his own," (*CCC*, no. 466). Because the two natures are intimately and integrally joined in Jesus, it is entirely appropriate to call Mary *Mother of God*, as she bore a human son whose nature was united in the closest possible way with the nature of God. The Council of Ephesus formally approved the use of the title *Theotokos* (literally meaning, "the bearer of God") for Mary.

Why was this controversy important? Because Christian theology understands Jesus as the representative of all humans, this controversy had deep implications for the Christian understanding of human nature and salvation.

1. The Nestorian model, in insisting that the human and divine natures cannot have an essential connection, challenges the whole Christian understanding of salvation. In the orthodox Christian view, salvation occurs when the human and divine meet—Jesus truly takes on human nature and makes atonement for human sin. Such a connection is impossible in the Nestorian view.

2. The orthodox model shows the immense human potential for good. In Jesus, the divine and human nature do not exist side-by-side, but the human is fully "taken" up into the divine, without losing its human distinctiveness. This orthodox model points forward to the Christian belief that, in heaven, the human is raised up into an intimate connection with God, yet remains human.

The Monophysite Controversy   12.6.2.2

If the Nestorians separated too sharply the divine and human nature in Jesus, the Monophysite teaching, a theological error of the fifth century, tended to collapse the two together. The Monophysite teaching insisted that if the all-powerful divine nature of the Word had assumed human nature, then the weak human nature must have been overwhelmed, in effect leaving one (*mono*) nature (*physis*) in Christ. This teaching tends in a **Docetic** or Gnostic direction, implying that although the divine Jesus may have appeared to be human, he could not have been a weak, limited human.

The Monophysite view tends to degrade human nature: it is weak and is simply swallowed up by the divine. The orthodox view, in contrast, insists that human nature is valuable in its own right. As the Second Vatican Council taught, Jesus took on human nature and gave the nature of humanity divine dignity (see *GS*, no. 22).

In the fourth century, the bishop Apollinarius had put forth a teaching that shared some characteristics with the Monophysite view. Apollinarius argued that in the Incarnation, the divine mind or soul of the Son had replaced the human mind or soul of Jesus.

In arguing against Apollinarius, Bishop Gregory of Nazianzus wrote, "For that which He has not assumed He has not healed; but that which is united to His Godhead is also saved" (*Epistle* 101). In other words, if God the Son had only taken on a human body in the Incarnation, then only the human body would be saved. However, the orthodox view of salvation is holistic: the Son took on all aspects of humanity—body, mind, and soul—so that the whole human is saved.

True God and True Human: The Definition at the Council of Chalcedon   12.6.3

Reacting against the Monophysite view and emphasizing the dignity of human nature, the Council of Chalcedon (451 CE) published its classic definition[13] of the relationship between the human and divine natures of Jesus.[14] In Jesus are "two natures without confusion, change, division, or separation" (*CCC*, no. 467). Beyond all expectation, the Council insisted, the limited human and the all-powerful divine had joined in Jesus Christ, opening the way for all humans to overcome sin and join themselves again in harmony with God.

Christology and Art   12.7

Through the centuries, beliefs about Jesus have been expressed not only in theological writings but also through art. There is no physical description of Jesus in the canonical Gospels and only a few generalized descriptions of the heavenly Jesus in the Book of Revelation (e.g., Rev 1:12–16). Because there is no surviving portrait of the historical Jesus, artists have had free reign in creating images of Jesus.

Early images pictured Jesus as a beardless young man, as in a third-century depiction found on a catacomb wall showing Jesus as the Good Shepherd.[15]

By the fifth century, the image of Jesus as a bearded man with long hair began to become standardized.

Continued

13. Charles Gutenson discusses the Chalcedonian definition in a video accessible at *www.youtube.com/watch?v=LW2OM0qSZII* (time 0:08:54).

14. A small number of churches, known as Oriental Orthodox Churches (including the Coptic and Ethiopian Orthodox Churches) did not accept the Council of Chalcedon. Others have labeled them as "Monophysites," but they reject that label. Beginning in the twentieth century, both Eastern Orthodox and Catholic Churches have been in ecumenical dialogues with these churches.

15. This image is accessible at *http://en.wikipedia.org/wiki/File:Good_shepherd_02b_close.jpg*.

Christology and Art *Continued*

Korean School (20th century) / Private Collection / Photo © Bolin Picture Library / Bridgeman Images

This portrait by a Korean artist pictures Jesus and his mother with Korean features. Though the historical Jesus had Middle-Eastern features, portraits like this one capture the universal significance of the Incarnation.

In later artistic tradition, a favorite image was the depiction of Mary and the baby Jesus,[16] a portrayal emphasizing Jesus' true humanity.

Another favorite scene was the baptism of Jesus,[17] understood by Christians as a revelation of the Trinity, in which God the Father speaks from heaven and the Holy Spirit descends on Jesus.

Jesus' crucifixion was often painted, frequently with a realistic focus on Jesus' suffering. A striking variation is that of twentieth-century Russian-Jewish painter Marc Chagall depicting the crucifixion in a way that accentuates Jesus' identity as a Jew: he is wearing a prayer shawl, amid scenes of the persecution of the Jewish people.[18]

In Eastern Christianity, many images portray Jesus as Pantokrator,[19] the all-powerful ruler of the universe. Paintings known as icons have a special place in the Orthodox tradition—they are understood as special windows into the Divine and are treated with veneration.

The cultural background of the artist has always influenced his or her depictions. In Western art, Jesus is usually represented with typically European features; while artists of other backgrounds depict Jesus accordingly.

---

16. An example of this image is accessible at *http://en.wikipedia.org/wiki/Madonna_of_Palazzo_Medici-Riccardi#mediaviewer/File:Madonna_col_bambino,_palazzo_medici_riccardi,_filippo_lippi.jpg*.

17. An example of this image is accessible at *http://en.wikipedia.org/wiki/File:Baptism-of-Christ-xx-Francesco-Alban.JPG*.

18. This image is accessible at *www.artic.edu/aic/collections/artwork/59426*.

19. An example of an image of Jesus as Pantokrator is accessible at *http://en.wikipedia.org/wiki/File:Christ_Pantocrator_Deesis_mosaic_Hagia_Sophia.jpg*.

Christology, Orthodoxy, and Heresy   12.8

Orthodox beliefs about Jesus developed over time. This development often occurred in the context of a debate between the orthodox position and others that the orthodox labeled "errors." In traditional Christianity, such serious theological errors are termed *heresies*. The *Catechism* defines *heresy* as "the obstinate post-baptismal denial of some truth which must be believed with divine and catholic faith" (*CCC*, no. 2089). A heresy, then, is a Christian's persistent rejection of an essential truth of the Christian faith. Orthodoxy, in contrast, is the correct teaching of truth.

Some scholars of ancient Christianity have called for a redefinition of these traditional categories. Bart Ehrman, for example, writes,

> There were lots of early Christian groups. They all claimed to be right. . . . The group that won out did not represent the teachings of Jesus or of his apostles. For example, none of the apostles claimed that Jesus was "fully God and fully man," or that he was "begotten not made, of one substance with the Father," as the fourth-century Nicene Creed maintained. The victorious group called itself orthodox. But it was not the original form of Christianity, and it won its victory only after many hard-fought battles.[20]

In other words, according to Ehrman, no group has a better claim than any other to the truth about Jesus. Gnostic, Docetic, Arian, Modalist, Adoptionist, and what later became known as the orthodox view (labeled "proto-orthodox" by Ehrman)—all are on equal footing. It was only after the proto-orthodox group won the battle for converting more people than the others that the proto-orthodox rewrote history, defining themselves as "orthodox" from the beginning and labeling all other groups "heretics."

However, Ehrman's version of history is misleading. He is correct that Jesus' first apostles did not claim Jesus was "of one substance with the Father." The orthodox Christian view, however, does not claim the apostles described Jesus with that exact language. It does claim that the Nicene definition is a faithful expression, in philosophical terms, of the experience of those first apostles, who knew Jesus as a human who spoke and acted with the full authority of God.

The debate here is about the nature of truth. It seems, in Ehrman's view, that there is no truth about the actual historical person Jesus, just equal claims; and the historical "winners" define what is meant by truth. The traditional Christian view is that there is an objective truth about who Jesus was and is. The Church claims that it can trace the roots of its teaching back to Jesus and his

---

20. Ehrman, *Jesus, Interrupted*, 215.

first apostles and can show, reasonably, that its teaching is a faithful expression of that original teaching and experience.

The word *heresy* has a harsh ring to modern ears. It is an intolerant word in a modern society whose highest value is tolerance. But one must remember that when Athanasius, Gregory Nazianzus, and others labeled their theological opponents as heretics, what motivated them was not primarily a quest for power but a quest for proclaiming the truth about Jesus as Savior.

Orthodox Christians, like any other fallible humans, were at times also motivated by the desire for power, prestige, or other less-than-noble motivations. However, an honest look at history reveals that their primary passion was for truth. The orthodox labeled others as heretics because the orthodox were convinced that the others' teachings were leading people astray, away from the truth about how humans could be saved from a life of sin, misery, and death and attain eternal salvation.

With this in mind, the following sections return to a key point in orthodox Christology: Jesus' assumption of human nature. Discussion of this point should clarify some of the reasoning behind the scandalous Christian claim that the salvation of all people depends on one person: Jesus of Nazareth.

The Son's Assumption of Human Nature: Christ as the Second Adam   12.9

The *Catechism* teaches that the Son "assumed" human nature and "made it his own" (*CCC*, no. 466).[21]

In becoming human, the Word of God provided humans a new model of what it means to be human. Paul brings out this point by contrasting Adam—the representative of human nature enslaved to selfishness and sin—with Christ—the representative of human nature freed from sin. "For if, by the transgression of one person [referring to Adam], death came to reign through that one, how much more will those who receive the abundance of grace and of the gift of justification come to reign in life through the one person Jesus Christ" (Rom 5:17).

Christ is the goal of humanity. Adam symbolizes humanity in its incompleteness, and Christ represents humanity in its fullness and completeness. Paul writes, "Just as we have borne the image of the earthly one [Adam], we shall also bear the image of the heavenly one [Christ]" (1 Cor 15:49). Because Christ is the perfect image of the Father (Col 1:15 ; Heb 1:3) Christ is the model for restoring humanity's own image of God, distorted by sin, to its original destiny of perfect harmony with nature and God.

---

21. Henri de Lubac gives many references to this teaching, especially from the ancient Greek Fathers. See de Lubac, *Catholicism: Christ and the Common Destiny of Man* (San Francisco: Ignatius, 1988; orig. pub. 1947), 37–39.

Jesus Offers His Life as the Representative of All Humans
12.10

It is in this sense that Christians believe Jesus is the Savior of all people. God's Logos took on human nature in Jesus Christ. Because he is the Logos of God, however, Jesus as an individual can also represent humanity. What Jesus does as an individual, he does for all of humanity. Balthasar says that Christ "must somehow have adopted human nature as a whole. If this is so, it becomes credible that his work of atonement has affected the whole of human nature."[22] The *Catechism* declares, "the existence in Christ of the divine person of the Son, who at once surpasses and embraces all human persons . . . makes possible his redemptive sacrifice for all" (*CCC*, no. 616).

Understanding Jesus' Atoning Death: Anselm's Model
12.11

The Christian doctrine of atonement is an attempt to understand the earliest teaching of the Church that "Christ died for our sins" (1 Cor 15:3). As C. S. Lewis notes, however, different theological explanations of the atonement have been offered over the course of the centuries.[23] In the Catholic tradition, the primary model of understanding atonement is of satisfaction or substitution. The *Catechism* reads, "By his obedience unto death, Jesus accomplished the substitution of the Suffering Servant, who 'makes himself an *offering for sin.*'" . . . Jesus atoned for our faults and made satisfaction for our sins to the Father" (*CCC*, no. 615).

The classic form of this doctrine was expressed by the bishop and theologian Anselm of Canterbury[24] (ca. 1033–1109) in his work "Why God Became Man."[25]

Anselm defines sin as not giving God what is due. However, because God is the Creator, the source of all goodness, humans owe it to God to always obey his will (1.11). Whenever they lie, steal, or act selfishly, they sin, disturb the divine order of the universe, and put themselves in debt to God.

Clearly, no human could ever repay this debt. Everything a human has—intelligence, free will, talents, life itself—is a gift from God. In "paying back" something to God, one only gives to God what is already his (1.20).

---

22. Hans Urs von Balthasar, *Theo-Drama: Theological Dramatic Theory, Vol. 3, The Dramatis Personae: The Persons of Christ* (San Francisco: Ignatius Press, 1992), 203.

23. C. S. Lewis, *Mere Christianity* (London: HarperCollins, 2001; orig. pub. 1952), 53–59. See also James K. Beilby and Paul R. Eddy, *The Nature of the Atonement: Four Views* (Downer's Grove, IL: InterVarsity Press, 2006).

24. An overview of Anselm's life and work is accessible at *www.iep.utm.edu/anselm*.

25. Anselm's text is accessible at *www.ccel.org/ccel/anselm/basic_works.vi.html*.

Therefore, the only being in a position to repay the debt owed to God would be God himself. But logically, God does not owe himself a debt; humans do. So the only way for human debt to be paid is if God becomes human. As a human, he owes the debt to God; as God, he has the power to make the payment (2.7).

Critiques of the Doctrine of the Atonement 12.12

To avoid misunderstanding this central Christian doctrine, consider some reasonable questions and objections.

Why Can't God Just Forgive? 12.12.1

If God is merciful, why doesn't he forgive sins without demanding a payment of debt? Anselm answers that this would violate God's justice and disturb the divine order of justice in the world (1.12). The following reflections consider this point more fully.

While the idea that God could "forgive and forget" sounds plausible, this way of dealing with sin violates some strongly held human convictions. The sense that one must make up or atone for a wrong lies deeply within human consciousness.

As an example, imagine that someone like Adolf Hitler had a complete and genuine change of heart just before he died. What if, in the last days of World War II, Hitler had voluntarily given up power and asked the Jewish people for forgiveness? Despite his genuine repentance, wouldn't the human sense of justice demand that Hitler not be forgiven so easily? Wouldn't people have a deep sense that Hitler needed to atone for his crimes—if it were even possible—that forgiving and forgetting would be impossible for someone who had caused the suffering and death of millions of people?

At a more ordinary level, daily experience confirms the human need for atonement. As a hypothetical example, consider George and Claudia, who dated for a long time and got to know each other well. One day, they argue and George, losing his temper, says something hurtful that offends Claudia terribly. They don't speak to each other for days.

Once George has calmed down, he feels ashamed and wishes to apologize. Instinctively, he knows saying "I'm sorry" isn't enough. He's sure Claudia will accept his apology, yet George feels words alone aren't sufficient. Somehow, he needs to make up for it. He feels the need to do something positive, something generous and kind to show Claudia his sincerity and somehow make up for the wrong. Perhaps he'll buy flowers, take Claudia out to supper, or do some other act of kindness. George is feeling the need to atone.

The history of religions reveals how deeply embedded the need for atonement is within human nature. Nearly every ancient religion offered sacrifice as a way of worshiping their gods. The Hebrews offered sheep, cattle, grain, and wine. The Greeks and Romans offered bulls. The ancient Aztecs had human sacrifices. While sacrifices were not always done to make up for a sin—they might be given in thanksgiving or to appease the anger of a god—the need to offer something personal or precious as a sacrifice is a common theme across cultures.

The Old Testament Book of Leviticus connects the idea of atonement with the blood of an animal: "the life of the [animal's] flesh is in the blood, and I have given it to you to make atonement on the altar for yourselves" (Lev 17:11).

Across cultures, we see that humans have the sense that they must offer something precious to God (or other divine powers), especially when atoning for sin. The blood of animals is especially important, because it is symbolic of life, the most precious human gift. It is possible that animals were thought to represent the person who owned them. So, instead of a human paying for his sin with his life, it is possible that the ancient Hebrews, at least originally, believed God allowed humans to pay or atone for sin with the life of one of their animals.

While the human need to atone and offer sacrifice can be manipulated and distorted, it seems to be a genuine human need.

Why Did Jesus Have to Give His Life as Atonement?   12.12.2

Christians believe Christ, as the representative of all humans, has the power to offer atonement for the sins of all people because he is also divine. But why did Jesus have to die as atonement? Anselm argues that Christ's sinless life has the greatest value; therefore, he is able to pay the price for the sins of the entire world (*Why God Became Man?* 2.14). The following discussion considers this point.

Again, the Christian doctrine seems to touch something deep in the human psyche. All humans have the sense that the greatest gift one can offer another, the greatest sign of love, is the willingness to give up one's life. Throughout the world, cultures honor the memories of those willing to give up their lives for their nation in war or who, in other situations, were willing to make that ultimate sacrifice. Even though these situations are often not religious, the religious word *sacrifice* is often applied.

Jesus spoke of this sense, "No one has greater love than this, to lay down one's life for one's friends" (John 15:13). In the Christian understanding, not only Jesus' death but also his whole life was a sacrifice offered for the sake of others. The Son surrendered his perfect eternal life within the Trinity to become human. His life was dedicated to helping, healing, and teaching others. His death, for the sake of others, was the climax of a life lived for the sake of others.

If Christ's Death Atones for All Human Sins, Aren't All Human Sins Forgiven? 12.12.3

If Christ took on human nature, represents all humans and, furthermore, paid the price of atonement so humans sins could be forgiven, doesn't that mean humans should now be free of their sins?

Is the Doctrine of the Atonement a Type of Cosmic Child Abuse? 12.12.4

Some theologians, writing especially from feminist or womanist perspectives, have raised fundamental criticisms of the doctrine of Jesus' atonement, arguing that the thinking behind it can legitimate and promote violence and oppression. The divine Father sending his innocent Son to redeem the world "looks uncomfortably to some like a charter for child abuse, with an innocent son sent to bear the wrath of a 'heavenly father' to make things right for the entire extended family."[26]

These theologians point out the potential to distort the Christian message in certain interpretations. However, Balthasar and others have shown that the danger for distortion lies not so much in the doctrine as in certain interpretations of it:

> One thing we must never forget: the atonement wrought by Christ must not be interpreted as a penance imposed on the Son by the divine Father; rather, as we have often repeated, it goes back to that salvific decision made by the Trinity. Jesus Christ sees himself as coming forth from that decision in perfect freedom.[27]

In other words, the Father does not act as an abusive tyrant in ordering his Son to die. Rather, the Son is in such harmony with the Father's will that he makes his Father's will his own. The Son willingly and freely accepts his Incarnation, suffering, and death as part of the Father's plan for the salvation of the world. He willingly and freely lays down his life. As Jesus proclaims in the Gospel of John, "This is why the Father loves me, because I lay down my life in order to take it up again. No one takes it from me, but I lay it down on my own" (10:17–18).

---

26. See the summary in S. Mark Heim, *Saved from Sacrifice: A Theology of the Cross* (Grand Rapids, MI: Eerdmans, 2006), 26.

27. Balthasar, *Persons in Christ*, 242.

Not quite. In the Christian understanding, a further step is involved, one that requires some initiative on the part of humans. Christ has paid the price for forgiveness of sin, and God, through Christ, offers that free gift, or grace, of salvation to all people. Yet as the Catholic tradition expresses it, people must *cooperate* with that grace—repent of their sins and accept God's offer. A person must make some kind of active movement toward accepting God's grace.

In addition to this personal cooperation, a person must also join the Church. In the Catholic understanding, Christ has willed to make his grace available to people through the Church—his Body on Earth. It is through baptism that one joins this Church. When a crowd in Jerusalem asks Peter what they must do after hearing about God's offer of salvation through Jesus, Peter replies, "Repent and be baptized, every one of you, in the name of Jesus Christ for the forgiveness of your sins; and you will receive the gift of the holy Spirit" (Acts 2:38).

The apostle Paul writes, "Or are you unaware that we who were baptized into Christ Jesus were baptized into his death? We were indeed buried with him through baptism into death, so that, just as Christ was raised from the dead by the glory of the Father, we too might light to newness of life" (Rom 6:3–4).

As will be discussed in more depth in chapter 13, baptism is a sign of joining the Church, the Body of Christ. As Paul teaches, in baptism a person, in a mystical manner, participates in Christ's death. In this sense the person makes Christ's atonement his or her own, and applies it to personal sins. Once the person "dies" with Christ to a sinful way of life, that person is prepared, as Paul says, to "live in newness of life" with the resurrected Christ.

How Can Those Who Lived before Jesus' Atonement Be Saved?   12.12.5

Part of the scandal of particularity of the doctrine of the Incarnation is that it occurred at a specific time in history—approximately two thousand years ago. If the Second Person of the Trinity was going to unite himself with human nature to save it, why didn't he do so earlier, from the beginning of the human race? Does this imply that those who lived in the thousands of years of history before Jesus was born cannot be saved because they were born before the Savior?

In the Catholic understanding, the answer is no. Because the Son united himself to a concrete, individual human being, the Incarnation could only occur at a specific point in history. Yet because God's plan of salvation, as well as the Trinity itself, are outside of time, the effects of the Incarnation are not limited to one point or direction in time. Rather, the offer of salvation made through Christ's atoning death is available not only to the generations who lived after Christ's death but also to all generations who lived before. It is offered, without restriction, to everyone, in the Catholic view. As Balthasar says, "The assumption of 'flesh'—which, seen from eternity, is timeless—is already an integral part of the original world plan."[28]

Questions about the Text

1. Why is the particularity of Jesus as the Savior a shock and offense to many?
2. What are the two basic Christological questions that the Church had to work out over the course of the first few centuries?
3. Explain the basics of Justin's Logos Christology and how it uses Greek philosophy.
4. Explain why Catholics reject the claim that Greek philosophy corrupted earliest Christianity.
5. Summarize the three points of Logos Christology that show how it is compatible with reason.
6. Explain how the error of Modalism overemphasizes the unity of Father and Son.
7. Explain how subordinationism overemphasizes the distinctiveness of the Father and the Son.
8. Explain Arius's beliefs about the relationship of the Father and the Son, and the biblical evidence that Arius had for his views.
9. In the orthodox view, why is it necessary for salvation that Jesus should be fully divine and not just semidivine, as Arius believed?
10. What does the term *homoousios* mean, and why was it used in the Nicene Creed?
11. How does the analogy of the sun and its rays apply to the relationship of Father and Son in the Nicene Creed?
12. What is the Nestorian Controversy, and how is it connected with the title *Mother of God* for Mary, mother of Jesus?
13. Compare the description of the relationship between Jesus' human and divine nature as described by the Monophysites and as defined at the Council of Chalcedon.
14. Why does the New Testament refer to Christ as the second Adam?
15. Summarize Anselm's model of Jesus' atonement.
16. Explain how the doctrine of atonement is connected with justice and with the human need to make up for a sin.
17. Explain how the doctrine of atonement is connected with the New Testament teaching that sins are forgiven in baptism.

---

28. Ibid., 256.

18. Summarize some basic feminist and womanist critiques of the traditional doctrine of the atonement, as well as a traditional response to those critiques.

Discussion Questions

1. Have you ever found the Christian beliefs about Jesus to be shocking or offensive? Explain.

2. In your opinion, why was so much time and effort put into the early Christian debates about whether the Son is fully divine or how the human and divine nature of Christ relate to one another?

3. Do you agree with Ehrman that *orthodoxy* and *heresy* are later labels invented by the group that wins the most converts and that all early Christian groups had equally valid interpretations of Jesus? Why or why not?

4. Do you agree that humans have a deep need to make up or atone for a wrong they have committed? Why or why not?

5. Do you think that the doctrine of Jesus' atoning death for all humanity can be defended rationally or that it no longer makes sense in the modern world? Explain.

13

Ecclesiology

Ecclesiology: The Study of the Church 13.1

The branch of theology that reflects on the Church—the body of the followers of Christ—is known as *ecclesiology*. This English word derives from the standard Greek New Testament word for church, *ekklēsia*. This, in turn, derives from the verb *ekkalein*, literally meaning, "to call out." The verb evokes the image of Jesus "calling out" his first disciples—from their former lives in the world into a newly formed community. In an analogous way, the image applies to members of the Church. They are "called out" from the ordinary lifestyle of the world into a new community focused on bringing the kingdom of God to Earth.

Defining *Church* 13.2

What exactly is the Church? The *Catechism of the Catholic Church* notes three meanings for the word *church*: (1) the liturgical assembly (i.e., Christians gathered to worship; (2) the local community of believers (e.g., the apostle Paul refers "to the church of God that is in Corinth" (1 Cor 1:2); and (3) the whole universal community of believers. These meanings are inseparable, because the universal Church exists in local communities and is made real in worship gathering, especially in the Eucharist (*CCC*, no. 752). This chapter focuses on understanding the Church as the universal community of believers.

Challenges to the Catholic Concept of Church 13.3

The following are common, reasonable challenges to the Catholic concept of Church.

1. Why is an organized church even necessary? Many believe that spirituality is personal. People can worship God on their own time. Organized religions have too many rules and focus too much on money.

2. Leadership in the Catholic Church, with its pope, bishops, and priests, is too hierarchical, contradicting modern values of democracy and full participation of all.

3. The Catholic Church's claims that the Church "is necessary for salvation" (*LG*, no. 14) are arrogant. As there are literally thousands of other churches and non-Christian religions, how can the Catholic Church claim that it alone is necessary for salvation?

4. The Catholic Church is too ritualistic, placing too much importance on rituals such as baptism and the Lord's Supper.

5. The Church claims that the pope is inerrant, that is, incapable of making a mistake. How can any human claim to be inerrant?

This chapter responds to these challenges. The following section addresses the first: Why is an organized church necessary for one's relationship with God?

The Social Character of Salvation 13.4

The purpose of any religion is to lead people to salvation. As noted in chapter 1, humans have a sense that there is a "deep meaning to life," that a transcendent reality that gives fuller and ultimate meaning to life in this world does exist. Religion, then, is a means of putting humans in touch with the transcendent, and helping them reach salvation.

An essential ingredient for a full and meaningful life, however, is interpersonal relationships. The capacity to make friends, communicate with, love, and care for others is essential to happiness and, ultimately, salvation.

Conversely, the root of sin, in the Christian view, is the tendency to isolate oneself, treat others as less than human, and be antisocial or anti-community. Pope Benedict XVI teaches that sin "is understood by the Fathers as the destruction of the unity of the human race, as fragmentation and division" (*Spe Salvi*, no. 14). The original unity of humanity, based on the premise that people have God as Father and are created in God's image, "was shattered into a thousand pieces" by sin.[1] Salvation, then, is "the recovery of supernatural unity of man with God, but equally of the unity of men among themselves."[2]

In the Christian imagination, judgment and final destiny are pictured in social terms. On the Day of Judgment, *all* people will be raised. The kingdom of God is pictured as a banquet (Matt 8:11) and heaven as a city (Heb 11:10; Rev 21:9–27).[3] Eternal life is participation in the community of love within the

---

1. Quotation from Maximus the Confessor (ca. 580–662 CE) in Henri de Lubac, *Catholicism: Christ and the Common Destiny of Man* (San Francisco: Ignatius, 1988), 33.

2. De Lubac, *Catholicism*, 35.

3. On the social understanding of eternal salvation, see de Lubac, *Catholicism*, 51–63.

Trinity. Aquinas taught that the final destiny of humans is "is to arrive at beatitude [perfect happiness], and this cannot be save in the kingdom of God. And this, in turn, is nothing but the ordered society of those who enjoy the divine vision" (*SCG* 4.50). Only hell—the loss of God and salvation—is without community. The Second Vatican Council teaches,

> God, however, does not make men holy and save them merely as individuals, without bond or link between one another. Rather has it pleased Him to bring men together as one people, a people which acknowledges Him in truth and serves Him in holiness. (*LG*, no. 9)

This statement does not imply that an individual Christian has no personal responsibility. On the contrary, the individual's free personal choice is essential for salvation. The Catholic teaching, however, is that this personal choice can only occur within the larger context of the social gathering of the Church.

Social Salvation: God's Covenant with Israel   13.5

Consider some biblical examples that illustrate the social character of salvation. God called Abraham (Gen. 12:2) not to save him as an individual but so Abraham could become father of a community, Israel. In the desert, God established a covenant not with Moses as an individual but with the people as a whole: "The Lord, our God, made a covenant with us at Horeb; not with our ancestors did the Lord make this covenant, but with us, all of us who are alive here this day" (Deut 5:2–3). Jesus, from the beginning, preached about a communal concept of salvation, the kingdom of God, and took concrete steps to establish a new community around himself, led by the Twelve. Salvation would come by joining his community, the renewed Israel.

Jesus and his Disciples: The Beginning of the Church   13.6

In the Christian understanding, Jesus is the key to salvation. It is crucial, then, to clarify the relationship between Jesus and the Church. According to the Scriptures, Jesus understood himself as God's Messiah, sent to establish the kingdom of God on Earth. In choosing the twelve disciples, he understood himself to be gathering the renewed people of God—eschatological Israel (sec. 11.5.2). This community, led by the twelve, grew and developed into the early Church.

The Role of Jesus' Apostles in the Church 13.7

According to the Scriptures, Jesus understood himself, in his authoritative teaching about the Torah (sec. 11.5.3) and in his supernatural healing and exorcisms (sec. 11.5.1) to act with the full power and authority of God.

Jesus, in turn, gave this authority to the Twelve, saying to his apostles, "Whoever receives you receives me, and whoever receives me receives the one who sent me" (Matt 10:40). This authority included teaching, healing, casting out demons, and even forgiving sins. Consider the following passages:

- Mark 6:7–13: "He summoned the Twelve and began to send them out two by two and gave them authority over unclean spirits. . . . They went off and preached repentance. They drove out many demons, and they anointed with oil many who were sick and cured them."
- John 20:21–23: "[Jesus] said to them [his disciples] again, 'Peace be with you. As the Father has sent me, so I send you.' And when he had said this, he breathed on them and said to them, 'Receive the holy Spirit. Whose sins you forgive are forgiven them, and whose sins you retain are retained.'"

The Acts of the Apostles, a history of the early Church, shows that the apostles did, in fact, act with this authority. The apostle Peter, for example, heals a man who is crippled (Acts 3) and even raises a woman from the dead (Acts 9:36–42).

None of these actions are done by the apostles' own authority; they always teach and act by the power and authority of Jesus. As Peter says to the man who was crippled, "in the name of Jesus Christ the Nazorean, [rise and] walk" (Acts 3:6).

Peter's Leadership of the Apostles 13.8

Within the Twelve, certain disciples were given more authority than others. Peter's role is especially prominent. In the lists of the Twelve given in the Synoptic Gospels, for example, Peter's name is always listed first (Mark 3:16 par.)

Several passages give Peter a unique leadership role over the other disciples (Luke 22:31–32; John 21:15–19).

Peter's leadership role is clearest, however, in Matthew 16:13–16. In reply to Jesus' question, "Who do people say that the Son of Man is?" Peter gives the definitive answer, "You are the Messiah, the Son of the living God." Jesus then tells Peter,

And so I say to you, you are Peter, and upon this rock I will build my church, and the gates of the netherworld shall not prevail against it. I will give you the keys to the kingdom of heaven. Whatever you bind on earth shall be bound in heaven; and whatever you loose on earth shall be loosed in heaven." (Matt 16:18–19)

Many scholars have rejected the historicity of this passage, seeing it as a creation of the early Church.[4] Other historical Jesus scholars, however, give persuasive arguments about how such a passage makes sense within Second Temple Jewish thought. The church is the gathering together of eschatological Israel. The name Jesus gave to Peter (*Petros* in Greek and *Cephas* in Aramaic mean "rock") alludes to the solid foundation of the new community gathered by Jesus—the eschatological Temple. Peter, originally named Simon, will be the solid foundation stone of renewed Israel.[5]

What does it mean that Jesus gives Peter the "keys to the kingdom of heaven" and the power to "bind and loose"? The *Catechism* states that the power of the keys "designates authority to govern the house of God, which is the Church" and the power "to bind and loose," "connotes the authority to absolve sins, to pronounce doctrinal judgments, and to make disciplinary decisions in the Church" (*CCC*, no. 553). The majority of historical-critical scholars concur that "binding and loosing," in the historical context of Second Temple Judaism, would apply especially to a teacher's authority to declare what is permissible and impermissible among his followers.[6] This authority of binding and loosing is also given to the rest of the disciples (Matt 18:18), but it is clear that Peter has a special role.

In the Catholic understanding, Jesus set up the basic structure of the Church when he chose the twelve disciples with Peter at their head as leaders of eschatological Israel. This structure continues to this day, with the bishops continuing the role of the original twelve disciples, and the pope in the role of Peter as the single head of the Church (*CCC*, no. 880).

The Church and the Eucharist 13.9

A particularly decisive moment in Jesus' foundation of the Church occurs at the Last Supper. The Scripture texts present Jesus clearly stating that his actions, so closely connected with his imminent death, establish the new covenant that will form the new community. "Then he took a cup, gave thanks, and gave it to them, and they all drank from it. He said to them, 'This is my blood of the covenant, which will be shed for many'" (Mark 14:24 par.). As Joseph Ratzinger, later Pope Benedict XVI, concludes, "It is the making of a covenant and, as such, is the

---

4. John Meier, for example, judges it to be a resurrection appearance to Peter that was retrojected back into the life of the historical Jesus (*A Marginal Jew: Rethinking the Historical Jesus: Vol. 3: Three: Companions and Competitors* (New York: Doubleday, 2001), 228–35.

5. See Ben F. Meyer, *The Aims of Jesus* (San Jose, CA: Pickwick, 2002), 185–97.

6. See W. D. Davies and D. C. Allison, *The Gospel According to St. Matthew, Vol. 2: Matthew 8–18*) (London: T & T Clark, 1991), 639.

concrete foundation of the new people: the people comes into being through its covenant relation to God."[7]

The Church as the Body of Christ   13.10

One of the most ancient names of the Church is "the Body of Christ." The apostle Paul says to the church in Corinth, "Now you are Christ's body, and individually parts of it" (1 Cor 12:27). Paul compares the individual parts of the human body (eye, hand) with the individual members of the Corinthian church: all parts/members must work together so the whole body can function properly. The phrase emphasizes the *unity* of the church members—they should be united as one.

The phrase *Body of Christ* also implies the unity of local churches throughout the world. The Letter to the Ephesians speaks of Christ's body as "the fullness of the one who fills all things in every way" (Eph 1:23), and later proclaims that all believers everywhere are united by "one Lord, one faith, one baptism" (Eph 4:5).

The Meanings of *Body of Christ*   13.11

The term *Body of Christ* has a profoundly rich meaning for Christians. As noted, Paul uses it to refer to the whole community gathered together, both locally and throughout the world. At the same time, it alludes to Jesus' atoning sacrifice of his body on the cross for the sake of forgiveness of sins. Paul reminds the Corinthians of the tradition:

> [T]he Lord Jesus, on the night he was handed over, took bread, and, after he had given thanks, broke it and said, "This is my body that is for you. Do this in remembrance of me." (1 Cor 11:23–24)

Finally, the *Body of Christ* can refer also to the bread shared by the community in the Lord's Supper. Paul asks, "The bread that we break, is it not a participation in the body of Christ?" (1 Cor 10:16). The meanings are closely linked: The breaking and eating of the bread (Body of Christ) links the church members (Body of Christ) to Christ himself, especially in his offering of his own body (Body of Christ) as an atoning sacrifice.

Paul further links the terms in his next comment, "Because the loaf of bread is one, we, though many, are one body, for we all partake of the one loaf" (1 Cor 10:17). Once again, the bread (Body of Christ) is linked to the community (Body of Christ) in the celebration of the Lord's Supper.[8]

---

7. Ratzinger, *Called to Communion: Understanding the Church Today* (San Francisco: Ignatius, 1996), 28.

8. See the further close links between the various meanings of the "Body of Christ" in 1 Cor 11:27–29.

Body of Christ: Real Presence[9] in the Sacrifice of the Mass

13.12

In Catholic Eucharistic theology, the concept of the Church as the Body of Christ is closely connected with the presence of Christ in the assembly of people gathered for worship. At every Mass, Christ is present in the person of the priest or bishop who presides (*CCC*, no. 1348). Christ is also present in the Word proclaimed at Mass. Above all, Christ is fully present in consecrated bread and wine, not merely symbolically but in such a way that in the Eucharist the "whole Christ is truly, really, and substantially contained" (*CCC*, no. 1374).

In Catholic theology, the Eucharist is called a sacrifice "because it re-presents (makes present) the sacrifice of the cross" (*CCC*, no. 1366). This does not mean that Christ is re-crucified at every Mass. Rather, it means that the sacrifice that Jesus made on the cross is made present whenever the Eucharist is celebrated.

Again, Catholic theology closely links the different senses of the Body of Christ—when the Body of Christ is gathered as a church, it celebrates by eating and drinking the Body and Blood of Christ (transformed bread and wine), an action that makes present the atoning sacrifice of Jesus' body on the cross.

The Catholic Church places great emphasis on the Eucharist because it is at the heart of the New Testament's understanding of what the Church is.

The Church as Sacrament

13.13

In Catholic theology, sacraments are central to God's plan of salvation. The sacraments, as Newman saw, are a logical development of the Incarnation: God using physical means to communicate supernatural benefits (grace).[10] Both the Incarnation and the sacramental system are radical affirmations of the Christian belief in the goodness of God's creation (sec. 7.6.2).

The *Catechism* defines sacraments as "efficacious signs of grace, instituted by Christ and entrusted to the Church, by which divine life is dispensed to us" (*CCC*, no. 1131). The "signs" are physical, Aquinas teaches, since it "is part of man's nature to acquire knowledge of the intelligible from the sensible" (*ST* 3.60.4). People learn things through their senses. In the Catholic view, a sacrament, however, is not only an external symbol of a spiritual reality, it is "efficacious" in that it brings about the reality of the thing signified. "Celebrated worthily in faith, the sacraments confer the grace that they signify. They are efficacious because in them Christ himself is at work" (*CCC*, no. 1127). In the

---

9. Fr. Robert Barron explains the Catholic Church's understanding of the doctrine of the real presence of Christ in a video accessible at *www.youtube.com/watch?v=bJjW3LXuHzo* (time 0:11:04).

10. John Henry Newman, *An Essay on the Development of Christian Doctrine* (Westminster, MD: Christian Classics, 1968), 93–94, is accessible at *www.newmanreader.org/works/development/chapter2 .html#section3*.

Catholic understanding of the sacrament of baptism, for example, the spiritual grace of Christ works through the physical means of water to cleanse sins. The water, then, is not a symbolic extra—it is essential, because God has chosen to work through the physical.

Logically, before the seven sacraments, however, the Church itself is a sacrament (see *LG*, nos. 1, 48). In the Catholic view, the Church, as a visible, physical institution, continues to be the physical instrument of Christ's spiritual grace long after Christ is no longer physically in the world.

Catholics believe that as God was truly present in the physical person of Jesus, so Jesus is present in the physical church. De Lubac writes,

> If Christ is the sacrament of God, the Church is for us the sacrament of Christ; she represents him, in the full and ancient meaning of the term, she really makes him present. She not only carries on his work, but she is his very continuation, in a sense far more real than that in which it can be said that any human institution is its founder's continuation.[11]

The Church and the Sacrament of Baptism   13.14

Another sacrament that lies at the heart of the Church's identity is baptism. It is through this sacrament that a person joins the Body of Christ: "For in one Spirit we were all baptized into one body" (1 Cor. 12:13).

Again, the Catholic understanding moves far beyond symbolism. By joining the Body of Christ—the Church—a person is united with Christ in a mystical way. Paul writes, "Or are you unaware that we who were baptized into Christ Jesus were baptized into his death?" (Rom 6:3). The idea that the believer is united with Christ in his death is one way to understand how Jesus' atoning death brings about forgiveness for the sins of the individual: The person joins himself to Christ's death, allowing Christ's atoning sacrifice to cleanse his or her personal sins. "We know that our old self was crucified with him, so that our sinful body might be done away with, that we might no longer be in slavery to sin" (Rom 6:6).

Paul's thought draws out a specific reason why the Church is necessary for salvation. It is only through joining oneself to Christ's Body, the Church, that a person's sinful way of life can "die with Christ," allowing the person to begin living a new life.

The Unity of the Church   13.15

The Nicene Creed describes the Church as "one, holy, catholic, and apostolic." The oneness, the unity of the Church, is emphasized in Scripture, as noted in

---

11. De Lubac, *Catholicism*, 29.

the discussion on the Body of Christ (sec. 13.10). Paul writes, "There is neither Jew nor Greek, there is neither slave nor free person, there is not male and female; for you are all one in Christ Jesus" (Gal 3:28). This unity of the followers of Christ is also stressed in Jesus' prayer before his death: "that they may all be one, as you, Father, are in me and I in you, that they also may be in us, that the world may believe that you sent me" (John 17:21). Vatican II's *Decree on Ecumenism* reiterates this belief, "Christ the Lord founded one Church and one Church only" (*UR*, no. 1).

The Visible, Hierarchical Church and the Mystical Body of Christ 13.16

How does the Catholic tradition understand this one Church? *Lumen Gentium* compares the Church to the incarnate Logos, in the sense that it has both human and divine elements. The Church is hierarchical, visible, and earthly; at the same time, it is the "Mystical Body of Christ," "a spiritual house," and a "Church enriched with heavenly things." The visible, hierarchical structure of the Church and the mystical body are not to be considered two realities; rather they form "one complex reality" (*LG*, no. 8).

By "visible structure," *Lumen Gentium* means especially the hierarchical structure of the Catholic Church: The pope is the head, governing the Church in union with the bishops. The mystical aspect of the Church involves the belief that God's Holy Spirit, the supernatural power of God, also works through these visible, human structures (see Pope Pius XII's encyclical *Mystici Corpis Christi*, no. 63).

The One, Holy, Catholic, and Apostolic Church 13.17

Many passages in the Vatican II documents are complimentary toward and open to dialogue with other Christian and non-Christian faiths. However, in the clear words of the Council's *Decree on Ecumenism*, "For it is only through Christ's Catholic Church, which is 'the all-embracing means of salvation,' that they can benefit fully from the means of salvation" (*UR*, no. 3).

Referring to the "one, holy, catholic, and apostolic" Church described in the Nicene Creed, the Vatican II Council taught,

> This Church constituted and organized in the world as a society, subsists in the Catholic Church, which is governed by the successor of Peter and by the Bishops in communion with him, although many elements of sanctification and of truth are found outside its visible structure. (*LG*, no. 8)

The Meaning of *Subsists In* 13.17.1

Since Vatican II, many have questioned why the bishops chose to say that the one Church "subsists in" the Catholic Church, and did not simply say that the one Church *is* the Catholic Church. In 2007, the Vatican's Congregation for the Doctrine of the Faith (CDF) issued *Responses to Some Questions Regarding Certain Aspects of the Doctrine on the Church.* The CDF also published an accompanying commentary.[12] The documents make two key points:

1. The phrase "subsists in" means there is an "essential identity" between the one, holy, catholic, and apostolic Church and the Catholic Church.[13] The Catholic Church is different from all other Christian churches in two ways: (a) it is the only Church that was clearly founded historically by Jesus, that has endured throughout history as a "visible and spiritual community," and that will endure until the end of time; and (b) it is the one Church "in which alone are found all the elements that Christ himself instituted."[14]

   The CDF's 2000 document, *Dominus Iesus*, similarly teaches that "the Church of Christ . . . continues to exist fully only in the Catholic Church" and that "there is an historical continuity—rooted in the apostolic succession—between the Church founded by Christ and the Catholic Church" (no. 16).

2. Nevertheless, there are "numerous elements of sanctification and truth" in non-Catholic churches and communities. Therefore, Catholic teaching declares that the one "Church of Christ is present and operative" in these other churches but not as fully as in the Roman Catholic Church.[15]

   The phrase "subsists in," therefore, "signifies a greater openness to the ecumenical desire to recognize truly ecclesial characteristics and dimensions in the Christian communities not in full communion with the Catholic Church."[16]

Further details on the Catholic understanding of its relationship with other Christians will be discussed in chapter 14.

---

12. CDF, *Commentary on the Document "Responses to Some Questions Regarding Certain Aspects of the Doctrine of the Church,"* accessible at *www.vatican.va/roman_curia/congregations/cfaith/documents/rc_con_cfaith_doc_20070629_commento-responsa_en.html.*

13. Ibid.

14. CDF, *Responses to Some Questions Regarding Certain Aspects of the Doctrine of the Church,* accessible at *www.vatican.va/roman_curia/congregations/cfaith/documents/rc_con_cfaith_doc_20070629_responsa-quaestiones_en.html.*

15. Ibid.

16. CDF, *Commentary on the Document,* accessible at *www.vatican.va/roman_curia/congregations/cfaith/documents/rc_con_cfaith_doc_20070629_commento-responsa_en.html.*

An Arrogant Claim by the Catholic Church?   13.17.2

The Catholic Church claims that it alone has the fullness of the Christian faith and that it alone can be identified, in its essentials, with the one, holy, catholic, and apostolic Church. This claim may seem unbelievably arrogant. Out of the hundreds of Christian denominations existing today, how can one claim to have the "fullness" of the one Church of the Creeds?

To answer this, one must refer once again to the doctrine of the Incarnation and its particularity. In Christian belief, God was reconciled with the human in the one man, Jesus, at a particular time and place in history. Jesus, in turn, established a specific, visible community led by twelve apostles, with Peter at its head, sharing his authority and passing on to them his teaching (secs. 13.7–13.8). The apostles and their associates, through the **apostolic succession,** passed down this teaching and authority to their successors, in particular the bishops (sec. 13.19).

In the Catholic understanding, only certain Christian bodies—that is, churches within the Catholic and the Orthodox traditions—can show, in a specifically concrete and historical way, that they are in continuity with this apostolic tradition that goes back to Jesus. Only the Catholic Church, led by the pope in Peter's role as the one head of the Church, is in full continuity with this apostolic tradition.

This Catholic insistence on visible, historical continuity is consistent with the great Christian principles of the Incarnation and the sacramental nature of the Church. The common threads are the convictions that God works through the concrete, the spiritual flows through the physical, and the divine plans works through real humans and institutions.

The Visible and the Invisible Church   13.18

Briefly considering an alternative view of the one Church may help clarify the Catholic teaching. Avery Dulles sums up the thought of the influential Protestant theologian Paul Tillich regarding the one Church:

> Tillich made a sharp distinction between the "Spiritual Community," which he viewed as one and undivided, and the "churches," which he regarded as mutually disunited human organizations. He refused even to use the term *Church* with a capital *C*, for he looked upon the "Spiritual Community" not as an organized body but as a mystical reality latent in and behind the visible churches.[17]

In the Catholic view, however, conceptions such as Tillich's come dangerously close to a Gnostic separation of the spiritual from the earthly, bodily, and historical realm. As *Lumen Gentium* (no. 8) taught, one cannot separate the

---

17. Avery Dulles, *Models of the Church*, expanded ed. (Garden City, NY: Image Books, 1987), 144–45.

"spiritual community" from the concrete, physical structures of church hierarchy, just as the body and the soul cannot naturally be separated from each other.

In the Catholic understanding, this is also the only way to safeguard the oneness of the Church. It is essential to have a clear, discernable sign of that oneness in the visible structure of the Catholic Church. Otherwise, how could one describe the oneness of the Church? Would it be a vague idea of the sum total of all churches that call themselves Christian? If so, in what sense are they "one," as their beliefs and practices are often quite different?

The concern to identify the visible structure and unity of the Church is not solely a Catholic one. The great Protestant theologian Karl Barth wrote, "If we seek to solve the question of the unity of the Church by appealing to an invisible church, we speculate as Platonists instead of listening to Christ."[18] Ola Tjørhom shows that the Reformers were also concerned to maintain visible structures of the Church, including visible sacraments and an ordained ministry.[19]

Catholic theology insists that the Church exists fully only in communities able, in a visible and historical way, to trace their beliefs, practice, and structure back to the first community of apostles founded by Jesus. This continuity between the church of today and the church of Jesus and his apostles is known as "apostolic succession."

Apostolic Succession   13.19

The *Catechism* defines "apostolic succession" as "the handing on of apostolic preaching and authority from the Apostles to their successors the bishops through the laying on of hands, as a permanent office in the Church." The following sections consider this definition in detail.

The Authoritative Handing Down of Apostolic Tradition   3.19.1

Section 9.11.1 pointed out the central importance of apostolic tradition for the Church. A key point is that long before Church leaders officially recognized the body (canon) of Christian Scripture, the Church existed fully. In the earliest Church, the essential teachings by and about Jesus, together with the essential practices of the Church, including the Lord's Supper and baptism, were passed down by the oral apostolic tradition.

The early Church handed down the traditions from and about Jesus in an organized, systematic fashion (sec. 10.5.2). What was true of the Jesus tradition in particular, applies to the apostolic tradition in general.

---

18. Quoted in de Lubac, *Catholicism*, 25.

19. Ola Tjørhom, *Visible Church, Visible Unity: Ecumenical Ecclesiology and the "Great Tradition of the Church,"* Unitas Books (Collegeville, MN: Liturgical Press, 2004), 3–4, 11.

J.N.D. Kelly, a well-known historian of early Christian creeds, concludes that at a very early date, orthodox Christians developed summaries of their basic beliefs, which were carefully passed down. Such summaries were called by a variety of names: the gospel, the preaching (*kerygma* in Greek), the faith, and the trust (*parathēkē* in Greek; literally: "that which is handed down"). After reviewing the evidence, Kelly concludes, "it is impossible to overlook the emphasis on the transmission of authoritative doctrine which is found everywhere in the New Testament."[20] Following are a few examples that illustrate this process:

- Paul encourages his church, "Therefore, brothers, stand firm and hold fast to the traditions that you were taught, either by an oral statement or by a letter of ours" (2 Thess 2:15).
- Jude speaks of "the faith that was once for all handed down to the holy ones" (Jude 1:3).
- The apostle Paul tells his disciple Timothy, "Guard this rich trust [literally: "what has been handed down"] with the help of the holy Spirit that dwells within us (2 Tim 1:14).[21] (sec. 9.11.1)

Apostolic Tradition and Apostolic Succession: Who Handed Down the Tradition? 13.19.2

For traditions to have authority, teachers who have authority must hand them down. The Twelve apostles and their associates were authoritative eyewitnesses to the traditions about Jesus (sec. 10.5). *Lumen Gentium* teaches that Jesus appointed the Twelve, whom "[h]e would send to preach the kingdom of God; and these apostles He formed after the manner of a college or a stable group, over which He placed Peter chosen from among them" (no. 19).

Bishops, in turn, are seen as the successors to the apostles, the "passers-on of the apostolic seed" (*LG*, no. 20). "[T]o keep the Gospel forever whole and alive within the Church, the apostles left bishops as their successors, 'handing over' to them 'the authority to teach in their own place'" (*DV*, no. 7).

The following points add some specific details to the general outline sketched by *Dei Verbum*:

1. The apostles included more than the Twelve. The most obvious example is the apostle Paul, who did not know the earthly Jesus. Barnabas is also called an apostle in Acts 14:14. The key qualifications of the twelve apostles were that Jesus chose them, and they were eyewitnesses to his actions and

---

20. Kelly, *Early Christian Creeds* (3rd ed. orig. pub. 1972; London: Continuum, 2006), 8.

21. Many historical-critical scholars judge that 1 and 2 Timothy and Titus were not written by the apostle Paul himself but by later disciples who wrote in his name and authority. Even if this judgment is accepted, it does not change the essential point made here: early Christians passed down authoritative summaries of the faith.

teaching. The essential qualification for later apostles, such as Paul, is that they were witnesses of Jesus' Resurrection and were called by the risen Jesus (*CCC*, no. 860; see 1 Cor 15:3–9; Acts 26:12–18).

2. The various church offices—such as prophet, teacher, deacon, elder, and bishop—were not always clearly distinguished in the early Church.[22] For example, the leaders of the Ephesian church, to whom Paul first preached the gospel, are called both presbyters (Greek: *presbyteroi*; Acts 20:17) and bishops (Greek: *episkopoi*; Acts 20:28). Although the Greek word *episkopos* is generally translated as "bishop," in a passage such as Acts 20:28, it is better to translate the word as "overseer," as it does not have the later connotation of a single religious authority heading a particular geographical area.

3. The office of bishop did, however, develop quickly. In the letters of Ignatius of Antioch, who was martyred around the year 107 CE, for example, the bishop of a particular church is its single head and a sign of its unity: "Let nothing exist among you that may divide you; but be ye united with your bishop, and those that preside over you" (*Letter to the Magnesians* 6).

4. By the end of the first century, writers clearly connect the apostolic succession with the bishops. Clement of Rome, writing around the year 100, speaks of the apostles appointing bishops and deacons (*1 Clem.* 42–44). Irenaeus (ca. 130–ca. 200 CE) writes that orthodox churches are able to trace the succession of their bishops back to the apostles. As an example, Irenaeus gives the names of the line of bishops of Rome from the time of the apostles Peter and Paul until his own day (*Against the Heresies* 3.3.3).

Tertullian (ca. 155–ca. 222 CE) likewise gives examples of apostolic churches: the apostle John founded Smyrna and appointed the bishop Polycarp; Peter appointed Clement at Rome. Tertullian presents two criteria for a church to be considered apostolic: (1) "apostles or apostolic men" must have founded it; and/or (2) it must have taught the same doctrine as the apostolically founded churches (*Prescription against Heresies* 32).

The Apostolic Churches and the Church of Rome   13.20

Certain churches, then, such as those at Smyrna, Corinth, Philippi, and Ephesus, had special authority because they could trace their roots back to the apostles (*Prescription against Heresies* 32, 36). The special authority of the ancient churches of Antioch, Alexandria, and Rome were recognized at the Council of Nicaea (canon 6). By the sixth century, the bishops, known in the East as patriarchs, of five churches were seen as having authority over their respective areas: Rome, Alexandria, Antioch, Jerusalem, and Constantinople.

---

22. Ratzinger, *Called to Communion*, 121.

Saint Peter's Basilica in Vatican City is a recognized symbol of the Roman Catholic Church. It is built on the traditional site of the tomb of Peter, the first pope and bishop of Rome. Emperor Constantine authorized the building of the original church at this site in 324; the current basilica was designed by the greatest Renaissance architects, including Michelangelo and Bernini. Vatican Councils I and II were held here.

At an early stage, however, many recognized the special apostolic authority of the church at Rome. Tertullian emphasizes Rome in his discussion of apostolic churches, since two foundational apostles, Peter and Paul, were martyred there (*Prescription against Heretics* 36). Irenaeus also writes of the Roman church, "For it is a matter of necessity that every church should agree with this church, on account of its pre-eminent authority" (*Against Heresies* 3.3.2). The Council of Constantinople (381 CE), declares, "The Bishop of Constantinople, however, shall have the prerogative of honour after the Bishop of Rome; because Constantinople is New Rome," implying the pre-eminence of the Bishop of Rome (canon 3).

The authority of the Roman church as a defender of the orthodox faith developed gradually, especially in the West, during the early centuries of Christianity; the Roman church often served to settle disputes between Western churches.[23]

---

23. See Robert B. Eno, "Some Elements in the Pre-History of Papal Infallibility," in *Teaching Authority and Infallibility in the Church*, eds. P. C. Empie, et. al., Lutherans and Catholics in Dialogue 6 (Minneapolis: Augsburg Publishing House, 1980), 238–58.

Apostolic Succession and the Ordination of Bishops   13.21

As noted, the *Catechism*'s definition of "apostolic succession" is "the handing on of apostolic preaching and authority from the Apostles to their successors the bishops through the laying on of hands, as a permanent office in the Church." Note the phrase, "laying on of hands." This refers to a central part of the ritual in which a man is ordained as a bishop in the Catholic Church (ordination is also known as the sacrament of Holy Orders) (*CCC*, nos. 1537–38).

The Church here emphasizes that apostolic succession is more than passing down teaching. It does include teaching—a central role of Catholic bishops is to be teachers of the faith. However, Catholic sacramental theology teaches that through the action of ordination, the bishops receive the spiritual authority of the apostles, the "gift of the Holy Spirit," as well. The bishops then have the authority to ordain others in the line of apostolic succession. As the *Catechism* teaches, the bishops "hand on the 'gift of the Spirit,' 'the apostolic line'" (*CCC*, no. 1576). This apostolic spiritual authority includes the authority to forgive sins by the power of Christ (cf. John 20:21–23; *CCC*, no. 1448) and to preside at the Eucharist in which Christ is present.

The New Testament refers to the laying on of hands ritual as a means of passing on spiritual authority. At this early stage, the centrality of the bishop's office had not yet developed. However, the general pattern of passing down the spiritual authority of the apostles is clear:

- [Paul writes to Timothy]: "Do not neglect the gift you have, which was conferred on you through the prophetic word with the imposition of hands of the presbyterate (1 Tim 4:14).

- [Paul writes to Timothy]: "For this reason, I remind you to stir into flame the gift of God that you have through the imposition of my hands" (2 Tim 1:6).

- [The Twelve ordain deacons]: "They presented these men to the apostles who prayed and laid hands on them" (Acts 6:6).

Many non-Catholic churches also have recognized the importance of apostolic succession as a standard for ensuring that the faith has been passed down accurately. In 1982, the World Council of Churches,[24] an alliance of churches from around the world, including most Orthodox churches and many churches with roots in the Reformation, issued "Baptism, Eucharist, and Ministry," a statement that recognized the importance of apostolic tradition and the historic succession of bishops as an important witness to retaining continuity with the apostolic church. The statement did, however, also argue that there are other means of preserving the apostolicity of the churches besides the succession of bishops (nos. 34–38).

---

24. To learn about the World Council of Churches, visit *www.oikoumene.org/en/about-us*.

The Indefectibility and Infallibility of the Church   13.22

The Catholic Church claims the gift of **infallibility**: "Christ endowed the Church's shepherds with the charism of infallibility in matters of faith and morals" (*CCC*, no. 890). How can a merely human institution be infallible—incapable of making a mistake?

Is the Church's Claim of Infallibility Reasonable?   13.22.1

John Henry Newman shows that the Church's claim to infallibility is a logical development of Christianity's basic claim that God revealed himself in Jesus.

Christianity claims to be a recipient of supernatural revelation of specific doctrines, including the basic teachings on the Trinity, the Incarnation, and Jesus' atoning death and Resurrection.

As Newman shows, the nature of any doctrine is to develop as its implications are drawn out—obscure points are clarified, new situations addressed, outside challenges answered, or the doctrine is compared with other systems of thought (secs. 9.15 and 12.2.4).[25]

If one accepts that God reveals doctrine, especially involving human salvation, Newman continues, it is logical that God would also want to give some kind of authority to protect that doctrine from becoming corrupted or misunderstood as it developed.

Newman, therefore, saw it as a logical necessity that God, along with the revelation, would provide an external authority to judge which of the inevitable developments of thought and practice are legitimate and which apparent developments are actually corruptions.[26]

Newman's point is that if one takes seriously the belief that the transcendent God has revealed a true teaching, then a logical extension of that belief is that God would also provide a completely reliable, infallible, means of protecting that revelation from corruption and misinterpretation.

Indefectibility and Infallibility in Ecumenical Perspective   13.22.2

The belief that there must be an infallible guide to revelation is not a particularly Catholic claim: Virtually all Christians make it. Many Christian traditions claim the Bible is the infallible guide that ensures God's revelation in Jesus is not corrupted. In the Catholic understanding, however, such a claim by itself cannot be adequate

---

25. Newman, *Development of Christian Doctrine*, 55–75, is accessible at *www.newmanreader.org /works/development/chapter2.html#section1*.

26. Ibid., 75–92.

because the Church recognized which books should be included in the canon. If the Bible is infallible, it can only be so because of a prior infallibility belonging to the Church that decided which books to include in the Bible (sec. 9.11.2).

In addition to claims of the Bible's infallibility, other Christian traditions accept the general concept of the Church's need for a trustworthy authority as a protection from false teaching. The Lutheran tradition, for example, speaks of the Church's "indefectibility"—that is, a divine guarantee of "the continued existence of the Church in all its essential aspects, including its faith."[27] The idea that God protects the Church "from falling away from the truth of the gospel" has been widely held by Christians throughout the centuries, including the Reformers Luther, Calvin, Melancthon, and Zwingli.[28] In a modern Lutheran-Catholic theological dialogue, both parties agreed in the belief that "in accordance with the promises given in the Scriptures and because of the continued assistance of the risen Christ through the Holy Spirit, the Church will remain to the end of time;" and will persevere "in the truth of the gospel, in its mission, and in its life of faith."[29]

From this common standpoint, the following section returns to a particularly Catholic understanding of the Church's gift of infallibility.

Infallibility of the Bishops and the Pope   13.23

In the Catholic understanding, the worldwide group, or college, of Roman Catholic bishops in union with the bishop of Rome, the pope, possesses the divine gift of infallibility. As the primary teachers and pastors of the Church, it is their responsibility to pass down the faith accurately. "In order to preserve the Church in the purity of the faith handed on by the apostles, Christ who is Truth willed to confer on her a share in his own infallibility" (*CCC*, no. 889).

The gift of infallibility is expressed by the bishops "whenever, even though dispersed through the world, but still maintaining the bond of communion among themselves and with the successor of Peter, and authentically teaching matters of faith and morals, they are in agreement on one position as definitively to be held" (*LG*, no. 25). This authority is especially clear when the bishops teach in an **ecumenical council**, such as the councils of Nicaea, Constantinople, Ephesus, and Chalcedon. During the great Christological controversies of the fourth century the need for an absolute, decisive authority became apparent. Christians were divided on essential issues involving salvation, and all parties argued that their position was supported by scriptural evidence. There would have been continuous conflict and confusion unless a single, authoritative voice had spoken.

---

27. Lutheran-Roman Catholic Dialogue. "Teaching Authority and Infallibility in the Church: Common Statement" *Theological Studies* 40 (1979), 113–66, no. 28.

28. Avery Dulles, "Infallibility: The Terminology," in Empie, *Authority and Infallibility*, 75–76.

29. Lutheran-Roman Catholic Dialogue, "Common Statement," no. 41.

Eastern Orthodox, Catholic, and many other Western traditions recognize the authority of the first seven ecumenical councils.[30] The Catholic Church recognizes the authority of fourteen additional councils,[31] up to and including the Second Vatican Council.

The authority of the bishops, in the Catholic view, however, is not independent of the authority of the pope: "The college or body of bishops has no authority unless it is understood together with the Roman Pontiff" (*LG*, no. 22).

Papal Infallibility   13.24

The pope has a unique authority to teach infallibly: "the Roman Pontiff, the head of the college of bishops, enjoys [the gift of infallibility] in virtue of his office, when, as the supreme shepherd and teacher of all the faithful, who confirms his brethren in their faith, by a definitive act he proclaims a doctrine of faith or morals" (*LG*, no. 25).

Although this doctrine at first glance may seem unreasonable (how can a fallible human have the gift of infallibility?), the following points help to demonstrate its reasonableness.

First, papal infallibility is based on, and is only an expression of, the wider infallibility given to the Church. The belief that the Church has infallibility or indefectibility seems a necessary correlate of the belief that a divine revelation was made in Jesus (sec.13.22.1).

Second, in the Catholic understanding, the pope is the successor to Peter, who had a unique authority as the head of the apostles. It was to Peter alone that the keys of the kingdom of heaven were given (Matt 16:18; sec. 13.8). As Peter's successor, the pope continues to exercise that unique authority.

Third, the pope has authority as bishop of Rome—a church with ancient claims to apostolic authority. It was seen by authors such as Irenaeus (*Against Heresies* 3.3.2) as the model of orthodox belief (sec. 13.20).

Clarifying the Meaning of Papal Infallibility   13.24.1

Part of the scandal caused by the doctrine of papal infallibility is a misunderstanding of its scope. The following points show the limits of the doctrine.

The doctrine of papal infallibility does *not* claim that a pope is perfect and never makes mistakes nor does it imply that the pope is without sin. In Catholic theology, the pope is an ordinary, fallible human who sins and stands in need of Christ's forgiveness along with all people.

---

30. The documents produced by these councils are accessible at *www.ccel.org/ccel/schaff/npnf214 .toc.html*.

31. Many documents from these additional councils are accessible at *www.ewtn.com/library /indexes/COUNCILS.htm*.

The pope does not have the authority to contradict the Bible or essential Church teachings. Every teaching of the pope, or bishops, must be "in accordance with Revelation itself, which all are obliged to abide by and be in conformity with" (*LG*, no. 25). The pope has no authority to announce a new teaching revealed to him personally: he only has the authority to define more clearly what has already been revealed. As *Dei Verbum* declares, "no further new public revelation" is expected before "the glorious manifestation of our Lord" (i.e., the end of history) (no. 4).

Not every public statement a pope makes is considered infallible. On the contrary, the occasions under which a pope can make an officially recognized infallible statement are tightly limited. Theologian Avery Dulles summarizes the following conditions:

1. The pope must be speaking in his office as "supreme pastor and teacher of all Christians," not as a private person.
2. He must appeal to his authority as successor of Peter, the head of the Church.
3. He must be defining or clarifying a doctrine of faith or morality.
4. He must intend that the whole Church accept the doctrine.[32]

There is some disagreement among Catholic theologians concerning how often this strictly defined papal authority has been used. The doctrine of papal infallibility was not officially defined until the First Vatican Council in 1870, although belief in the doctrine preceded its formal definition.

The following are undisputed examples of popes using their gift of infallibility to define a teaching:

- Pope Pius IX's definition (1854) in the apostolic constitution *Ineffabilis Deus* of the Immaculate Conception of Mary,[33] the teaching that Mary, in view of her unique role as Mother of God, was protected from original sin.
- Pope Pius XII's definition (1950) in his apostolic constitution *Munificentissimus Deus* of the Assumption of Mary, the belief that, at the end of her life, Mary was taken body and soul into heaven.

In both cases, the popes were officially defining beliefs that, although not found in Scripture, had been held though Church tradition for centuries.[34]

---

32. See Avery Dulles, "Moderate Infallibilism," in Empie, *Authority and Infallibility*, 85–87. See also John Henry Newman's classic discussion on the limitations of papal infallibility in his 1875 "Letter to the Duke of Norfolk," accessible at *www.newmanreader.org/works/anglicans/volume2/gladstone/section9.html.*

33. Robert Christian explains the development of dogma of the Immaculate Conception of Mary in a video accessible at *www.youtube.com/watch?v=0WorFUig9do* (time 0:03:29).

34. See "Teaching Authority and Infallibility in the Church: Roman Catholic Reflections," in Empie, *Infallibility in the Church*, 52.

The Pope as the Sign of Christian Unity   13.25

In his 1995 encyclical *Ut Unum Sint* (*That They May Be One*), Pope John Paul II reiterated the Catholic tradition's belief that the ministry of the pope is the "perpetual and visible principle and foundation of unity" (referring to *LG*, no. 23) and that the pope is "the visible sign and guarantor of unity" (no. 88).

The Church is one, according to Scripture and the Nicene Creed. The pope's role is to be the visible center and sign of that unity. This ministry, John Paul II taught, is not one of power but of service to other Christians: The visible head of the Church should be the "servant of the servants." He emphasized that he, like Peter, is humanly weak and frail and, therefore, must depend completely on God's grace to fulfill this ministry (nos. 4, 91).

The Pope as Visible Representative of Christian Values   13.26

In a time when Christian voices are increasingly marginalized, the pope serves as an important symbol of, and spokesperson for, Christian values. Following are just a few examples of how popes have served that role:

Through their encyclicals, popes since Leo XIII (1878–1903) have developed a distinctive Catholic social teaching[35] that offers a clear vision of a society and economy based on the transcendent dignity and value of the human person. In developing this vision, they have vigorously opposed the collectivist and atheistic elements in socialism and communism, and condemned the abuses of unbridled capitalism and the consumerist and materialist societies it can foster.[36]

Popes have also served as prophetic voices unafraid to criticize the values of mainstream societies. Pope John Paul II, for example, bluntly labels a modern society that views abortion and euthanasia as acceptable methods of dealing with social problems as a "culture of death." As an alternative vision, John Paul II offers the Church's "Gospel of Life."[37]

Continued

---

35. A thematic summary of Catholic social teaching prepared by the US Conferences of Catholic Bishops is accessible at *www.usccb.org/beliefs-and-teachings/what-we-believe/catholic-social-teaching /seven-themes-of-catholic-social-teaching.cfm*.

36. See the summary of papal and Church teaching in the Pontifical Council for Justice and Peace's *Compendium of the Social Doctrine of the Church* (Vatican: *Libreria Editrice Vaticana*, 2004).

37. See, for example, John Paul's encyclical, *The Gospel of Life: On the Value and Inviolability of Human Life* (*Evangelium Vitae*) (Vatican: Libreria Editrice Vaticana; Washington, DC: USCC, 1995), accessible at *www .vatican.va/holy_father/john_paul_ii/encyclicals/documents/hf_jp-ii_enc_25031995_evangelium-vitae_en.html*.

The Pope as Visible Representative *Continued*

In this Christian vision, the weakest and most defenseless members of society (the unborn, sick, and elderly) are treated with special concern and dignity, not as "social problems" that need to be eliminated.

Pope Paul VI's encyclical *Humanae Vitae* (1968), upholding the Catholic Church's condemnation of artificial birth control, was widely criticized as regressive. Now, however, many see the pope's warnings as prophetic. He had predicted that a contraceptive culture would lead to increasing sexual promiscuity and lack of respect for women considered merely as sexual objects. Many see John Paul II's "Theology of the Body"[38] as a positive way of helping modern societies recover a sense of the dignity of the body and the sacred nature of sexual relations.

In his 2008 address[39] to the United Nations, Pope Benedict XVI was a voice of conscience, reminding the world community that moral relativism is a threat to basic human rights. If one denies that universal standards of right and wrong based on a common human nature exist, the pope declared, then there is no solid basis for defending human rights (sec. 7.19.1).

Non-Catholics are aware of the power of the papal platform. Explaining why *Time Magazine* named Pope Francis "Person of the Year"[40] for 2013, managing editor Nancy Gibbs remarks,

"The world is getting smaller; individual voices are getting louder; technology is turning virtue viral, so his pulpit is visible to the ends of the earth. When he kisses the face[41] of a disfigured man or washes the feet[42] of a Muslim woman, the image resonates far beyond the boundaries of the Catholic Church."[43]

---

38. A video overview of John Paul II's Theology of the Body by Rome Reports is accessible at *www.youtube.com/watch?v=P0-iG3pyUWQ* (time 0:02:05).

39. A video report by the Catholic News Agency on Benedict's address to the UN is accessible at *www.youtube.com/watch?v=_c4MgDupQWU* (time 0:01:23).

40. A video report by the Catholic News Agency on the naming of Francis as "Person of the Year" is accessible at *www.youtube.com/watch?v=L6DsM4ydkLs* (time 0:01:40).

41. A video report by CNN on Francis kissing the face of a disfigured man is accessible at *www.youtube.com/watch?v=UebCg9HuTiI* (time 0:02:59).

42. A video report by CNN on Francis washing the feet of prisoners is accessible at *www.youtube.com/watch?v=7vXOVe6nM_c* (time 0:02:36).

43. Gibbs, "Pope Francis: The Choice," accessible at *http://poy.time.com/2013/12/11/pope-francis-the-choice/*.

John Paul II notes that many recent ecumenical dialogues, including the Faith and Order Commission of the World Council of Churches, as well as Roman Catholic dialogues with Anglicans, Lutherans, and the Orthodox, have focused on the question of a "universal ministry" that would visibly demonstrate Christian unity (no. 89). The Lutheran-Catholic document, "Teaching Authority and Infallibility in the Church: Common Statement," agrees that "there may appropriately be a Ministry in the universal Church charged with primary responsibility for the unity of the people of God in their mission to the world" (no. 41).

The Role of the People in the Church's Infallibility　　13.27

In the Catholic view, the Church's gift of infallibility is normally expressed through the Magisterium, the teaching authority of the Church embodied in the pope in union with the bishops. The "ordinary" faithful of the Church, however, also play a role. The Council taught,

> The entire body of the faithful, anointed as they are by the Holy One, cannot err in matters of belief. They manifest this special property by means of the whole peoples' supernatural discernment in matters of faith (*sensus fidei*) when "from the Bishops down to the last of the lay faithful" they show universal agreement in matters of faith and morals. (*LG*, no. 12)

One of the chief characteristics of the Vatican II Council was its emphasis on understanding the Church not primarily in terms of its visible hierarchical structure but in terms of the whole community of the faithful. Some key images of the Church in *Lumen Gentium*, are the Church as "The People of God" and as a "Pilgrim Church."[44] The Council stressed that the **laity**, those not ordained or in religious orders, has its own particular apostolate, or mission, in proclaiming the Christian message to the world through their ordinary occupations and activities. Laypersons are also called, in their own way, to a life of holiness.[45]

The *Sensus Fidelium*　　13.27.1

Newman taught that the *sensus fidelium*, "the sense of the faithful," was one important way in which the apostolic tradition is clarified.

> I think I am right in saying that the tradition of the Apostles . . . manifests itself variously at various times: sometimes by the mouth of the episcopacy, sometimes by the doctors, sometimes by the people,

---

44. See further, Yves Congar, "The People of God," in *Vatican II: Interfaith Appraisal*, ed. J. H. Miller (Notre Dame: University of Notre Dame Press, 1966), 200.

45. See *LG*, nos. 4 and 5.

sometimes by liturgies, rites, ceremonies, and customs, by events, disputes, movements, and all those other phenomena which are comprised
under the name of history.[46]

Newman's understanding of the "sense of the people" is related to his "illative
sense," the more personal, implicit, and not strictly logical way of knowing that
forms the basis of many of our actions and decisions (sec. 2.4.1.3).

The Tradition is preserved in many different ways, and the faith of the people as a whole is an important witness to the Tradition. Before declaring the
belief in the Immaculate Conception of Mary an official teaching of the Church
(1854), Pope Pius IX asked the bishops of the world to determine the beliefs of
the common people. This *sensus fidelium* was an important factor in determining
whether the belief should be officially defined.[47] Similarly, Pope Pius XII wrote
to the world's bishops to determine their sense and the sense of their people
before defining the Assumption of Mary as an official Catholic belief.[48]

In the end, the bishops have the duty of discerning, judging, and teaching
the faith, but Newman believed it was important for them to have a good sense
of the actual beliefs of the people. In fact, Newman argues, at times, the faithful
sense of the people has been more reliable than the teachings of the bishops as
a whole. This was the case during the Arian controversy: at a time when most
bishops were following Arian teaching, the faithful preserved the correct understanding of the fully divine nature of Christ in their worship of him.[49]

The Role of the Faithful: "Reception" of Church Teaching   13.27.2

In Catholic thought, when a teaching is declared infallible by the pope, the
assent of the Church is not necessary in order to make it a valid teaching, because the Holy Spirit validated the teaching. At the same time, the
Council also taught that "the assent of the Church can never be lacking to
such definitions on account of the same Holy Spirit's influence" (*LG*, no.
25). Contemporary American Catholic theologian Avery Dulles, therefore,
concludes that one expects an infallible teaching will correspond with the
people's sense of faith "and will therefore evoke assent, at least eventually."
He writes carefully,

46. John Henry Newman, *On Consulting the Faithful in Matters of Doctrine* (New York: Sheed
and Ward, 1962), 63, accessible at *www.newmanreader.org/works/rambler/consulting.html*.

47. See Michael Sharkey, "Newman on the Laity," *Gregorianum*, 68 1–2 (1986): 339–46, accessible at *www.ewtn.com/library/Theology/newmnlay.htm*.

48. Pius XII, *Munificentissimus Deus*, no. 11–12 is accessible at *www.vatican.va/holy_father
/pius_xii/apost_constitutions/documents/hf_p-xii_apc_19501101_munificentissimus-deus_en.html*.

49. See John Henry Newman, *The Arians of the Fourth Century* (London: Longmans, Green, and
Co., 1908), 445–68, accessible at *www.newmanreader.org/works/arians/note5.html*.

If in a given instance the assent of the Church were evidently not forthcoming, this could be interpreted as a signal that the pope has perhaps exceeded his competence and that some necessary condition for an infallible act had not been fulfilled.[50]

The role and significance of the faithful in "receiving" Church teaching is an ongoing topic of discussion in Catholic theology.

To sum up, the doctrine of infallibility is by no means irrational. If one accepts that God has revealed the truth about human salvation in Jesus Christ, then it follows logically that God would provide a means for that revelation to be passed down without corruption. In traditional Christian, not only Catholic, understanding, the Church was given divine authority to protect that revelation. In the Catholic view, the bishops and especially the pope have the final responsibility for clarifying that revelation in their teaching, but the role of the people in preserving the revelation is not merely passive.

Questions about the Text

1. What is the root meaning of *ekklēsia*, the ancient Greek word for "church"?
2. What does it mean to say that salvation has a social character in the Catholic understanding? What are some biblical examples that illustrate this belief?
3. Explain in what way the "the chosen people" (either Israel or the Church) is understood to be an "instrument of salvation" for the rest of the world.
4. In what sense did the historical Jesus begin the Church?
5. Give some examples of the power and authority that Jesus gave to his apostles.
6. Give some examples of Peter's leadership over the Twelve. In Catholic understanding, what is the significance of Jesus giving Peter the "keys to the kingdom of Heaven"?
7. Identify the three basic meanings of the phrase, "Body of Christ" in the New Testament, and show how they are connected in Catholic theology.
8. Give the basic Catholic understanding of a sacrament. Why is it important that sacraments have a physical aspect?
9. Discuss the biblical evidence for the claim that there is only one Church of Christ.
10. What do Catholics mean by the "visible Church" and the "Mystical Body of Christ"? How are the two related?
11. What is the meaning of *Lumen Gentium's* statement that the one Church of Christ *subsists in* the Catholic Church? Why was this phrase used?

---

50. Avery Dulles, "Moderate Infallibilism," in Empie, *Authority and Infallibility*, 88–89.

12. Define "apostolic succession." In the Catholic view, why is it necessary? Understand specifically the bishops as the successors of the apostles and the pope as the successor of Peter.

13. Discuss some of the evidence that apostolic traditions were passed down in the early Church in an organized, systematic way.

14. Describe how leadership roles were more fluid in the first-century Church, with the clear leadership role of bishops emerging in the second century.

15. Explain the importance that Irenaeus and Tertullian place on the apostolic succession of bishops in apostolic churches in their struggles against Gnostic and other heretical claims.

16. In what sense does ordination pass on the "spiritual authority" of the apostles, according to Catholic thought?

17. Describe how some non-Catholic churches also recognize the importance of apostolic succession.

18. According to Newman, why is it logical that the Church would claim to have the gift of infallibility?

19. Why do all Christians identify some source of teaching that they regard as infallible?

20. Explain the Catholic view that both ecumenical councils and the pope have the gift of infallible teaching.

21. Explain the Catholic Church's understanding of papal infallibility. Name the two occasions when this authority was clearly used.

22. In Catholic theology, why is the pope's role as a visible sign of the unity of the whole Church important?

23. Explain the role of the laity in the Church's gift of infallibility.

Discussion Questions

1. Why do you think the Bible emphasizes the "social aspect" of salvation so strongly?

2. Besides the apostolic succession, are there other ways by which a Christian could be confident that the original teachings of Jesus have been handed down without being corrupted?

3. Besides the episcopal structure based on the leadership of bishops, are you familiar with other ways of structuring or governing a church? If so, what are the advantages and disadvantages of different structures?

4. What is your impression of the current pope? Do you agree that he can be a visible sign of the unity of the Church? Can he rightly act as a spokesperson for all Christians?

The Catholic Church and the World

The Claims of the Church in a Pluralistic World 14.1

This final chapter, building on the previous discussion regarding the Catholic understanding of the nature of the Church, considers the relationship of the Church with the rest of the world. The scandal of particularity is at the forefront. Just as the proclamation that Jesus is the only means of salvation is seen as a scandal, so too the universal claims (sec. 13.17.2) of the Catholic Church are considered a scandal in an increasingly pluralistic world.

Specifically, this chapter addresses Catholic views on (1) the universality, or "catholicity," of the Church; (2) the Catholic Church's relationship with other Christian communities; (3) the Catholic Church's relationship with non-Christian religions; and (4) the Catholic Church's relationship with secular society.

Catholicity and the Catholic Church 14.2

The Nicene Creed speaks of the one, holy, catholic, and apostolic Church. The word *catholic, katholikos* in Greek, is sometimes translated as "universal." This translation, however, does not fully capture the two essential meanings of the word.

1. The word means "according to the totality" or "in keeping with the whole." This sense can be related to Catholic Church's claim to possess the fullness of doctrine, the fullness of the sacraments, and an ordained ministry fully within the apostolic succession; in other words, everything that is needed for salvation (*CCC*, no. 830). In this sense of *catholic*, then, every local Catholic church is fully catholic, because if possesses the fullness of the faith.

2. The second aspect is more properly universal in the sense that the Church has been sent by Christ on a mission to the whole world. (*CCC*, no. 831). Just as humans are one through their common human nature, they are called to join in the oneness of the Church. Cyril of Jerusalem (ca. 315–387 CE) writes, "It is called Catholic then because it extends over all the world, from one end of the earth to the other; and because it teaches universally and completely one and all the doctrines which ought to come to men's knowledge; and because it brings into subjection to godliness the whole race of mankind . . . and because it universally treats and heals the whole class of sins . . ." (*Catechetical Lectures* 18.23).

The Catholic claim, then, is that this "catholic" Church "subsists in" the Catholic Church governed by the pope and the bishops in communion with him (sec. 13.17.1). With this understanding of the word *catholic*, the relationship between the Catholic Church and other Christians can be considered. Because the Catholic understanding of its relationship with Eastern Orthodox churches differs from that of its relationship with communities that grew out of the Reformation, the following sections deal with those topics separately.

The Church's Relationships with Protestant and Evangelical Christians   14.3

Despite the historically antagonistic relations between Catholics and the communities that grew out of the Reformation, Vatican II speaks of these communities with high regard. The Church declares that the one "Church of Christ is present and operative" in these churches, although not as fully as in the Catholic Church.[1] Following are some key points regarding the Catholic understanding of these other Christian communities:

1. **Baptism unites Catholics and other Christians.** Christians who are properly baptized "are put in some, though imperfect, communion with the Catholic Church." Baptism "constitutes the foundation of communion among all Christians, including those who are not yet in full communion with the Catholic Church" (*CCC*, no. 1271).

2. **All who are baptized are rightly called Christians, members of Christ's body, and should be accepted as brothers and sisters by Catholics** (*CCC*, no. 1271; *UR*, no. 3).

---

1. CDF, *Reponses to Some Questions Regarding Certain Aspects of the Doctrine of the Church. Response to Second Question* is accessible at *www.vatican.va/roman_curia/congregations/cfaith/documents /rc_con_cfaith_doc_20070629_responsa-quaestiones_en.html.*

3. **The Holy Spirit is present in these non-Catholic communities, and their members can be saved through these communities**. "For the Spirit of Christ has not refrained from using them [non-Catholic Christian denominations] as means of salvation" (*UR*, no. 3); their "liturgical actions must be regarded as capable of giving access to the community of salvation" (*UR*, no. 3).

4. **These communities have "many elements of sanctification and of truth"** (*LG*, no. 8). Such elements include "the written word of God; the life of grace; faith, hope and charity, with the other interior gifts of the Holy Spirit" (*UR*, no. 3). The Holy Spirit "is operative among them with His sanctifying power" (*LG*, no. 15).

Nevertheless, the ability of non-Catholic communities to offer salvation to their members depends on the Catholic Church, because the Church "is necessary for salvation" (*LG*, no. 14). Because the fullness of Christ's saving presence is in the Catholic Church alone, these other Christian communities, in a sense, draw from this fullness to offer salvation to their members.

Key Issues Separating Protestants and Evangelicals from the Catholic Church 14.4

The Church recognizes Protestants and evangelicals as fellow Christians. From a Catholic perspective, then, what key issues still divide Catholics from other Christians?

Doctrinal differences, often involving a different understanding of the relationship between Scripture and Tradition (secs. 9.10–9.11), divide some Christians. At a more fundamental level, however, the key issues dividing Christians, from the Catholic view, involve apostolic succession and the full validity of the sacraments. The belief in apostolic succession is at the heart of Catholic ecclesiology (sec. 13.19). This visible, unbroken line of authority, traceable to the apostles, guarantees that the Church is still following the teaching and example of Jesus. The apostolic succession further gives a bishop or priest the spiritual, mystical authority to preside during the consecration at the Eucharist and administer other sacraments. Many communities with roots in the Reformation have a radically different theological understanding of the nature of church leadership, and many reject the belief in apostolic succession. In the Catholic Church's eyes, therefore, the communities deriving from the Reformation "do not enjoy apostolic succession in the sacrament of Orders, and are, therefore, deprived of a constitutive element of the Church."[2]

---

2. CDF, *Reponses to Some Questions Regarding Certain Aspects of the Doctrine of the Church. Response to Question 5* is accessible at *www.vatican.va/roman_curia/congregations/cfaith/documents /rc_con_cfaith_doc_20070629_responsa-quaestiones_en.html.*

Communities in the Protestant and evangelical traditions tend to see church leaders primarily as teachers and preachers of the gospel. While the Catholic tradition agrees that this role is essential, it insists that Jesus also instituted another essential dimension of Church leadership: the mystical. This dimension is apparent, for example, in Jesus' granting his apostles the spiritual authority to forgive sins (see, e.g., John 20:22–23). Such mystical authority is passed down by the sacrament of Holy Orders.

Lacking this understanding of apostolic succession and the mystical dimension of church offices, typical Protestant and evangelical views of the sacraments are also different. Jesus' presence in the celebration of the Lord's Supper, for example, often is understood as symbolic rather than real as the Catholic Church teaches. Vatican II holds that the communities of the Reformation tradition "have not retained the proper reality of the eucharistic mystery in its fullness, especially because of the absence of the sacrament of Orders" (*UR*, no. 22). In the Catholic understanding, part of the mystical authority of the priest or bishop given in Holy Orders is to act as Christ's representative when the bread and wine are transformed into the Body and Blood of Christ at the consecration of the Eucharist.

In Catholic understanding, the celebrations of the Lord's Supper in Reformation communities lack the conversion of bread and wine into the Body and Blood of Christ. Given the importance Catholics place on the Real Presence of Christ in the Eucharist, this is a significant difference. The belief in the Real Presence is essential for the Catholic understanding of Church as the ongoing presence of Jesus in the world. The Church, as the Body of Christ, participates in the Eucharist; the Eucharist, itself, participates in Christ's atoning sacrifice of his body (secs. 13.10–13.12).

These considerations are behind Catholic decisions regarding terminology. Because they "have not preserved the apostolic succession or the valid celebration of the Eucharist," the communities with their roots in the Reformation are "not Churches in the proper sense of the word" but rather "ecclesial Communities."[3] Such terminology is not meant to denigrate the Protestant or evangelical communions but to protect the strongly mystical and sacramental Catholic understanding of the Church.

Despite these differences, the Catholic Church remains committed to an ongoing relationship and dialogue with Protestant and evangelical communities. Beyond the level of theological dialogue, the Church emphasizes the importance of face-to-face encounters between Catholics and other Christians to promote better understanding, cooperation in prayer, and cooperation in helping the poor and working for a peaceful and just society (*UR*, nos. 4, 12; *UUS*, nos. 71–76).

---

3. CDF, *Commentary on the Document "Responses to Some Questions Regarding Certain Aspects of the Doctrine on the Church"* is accessible *at www.vatican.va/roman_curia/congregations/cfaith/documents/rc_con_cfaith_doc_20070629_commento-responsa_en.html*; *UR*, no. 22 is accessible at *www.vatican.va/archive/hist_councils/ii_vatican_council/documents/vat-ii_decree_19641121_unitatis-redintegratio_en.html*.

One Church Sharing the Body of Christ? 14.4.1

Many Christian bodies, such as the Evangelical Lutheran Church of America and the United Methodist Church, practice an "open communion" policy, whereby baptized and believing members of any Christian denomination are invited to participate in the Lord's Supper. In contrast to this inclusiveness, the Roman Catholic policy that only Catholics should receive the Eucharist at Mass strikes many people as narrow-minded, arrogant, or even un-Christian.

The US Conference of Catholic Bishops explains the reasoning, "Because Catholics believe that the celebration of the Eucharist is a sign of the reality of the oneness of faith, life, and worship, members of those churches with whom we are not yet fully united are ordinarily not admitted to Holy Communion."[4]

Catholics understand the Eucharist, the Body of Christ, as a sign of unity, as Paul taught (1 Cor 10:17). The different Christian communities are not united, however, and their differences include strikingly different understandings of the Eucharist (i.e., some Christians see it as symbolic only, in contrast to a belief in the Real Presence) as well as the nature of Church leadership and apostolic succession (sec. 14.4). In the Catholic view, it would be dishonest for Christians who are not united to share in this sign of unity.

The Church and Martyrs 14.5

John Paul II recognizes that the Catholic Church has a "real but imperfect communion" with non-Catholic Christians. Thinking of those Catholic and non-Catholic Christians who were willing to give their lives as martyrs, however, he goes further, "I now add that this communion is already perfect in what we all consider the highest point of the life of grace, *martyria* unto death, the truest communion possible with Christ who shed his Blood, and by that sacrifice brings near those who once were far off" (cf. Eph 2:13; *UUS*, no. 84). This common "witness" (the basic meaning of the Greek word *martyria*) of those who have been willing to die for their faith is a foreshadowing of the end of time when the Church will achieve perfect unity.

---

4. USCCB, "Guidelines for the Reception of Communion," accessible at *www.usccb.org/prayer-and-worship/the-mass/order-of-mass/liturgy-of-the-eucharist/guidelines-for-the-reception-of-communion.cfm.*

Dietrich Bonhoeffer: Martyr for the Faith

14.5.1

© James Brittain / Bridgeman Images

These Westminster Abbey statues depict the martyrs Martin Luther King, Oscar Romero, Bonhoeffer, and Esther John, a Pakistani nurse and convert to Christianity.

In referring to those willing to shed their blood for their faith in Jesus Christ, John Paul II may well have considered people such as Dietrich Bonhoeffer (1906–1945), a German Lutheran pastor and theologian. Bonhoeffer was involved in the ecumenical movement, studied at Union Seminary in New York and pastored German churches in London.

From the moment the Nazi regime came to power, Bonhoeffer opposed it. Lecturing in the United States shortly before World War II, he had the opportunity to stay in America but chose to return to Germany to share the fate of his people. After first believing the Nazis could be resisted nonviolently, he became convinced that Nazi evil could only be stopped by force and became involved in a failed attempt to assassinate Hitler.

He was arrested and spent two years in prison, where he ministered as well as he could to the emotional and spiritual needs of his fellow prisoners. On the day of his execution, he was seen praying fervently. His last recorded words were, "This is the end—for me, the beginning of life." The Nazis hanged him on April 9, 1945.

Statues at Westminster Abbey in London honor Bonhoeffer, along with nine other witnesses to the faith (including the Baptist Martin Luther King, the Catholic Archbishop Oscar Romero, the Catholic priest Maximilian Kolbe, the Orthodox grand duchess Elizabeth of Russia, and the Anglican Lucian Tapiedi as twentieth-century martyrs.

This monument to the martyrs[5] is a visible symbol of John Paul II's vision of the perfect unity among Christian denominations already achieved by those who shed their blood for their faith.

---

5. A 1998 BBC news article about the unveiling of the monument to the martyrs at Westminster Abbey is accessible at *http://news.bbc.co.uk/2/hi/uk/129587.stm*.

The Catholic Church and Eastern Orthodox Churches 14.6

The two factors that distance the Catholic Church from communities of the Reformation also make it closer to the Eastern Orthodox traditions. "These Churches, although separated from us, possess true sacraments, above all by apostolic succession, the priesthood and the Eucharist, whereby they are linked with us in closest intimacy" (*UR*, no. 15). The Orthodox understanding of the sacramental, mystical nature of the Church, and Orthodoxy's deep roots in apostolic tradition unite them with the Catholic Church.

Vatican II emphasized the importance of the common past shared by the Catholic and Orthodox Churches and noted the Catholic debt to the East:

> [I]t must not be forgotten that from the beginning the Churches of the East have had a treasury from which the Western Church has drawn extensively—in liturgical practice, spiritual tradition, and law. Nor must we undervalue the fact that it was the ecumenical councils held in the East that defined the basic dogmas of the Christian faith, on the Trinity, on the Word of God Who took flesh of the Virgin Mary. (*UR*, no. 14)

The Eastern Orthodox and the Western Roman Catholic Churches have long had distinctive cultural and theological approaches, and certain tensions developed between them. These included the *filioque* controversy (sec. 6.17), a debate over the use of leavened or unleavened bread for the Eucharist, and the debate over the primacy of the pope. An official break in Orthodox-Catholic communion, technically known as a schism, is usually dated to 1054, when a Roman Catholic delegation and the Orthodox patriarch in Constantinople mutually excommunicated each other.

A key issue that continues to separate Catholics and the Orthodox involves ecclesiology and the role of papal primacy. In Orthodox understanding, each particular church, under its own bishop, is a complete church when it celebrates the Eucharist. In Catholic understanding, this vision lacks the universal dimension of the Church. It is essential that each individual church also recognize its unity with other churches around the globe. In the Catholic view, a church's recognition of the primacy of the pope—the visible symbol of the unity of Christians—achieves this universal dimension.

The Catholic Church teaches that "these venerable Christian communities lack something in their condition as particular churches."[6] Nevertheless, the communion between the Catholic Church and the Orthodox "is so profound 'that it lacks little to attain the fullness that would permit a common celebration of the Lord's Eucharist'" (*CCC*, no. 838).

---

6. CDF, *Commentary on the Document "Responses to Some Questions Regarding Certain Aspects of the Doctrine on the Church"* is accessible at *www.vatican.va/roman_curia/congregations/cfaith/documents /rc_con_cfaith_doc_20070629_commento-responsa_en.html*; CDF, Declaration *Dominus Iesus* on the Unicity and Salvific Universality of Jesus Christ and the Church, no. 17 is accessible at *www.vatican .va/roman_curia/congregations/cfaith/documents/rc_con_cfaith_doc_20000806_dominus-iesus_en.html*.

In 1979, the Joint International Commission for Theological Dialogue Between the Catholic Church and the Orthodox Church was established. It has published several documents[7] as the ecumenical dialogue[8] continues.

Roman Catholic Relations with Anglicanism   14.7

Anglicanism is sometimes considered a middle way between Catholicism and Protestantism. Although the Anglican tradition began, historically, at the time of the Reformation, it understands its bishops to be within the line of apostolic succession. A decree by Pope Leo XIII in 1896, however, rejected this claim. Shortly after the Vatican II Council, the Catholic Church and the Anglican community began a theological dialogue that continues today.

Roman and Eastern Catholic Churches 14.8

Roman Catholic relations with Eastern Catholic Churches are an important example of how legitimate diversity may exist within the one Body of Christ. Twenty-one Eastern Catholic Churches are in full communion with the Roman Catholic Church, recognizing the primacy of the pope. Each, however, has its own liturgical, legal, and other traditions. Among these Churches are the Maronite Church (Lebanon), Coptic Catholic Church (Egypt), Ukrainian Greek Catholic Church, and the Chaldean Catholic Church (Iraq). Some of their distinctive liturgical traditions include

- Use of icons as an essential part of worship.
- When infants are baptized, they also receive the sacraments of confirmation and the Eucharist—given by means of a few drops of the consecrated wine.
- Married men can be ordained to the priesthood.

Vatican II reaffirmed that these Churches have the full right to rule themselves and practice their unique liturgies, in union with the pope (*Orientalium Ecclesiarum*, no. 5). These Churches have a special role in promoting the unity of Christians, especially with the Eastern Orthodox (*Orientalium Ecclesiarum*, no.24).

---

7. The documents of the Joint International Commission for Theological Dialogue Between the Catholic Church and the Orthodox Church are accessible at *www.vatican.va/roman_curia/pontifical_councils/chrstuni/sub-index/index_orthodox-ch.htm*.

8. A video report on Catholic and Orthodox talks on the papacy is accessible at *www.youtube.com/watch?v=EvegX1ta74M* (time 00:02:02).

Catholic Commitment to the Ecumenical Movement 14.9

In his encyclical *Ut Unum Sint*, Pope John Paul II declared that, at "the Second Vatican Council, the Catholic Church committed herself *irrevocably* to following the path of the ecumenical venture" (no. 3, emphasis original).

Since its beginning, the ecumenical movement has produced concrete results. Two examples follow:

- In 1965, Pope Paul VI and the Orthodox Patriarch of Constantinople Athenagoras declared that both the Catholic and Orthodox Church "regret and remove both from memory and from the midst of the Church the sentences of excommunication" (*Joint Catholic-Orthodox Declaration*) that marked the split between Eastern and Western Christianity in 1054.
- In 1999, the Lutheran World Federation and the Catholic Church issued a *Joint Declaration on the Doctrine of Justification* (sec. 7.13.3). This document showed that "a consensus in basic truths of the doctrine of justification exists between Lutherans and Catholics" (no. 40)—a significant achievement, because the dispute over this doctrine was a major factor in the original separation of Lutherans and Catholics.

Pope John Paul II (*UUS*, no. 79) outlines some key areas for continued ecumenical dialogue:

1. The relationship between sacred Scripture and sacred Tradition.
2. The sacramental understanding of the Eucharist.
3. Ordination as a sacrament.
4. The role of the Magisterium of the Church as an authority for "teaching and safeguarding the faith."
5. The theological understanding of the Virgin Mary.

The pope also identified the primacy of Peter as a key topic for ecumenical discussion (*UUS*, nos. 88–96).

The goal of ecumenical dialogue, from the Catholic perspective, is not merely better relationships or understanding between Christian churches, although these may be considered intermediate goals. As John Paul II wrote, the Catholic Church asks "the Lord to increase the unity of all Christians until they reach full communion" (*UUS*, no. 3). Full unity would be expressed through a full sharing of beliefs and sacraments in worship.

For John Paul II, Christian unity is to be a reflection of the unity of the Trinity: "Christian unity . . . has its divine source in the Trinitarian unity of the Father, the Son and the Holy Spirit. . . . The faithful are *one* because, in the Spirit, they are in *communion* with the Son and, in him, share in his *communion* with the Father" (*UUS*, nos. 8–9; emphasis original).

Christianity and Non-Christian Religions   14.10

The following sections turn to the Catholic understanding of the relationship between the Church and non-Christian religions—a central issue in today's pluralistic world. Once again, the claim that salvation is possible *only* through Jesus Christ and his Church must be considered. How is such a claim reasonable in the face of the billions of people in the world who are not Christians and the many who have never even heard of the name of Jesus?[9]

First, several theological proposals to this dilemma are considered: Karl Rahner's anonymous Christians theory, the pluralist position, the reflections of Joseph Ratzinger, and the proposals of Gavin D'Costa. Next, key elements of Vatican II's teaching on the Church's relations with other religions are applied to this question. The chapter concludes with a reflection on the Church's relationship with the secular world.

Rahner's Theory of Anonymous Christians   14.10.1

Regarding Christian relations with non-Christian religions, Karl Rahner identified the following key points:[10]

1. The logical conclusion of Christian belief is that Christianity is the one true religion. If one believes that humans cannot free themselves from sin and, therefore, are only saved through the union of the human and divine in Jesus, it follows that Christianity is the one path to salvation.

2. Billions of people, however, have never heard the Christian message, either because they lived before the Incarnation or because they lived in parts of the world dominated by non-Christian religions.

3. It is impossible that God would give billions of non-Christians no chance at salvation, because God created them out of a free act of love and because "God our savior . . . wills everyone to be saved" (1 Tim 2:3–4). Therefore, God must have presented to them, in some way, the offer of supernatural grace through Christ.

4. This kind of supernatural offer, however, cannot have been made solely to each isolated individual, as religion and salvation are essentially social (sec. 13.4). Therefore, the offer of God's supernatural grace must have been made through every non-Christian's cultural and religious traditions.

---

9. Answers to this theological dilemma are sometimes divided into exclusivist, inclusivist, and pluralist categories. For a summary and critique of these categories, see Gavin D'Costa, *Christianity and World Religions: Disputed Questions in the Theology of Religions* (Chichester, UK: Wiley-Blackwell, 2009), 3–32.

10. Rahner, "Christianity and the Non-Christian Religions," in *Theological Investigations*, vol. 5, *Later Writings* (Baltimore: Helicon; London: Darton, Longman & Todd, 1966), 115–34.

5. The number of non-Christians who accept God's supernatural offer of salvation cannot be slight. While each person is free to accept or reject the offer, it seems to contradict God's loving plan of creation and redemption to think that only a tiny percentage of the billions of non-Christians would actually be saved.

6. Because salvation comes only through Christ, and God makes offers of salvation through non-Christian religions, those who accept the offer can justifiably be called "anonymous Christians." They are saved through accepting God's supernatural offer of grace through Christ, even though they are not explicitly aware of Christ.

In support of his theory, Rahner refers to the account of Paul's preaching in Athens. Speaking to the polytheistic Athenians, Paul declares,

> You Athenians, I see that in every respect you are very religious. For as I walked around looking carefully at your shrines, I even discovered an altar inscribed, "To an Unknown God." What therefore you *unknowingly worship*, I proclaim to you. (Acts 17:22–23, emphasis added)

The key point revealed in the Acts passage for Rahner's theory, is that people can have a relationship with God and worship God without knowing explicitly that they are doing so. One could thus also implicitly accept the offer of salvation through Christ without knowing Christ directly.

The Pluralist Position   14.10.2

The philosopher and theologian John Hick[11] represents a solution to this dilemma that moves beyond traditional Christianity. Hick was influenced by the philosophy of Immanuel Kant, who teaches that people can never know reality but only their own perception of reality. Hick concludes from this that no one knows God in himself—only various perceptions of God. The transcendent does exist, but because no one has direct access to it, varied perceptions of the transcendent arise in the various world religions. Such perceptions are shaped by different historical and cultural influences. Different religious traditions "have developed to meet the needs of the range of mentalities expressed in the different human cultures."[12]

Therefore, no one religious tradition can claim to be "truer" than another, as they are merely perceptions. All religions are equal paths to the transcendent, and Christianity cannot be privileged over any other.

---

11. David Cheetham discusses John Hick's life and thought in a video accessible at *www.youtube.com/watch?v=C79JmHZ4QB8* (time 00:13:24).

12. Hick, *God Has Many Names* (Philadelphia: Westminster, 1980), 21.

A Critique of Rahner and Hick: Ratzinger's Approach to World Religions   14.11

Joseph Ratzinger, later Pope Benedict XVI, shows that both Rahner's and Hick's approaches involve questionable presuppositions. By classifying religions into only two categories, Christian and non-Christian, Rahner assumes there are no essential differences among non-Christian religions, while Hick assumes all religions are fundamentally similar quests for the divine. Is this true?

Rather than assuming similarity, Ratzinger suggests that one should begin by analyzing individual religions and determining if they fall into certain patterns. One could then locate the place of Christianity within those patterns.[13]

Ratzinger analyzes two basic categories of religions: the great mystical religions of the East (e.g., Hinduism and Buddhism) and the great monotheistic religions that arose in the Middle East (Judaism, Christianity, and Islam). The following chart is built on Ratzinger's analysis.

Mystical Religions	Monotheistic Religions
Ultimate reality is a transcendent One who is beyond human conception.	Ultimate reality is a personal God who can be known by analogy.
Salvation involves losing one's personal identity and uniting oneself to the One.	Salvation involves purifying one's identity and entering into an eternal relationship with God, while retaining one's identity.
Time is an endless cycle of death and rebirth.	Time and history move toward a definite climax on the Day of Judgment.
Humans are born and reborn into numerous lives; salvation ends this cycle of rebirth.	Humans live a single life and then face a final judgment.

Such differences are not minor; they involve fundamentally different ways not only of looking at the divine but also of thinking about what it means to be a human. These differences in belief, Ratzinger adds, have practical social

---

13. Joseph Ratzinger, *Truth and Tolerance: Christian Belief and World Religions* (San Francisco: Ignatius Press, 2004), 17–18.

consequences. In Hinduism, for example, it is not clear that there is a solid basis for the dignity of the individual person, because a person's destiny is to be reincarnated for endless ages, ultimately to be absorbed into the Absolute. Some writers have claimed that modern Hindu reform movements based on individual rights and dignity were only able to arise when the Hindu reformers borrowed the Christian concept of person.[14]

Are all religions the same? Ratzinger's response to such a position is blunt:

That is by no means the case. There are in fact sick and degenerate forms of religion, which do not edify people but alienate them. . . . And even religions whose moral value we must recognize, and which are on their way toward the truth, may become diseased here and there. . . . In Hinduism . . . there are some marvelous elements—but there are also negative aspects: involvement with the caste system; suttee [self-immolation] for widows.

Even Islam, with all the greatness it represents, is always in danger of losing balance, of letting violence have a place and letting religion slide away into mere outward observance and ritualism. And there are of course, as we all know but too well, diseased forms of Christianity— such as when the crusaders, on capturing the holy city of Jerusalem, where Christ died for all men, for their part indulged in a bloodbath of Moslems and Jews.[15]

Brief comments cannot do justice to the complex reality of religions such as Hinduism and Islam, as Ratzinger himself acknowledges. Yet his reflections are enough to suggest that it is misleading to claim that religions are fundamentally the same. There are, in fact, profound differences between them; and these differences, in turn, have profound effects on how people live their daily lives.

A Question of Truth 14.11.1

Ratzinger notes that the question of world religions raises the question of truth. For the pluralist, objective truth is an illusion. It is impossible for people to get beyond their subjective perceptions—shaped by their cultural experiences—to attain the "objective" truth about who God is. For the pluralist, truth is always relative: Each cultural tradition has its own truth about God.

Ratzinger, however, shows that if individuals wish to have a true dialogue with a believer from another religion or even look honestly at their own religion, they cannot do so on the basis of a relativistic concept of truth. How can people

14. Ibid., 47.
15. Ibid., 204.

make an honest analysis of healthy and diseased elements in their own or in another's religious traditions if they have no objective standards?

How Are Non-Christians Saved?   14.11.2

As a Christian, Ratzinger believes it is objectively true that people can only be saved through Jesus and his Church. Yet Ratzinger also accepts the Church teaching (e.g., *LG*, no. 8) that it is possible for one who has never heard of Christianity to be saved. If he is dissatisfied with Rahner's anonymous Christian proposal, how does Ratzinger solve the tension between the two beliefs?

Ratzinger is content to leave the question of how God saves non-Christians open, asking, "How do we know that the theme of salvation should only be tied to religions? . . . Do we necessarily have to invent a theory about how God can save people without abandoning the uniqueness of Christ?"[16] Ratzinger leaves the question of salvation to God, because God alone is judge of the world.[17] For Ratzinger, Christian theologians have the more humble task of patiently seeking the truth by means of their tradition, while remaining open to dialogue with other worldviews.

World Religions and Salvation: Retrieving the Tradition   14.12

The Catholic theologian Gavin D'Costa,[18] in contrast to Ratzinger, does offer a way to resolve the tension between (1) salvation through Christ alone and (2) the conviction that God's love, mercy, and justice must have provided an opportunity for salvation for those who have never heard of Christ.

D'Costa rejects the pluralist position, because it openly contradicts basic Christian teaching. He also rejects Rahner's inclusivist position for two basic reasons. First, he rejects the notion that non-Christian religions can save a person, because the Christian definition of salvation is human unity with the Triune God, and other religions do not teach a triune God. He is also critical of Rahner's notion that a person can implicitly choose to be a Christian—for D'Costa, the choice must be an explicit one.

D'Costa's solution is to retrieve a traditional Christian notion: Christ's descent into hell, found in the Apostle's Creed. According to a traditional interpretation of this phrase, Jesus descended to the realm of the dead after his death

---

16. Ibid., 53.

17. Ibid., 18.

18. Gavin D'Costa discusses theology of religions in a video accessible at *www.youtube.com /watch?v=Wa7HdJ7FI78* (time 0:09:57).

and before his Resurrection and there preached the gospel to all who had never had the chance to hear it in their earthly life (*CCC*, nos. 632–37).[19]

Vatican II on Salvation and Non-Christian Religions

14.13

Catholic theology has always stressed the centrality of the Church in salvation. The Church is Christ's continuing sacramental presence in the world: people are saved through joining themselves in faith to Christ's Body, the Church. Because the Church "is necessary for salvation" (*LG*, no. 14), it seems that any non-Christian who is saved would be saved through his or her connection, in some sense, to the Body of Christ.

In contrast to Rahner's focus on God's grace working through non-Christian religions, the Vatican II documents explore ways non-Christian religions are connected with the Church, a notion consistent with the understanding of the Church as a sacrament that works for the salvation of the whole world (*LG*, no. 48).

Lumen Gentium teaches, "Those who have not yet received the Gospel are related in various ways to the People of God" (no. 16). This relationship has taken on various historical forms: Christians have an especially close relationship with Jews and Muslims, their fellow monotheists. The Church is also related to those who have never heard the Christian message.

> Those also can attain to salvation who through no fault of their own do not know the Gospel of Christ or His Church, yet sincerely seek God and moved by grace strive by their deeds to do His will as it is known to them through the dictates of conscience. (*LG*, no. 16)

The statement adds that God does not deny "the helps necessary for salvation" to people in such a situation.

John Paul II echoes the teaching of the Council. For those who are not Christian, John Paul says,

> [S]alvation in Christ is accessible by virtue of a grace which, while having a mysterious relationship to the Church, does not make them formally part of the Church, but enlightens them in a way which is accommodated to their spiritual and material situation. This grace comes from Christ; it is the result of his Sacrifice and is communicated by the Holy Spirit. (*Redemptoris Missio*, no.10)

---

19. D'Costa, *Christianity and World Religions.*

Exactly how is the non-Christian in relationship to the Church? The Council was content to say God does this "in ways known to himself."[20] The CDF's *Dominus Iesus* taught that theologians are free to explore specific ways in which this relationship could be conceived. What a theologian could not say, however, is that the Church was only "*one way* [among many] of salvation" (no. 21, emphasis original).

Vatican II's Declaration on Non-Christian Religions 14.14

The *Declaration on the Relation of the Church to Non-Christian Religions (Nostra Aetate)* presents a positive view of non-Christian religions and encourages inter-religious dialogue.

Nostra Aetate balances respect for non-Christian religions with a sense of the Church's unique role and the centrality of Christ. The language parallels the image used in describing the relationship of the Catholic Church with other Christians: The Church contains the "fullness" of truth and holiness, while other religions contain elements of truth and holiness.

> The Catholic Church rejects nothing that is true and holy in these religions. She regards with sincere reverence those ways of conduct and of life, those precepts and teachings which, though differing in many aspects from the ones she holds and sets forth, nonetheless often reflect a ray of that Truth which enlightens all men. Indeed, she proclaims, and ever must proclaim Christ "the way, the truth, and the life" (John 14:6), in whom men may find the fullness of religious life, in whom God has reconciled all things to Himself. (*NA*, no. 2)

The Council singles out Hinduism and Buddhism, the two largest Eastern religions, for special comment (*NA*, no. 2):

- Hindus "contemplate the divine mystery and express it through an inexhaustible abundance of myths and through searching philosophical inquiry. They seek freedom from the anguish of our human condition either through ascetical practices or profound meditation or a flight to God with love and trust."

- Buddhism "realizes the radical insufficiency of this changeable world; it teaches a way by which men, in a devout and confident spirit, may be able

---

20. *Decree on the Church's Missionary Activity (Ad gentes)*, no. 7 is accessible at *www.vatican.va /archive/hist_councils/ii_vatican_council/documents/vat-ii_decree_19651207_ad-gentes_en.html*.

either to acquire the state of perfect liberation, or attain, by their own efforts or through higher help, supreme illumination."

The Church's Relationship with Islam 14.15

The Vatican II documents again emphasize the positive aspects of the Muslim-Catholic relationship (*LG*, no. 16; *NA*, no. 3). Muslims share with Catholics the following beliefs:

1. Muslims "along with us adore the one and merciful God" (*LG*, no. 16), the all-powerful creator of heaven and Earth. Muslims also recognize God's role as judge on the Day of Judgment when the dead are raised.

2. Muslims recognize the special role of Abraham; he models the believer who submits (the term *Muslim* means "one who submits") his will to God's will.

3. Although Muslims do not recognize Jesus' divinity, they revere him as a prophet. They also honor Mary. Mary is the only named woman in the Qur'an; an entire chapter, *surah maryam* (chap. 19), is dedicated to the story of her giving to birth to Jesus while still a virgin.

4. The Council calls on Muslims and Christians to forget past conflicts and work together toward mutual understanding and common efforts in peace and justice.

One unavoidable issue in Muslim-Christians relations is the current persecution of Christians, including violent attacks by extremists, in several Muslim-majority nations. In Iraq,[21] for example, flight from persecution has resulted in the Christian population dwindling from around one million in 1993 to a fraction of that number currently. Muslim populations have also suffered persecution from Christians in the recent past, most notably during the "ethnic cleansing" campaign during the Bosnian War (1992–95).

The Church's Relationship with Judaism 14.16

Vatican II recognized the Church's special relationship with the Jewish people, emphasizing the following points: (*LG*, no. 16; *NA*, no. 4).

1. **Christianity's Jewish heritage.** The Church's roots run deeply in Jewish soil. Jesus Christ, the savior, is of the Jewish people, as are the apostles. Christians are "Abraham's sons according to faith." The Church has received a great part of her Scripture, the Old Testament, from the Jewish people.

---

21. A video report by *The Telegraph* on Iraqi Christians is accessible at *www.youtube.com /watch?v=fACyQN0jJ6Y* (time 00:03:14).

2. **Israel's ongoing relationship with God.** The apostle Paul's discussion of his fellow Jews in Romans 9–11 is fundamental to the Church's current understanding of Catholic-Jewish relations. Of decisive importance is Romans 11:28–29: "but in respect to election, they [the Jewish people] are beloved because of the patriarchs. For the gifts and the call of God are irrevocable."

   The Church believes God still has a relationship with the people of Israel. Pope Francis says, "their covenant with God has never been revoked, for 'the gifts and the call of God are irrevocable' (Rom 11:29)" (*EG*, no. 247).

   The Council adds, "Although the Church is the new people of God, the Jews should not be presented as rejected or accursed by God, as if this followed from the Holy Scriptures" (*NA*, no. 4). This statement is historically significant because a common traditional Christian interpretation is that God's new covenant in Jesus implies God's covenant with the Jews is nullified, and the Jews are rejected as God's chosen people. Rather, as Pope Francis insists, "God continues to work among the people of the Old Covenant and bring forth treasures of wisdom which flow from their encounter with his word" (*EG*, no. 249).

3. **Ongoing cooperation.** The Council calls on Christians and Jews to engage in mutual scriptural and theological study, as well as dialogue. The Council condemns any hatred, persecution, or other form of anti-Semitism.

4. **Different views on Jesus.** At the same time, the Church recognizes the differences between Jews and Catholics: Pope Francis maintains "that the Church cannot refrain from proclaiming Jesus as Lord and Messiah" (*EG*, no. 249).

The Church's close relationship with Israel raises theological questions. If God's covenant with Israel is still valid after the new covenant in Christ, does this imply that the Jewish people can still be saved through the old covenant? If so, wouldn't this contradict the basic Christian principle that salvation is through Christ alone? Given the centrality of Christ, it would seem that Israel's salvation must, in some sense, be connected with Christ and his Church.

The apostle Paul, at the end of his reflections on the fate of Israel in God's plan, asserts, "I do not want you to be unaware of this mystery . . . a hardening has come upon Israel in part, until the full number of the Gentiles comes in, and thus all Israel will be saved" (Rom 11:25–26). In a mysterious way, Israel's fate remains tied up with the fate of the rest of the world (Gentiles). Paul remains unclear as to *how* Israel will be saved, but he asserts it as fact.

Pope John Paul II and the Jews 14.16.1

Pope John Paul II[22] had a particularly close relationship with the Jewish people. He grew up in Poland with close Jewish friends. In 1986,

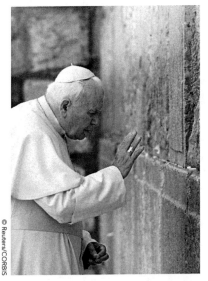

he became the first pope on record to visit a synagogue. At this visit to the Great Synagogue in Rome, he referred to the Jewish people as "elder brothers" in the faith of Abraham. He was also the first pope to visit Auschwitz. In 2000, John Paul II prayed in Jerusalem at Western Wall, also known as the Wailing Wall, a traditional Jewish site of prayer at the ruins of the Temple. As is customary, he left a written prayer at the Wall. This prayer reflects the Catholic sense of the close relationship with the Jewish people, the willingness to admit past wrongs (including a long history of Christian persecution of Jews), and the desire to build a strong future relationship:

Pope John Paul II prays at the Western Wall in Jerusalem. Jewish leaders have often praised him for his unequivocal condemnation of anti-Semitism and his persistent call for Jewish-Catholic dialogue and mutual respect.

© Reuters/CORBIS

> God of our Fathers,
> you chose Abraham and his descendants
> to bring your Name to the Nations:
> we are deeply saddened by the behavior of those
> who in the course of history
> have caused these children of yours to suffer,
> and asking your forgiveness we wish to commit ourselves
> to genuine brotherhood
> with the people of the Covenant.
> Amen

---

22. A video by *romereports.com* that chronicles John Paul II's relationship with Jews is accessible at *www.youtube.com/watch?v=0_VPa3F4AnM* (time 00:09:51).

Ongoing Commitment to Dialogue with Other Religions 14.17

The Catholic Church is committed to continuing dialogue and cooperative efforts with members of other world religions. This commitment was concretely expressed in Pope John Paul II's sponsorship of an interfaith gathering for a World Day of Prayer for Peace[23] in Assisi, the hometown of St. Francis, in 1986. Pope Benedict marked the twenty-fifth anniversary of that gathering by inviting leaders of world religions to Assisi for a day of dialogue.

The Church and Secular Society 14.18

A trend in modern, secular thought holds that religious convictions have no place in public discussions—whether political, economic, or social. This trend, a type of rationalism, seeks to relegate religious convictions to the private realm, arguing that religious convictions are purely subjective.

In an American context, this tendency is sometimes connected with the "separation of church and state" principle. In this interpretation, religious beliefs should remain in the realm of the church, and the state should be completely secular.

A Clarification of the American Context 14.18.1

The US Constitution, in fact, does not contain the phrase "separation of church and state." The relevant clause in the First Amendment reads, "Congress shall make no law respecting an establishment of religion, or prohibiting the free exercise thereof." What the American founders wished to avoid was an established religion—one that would receive the official recognition and support of the national government, as was the case with the Church of England in Great Britain.

Great American political movements have always been inspired by religious beliefs. The civil rights movement of the 1960s is one example. In his "I Have a Dream" speech, Baptist minister Martin Luther King Jr. quoted from Amos 5:24 and Isaiah 40:4–5 and ended his speech inspired by the words of an African American spiritual, "Free at last! Free at last! Thank God almighty, we are free at last."

The Role of the Church in Social Policies: Teaching Ethical Principles 14.18.2

In the Catholic view, the Church should not play a direct role in politics: It should not promote specific candidates, for example. Nevertheless, the Church

---

23. A video report on the World Day of Prayer for Peace in Assisi is accessible at *www.youtube.com/watch?v=M0QwubjjBXs* (time 0:04:27).

does have a right and a duty to clarify the ethical values behind public policies. As the US Bishops declared, "we bishops do not intend to tell Catholics for whom or against whom to vote. Our purpose is to help Catholics form their consciences in accordance with God's truth."[24] This teaching on moral truths can help guide not only Catholics but also society as a whole.

It is impossible to separate the political and social realm from the ethical. Political and social decisions are made on the basis of ethical values. If religiously motivated ethics are banned from public dialogue, ethical decisions will be made on another basis—the values of secular humanism or on a utilitarian or pragmatic basis, for example.

The Church does not seek to impose its ethical principles on society. As Vatican II taught, "The truth cannot impose itself except by virtue of its own truth, as it makes its entrance into the mind at once quietly and with power."[25] The Church, rather, must use reason to persuade people that its ethical values are truer and more just than alternative ethical values. However, the Church must be allowed a public voice in order to make its case.

The Catholic tradition, with its 2000 years of institutional experience, has much to offer current social and political discussions. Following are just a few examples:

- **Catholic Social Teaching**. The Church offers a well-developed social teaching that warns how socialism can endanger freedom and personal initiative, while, at the same time, critiques the consumerism and "idolatry of money" that a capitalist system can encourage (*EG*, no. 55–56).

- **Defense of the dignity and value of every life.** The utilitarian philosophy of Princeton professor Peter Singer teaches that the sanctity of human life is an outdated principle. He justifies abortion and the killing of disabled infants because, due to their early stages of development, they do not qualify as "human persons."[26] In teaching that every life is a gift from God, made in God's image, the Church offers an alternative vision (*CCC*, no. 1700).

- **Defense of human rights.** Offering a transcendent basis for basic human rights helps protect those rights. If the government gives rights, the government can also take them away. If God gives rights, no human can take them away. The Declaration of Independence recognized this truth in its declaration that all men are created equal, and that "they are endowed by their Creator with certain unalienable Rights, that among these are Life, Liberty, and the pursuit of Happiness" (sec. 7.19.1).

---

24. USCCB, "Forming Consciences for Faithful Citizenship," no. 7, is accessible at *www.usccb.org /issues-and-action/faithful-citizenship/forming-consciences-for-faithful-citizenship-part-one.cfm*.

25. *Dignitatis Humanae*, no. 1, is accessible at *www.vatican.va/archive/hist_councils/ii_ vatican_council/documents/vat-ii_decl_19651207_dignitatis-humanae_en.html*.

26. See Peter Singer, FAQ, under "Sanctity of Human Life," accessible at *www.princeton .edu/~psinger/faq.html*.

- **Natural Law**. The Catholic tradition offers a sophisticated tradition of reflecting on just law. When Martin Luther King Jr., for example, defended the distinction he made between (1) the duty to obey just laws and (2) the right to disobey unjust laws (such as the segregation laws in the South), he appealed, among other sources, to the teachings of Augustine and Thomas Aquinas. "I would agree with St. Augustine that 'an unjust law is no law at all' . . . To put it in the terms of St. Thomas Aquinas: An unjust law is a human law that is not rooted in eternal law and natural law."[27] Catholic teaching on a God-given natural law gives a standard for measuring the truth of human laws.

As Martin Luther King observed, the church is neither the master nor the servant of the state but its conscience, guide and critic.[28] The Catholic Church, with its experience of 2,000 years of tradition and its trust in the harmony of faith and human reason, is in a good position to offer that guidance.

Questions about the Text

1. In the Nicene Creed, what are the two main meanings of the word *catholic*?
2. In what specific ways, in the Catholic view, are Protestant and evangelical communities related to the Catholic Church? What elements of sanctification and truth do these communities have?
3. In the Catholic view, why is it significant that Protestant communities do not have apostolic succession in their leadership? How is this issue related to the Catholic belief that these communities do not have a "valid celebration of the Eucharist?"
4. How do the issues in question 3 relate to different understandings by both Catholics and Protestants of the Lord's Supper (real presence vs. symbolic)?
5. Why do Catholics believe the Catholic Church is more closely united with the Orthodox Churches than with Protestant communities?
6. What are some factors that led to the 1054 schism between Eastern and Western Churches? What is the one major issue that continues to separate Catholics and Orthodox?
7. Name some of the Eastern Catholic Churches. How are they similar to and different from the Orthodox churches?
8. What is the ecumenical movement? What is its ultimate goal? Name some concrete achievements of this movement.

27. Martin Luther King Jr., "Letter from Birmingham Jail," accessible at *www.africa.upenn.edu /Articles_Gen/Letter_Birmingham.html*.

28. Quoted in US Conference of Catholic Bishops, "Our First, Most Cherished Liberty" is accessible at *www.usccb.org/issues-and-action/religious-liberty/our-first-most-cherished-liberty.cfm*.

9. What are key issues that still divide Christian denominations from each other and from the Catholic Church?

10. Explain Rahner's "anonymous Christian" theory. Why is Acts 17:22–23 important for Rahner? What problems does this theory solve for Rahner?

11. What is the pluralist position regarding Christian and other world religions?

12. Explain how mystical religions differ from monotheistic ones. How do these differences challenge the pluralistic approach?

13. Explain why D'Costa rejects Rahner's anonymous Christian theory. How does D'Costa use Christ's descent to the dead to address the theological problem of how those who do not know Christ can still be saved?

14. According to *Lumen Gentium*, no. 16, how is it possible for a person who does not know Christ to be saved?

15. Summarize *Nostra Aetate's* (no. 2) view on respecting the truth and holiness found in non-Christian religions.

16. Summarize Vatican II's view of Islam.

17. Summarize Vatican II's view on Judaism, especially the theme of God's ongoing relationship with Israel.

18. In the Catholic view, what role should the Church play, directly or indirectly, in political and public policy debates?

19. Give some examples of how Catholic ethical principles can help form the basis for public policies.

Discussion Questions

1. Do you have personal experience of the relationships between different Christian denominations or churches? If so, how would you describe the relationships?

2. Do you have a personal experience of the relationships between different world religions, including Christianity, Judaism, Islam, Hinduism, and Buddhism? If so, how would you describe the relationships?

3. What is your view of the Catholic policy of allowing only Catholics to receive Communion at Mass?

4. Is the Christian view of the sanctity of every human life or Peter Singer's utilitarian view of human life a better ethical basis for establishing a more humane, compassionate society? Why?

5. In your view, what role should churches or other religious groups play in debates about public policies?

Glossary

analogy A description built on comparison. Using comparisons to natural realities to talk about God, based on the belief that God and other supernatural realities cannot be described directly, is an example of analogical language.

anthropomorphic Ascribing human characteristics to a nonhuman subject. Applied to God, these characteristics might be either physical (e.g., "God's arm") or emotional and psychological (e.g., "God's jealousy"). Theologically, these characteristics must be understood as analogies only.

anthropology The understanding of human nature. A Christian anthropology takes into account God's creation of humans in his image, original sin, and the eschatological destiny of humans.

apocalyptic A type of thinking or writing that deals with end-of-the-world themes; its language is often heavily symbolic and emphasizes God's direct intervention in human affairs.

apophatic approach Applied to theology, the belief that human language cannot describe God directly, but can say only what God is not.

apostolic succession The handing on of the beliefs, practices, and spiritual authority of Jesus' apostles to their successors, the bishops.

argument from design The argument that evidence of a planned design in nature, whether animate or inanimate, points toward a mind responsible for that design.

atonement An action that "pays for" or "makes up for" sin. A central Christian belief is that Jesus offered his life on the cross to make up for or pay for the sins of all humanity.

Babylonian Exile A period from approximately 587 to 538 BCE when the Judean people were in exile in Babylon after the destruction of the Jerusalem Temple.

canon, canonical The basic meaning of *canon* is "a standard or guide." In a Christian context, it refers to the books the Church has accepted as authoritative Scripture.

canonization Israel and the Church used the process of canonization to discern which books are authoritative Scripture. The Catholic Church also applies the term to the process of discerning whether an individual should be declared a saint.

Catholic v. catholic As used in this book, *Catholic* with a capital *C* generally refers to the Catholic Church headed by the bishops and pope; *catholic* with a lowercase *c* refers to the universal and holistic nature of the one, holy, and apostolic Church of Christ.

Christology The branch of theological study focused on Jesus Christ. Particularly important topics are the relationship of the Son and Father and the relationship of the human and divine nature in Jesus.

Church As used in this book, *Church* with a capital *C* generally refers to the one, holy, catholic, and apostolic Church referenced in the Nicene Creed. This one Church is found most fully in the Catholic Church but also exists in other Christian communities.

creed A short summary of basic Christian beliefs. The two most influential Christian creeds are the Apostles' Creed and the Nicene Creed.

Darwinian theory of evolution Scientific theory of evolution by natural selection; distinct from *evolutionism*, a materialistic, deterministic worldview.

determinism A worldview that denies human free will, believing all human actions are determined by forces such as genetics and environmental influences.

development of doctrine The belief that Christian teaching, including key Trinitarian and Christological doctrines, developed naturally and legitimately by deepening or clarifying earlier Christian teaching. An analogous development occurred in sacramental practice.

Docetic Of or relating to Docetism; the view that Jesus was a supernatural being who appeared to be human but, in reality, was not.

ecclesiology Systematic theological study of the nature of the Church.

economic trinity Persons of the Trinity as they are revealed in the world.

ecumenical council Gatherings of Christian bishops from around the world. Most Eastern and Western churches accept the authority of seven ecumenical councils: Nicaea I (325), Constantinople I (381), Ephesus (431), Chalcedon (451), Constantinople II (553), Constantinople III (680–681), Nicaea II (787). The Catholic Church recognizes the ecumenical authority of fourteen further councils, up to and including Vatican Council II.

ecumenical dialogue Official discussions between various Christian churches and communities with the aim of establishing better mutual understanding and cooperation. For some participants, the goal of the dialogue is full, visible unity of all Christian communities.

Enlightenment An influential European philosophical and cultural movement of the eighteenth century that promoted religious toleration and freedom of thought but also tended toward rationalism and Deism.

eschatological Having to do with the "last times," the fulfillment of earthly history, and final judgment.

ethical relativism The belief that no fixed standards of right and wrong exist; rather, ethical standards change according to particular circumstances.

evangelical A general term for independent Christian churches that proclaim a Bible-based message and do not belong to traditional Protestant denominations.

fallen human nature, the Fall The Christian belief that human nature, although created good, has become corrupt, with inherent tendencies toward sin and self-destructive behaviors.

fideism A belief system founded on religious feeling rather than on a reasoned faith. This belief is essentially equivalent to original sin.

Gnostic Religious and philosophical trend that tends to see the material world as evil and defines salvation as the spirit's escape from the material world. Christian Gnostics held a docetic view of Jesus and believed that salvation is attained through esoteric knowledge.

grace A supernatural gift of God that cannot be earned by any human efforts.

Hebrew and Jewish As ethnic designations, *Hebrew* generally names the tribes of Israel up until the time of the Babylonian captivity; *Jewish* is typically first applied to the Judean captives returning to Jerusalem.

Hellenistic Refers to the Greek culture spread throughout the eastern Mediterranean world after the conquests of Alexander the Great (356–323 BCE).

hermeneutic Guideline for determining the meaning and valid interpretation of classic texts, especially of the Bible.

historical-critical method A general approach that applies historical, cultural, and literary analysis to Scripture.

historical Jesus The human Jesus as known from using standard historical methods to study him in his historical and cultural context as a first-century Jew.

hypostatic union The belief that Jesus is one person in whom the divine and human natures are united.

immanent Trinity The relationship of the three Persons of the Trinity within the Godhead; contrasted with Economic Trinity.

Incarnation The belief that the Second Person of the Trinity became human as Jesus of Nazareth.

inerrancy The belief that God protected the writers of Scripture from error. *Strict inerrancy* is the belief that God protected the writers from any error, including historical or factual errors. *Limited inerrancy* is the belief that God protected the writers from essential theological or ethical errors related to salvation.

infallibility Belief that the Church has the divine gift of proclaiming essential truths of faith and morals without error. In the Catholic understanding, the pope and the bishops in union with him have the authority to proclaim infallible teachings.

inspiration The belief that the authors of biblical writings were guided by the Holy Spirit.

kingdom of God The eschatological culmination of history in which God's will is established fully. The Kingdom began to be established in the person of Jesus and in his founding of the Church.

laity Member of the Church who is not ordained or a member of a religious order.

logos A Greek philosophical term referring to the divine, rational order governing the universe and found in the human mind. Christian theology identifies the Logos (capital L) with the Second Person of the Trinity.

Magisterium In Catholic understanding, the official teaching authority of the Church, expressed through the bishops and the pope.

materialism Worldview that understands the physical, tangible universe as the only reality.

Modalism A tendency to overemphasize the unity within the Trinity. It pictures God as existing in different "modes," and not as three subsistent persons.

open historical-critical method Use of the historical-critical method that does not rule out the possibility of supernatural intervention in nature.

original sin *See* fallen human nature.

Orthodox and orthodox *Orthodox* with a capital *O* refers to a group of Eastern churches, such as the Greek and Russian Orthodox churches. *Orthodox* with a lowercase *o* literally means "right belief" refers generally to Christian belief and practice as expressed in the creeds and ecumenical councils.

rationalism A worldview holding that the only valid knowledge is scientifically verifiable knowledge; religious beliefs are seen as subjective opinion only.

Reformation A movement, beginning in the sixteenth century, in which reformers broke away from the Roman Catholic Church and established such communities as the Lutheran and Reformed churches. Churches with roots in the Reformation are typically called Protestant.

Revelation God making himself known to humanity in order to establish a saving relationship with them. General revelation is God's revelation through nature and conscience. Special revelation is God's direct communication to specific humans on special occasions.

sacrament A physical sign, instituted by Jesus, through which God's grace is channeled to humans. All traditional Christians recognize the Lord's Supper and baptism as sacraments; the Catholic Church recognizes seven sacraments.

salvation The human triumph over sin, suffering, and death and attainment of eternal happiness with God.

Second Temple Period Period of Jewish history from the end of the Babylonian Exile in 538 BCE until the destruction of the Jerusalem Temple by Rome in 70 CE.

secular Nonreligious.

Septuagint The Greek translation of the Old Testament"; most early Christians read and quoted from this version.

sola scriptura A Latin phrase describing the Protestant principle that Scripture alone is the basis for Church teaching and practice.

subordinationism The theological understanding of the Son as, by nature, subordinate to the Father. An example is the belief that the Father created the Son before he created the rest of the universe.

theology The rational study of faith from the perspective of a particular faith tradition.

Tradition and tradition *Tradition* with a capital *T* refers to the Christian faith as a whole, including Scripture and essential Christian beliefs and practices, as it has been passed down through generations. In Catholic theology, *Tradition* may also refer to essential teachings and practices not explicitly in Scripture. *Tradition* with a lowercase *t* may refer to denominational beliefs and practices (e.g., the Lutheran tradition) or to nonessential practices of various churches.

traditional The Christian faith as handed down by the apostles and expressed in the creeds and ecumenical Councils. The term is equivalent to *orthodox* as used in this book.

transcendent Supernatural reality beyond the empirical or natural world.

worldview A particular paradigm through which all reality is perceived and interpreted.

Index

An *italiczed* page number indicates an illustration.